INDIA AND ASIAN GEOPOLITICS

INDIA AND ASIAN GEOPOLITICS

THE PAST, PRESENT

SHIVSHANKAR MENON

BROOKINGS INSTITUTION PRESS
Washington, D.C.

The Brookings Institution is a private nonprofit organization devoted to research, education, and publication on important issues of domestic and foreign policy. Its principal purpose is to bring the highest quality independent research and analysis to bear on current and emerging policy problems. Interpretations or conclusions in Brookings publications should be understood to be solely those of the authors.

Library of Congress Control Number: 2021932887

ISBN 9780815737230 (pbk : alk. paper)
ISBN 9780815737247 (ebook)

9 8 7 6 5 4 3 2 1

Typeset in Adobe Jenson Pro

Composition by Cindy Stock

Contents

II. THE PRESENT

Acknowledgments

Like every book, this one owes debts of intellectual and physical gratitude to many friends and institutions.

The book was conceived at Ashoka University outside New Delhi. A huge debt and many thanks to Pratap Bhanu Mehta, Srinath Raghavan, Rudra Chaudhury, and Joanna Korey at Ashoka. Also thanks to my 2018 students, whose fresh eyes brought back some of the wonder of seeing familiar things for the first time.

Much of the writing was done at the Institute of South Asian Studies, National University of Singapore, where Gopinath Pillai, Raja Mohan, and many others gave me the perfect environment to write and to try out ideas. Two reviewers helped to clarify some of my confusions and greatly improved the text with their suggestions and comments. I could not have asked for more encouraging yet rigorous guides than Bill Finan at the Brookings Institution Press and Ranjana Sengupta at Penguin Random House India, who kept the faith in this manuscript and whose suggestions vastly improved it. My thanks also to Janet Walker Chirlin, whose painstaking hard work made this text readable.

Several friends, colleagues, and students have suffered my ideas and set me straight while I was working on this book, but I am solely responsible for what is in it, good, bad, and indifferent.

But most of all I am grateful to Mohini, who keeps me real and true, and without whom this book would never have been done.

This book is for my grandchildren, Kabir, Amaara, Samira, and Ahren. Their world will be quite different, and I hope that this book will give them a sense of what my generation's times were like.

India in Asia

Introduction

In spring 2018 I taught a course on Indian foreign policy at Ashoka University. My bright young students were mostly born in this century; I was born in the first half of the last one. They rapidly taught me that familiar events from my lifetime were ancient history to them. When I said Mrs. Gandhi meaning Indira Gandhi, they heard Sonia Gandhi, who had headed the Congress Party in their lifetimes. My vivid memories of walking about Delhi with friends during the 1965 war enforcing the blackout against air raids was something their generation would never know, now that GPS and precision sensing have made blackouts irrelevant. It is sobering to realize that the events that frame your conscious life have already faded into the fog of history. But my students' enthusiasm and interest in learning about and analyzing those events, no matter how remote they may have seemed to them, encouraged me to attempt this book.

At another level, my students only reflected the massive changes in India and Asia in the last seventy years. At the end of World War II India and Asia were still largely colonized. India was poor, backward, and weak, and Asia was little more than a geographical expression. Today, Asia is at the center of world politics, is the most dynamic and rapidly developing region in the world, and some Asian countries now worry about a middle-income trap. India and China have eliminated more poverty in a shorter amount of time than any other nations in history. Several Asian states have acquired agency in the international system unprecedented in their modern history.

This book is the story of India in that changing Asia, of how India has adapted to changes since Indian independence in 1947, when the modern Indian state came into being. While India is unique, and therefore a singular actor in many respects—geography, history, demography, culture—it has also always been a part of the Asian story and an active participant in it. Even as India experimented briefly after independence with an inward-looking approach in its quest to transform, develop, and strengthen itself, the country has consistently recognized that it must work with others in the international system to further its own interests. Paradoxically, as India has evolved and gathered power in the international system, its need for and dependence on the world have steadily increased. While India attempted from the start to pursue interests in partnership with other states and actors different from itself, it was often alone abroad because of the unique set of geopolitical compulsions and drivers for its foreign and security policies. Despite that, it was still able to achieve many of the nation's international goals not only because of its relative power or influence, hard or soft, but because of its use of the shifting geopolitical situation around the country, particularly in Asia. That recent past, along with the consequences of India's choices in Asia's geopolitics, is still with us. Hence, the title of this book. Today, India is more connected to and involved with the world around it than ever before, as its interests grow and change. That is the story this book attempts to tell.

While this book is not a history of Indian foreign policy, or comprehensive in any way, and should not be considered a work of scholarship or of international relations theory, despite its development through an international relations department course, it does attempt to look at Indian foreign policy with a wide-angle lens. It examines Indian foreign policy, not as an autonomous activity driven by personality and domestic politics and reacting to external stimuli, but as part of larger historical shifts in Asia and world geopolitics, of which India is a significant constituent. From the very outset, with independence in 1947, and even before that under the interim government from September 1946, India was not just a reactive or passive object of Asian geopolitics but an active participant, and it sought to shape the Asian environment. This proactive role was played by India's earliest leaders, Jawaharlal Nehru and Indira Gandhi, and by later heads of government, P. V. Narasimha Rao, Atal Behari Vajpayee, and Manmohan Singh.

As an Indian diplomat, it often seemed to me that the explanations advanced in the media and in scholarly studies of the country's policies were simplistic, unidimensional, or insufficient, no matter whether they were realist, liberal, or constructivist. Each of these approaches seemed to be useful but incomplete or unsatisfactory as an explanation of state and leader behavior. In my experience of diplomacy and policymaking, most of the brilliant thoughts, concepts, and ideas that analysts and historians discuss seldom influence the politicians and policymakers who make the decisions that are the raw material of history. At the same time, the better ones are acutely aware of how their decisions will appear to their constituencies and have a clear sense of the power equations and geopolitics around them. That brought me to the idea that it might be worth examining the geopolitics of India in Asia. Also, intellectual and other histories of geopolitics tend to overemphasize Europe and the Atlantic, and in an age of U.S. hegemony, the maritime domain. I wanted to explore Indian foreign policy through a geopolitical perspective for what it reveals about India's past, present, and, possibly, future behavior.

I should perhaps explain at the outset why and how I use the rather slippery term *geopolitics*, despite its unsavory and often tortured intellectual history. One definition of *geopolitics* is "the study of how the political views and aims of nations are affected by their geographical position."[1] In other words, geopolitics was, to begin with, the study of the influence of geography on the behavior of states and international relations. This was the sense in which Halford Mackinder and Alfred Mahan used the term in the late nineteenth and early twentieth century—Mackinder stressing the importance of the Eurasian world island and Mahan of control of the oceans and the rimland.[2]

In its early form in the years before World War I, the study of geopolitics was the outcome of three factors. One was the rise of economic nationalism and trade protectionism as imperial Britain, France, and Germany adjusted to an increasingly interconnected global economy. It was also a period when imperial accumulation of new territories had led to confrontations in Africa and in pursuit of the "Great Game" in central Asia—what Mackinder called the post-Columbian era, namely, when Europe's discovery of the world beginning with Columbus had come to an end. Geography was emerging in universities as an academic discipline in an era of rapid and major university expansion in Britain and Europe. The study of geopolitics was also an act of academic colonization of an activity previously conducted outside the academy in European chancelleries, foreign offices, and ministries of war in the eighteenth and nineteenth centuries.[3]

Geopolitics was ideologically suspect for quite some time due to the taint of its association with nazism and fascism and their associated policies of genocide, racism, spatial expansion, and domination of place. The German geographer Klaus Haushofer, described by *Life* magazine in November 1936 as the "guru of geopolitics" for the Nazis, and his Munich institute were regarded as having legitimized Nazi expansionism with the concept of *Lebensraum*, or "living space," and of using geopolitics to justify Nazi policies of racial extermi-nation. This was guilt by association rather than by commission, but the charge tarred the discipline for many years.[4]

The limited meaning in which geopolitics was used by Mackinder and his immediate followers has, however, long since been overtaken by the present-day use of the term to mean the study of the long-term drivers and factors that influence state behavior. *Geopolitics* is now defined as "a study of the influence of such factors as geography, economics, and demography on the politics and especially the foreign policy of a state."[5] Indeed, in popular parlance geopolitics is almost synonymous with power politics. It is in that broader sense of long-term drivers of a state's quest for power, such as geography, history, economics, and demography, that I use the term *geopolitics* in this book.

In my opinion, these drivers or geopolitical factors help to explain the strong continuity in the foreign and security policies of successive governments of India, no matter their political color—despite each, particularly the present one under Prime Minister Modi, claiming to be unique and different, better than its predecessors, and somehow special.

Of course, when you hear people speak today of the return of geopolitics, it is quite possible that they are using a polysyllabic word even more loosely, as a synonym for power politics, or possibly just politics itself, in order to impress and dress up some fairly pedestrian ideas. For some of us, geopolitics and power politics never went away. It was a strange conceit that the fall of the Soviet Union[6] meant the end of history or that what came immediately thereafter was now permanent, unlike everything that had come before. What is new today is indeed the fact that our politics and our international dealings have changed again, from the post-Cold War unipolar moment and the high tide of globaliza-tion that lasted until the 2008 global economic crisis. We are in flux, and this too shall pass.

The other difficulty with the term *geopolitics* lies in the determinism that some have ascribed to it. But the discipline cannot be blamed for the uses it is put to. As Braudel reminds us, "History is made not by geographical features but by the humans who control or discover them." Geography and landscape do crucially impact human perception and behavior. But geopolitics cannot and should not diminish our concentration on human agency and responsibility.

It seems to me that geopolitics is more than just the effects of geography, history, and demographics on a state's foreign and security policies. These are important, and a part of geopolitics, because they affect the perceptions of those who make those policies. There is a considerable subjective element involved in the making of policy. In studying geopolitics, therefore, we need to also get into the heads of those who made the decisions. To that extent, the preaching or morality of Indian policymakers in the 1950s and 1960s served a purpose. When coercive strategies were only available within the Indian subcontinent, conciliation and persuasion were what was left to be used beyond the inner ring. Morality, which every politician in every society professes, gave Indian policymakers another string to their bow. As other means have become available, and as the temperament of leaders has changed—from activist leaders of a freedom movement to today's statists—the use, but not the utility, of moral suasion has diminished. But morality is still essential if power is to be converted into authority and legitimized, whether in democracies like India or in authoritarian states like China and Russia.

I am acutely aware that the determinism that early European advocates of geopolitics professed or suggested was biased, reflecting their times and a faith in European hegemony and dominance rather than rigorous academic discipline or method. Nothing in geopolitics enables one to predict what a nation will do—no more than one can predict an individual's behavior based on knowledge of a situation and psychological profile. We make our own fate, and India must do so now if it is not to miss the bus to developing a prosperous and secure country for all its people.

Harold MacMillan, the British prime minister, was once asked what worried him and kept him awake. "Events, dear boy, events," was said to have been his answer. The answer to the thinking leader's nightmare of being driven by events, as MacMillan described it, is to use policy to shape and manage the environment and to try and increase his or her available options. This is, therefore, also the story of some significant events in India's dealings with the world since independence and of how India developed the capacity to shape events, obtaining increasing agency in the international system by going beyond events, working with others, and building partnerships and national capability while accumulating power.

To some extent, analysis of India's foreign and security policies suffered in the 1950s and 1960s from the hangover of a nonviolent freedom movement. Subsequently, a post-independence generation of younger scholars like Srinath Raghavan brought strategy, war, and peace into the study of independent India's foreign and security policies. They also took it to the next and, in my view, necessary level of analysis by adding geopolitics. Thus, one sees India as not just a reactive power, the object of others' actions, as it may have largely been soon after independence, but as a participant in Asian and ultimately global geopolitics. This volume, too, takes that point of view.

It is necessarily an Indocentric view and will be open to accusations that its internal logic stems from India's view of itself as central to the subcontinent and Asian affairs. The attempt, however, is to offer more than an Indian worldview and to examine the historical and geopolitical factors that have marked India's dealings with the world. In essence, I argue here that there is a broader Asia. Until recently, east and west Asia were so different that when outsiders referred to "Asia," they seldom meant the whole continent from the Mediterranean to the Pacific. In the West, Asia used to mean east and southeast Asia. Now it also includes India. In southeast Asia, Asia is often used to include eastern, south-eastern, and south Asia, but not west Asia. For reasons examined in chapter 10, this is no longer a workable way of considering politics. Asia is now physically tied together by infrastructure, trade, and investment. Globalization means that the prosperity of east Asia depends and can be threatened by what happens in west Asia. Radical ideologies and terrorism, which get their financing and inspiration from west Asia, are spreading to south and southeast Asia, as we see in India, the subcontinent, the Philippines, southern Thailand, with the Rohingya, and even in Indonesia. It is Asia, with its 4.4 billion people, about 60 percent of the world's population in forty-nine nations, that increasingly drives global growth and affects global security. Asia matters, and its internal linkages mean that all of Asia will be the primary determinant of the external environment in which India must operate.

In writing this book I came to see that India is very much a part of the Asian story and always has been. Indian policymakers have not just been the objects of others' policies but have exercised agency and worked actively to shape trends and developments in Asia, from the inception of independent India. The record also shows that India is not an island but an interdependent part of that Asia and has been most successful when most connected to that world.

In telling this story from India's independence in 1947 to the present day, I have chosen to do so chronologically. "The Past," which is examined in chapters 2 through 8, attempts to describe India's role and responses to the major trends of the time, including decolonization, the reshaping of borders in the subcontinent, the Cold War, the Sino-Soviet split, the tacit U.S.-China alliance after 1971, the collapse of the Soviet Union, and the rise of China. While the division of chapters by decades may seem arbitrary, when elastically defined the decades actually coincided with changes in the Asian environment and with phases of

Indian policy. By describing policy over time, I hope to convey a sense of the times, of the simultaneity of major events as history evolves, which is, in fact, how policymakers perceive the world. The second part of the book, "The Present," from chapters 9 onward, is a thematic treatment of the present situation, as I see it, of a globalized world, with China risen and other powers rising, in a crowded Asian environment. Finally, chapter 13 looks forward, as diplomats are wont to do, attempting to predict and prescribe India's future course in an Asia that faces multiple likely futures, ranging from a set of multiverses to the more familiar pattern of several states of varying size, power, and capabilities contending to defend their interests in a globalized world.

PART I

The Past

1

The Stage and Inheritance

The Indian subcontinent is the only subcontinent in the world. That in itself tells us that India possesses a unique geography while also being intrinsically linked to the larger continent, Asia. These two impulses, a pull toward engagement as part of a larger whole and a push to be apart due to a unique geography, have influenced India's history and behavior through the ages and have determined the nature of her engagement with the world. Geography matters because it has consequences for policy, worldviews, and history.

The "big geography" of Eurasia, to which the Indian subcontinent is attached, divides that landmass into a series of roughly parallel ecological zones, determined largely by latitude, ranging from tropical forest in the south to northern tundra. In between these extremes, are temperate woodlands and grasslands, desert-steppe, forest-steppe, the forest, and more open taiga. The zone of mixed grassland and woodland was the ecological niche for settled agriculture to develop in two areas—in southwest Asia, from the Nile valley to the Indus valley, and in southeast Asia including China—where civilizations, states, and empires grew.

Of the two, its geography enabled southwest Asia to communicate easily. Throughout history, from the Nile to the Indus and later the Ganga, exchanges, migrations, and change were the rule with civilizations growing and developing in contact with one another even though they were separate geographically.[1]

The topography of the Indian subcontinent is open on three sides: the west, south, and east and is blocked off to the north by the Himalayan range. It is through the Makran coast that human beings first came to the subcontinent after it had been wiped clean of life as it traveled over the Reunion volcanoes on its 6,500-kilometer journey to collide with the Eurasian plate, thus forming the Himalayas, which are still rising at about 5 millimeters every year. When early humans migrated into the subcontinent, the Makran coast was part of a grassland or scrubland corridor that stretched across Asia. By the time Alexander retreated along the same corridor in 321 BCE, it was already a dry, inhospitable desert to which he lost many men.

The Indian subcontinent, bounded by the world's highest mountains and the Indian Ocean, was given a unity by geographical features within which cultural, political, and economic processes of integration could occur. Successive waves of migrants, immigrants, and invaders were assimilated and absorbed into the subcontinental mix, until the English chose to be indigestible. For most of history, until technology gave us the means, geography represented unalterable facts that humans had to work around in war and peace. Today, technology has given us the means to overcome the tyranny of distance, to cross mountains like the Himalayas, and to even fight wars in them.

The Indian subcontinent's location made it both the pivot of the Indian Ocean world and one of the crossroads of Asia. Writing in 1922, Halford Mackinder remarked, "In all the British empire there is but one land frontier on which war-like preparation must ever be ready. It is the north-west frontier of India."[2] He then described the physical geography of the single plateau of Persia, Afghanistan, and Baluchistan as not as lofty as Tibet, but still, he remarked, one of the great natural features of Asia, bounded by escarpment. Near Kabul is the dividing watershed between drainage going west (the Helmand flowing to Iran), north (the Amu Darya), and south (the Kabul River flowing into the Indus). The towering Hindu Kush separates central Asia from the Indus valley and is crossed by a few passes. As he noted, there is no obvious border between Persia and Afghanistan, nor between Iran and Baluchistan. As a result, the histories of India, Afghanistan, and Persia have long been intertwined.[3]

Without obvious borders in the northwest, a long search by the Raj (India under the British yoke) for a secure northwestern frontier produced a multilayered result: a boundary between Russia and Afghanistan; a buffer or client state of the Raj in Afghanistan and the North West Frontier Province; and a border province of British India without the laws or administration of other Indian provinces. On the other open land frontier of the northeast as well, the Raj created, in fits and starts, a multilayered frontier: occupying Burma in the late nineteenth century and ruling it from Calcutta until 1936; a frontier zone of British India up to the Himalayas without Indian laws and administrative structures; and a boundary with Tibet as a de facto buffer between India and a weak China.

In the Indian Ocean and its littoral, the Indian subcontinent's pivotal role was established early in history by the predictable cyclic weather pattern dominated by the monsoon winds. Between April to August low pressure over the

Himalayas draws in air from the south, creating southeast trade winds that, crossing the equator and picking up moisture, become the southwest monsoon. Between December and March, in the second half of the year, high pressure over central Asia gives rise to the northeast monsoon as the winds blow south to the equator.

Thanks to this regular pattern of monsoon winds, the Indian Ocean did not have to wait for the age of steam in the eighteenth century for deep water navigation and sailing. As early as 57 CE. "Periplus of the Erythraean Sea," a handbook for pilots, told navigators when and where to catch the winds to sail between Red Sea ports and India. It credited Hippalus as "the pilot who first discovered how to lay his course straight across the ocean," but this must have been preceded by centuries of experience as shown by the Indus valley civilization's docks at Lothal and the evidence of traded goods found in Indus valley sites and in Mesopotamia going back to the third millennium BCE.

The pattern of revolving winds to India's east and west made the Malabar and Coromandel coasts a commercial crossroads where goods from Egypt, the Levant, and Persia were exchanged for those from India, southeast Asia, and China. The Straits of Malacca are the junction of the southwest and the northwest monsoon winds. The Chinese called Malacca "where the winds end." A revolving wind pattern allowed ships sailing southwest from China through the South China Sea and southeast from India to meet in the straits and on the Malay peninsula where they exchanged goods. In each case, they would sail back when the winds reversed (in January-February and April-May). The Indonesians traded with India by 500 BCE, China by 400 BCE, and Egypt and Mesopotamia as early as 2600 BCE.

The subcontinent was thus both the pivot of the Indian Ocean world and also a self-contained geopolitical unit and could choose its engagement with the rest of the world. Not all routes across the Indian Ocean had to pass through India, unlike, say, the Mediterranean, where routes all passed through the Levant. When the Melanesian ancestors of today's Indonesians sailed right across the Indian Ocean in the sixth to ninth century CE to become the first humans to settle and colonize Madagascar, they did not have to touch India. By that time sailing long distances in the Indian Ocean was normal.

Nehru's summary of the effects of geography was that "we are geographically so situated that we are not drawn into controversies with that passionate fury that some other countries are. This is not due to our goodness or badness, but it is a matter of geography."[4] For him, India "is the natural centre and focal point of the many forces at work in Asia. Geography is the compelling factor, and geographically she is so situated as to be the meeting point of Western and Northern and Eastern and South-East Asia. Because of this, the history of India is a long history of her relations with the other countries of Asia."[5]

~

The other long-term driver of India's behavior in the world has been its demography.

India has always supported a relatively large population on a limited arable landmass. Today it occupies 2.41 percent of the world's land area but supports over 18 percent of the world's population. At the 2001 census, 72.2 percent of the population lived in about 638,000 villages, and the remaining 27.8 lived in more than 5,100 towns and more than 380 urban concentrations. More than half the population is under 25 years of age, which adds over 11 million people to the job market every year.

Historically three waves of urbanization—during the Indus valley civilization, 2600–1500 BCE, from the sixth century BCE to the second century CE, and during the Mughal period—were both a consequence and a cause of periods of rapid population growth. The subcontinent's population grew steadily from the stone age in 10,000 BCE until the Mauryan empire in the second century BCE, before slowing in the classical era up to 500 CE, and then staying generally stagnant up to about 1000 CE. Population growth resumed during the Delhi Sultanate from 1000 to 1500 CE. The Mughal empire, between the sixteenth and eighteenth centuries, saw higher population growth rates than any previous period in Indian history. Agrarian reforms, intensified agricultural production, and proto-industrialization established India as the most important global source of manufactured goods. Some 15 percent of the population lived in urban centers, higher than the percentage of the urban population in nineteenth-century British India, much higher than other societies except China, and a level that Europe only reached in the nineteenth century.[6]

Among the enduring practical consequences of this demography, of a large population on a limited landmass, was for India to become one of the first areas in the world to undergo proto-industrialization. It was also the largest military manpower market in the world for the greater part of history and one of the world's significant sources of advanced weapons. While it depended on central Asia for the horses that provided military mobility, it was a major source of military manpower in its periphery. For instance, India provided the skilled manpower and elephants that constituted half of Mahmud of Ghazni's troops when he conquered Samarkand and Bokhara in the thirteenth century.

The population of India under the Raj, including areas that are now Pakistan and Bangladesh, grew sporadically but steadily from approximately 239 million to 389 million between 1871 and 1941. In the 1920s India's population was around 275 million. Only 0.6 percent of the population was enrolled in secondary education and 0.03 percent in universities. Primary education was even worse with less than 4 percent of the population in any form of instruction. The literacy rate was about 10 percent and education formed tiny islands of privilege in a sea of ignorance. Seventy percent of the population were dependent on agriculture and 90 percent lived in villages.

The British altered the geography of India in many ways, through deindustrialization, by building railways, by making the economy a colonial appendage to their own, and by adding new port cities to the periphery of the subcontinent. The bulk of India's population is now concentrated along the coasts and in the Gangetic valley.

~

Another abiding influence has been India's resource endowment and the economy that it has shaped. Resources around the world are very unevenly distributed and, along with climate change and demography, set up the pervading rhythms of life. While India is a fertile and rich land agriculturally, throughout history it has needed resources from abroad. The country is people rich but resource poor. Today, the country is resource poor in energy and nonferrous metals. Over 80 percent of its imports are maintenance imports—of nonferrous metals, of fertilizer, of crude oil, of even lentils for a basic dish, dal, and we have no choice but to buy from the world.

Because of its resource endowment India has always been a trading nation. Throughout history India has been most successful and prosperous when it was most connected to the rest of the world. Buddhism spread to the rest of Asia along trade routes between India and west, central, and east Asia, and it was initially a religion of the trading classes, with the guilds and *sangha* (or monks) working hand in hand. When India exported its ideology, as was done with Buddhism and Hinduism, or military power in the Indian Ocean region (becoming what would now be called a net provider of knowledge and security), it was also promoting its own prosperity. It was these links abroad that made India one of the most prosperous and advanced societies in the world. When the country stopped doing so, from the eighteenth century onward, and closed its mind as well, it entered a long and precipitate decline.

~

The postmodernists would like us to believe that Indian history is what we make it or are the narratives that we choose to tell ourselves and believe. I beg to differ. History is like a map, an imperfect reflection of a larger objective reality that, over time and with improvements in the historian's art, becomes clearer and more representative of an objective reality that did exist and certainly seemed to exist to earlier generations in history. That map is important to us in looking at India's foreign and security policies because we choose, decide, and act on the basis of the map of our own experience, or the history, that we carry in our heads. Perception matters. And when perception does not match objective reality, policy errs or fails.

The problem is that several generations in India have been taught a version of history that ignores that India has for much of its past been well connected to the world and its prosperity and security have waxed and waned in direct proportion to that link. That may be because the regions that undertook these contacts with the rest of the world, what historians call coherent core areas, that is, areas characterized by stable, long-term political and cultural institutions, such as Bengal and Gujarat and the Malabar and Coromandel coasts, have been ignored or downplayed in these historical narratives in favor of the relatively insular Indo-Gangetic plain and the region around Delhi, partly because a version of Indian history written by those loyal to the British empire dominated the field. It is only in the last few years that younger scholars have begun to study these less recognized regions seriously.

The simplistic history written by historians loyal to the British empire legitimized British rule by making Indian history a continuous sequence of alien empires and conquerors. This saga of empires was periodized by religion, and caste was emphasized, disregarding the fact that the ruling elite was always of mixed religious persuasion and origins, and that assimilation and social mobility were both possible and practiced.

It amazes me that some Indians—despite having been shown alternative and more cogent lines of enquiry—persist in this religious characterization and accept the simplified history foisted on us. Certain historians and writers in India still contribute to the misrepresentation of India in history as an autonomous world apart, driven by religion and its own logic, and different from the rest of the world. One has only to look at the practice and the linkages with the world of the Mauryas, Kushanas, Guptas, Delhi Sultanate, and Moghuls to see how misleading this representation is. And these entities were carrying on a tradition of engagement stretching from the Indian subcontinent to the Middle East, the Roman empire and the Mediterranean Sea, central Asia, China, and southeast Asia inherited from the Indus valley civilization in the third and second millennium BCE. India was not "a world apart," but a complex civilization involved in myriad exchanges—of goods, ideas, and peoples—with the surrounding world.[7]

But this is only one part of India's true geopolitical inheritance. Kalidasa described the ideal rulers of the Raghukula as *asamudra kshitiesanam*, or those whose territories extended to the sea shore. The Satavahanas used the title *Trisamudrapati*, or Lords of the Three Seas. Including the history of the other regions in our consideration gives us a very different historical legacy that forms an increasingly important element of our strategic culture and driver of our policy choices. If you see Indian history as Delhi-centered, you will make the mistake that many of us make, of believing, as K. M. Panikkar said, that "India has, throughout history, had trouble arousing much interest in the world beyond its borders," which he contrasted to British attentiveness to developments around the Raj.[8] The coastal tradition in India, on the other hand, has seen outward projections of power, influence, and culture throughout its history.

Once you include southern and western India and Bengal and Orissa, the strength of India's links with the rest of the world, going back to 2600 BCE, become clear. Ptolemy attests to this in the second century CE, while Pliny in mid-first century CE grumbles about gold and silver draining away to India from the Roman empire for luxury goods, a problem that the British also had in the early days of trading with India, until they discovered the uses of opium. The reach and extent of the soft and hard power of non-Gangetic regions of India in both mainland and archipelagic southeast Asia are visible to this day in the great ruins of Angkor Wat and Borobudur, on the walls of the Vaikuntha Perumal temple in Kanchipuram and in Hampi, and in the living culture of our countries. The Cholas' activist external policies and willing militarism enabled them to last from the third century BCE to the thirteenth century CE, longer than any dynasty in the Gangetic valley. Their example was actively followed by the Pandyan (sixth century BCE to twelfth century CE) and Pallava (third to ninth century CE) dynasties. The same is also true of the reach and influence of some Gangetic or Indus valley-based political entities like the Mauryas or Kushanas as the spread of Buddhism overland to the Pacific and the Mediterranean attests. Vijayanagara flourished and grew prosperous on its trade with central, west, and southeast Asia. The Mughals, for their part, played an active role in central Asian politics, too. This is a strong, continuous, and abiding legacy of engagement beyond the subcontinent. As long as the Indian Ocean was an open, competitive space, peninsular India was relatively secure. The Mughals punished the Portuguese for piracy by limiting their activity on land, advantaging their competitors, the English, French, Dutch, and Danes. When Britain managed a relative monopoly on trade in the Indian Ocean following the Carnatic Wars with the French, it became possible for Britain to translate maritime control into predominance on land.

~

Until almost 1800, little differentiated the development of western Europe from India or eastern Europe or China, or, to be more precise, portions of each of these regions from one another. The areas in India where living standards were similar to those in advanced parts of China and western Europe and where proto-industrialization had taken place were precisely those most connected to the world mentioned earlier—Bengal, Gujarat, the Malabar, and Coromandel coasts. It was only later that the great divergence, as it is now called, took place with western Europe's economic and technical advancement creating a Europe-centered world. As Pomeranz says, "We cannot understand pre-1800 global conjunctures in terms of a Europe-centered world system; we have, instead, a polycentric world with no dominant centre."[9]

Angus Maddison's estimates of GDP bear this out and show how late the great divergence actually took place (see table 1-1).[10] For our purposes, these figures are interesting, not because they show what the British empire did to a once prosperous and advanced society in Asia, nor to create a narrative of historical humiliation to justify present-day bad behavior as today's Chinese regime does. Instead, they show the existence of a polycentric world through most of history and how unusual were the bipolar, then unipolar, and now the confused world orders that Indians have operated in since independence in 1947.

TABLE 1-1. *Distribution of Population and Income in World Economy, 1000–1820* (Percent)

Period	World population			World GDP		
	1000	1700	1820	1000	1700	1820
Asia (total)	65.5	62.1	65.2	68.2	57.7	56.5
China	22.1	22.9	36.6	22.7	22.3	33.0
India	28.1	27.3	20.1	27.8	24.5	16.1
Western Europe	9.6	13.5	12.8	9.0	21.8	22.9

Source: Deepak Nayyar, *Catch Up: Developing Countries in the World Economy* (Oxford University Press, 2013), p. 13.

The data also show that the Indian Ocean region was the center of world affairs and of the global economy for centuries. It remained so after Vasco da Gama reached India in 1498, even as the New World made the Mediterranean a backwater and the Atlantic became more important. In 1667 the Dutch considered it a great victory when they forced the English to hand over the tiny nutmeg-growing island of Run in the East Indies for a much larger island on North America's eastern seaboard, Manhattan.[11] By the nineteenth century this position was reversed. The Atlantic was the new center of the global economy and world affairs. In the second half of the twentieth century the center of gravity shifted again to the Pacific rim, with the growing importance of the economies of the U.S. state of California, Japan, Taiwan, Korea, and ultimately China. The Indian Ocean was mainly a transit route for shipping passing through to other places, a spectator to history. Today, with the rise of India, and the growing importance of Indian Ocean rim economies like Singapore, Indonesia, Australia, Iran, and others, the Indian Ocean could return to its earlier preeminence if it were to manage its demography, natural resource endowments, and politics, while also continuing its present economic course.

For most of its history, the world system, when one could speak of one, was essentially made up of parallel multiverses trading and exchanging people, goods, and ideas, but disconnected in terms of security and internal order.[12] Before the nineteenth century, technology and geography did not permit involvement with each other's polity or security on a sustained basis, except for short, exceptional periods of war. In Asia, before the sixteenth century, these multiverses were centered on Egypt and Persia in the west, India in the Indian Ocean region, the maritime empires of Srivijaya and its successors in southeast Asia, and on China in northeast Asia. The Khmer and other empires on the southeast Asian mainland coexisted with and traded with the other centers in uneasy and unstable relationships. This, to my mind, was the historical norm in Asian geopolitics and is one possible future that we might return to after the aberrations of the last two centuries.

∼

For fifteenth century Europeans, starting with the Iberians and later other European powers, sea power was a way to get around the great overwhelming land power of Islam in the Middle East and to break out of the "prison of the Mediterranean." After Vasco da Gama's first landing at Calicut in 1498, maritime power became a 400-year European monopoly, allowing European hegemony over the land masses of continental Asia. Only in the mid-twentieth century did that monopoly weaken with Japan's rise, the growth of nationalism in Asia—particularly in India and China—and Europe's own weakness after its fratricidal world wars, following which Europe failed to reconquer and hold Asia. That failure is also an example of the limitations of sea power. Hilaire Belloc wrote: "Dependence on sea power in military affairs is a lure leading to ultimate disappointment. In the final and decisive main duels of history, the party which begins with the high sea power is defeated by the land power; whether that sea power be called Carthage or Athens or the Phoenician fleet of the Great King, it loses in the long run and land power wins." But this might be too one-sided a judgment, because the record is mixed in Asia. Japan's naval power was defeated in World War II, only because of the superior naval force of the United States, and it was not overcome by land powers China and Russia. On land, Japan was outfought by the Indian Army of a maritime British empire.

Today, Asia sees a land power, China, trying for the first time in its history to become a maritime power, increasingly confronting the world's greatest maritime power, the United States. It is far from clear who will prevail and whether China will be able to make that transition. Historical analogy and experience suggest that the different geographies of Asia's seas will produce different results, whether it is the Indian Ocean, the South China Sea, or the western Pacific. The Indian Ocean has historically been an open area where attempts to dominate the trade or build monopolies have always failed, such as when Admiral Zheng He tried to monopolize the trade in porcelain and pepper during the Ming dynasty in the fifteenth century.

~

The classical geopoliticians were children of their age and looked at Asian geopolitics through a late nineteenth-century European or British lens, concentrating on the European hegemony that followed the breakup or decline of the classical Asian empires, namely, the Mughals in India, the Ming and early Qing in China, the Ottomans in Turkey, and the Safavids in Iran.

British geographer Halford Mackinder attempted to provide a theoretical explanation for events and relationships through his theory of what he called "the heartland" of Eurasia in a 1904 paper, "The Geographical Pivot of History." Here he detailed his version of the histories of the peripheries of the Eurasian landmass, Europe, and China in response to the pressure of successive waves of Asiatic nomads—Huns, Avars, Bulgarians, Cumans, Magyars, Mongols, Kalmuks, and others. He described the heartland of Eurasia as a citadel, radiating influence but not subject to invasion itself, because water transport along the periphery remained much easier than land transport until the coming of the railways. Physical geography meant that the horse ruled the steppe, the Pivot areas, denying the peripheral world the use of its waterborne transport except in the Outer Crescent of the maritime states and the oceans around Eurasia.[13] Later writers revised and added to Mackinder's vision in terms of trade and culture. But the basic Mackinder view of the world informed British, American, and both Czarist and Soviet foreign policy for years, and, as Robert Kaplan points out, is still influential in the West.[14]

In this view, the Indian subcontinent is unique and distinctive. Cohen classifies it as an independent geopolitical region, not contained within either of the geostrategic regions.[15] It is big enough to be a subcontinent in its own right, guarded from Eurasian power by the Himalayas, from the Middle East by the Hindu Kush and other mountains, and from Myanmar and Indochina by lower but heavily forested mountains. If united, the subcontinent has clear lines of defense, and it has the options of self-sufficiency or access to the trade-dependent maritime world. But if divided, scenarios change fundamentally. When the British left India they bequeathed a Joint Defense Council to India and Pakistan that did not survive the war in Kashmir. When divided, subcontinental powers have sought outside balancers and patrons, and the alignments between India and Pakistan and the three outside powers most involved in subcontinental affairs—Russia, China, and the United States—often reflect a continuation of Mackinder's imperatives. The early 1950s were a period of many open opportunities and few binding commitments, but Pakistan, seeking weapons and support from the United States, as well as membership in CENTO and SEATO, took advantage of the U.S. goal to complete the rimland containment of the Eurasian heartland controlled by the Soviet Union.

~

The nineteenth- and early twentieth-century British Raj in India saw a bogey in Russia, first imperial then revolutionary, threatening the northwest of India, and repeatedly intervened in Afghanistan to preempt that fear from becoming reality. Despite policy based on false premises, and suffering repeated tactical setbacks in Afghanistan and elsewhere, the British in India did succeed in keeping external powers at bay and away from India itself. British forces also countered a Japanese threat in the northeast when Japan took Burma and sought to enter India in World War II.

The phrase the "Great Game" was reputedly coined by British officer Arthur Connolly around 1840, and popularized by Rudyard Kipling. And it led to the British "Forward School" approach to military conquest or annexa-tion of land to ensure security. It described the nineteenth-century contest be-tween Great Britain and Russia for mastery in continental Asia or Eurasia and inflated the concern about a Russian invasion of India. Three generations of Britons believed that the Russian empire, which had been expanding for four centuries at a rate of 20,000 square miles a year, was poised to invade and seize India from Britain. British Foreign Secretary Palmerston argued in 1840 that since the Russian and the British armies were bound to meet one day, it was best to ensure that the meeting took place as far as possible from India, instead of "staying at home to receive the visit." This logic led to a demand for Brit-ish garrisons in Afghanistan. The Forward School saw "masterly inactivity" as encouraging Russian invasion and Indian rebellion. The 1839 British invasion of Afghanistan led to the annihilation of the occupying British forces and the death of British proxies. But by 1878 Britain was ready to try again. Again, mil-itary disaster resulted but its political fruits were averted by diplomatic skill and flexibility. This time the result was a buffer state run by a strong and subsidized ruler in Afghanistan, Abdur Rahman, friendly to the British and a claimant to the throne who had also been backed by the Russians.

In 1893 Mortimer Durand, foreign secretary to the government of India, 1885–1894, negotiated a unique and peculiar agreement with Afghanistan that gave India a double border. The "Durand Line" (which Pakistan today regards as its international border with Afghanistan) ran through tribal areas, eliminat-ing the no-man's-land and dividing it into spheres of influence loosely attached to Kabul and Lahore. But behind it to the east, resting for the most part on the Indus, lay the administrative border. Between the two lines tribes lived under British protection but not as British subjects; they came under the supervision of political agents and not the direct rule of deputy commissioners; their crimes were dealt with under tribal and Islamic law, not the British-Indian Code of Criminal Procedure.

In 1900 Lord Curzon, viceroy of India, who had long proclaimed the Rus-sian threat, traveled to the northwestern region and revised what he considered the empire's deeply flawed frontier policy. He withdrew regular troops from ad-vanced positions on the Khyber Pass and concentrated them in the rear, instead employing tribal forces recruited by British officers, such as the Khyber Rifles and Khurram Militia, to police the tribal country. In his own words, Curzon's way of managing the Pathan tribesman was "to pay him and humor him when he behaves, but to lay him out flat when he does not." He also detached Punjab's frontier districts and united them to the transborder tracts between the Indus

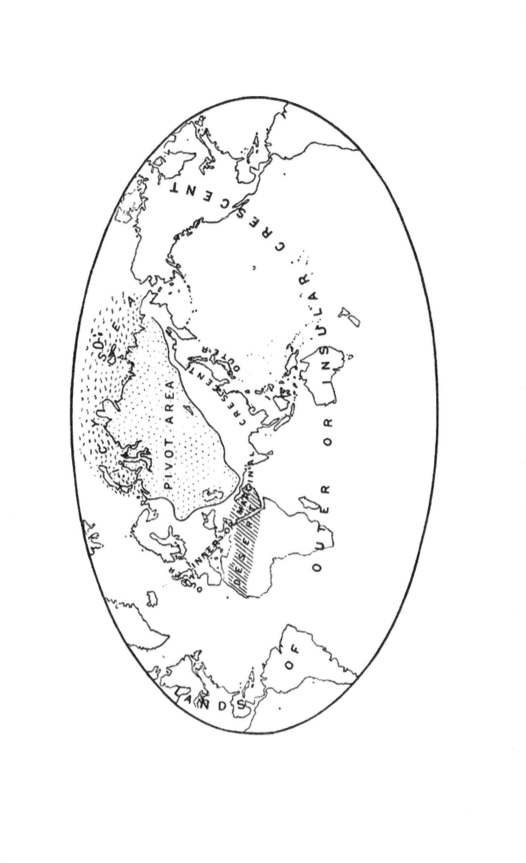

and Durand Line creating the North-West Frontier Province in 1901. Curzon had created a frontier that John Masters described as "a betwixt and between place, part India, part central Asia."

The Victorian British view of India's role in Asia was of "sub-imperial" diplomacy, or what some call the "empire of the Raj." Mortimer Durand imagined India's role in Asia in his 1885 "Memorandum on the External Relations of the Government of India." He proposed that the government of India ought to control England's relations with "all the purely Asian continental powers" from Persia and Siam to China and Korea. Although this grand vision was never implemented or accepted in London, bureaucrats in Simla, summer capital of British India, exercised considerable authority over much of the Middle East, appointing residents at Gulf and Persian courts, and through the agency of the Bombay Presidency at the Aden and Zanzibar outposts. Relations with Afghanistan and central Asia too, as part of the Great Game, fell under the control of the Indian Foreign Department. Some of India's neighbors suspect that such thinking is still not entirely dead in New Delhi, 150 years later.

From 1875 on, the British empire grew rapidly both in Africa and in southeast Asia. In that expansion from northern Nigeria to Fiji, British principals looked to India and Indian models and used the Indian Army. The use of the Indian Army to extend and secure Britain's empire "east of Suez" was not a new phenomenon of the late nineteenth century. The East India Company had deployed Indian troops in Manila, Sumatra, Malacca, Mauritius, the Persian Gulf, and Aden from its very first conquests. Company troops participated in both opium wars with China, the 1855 Persian war, and successive campaigns in Burma. With the abolition of the East India Company in 1858, and the subsequent reorganization of the Indian Army, deployment abroad became a regular feature. (Unlike the deployment of British troops, it required no parliamentary approval in London.) India was, of course, a subordinate partner in the imperial enterprise, but the construction of the arc of power extending throughout the Indian Ocean rim from Africa to eastern Asia centered on India was made possible by the Indian Army. This had its consequences: those living in most other British colonies in southeast Asia, west Asia, and Africa viewed Indians, and the Indian Army particularly, as subordinate colonizers or instruments of their imperial masters, thus complicating independent India's foreign policy task. At the same time, until World War I the British ensured that Indian troops were never used against whites, lest they realize that they could defeat the British and rule themselves. The Boer war even saw Indian cavalry horses used without their Indian riders, in order to keep it a "white man's war"—in what is proudly described in Jodhpur as "the only time the Jodhpur Lancers were unhorsed." At the same time, at the peak of the Boxer expedition in 1900–1902, 15,000 Indian troops were in action in China. After World War I Britain was unable to sustain such commitments. By 1920 colonial Indian contingents had ceased to exist outside Hong Kong and the Chinese treaty ports. But the Indian police presence abroad remained. At the outbreak of World War II in 1939, Indians still formed some 35 percent of the Hong Kong police. With Indian independence, a process began to end all recruitment of Indians for colonial police service by the 1960s. As Metcalf says: "Everywhere in the empire, Indians were viewed with suspicion and disdained as rivals and competitors—by whites in south and east Africa, blacks throughout Africa, Arabs in Iraq, and Malays in south-east Asia."[16]

~

The later decades of the nineteenth century leading up to World War I saw the emergence of a truly global economy. The early modern era, with the extension of Portuguese and later British power into the Indian Ocean and subsequently the South China Sea marked the origins of this wave of globalization. That was an era of proto-globalization, when an integrated Eurasian economy was created but trade was still limited, for the most part, to luxury goods—spices, tea, silk, and handwoven textiles—and limited by the high cost of carriage in sailing ships traveling the long way around the Cape of Good Hope. It is estimated that trade with Europe grew steadily by some 1.1 percent a year over three centuries, 1300–1800, with an annual 50,000 tons of goods shipped to Europe by 1800. Europe's trade with Asia was dwarfed by the Atlantic trade, which grew at twice the rate of the Asian. Mature globalization was a product of the nineteenth century, pushed by technical innovation, the telegraph, railways, steamships, undersea cables, and the Industrial Revolution. By the end of the nineteenth century the "modern" global economy encompassed the entire world, with capital and goods flows creating the first truly globalized economy. The high point of that process of globalization coincided with the fullest development of the India-centered subimperial system.[17]

That era of truly global integration came to an end after the First World War and arrived hand in hand with the decline and ultimate collapse of the India-centered Indian Ocean British imperial system.[18] Indians too lost faith in the British empire, from Ranade to Gandhi to Gokhale, and moderates in the Indian freedom struggle were disenchanted, eclipsed, or discredited. British favoritism to the white Dominions (Canada, Australia, and South Africa), discrimination against Indians in white settler dominated states, and the treatment of Indian indentured labor in British sugar colonies outraged Indian sentiment. Over roughly eighty years, from 1840 to 1920, a total of just over 1.3 million Indians went overseas as indentured laborers. A beleaguered Britain reverted to the narrower imperialism of race, which revealed for all to see the racial hierarchies and institutionalized violence that sustained colonialism.

Until 1914 passports did not exist as a confirmation of citizenship, and where similar documents were produced, their use was often not enforced. Within the British empire, restrictive immigration policies were first enunciated by the British colony of Natal in South Africa in the mid-1880s, and these in turn inspired similar restrictions in Australia and Canada after 1900. In India a reluctant Raj government implemented a passport officially certifying that its holder was "Indian" by the 1920s. It might get a reputable holder temporary entry into Australia, but there was no longer the concept of an "imperial citizen." World War I brought increased surveillance of travelers and the enforcement of passport regulations in Europe as well as in India. Codified in the Indian Passports Act of 1920, the restrictions were justified in the name of keeping out "mischievous persons," Bolsheviks, and revolutionary conspirators.

With the Depression and protectionism, deglobalization gathered pace after the war. In 1931 Britain formally abandoned the gold standard and, with it, free trade. India was allowed to raise its own tariff barriers, first on steel in 1920, and then in the 1930s on cotton textiles. With India's struggle for freedom and subsequent concentration on its own development, India was cut loose from the "global" order during the Cold War, much of it at India's insistence. It was only at the beginning of the 2000s, and after, that levels of international trade and investment as a proportion of economic output for India once again reached those of a hundred years before.

The British made some gestures toward giving India's foreign relations something of an Indian face after World War I but still controlled completely by Britain. At the Versailles peace conference in 1919 India was represented, effectively giving Britain a second seat in the form of the submissive and exotic figure of Maharajah of Bikaner. This led to India's role as a founder member of both the League of Nations and the United Nations after World War II. An agent of the government of India had been sent to South Africa in the 1920s, and during the Second World War the government of India sent representatives to Chungking, Washington, and Xinjiang.

World War II changed everything for Britain in Asia. The fall of Singapore and Burma to Japan in 1942 was the final blow. Empire had collapsed abjectly, and even Indians who had served and prospered under it had no choice but to seek their own destiny. This was a final parting of the ways, exemplified by Indian soldiers who chose to join the Indian National Army to fight with Japan against Britain.

Although the economic basis for India at the center of an imperial Indian Ocean system no longer existed after the 1920s and the Great Depression, British strategic thought and planning did not make that transition until much later. Late British strategy in India was perhaps best exemplified by the work and writings of Olaf Caroe, a true successor to Lord Curzon. Caroe was foreign secretary to the Indian government during World War II and a lifelong practitioner of the Great Game. The concept of "buffer states" from the 1880s onward, a British-Indian coinage, sought to interpose a protected state between the area actually administered and the possessions of adversarial neighbors, Russia and China, who were to be kept at arm's length. Curzon called this outer periphery a "glacis," literally a gentle slope. "We do not want to occupy it but we cannot see it occupied by our foes," Curzon said. This was not a neutral space but one that excluded all outside influences in its foreign relations. Britain built a series of buffers along the landward periphery of the Indian subcontinent, a system that the Raj called "the ring fence." As Caroe put it, this stretched from the Persian Gulf to Burma in "a double line of inner and outer entrenchments." The inner ring included Nepal, Bhutan, and Sikkim. The outer ring consisted of countries and territories that Britain nominally recognized as independent or at least autonomous—Persia, Afghanistan, Tibet, and Siam—which it sought to keep free of outside influence and hostile powers. India was, as Caroe said, "a kernel within an outer shell and an inner husk." Today's flash points and headlines continue to light up those same places in an arc from the Persian Gulf to Persia to Afghanistan, to Kashmir to Nepal to Burma. For Curzon, Caroe, and other British strategists, India commanded the strategic center, and the Asian balance hinged on India's power and the overall stability of the subcontinent.

Caroe formed a Viceroy's Study Group during the war to devise a strategy for the time when India would become independent. He saw control of the "Indian Ocean theatre" as critical to check Russia's piecemeal absorption of more than half the colossal "Central Land Mass theatre," enabling Britain to link the Pacific and European theatres. Control of the Cape of Good Hope, Egypt, and Malacca secured what Edwardian Admiral Fisher had called "the keys." But these keys did not lock all doors. Military power based on India was the only sure way to seal out the most dangerous re-entrants in Afghanistan and Persia.[19] The ultimate goal for British officials like Caroe in the 1940s was to ensure that the subcontinent remained a secure base of power for Britain in the wider Asian balance after India's independence. For them the Great Game did not end with British rule in August 1947, and they did not expect it to. They intuited that the imperatives of Asian defense reflected the permanence of geography versus the vicissitudes of empire and ideology. The landscape would endure. As Soviet, and increasingly Chinese, power consolidated in the Asian heartland, they expected that India would remain pivotal to the maintenance of global balance between land and sea power. India had historically formed and would continue to be a "central bastion" of world power well beyond the end of British rule, Caroe wrote.

~

What also matters for our purposes is the Indian elite's sense of self and view of their place in the world, as broadly formed in the early twentieth century in the course of a national movement seeking independence from Great Britain. It was an awareness born of 5,000 years of history, of India's geographic advantages and demographic weight, and of its civilizational contributions that helped to shape the thinking of the leaders of the freedom movement when they turned their minds to foreign policy. Or perhaps I should use the singular and say "leader," because to a great extent it was Jawaharlal Nehru and his ideas that formed the core of Indian foreign and security policy thinking during his lifetime. And his ideas played that role until the late 1980s, for more than twenty years after his death, and still influence thinking today. Others in the national movement, however, also thought deeply on these questions and not always in line with Nehru.

Nehru's thinking was a mixture of realism and idealism, although he would describe himself as a realist with a longer strategy than that of the tactical geopoliticians. His understanding of India's civilizational greatness and of the importance of the subcontinent as a geopolitical unit led him to continue several British Indian policies. After independence in 1948, the treaties India signed with Bhutan in 1949 and Afghanistan in 1950 were very similar to earlier ones signed by these countries with British India. He was also willing to intervene in affairs in the subcontinent, as in Nepal in 1950, to an extent that he was not willing to consider outside it. But by far the greater influence in his thinking was the nationalist and anti-imperialist strand. Hence his early pan-Asianism and his attempt to manage India's "civilizational sphere of influence."[20]

Nehru was deeply influenced by the conviction, not unreasonable in midcentury, that power politics in the name of realism and geopolitics had led the world to two world wars and disaster, and that there had to be another basis for international politics. He makes his arguments in detail in his book, *The Discovery of India*, where he sees geopolitics and power politics as handmaidens of fascism, national socialism, and imperialism.[21] Writing in jail during the final stages of the Second World War in 1944–1945, Nehru saw geopolitics and realism as continuations of the power politics and practices that had caused the disasters of the two world wars. He saw geopolitics as "the anchor of the realist," and "its jargon of 'heartland' and 'rimland'" as a "partial truth [which] is sometimes more dangerous than a falsehood" and as "the old policy of expansion and empire and the balance of power which inevitably leads to conflict and war." He believed, "Civilization is no longer confined to the oceanic fringes and tends to become universal in its scope and content." He felt that "Mr. Walter Lippman's vision of a three or four orbits encompassing the globe—the Atlantic community, the Russian, the Chinese, and later the Hindu-Muslim in South Asia—is a continuation of power politics on a vaster scale, and it is difficult to understand how one can see any world peace or cooperation emerging out of it."[22] But Nehru was practical enough to say on the same page, "Realism of course there must be, for no nation can base its domestic or foreign policy on mere goodwill and flights of the imagination. But it is a curious realism that sticks to the empty shell of the past and ignores or refuses to understand the hard facts of the present"—meaning the desires of the colonized and the destructive power of modern war. These beliefs were reinforced by the use of U.S. atom bombs to end the war with Japan. Nehru therefore saw building an area of peace, as he called it, in Asia as the only truly practical and realistic goal if mankind was to avoid annihilation.

Nehru's anti-imperialist and socialist inclinations were evident as early as 1927 when he attended a Brussels conference of oppressed peoples organized by the leftist League Against Imperialism, of which Nehru was elected an Executive Council member. In Brussels, Nehru was convinced that independence from Britain had to be a multinational effort by all the oppressed and colonized throughout Asia and the world. He then visited the Soviet Union in the 1930s. He was not swept off his feet by what he saw there, or by the propaganda, but recognized an alternative to the economic and political system that had enslaved India. He was therefore willing to grant the Soviets equal or greater validity and to work with them. This also accorded with his instinctive faith in socialist solutions to India's abject socioeconomic condition. Nehru broke with his colleague and sometime rival in the Congress Party, Subhash Chandra Bose, in the late 1930s on the question of working with the fascist regimes in Europe. He refused to meet Benito Mussolini while in Italy in the 1930s and visited Spain along with V. K. Krishna Menon to support the Republicans in the Spanish Civil War. Nehru organized support and a medical mission to China, when China was fighting the Japanese invasion in 1938. Bose, as president of the Congress, was not in favor of steps hostile to Japan and Germany but chose to allow the medical mission to China to proceed while he did not associate with it in any way.

When World War II broke out and it came to choosing sides, Nehru and the Congress made it clear that India's place was with the democracies but that it could only fight as a free country. In this Nehru and Gandhi differed from Bose, who, on the principle that "my enemy's enemy is my friend," wanted to work with and fight alongside the Axis to win freedom for India. Indeed, this was the significant ideological cleavage in the Congress, before, during, and after the war. When the British viceroy declared India a belligerent within hours of Britain's declaration of war on Germany without consulting either the Central Assembly or the easily identifiable leaders of Indian opinion, the Congress leadership was divided. Many sympathized with Bose's anti-British stand, which called the war imperialist. Moderates, led by C. Rajagopalachari, were for Congress giving "whole-hearted support to Britain in the fight against gangsterism personified."[23] That was also the stand of the Hindu right, which worked with the Raj through the war. Nehru was between the two extremes, saying that "Indians will not participate [in the war] as slaves."[24] Ultimately, Congress under Nehru and Gandhi's influence made it clear that they stood against the fascists, but were not willing to stand with Britain unless India was promised freedom at the end of the war—a promise that Churchill was unwilling to make even in the desperate straits that Britain was reduced to in 1940–1941. Nehru made his ideological position clear, stressing that India could not support a war in the name of democracy and freedom when this was denied to India by Britain. He managed to do so with a remarkable absence of personal rancor against the British, despite his extended imprisonment during the war. He showed equal equanimity in his attitude toward those Indians who differed from him politically. When it came to the trials for treason after the war of Bose's Indian National Army followers, Nehru chose to defend his political opponents himself and later accommodated many leaders in the Indian National Army in the new Indian Foreign Service and in politics, but not in the armed forces.

Writing in Allahabad jail in 1944 Nehru foresaw that "an entirely new situation would arise after the war, with two dominating world powers—the USA and the USSR—and the rest a good distance behind them unless they form some kind of a bloc."

~

Nehru's belief in the rise of Asia and pan-Asian unity was not unique or an unreasonable reaction to what Asia had experienced under European hegemony.

If there ever was a moment when minds all across Asia were electrified, when Asia began to believe that it might have a future other than one under Western subjugation, and when the rise of Asia began, it was during two days in May 1905 when Admiral Togo Heihachiro's Japanese ships annihilated the Imperial Russian navy in the Tsushima Strait. A non-European country, and an Asian one at that, had vanquished a European power at sea. From Egypt to China Asians celebrated. A sixteen-year-old schoolboy then, Nehru heard the news on a train to his British school, Harrow, and was elated and "in high good humor," as he put it. Returning to China later that year, Sun Yat-sen was congratulated by Arab port workers at the Suez Canal who thought he was Japanese. In Damascus a young Ottoman soldier, Mustafa Kemal, was thrilled and felt vindicated. As Pankaj Mishra said, "They all drew the same lesson from Japan's victory: white men, conquerors of the world, were no longer invincible. A hundred fantasies—of national freedom, racial dignity, or simple vengefulness—now bloomed in hearts and minds that had sullenly endured European authority over their lands."[25]

If Japan's rise kindled hope, the carnage of the world wars extinguished any lingering respect for Western superiority in Asian minds. In its place rose pan-Asianist sentiment, the belief that Asian fates were linked and that Asians would take charge of their own destinies together in a way that Japan had shown was possible. Pan-Asianism was part of the reaction to imperialism and colonialism and to the impact of the West on Asian societies. Indian poet Rabindranath Tagore, for instance, developed serious differences with Gandhi over what he saw as the xenophobic side of the anti-colonial movement and nationalism in India and elsewhere. Pan-Asianism seemed to offer Tagore, Liang Qichao, Okakura Kakuzo, and others across Asia self-respect and an answer to the humiliation and racism inflicted on what the West considered to be backward societies. They sought to establish a cultural basis in Asian spiritualism and ideals, contrasted with Western power and materialism, and stressed the old maritime and Silk Road links, arts, and a shared legacy of Buddhism in India, China, and Japan.

By the mid-1930s, however, pan-Asianists in Japan who were also ultranationalists were dreaming of an Asia revitalized and dominated by Japan. Okawa Shumei, for instance, outlined a Japanese version of the Monroe Doctrine for

Asia. (In 1946 he would be indicted as the chief ideologist of Japanese expansionism by the Tokyo War Crimes Tribunal.) After the 1931 invasion of Manchuria, Tagore and Chinese victims of Japanese aggression broke with the pro-Japan freedom movement across Asia. The movement split between those who saw pan-Asianism as part of a larger, humanist return to a mythical Asian peace, such as Nehru and Tagore on the one hand, and Japan-sponsored Asian freedom fighters on the other hand, who saw military power as offering them the way forward. By 1940, sitting in a British prison in India, Nehru would say, "My own picture of the future is a federation which includes China and India, Burma and Ceylon, Afghanistan and possibly other countries."[26]

In a little more than ninety days beginning on December 8, 1941, Japan's military offensive through Asia dispossessed the United Kingdom, United States, Netherlands, and France and took the Philippines, Singapore, Malaya, Hong Kong, the Dutch East Indies, much of China, Indochina, and Burma. "There are few examples in history of such dramatic humiliation of established powers."[27] In each Asian country nationalists were faced with a choice of whether to work with the Japanese, who promised liberation from the old colonial masters, or whether to oppose them as new masters. In April 1943 the "liberation of Asia" became Japan's official war objective. Despite the undoubted brutality that accompanied Japanese occupation, occupying forces set up friendly regimes across almost all of occupied Asia and actively boosted nationalist movements in Burma and Indonesia and galvanized anti-Western feeling. Aung San in Burma, Ibrahim bin Haji Yaacob in Malaya, and Sukarno in Java, like Bose of India, all received encouragement and were actively boosted by Colonel Suzuki Keiji, often called Japan's Lawrence of Arabia. The first generation of postcolonial leaders had been trained and tasted power thanks to Japan. Ba Maw, the Burmese leader, said he felt the "call of Asiatic blood," and, "We were Asians rediscovering Asia."[28]

The strength and effect of pan-Asian sentiment should not be underestimated just because its unchallenged life was short and it was quenched in China by Japanese behavior in the 1930s. For one thing, nationalist leaders supported by Japan, all believers all in one form or another of pan-Asianism, made a return to prewar empire impossible, from Vietnam through Indonesia to Burma and India. The speed of decolonization in Asia was spectacular. Britain departed from a partitioned subcontinent in August 1947, Burma became free in 1948, Indonesians threw out the Dutch in 1949. Malaya and Singapore were plunged into postwar chaos that lasted years, but the British departure was clearly inevitable and never in doubt. Where empire tried to hold on to its privileges, as in

Iran with the Anglo-American coup against Mosaddegh in 1953, the seeds of future foment lay in wait.

Besides, it was these pan-Asianists—Aung San, Sukarno, and others—who led the new Asian states that emerged from decolonization and produced the new rulers of Asia. There was a direct line from the 1943 Greater East Asian Congress in Tokyo to the 1955 Bandung Conference of the Afro-Asian states. The Asia for the Asians sentiment of those conferences still resonates today, for instance, with China's Xi Jinping tapping into an idea with deep and abiding roots.

~

The significant strands in Nehru's thinking—anti-imperialism, subcontinental leadership, cultural and political pan-Asianism—can be traced back to Nehru's experiences before independence. What underlay them all was his conviction that "India is not a poor country. She is abundantly supplied with everything that makes a country rich, and yet her people are very poor. She has a noble heritage of culture-forms and her culture-potential is very great; but many new developments and the accessories of culture are lacking." He was prescient in saying in 1946 that "only two factors may come in the way: international developments and external pressure on India, and lack of a common objective within the country. Unfortunately, it is the latter alone that will count. If India is split up into two or more parts and can no longer function as a political and economic unit, her progress will be seriously affected. There will be the direct weakening effect, but much worse will be the inner psychological conflict between those who wish to reunite her and those who oppose this."[29]

If the ideological basis of the new India's foreign policy was nationalist, anti-colonial, and pan-Asianist, the foreign policy and security instruments that the republic inherited were the creation of the Raj, were limited in nature, and brought along a set of attitudes and habits, too. The Foreign and Political department, which became the Ministry of External Affairs, the Indian Army, and the government of India missions and posts abroad, as well as seats in the United Nations and International Labor Organization, were all legacies of British India. They were also the least "Indianized" of the Raj's instruments. That did not prevent Nehru from remaking and repurposing them. Deputy Prime Minister and Home Minister Vallabhbhai Patel did the same for the state's internal instruments. It is interesting to consider which of them was more successful in making the apparat inherited from the Raj fit for the new democratic republic's purpose. Nehru had a cleaner slate to work with in foreign affairs.

His instruments, such as the Indian Army and the Indian Foreign Service, have shown an ability to adapt and evolve with India's needs. Patel was probably dealing with more intractable internal structures left by the Raj, such as the police and the civil services, all of which today require drastic overhauling. Nehru was pragmatic enough from the start to turn and use these instruments for his own purposes. For instance, when the process of integrating the princely states was about to begin and some rulers were toying with the idea of independence, Nehru said in July 1946 that no princely state could prevail militarily against the army of independent India, implicitly threatening them with an imperial instrument for a national purpose.

While the British like to be remembered for their contributions to India of administration—civil service, the army, posts, telegraphs, banking systems, irrigation schemes, and, most of all, the railways—it was a state run for Britain, by Britons who, unlike all previous invaders, never made their home in India, never assimilated, and were never committed to India's interests before Britain's imperial interests. The British Raj, however, was an Indian state in that most of its personnel were Indian. Only 4,000 British officers were stationed with the civil service, the police, the railways, and in forestry in the 1930s. Perhaps a maximum of 30,000 civilian Britons in India worked as traders, tea planters, bankers, and so on. Units of the British Army in India peaked at 70,000. As against this, the British Indian Army composed of Indian soldiers with British and Indian officers raised voluntarily had 1.3 million men serve in World War I and 2.5 million in World War II. Given the fragility of their hold, the British obsessed about staying in power, particularly after 1857, and the imperial state failed to do what it might have in education, public health, and industry. This made them more determined than ever to keep the higher functions of the state—war, diplomacy, and intelligence—in British hands, and these were the last portions of the Raj to be "Indianized."

During the Raj, India enabled Britain to overcome its limited size, small population, and lack of natural resources to hold on to its global empire. The Indian Army was used by the empire from Africa (Natal, Somaliland, Uganda, Rhodesia, Sudan, Mauritius, Egypt) to the Middle East (Iraq, Iran, Palestine, Aden) to Asia (China, repeatedly, Tibet, Singapore, Indonesia, Hong Kong). For Curzon and British followers of Mahan and Mackinder, control of the sea was critical. They believed that their security in India would be materially affected by an adverse change in political control of the Persian Gulf, that they had to ensure the safety of "the great sea route, commercial and military, to India and the Further East." British policies in Persia, Afghanistan, Tibet,

China, Burma, and the Middle East were all influenced by the security and geopolitical advantages of the base in India. Churchill recognized that without India, the British empire would not survive and Britain would no longer be a global player. "The loss of India would be final and fatal" for Britain and "reduce us to the scale of a minor power," he said on January 30, 1931. A significant factor in the British decision to leave India was a concern about the loyalty of the Indian Army after World War II and the Royal Indian Navy mutiny of February 1946, which spread from Bombay to Karachi, Cochin, and Calcutta. The mutiny was joined by elements of the Royal Indian Air Force and police and had to be suppressed by force by British troops and Royal Navy warships. There was also some unrest in Indian Army garrisons in Poona and Madras.

Nehru took a very different view. He was deeply opposed to what he saw as imperial adventures that Britain had dragged India into and was against the use of Indian soldiers as cannon fodder in Britain's fights, as in the First World War. In this he differed from K. M. Panikkar, and senior Congress politicians like C. Rajagopalachari and T. T. Krishnamachari, who saw independent India playing the same role as it had under the Raj, but now for India alone, as a security provider in southeast Asia, the Middle East, and elsewhere, and were willing to rely on and work with British maritime power, which India lacked. They also saw India as a key economic power in an extended neighborhood. In 1948 Panikkar argued for a regional organization with a defense council from Iraq and Iran to Australia, including Indochina, Thailand, and all the other countries in between, centered on India and involving Britain as well. In this he was supported by C. Rajagopalachari. This was a very different view from what finally prevailed in independent India, as we shall see.

The imperial uses and origin of the Indian Army had left a layer of mistrust of that body in independent India's first generation of political leaders. They had seen the army used against themselves in internal security duties. For a short while after World War II it was Bose's Indian National Army that was the national army of India in the popular mind. But the role of the armed forces in handling the communal violence that accompanied Partition and, more significantly, the army's response to Pakistani raiders and then regular armed forces invading Jammu and Kashmir in 1947–1948 helped to make it the national army of India in the popular imagination and to smooth its relationship with the political leadership, most of whom had no experience or familiarity with the military. Today, after years of an apolitical army that has stayed away from politics, unlike its siblings in the neighborhood, the concerns of those days about civil-military relations are hard to credit.

~

This broad-brush look at India's past suggests that though India is unique in several respects, and has been so for much of her history, the country has also been connected to the world and its fate, and prosperity has depended on that connection. The nature of India's engagement with the world is a logical result of its geography, resource endowment, demography, and history. No other country in the world has the same combination of size, location, present-day backwardness with some effective power, and voice as India. It is therefore not surprising that India has had to walk a lonely path for much of its independent existence as a modern state since 1947, but, where possible, chose to do it with other partners, among the nonaligned and the major powers. Indian exceptionalism has some basis in geography, history, and condition, but remains an incomplete and unsatisfactory frame to understand India's behavior. No other country shares India's interests to such an extent that an alliance is natural or inevitable. At the same time India's interests and weaknesses make partnership and cooperation abroad essential and inevitable. It is through the search for congruence of interest and partnerships short of alliance that India has sought to engage the world.

Not surprisingly, in order to further its unique set of interests, every Indian government since 1947 has chosen to pursue strategic autonomy, by one name or another—whether one calls it nonalignment or genuine nonalignment or a multidirectional foreign policy, or anything else. There has also naturally been an internal focus on remaking the institutions of governance and creating instruments of state to concentrate on the primary task of transforming India into a strong, prosperous modern country where every Indian can achieve his or her potential.

In 1947 the new state's inheritance was a complex one of some instruments and attitudes that the new leadership sought consciously to reject or change; of limited capacity to drive foreign and security policy; of an Asia that was clearly evolving but in an uncertain direction; and of overwhelming domestic priorities for the new state of India. At the same time, India's independence in 1947 and China's revolution in 1949 radically altered the basis of Asia's relationship with the world, dealings among the countries of Asia, and also India's role and policies. The rest of this book is about that change, and its evolution over seven decades, a story of incredible and improbable events that have led us to where we are.

2

Independence

India became independent at midnight on August 14, 1947.[1]

Spare a thought for Jawaharlal Nehru and the leaders of independent India. Between September 1946, when Nehru took over the interim government of India, and 1950, when the country became a republic, many tasks awaited: to build a country by combining British India with 564 or so sovereign or semi-sovereign princely states; deal with the horrendous consequences of Partition, including the greatest mass migration in history until Bangladesh in 1971; begin changing the abject condition of the people of India; fight a war with Pakistan in Kashmir; and build new instruments of state such as the Indian Foreign Service and repurpose old ones like the Indian Army, the Intelligence Bureau, and the police. Even Indian Standard Time was only introduced on September 1, 1947. Before this, different provinces and princely states had their own times, and reading an Indian railway timetable was a complex skill. Frontiers and boundaries needed to be established and administration extended to every corner of the new state of India. Those involved in the transition had to draft a constitution for the new republic; suppress an armed communist revolution in Telangana; and deal with China's occupation of Tibet—for the first time in history China had become India's neighbor. Nehru faced all this simultaneously and without the experience of ever having run even a municipal government. That so much of what was done in those initial days has stood the test of time and has been carried on by the leaders' successors, not all of whom shared their ideas and preferences, says a great deal about those men and women, their ideas, and their understanding of India. They managed to accomplish much despite disagreements among themselves, largely because of the leadership that Jawaharlal Nehru provided.

In the midst of the chaos of independence, Nehru made one of the great speeches in history about India's tryst with destiny. As freedom came at midnight on August 14, he spoke about India and the world:

> That future is not one of ease or resting but of incessant striving so that we may fulfil the pledges we have so often taken and the one we shall take today. The service of India means the service of the millions who suffer. It means the ending of poverty, ignorance, disease and inequality of opportunity. The ambition of the greatest man of our generation has been to wipe every tear from every eye. That may be beyond us, but as long as there are tears and suffering, so long our work will not be over.
>
> And so we have to labour and to work, and work hard, to give reality to our dreams. Those dreams are for India, but they are also for the world, for all the nations and peoples are too closely knit together today for any one of them to imagine that it can live apart. Peace has been said to be indivisible; so is freedom, so is prosperity now, and so also is disaster in this One World that can no longer be split into isolated fragments.
> (J. Nehru, "Tryst with Destiny" speech, August 14, 1947)

In that speech we see at the very inception some of the ideas that drove a Nehruvian foreign policy: the overriding priority of ending India's poverty and backwardness, that peace, freedom, and prosperity for India are linked to that of the world, and that this is now "One World." Nehru already saw India's foreign and domestic policies as linked.

These were prescient remarks. As he spoke, most of Asia was still reeling from the aftereffects of World War II and from the vain attempt by colonial powers to reimpose their empires in Asia. China was in the throes of civil war, Japan under occupation, and Indochina, Malaya, Burma, and Indonesia saw colonial masters using brute force against an aroused nationalism that would not be denied. It is difficult to speak of Asian geopolitics in the first few years of the Indian republic. When India became free, southeast Asia was still colonized, except for the Philippines and Thailand, and west Asian countries like Persia were undergoing their own internal convulsions. Yet, rather than being distracted by daily headlines and preoccupations, Nehru already saw Asia free and potentially one political, economic, and strategic space. And he saw the outlines of the three trends that were to shape India's world in the decade to come: decolonization, the reshaping of subcontinental borders, and the Cold War.

Nehru's first thought, however, was for "the millions who suffer" in India. India's condition at independence in 1947 was truly abject. The new government had its hands full dealing with the political, social, and economic consequences of Partition, with a stagnant economy and a country wracked by communal violence and other tensions. Some basic figures show the challenges faced and how far India has had to come. Between 1900 and 1950, India's GDP grew by less than 1 percent a year, while agricultural and food grain output grew at just 0.5 percent a year. The structure of the economy was colonial, with 49 percent of GDP from agriculture, 7 percent large-scale industry, 10 percent small and medium industry, and 34 percent from services and construction. Some 72 percent of the workforce was in agriculture and only 2.5 percent was employed in factories and mines. According to the 1951 census, only 16 percent of the population as a whole was literate (just 8 percent of girls and women were literate), and the average life expectancy of an Indian born in 1947 was thirty-two years. The country generated only 3,000 megawatts of electricity, and the infant mortality rate was 150/1,000 live births. This was a country that was poor, backward, that could barely feed itself, and that was racked by disease and hunger. It was therefore only natural that government's priority was internal, on economic development and social transformation.

Two years after independence when the constitution was adopted, B. R. Ambedkar, jurist, economist, and politician, said: "On the 26th of January 1950 we are going to enter into a life of contradictions. In politics we will have equality, and in social and economic life we will have inequality. How long shall we continue to live this life of contradictions?"[2]

One might have added to Ambedkar's contradictions that of India's idea of itself as an important world-class civilization, on the one hand, and the actual weakness and condition of its people and the inherited instruments of governance, on the other. The gap between the idea of India and its reality in 1947 was vast. Domestic consolidation had to be the first priority.

Remarkably, the nascent republic was able to integrate itself and stand on its feet despite myriad distractions, war, and crises. Politically, the cartographic reconstruction of India needed immediate attention after Partition and the Radcliffe Award, which drew the boundary between India and Pakistan.[3] In 1947 India acquired 81 percent of the British India's population but only 72 percent of the area, and that needed to be unified and integrated. India's internal political integration took from 1947 to 1956. The princely states' territories encompassed some 40 percent of the subcontinent's area and over a quarter of the population. It took prodigious effort by Deputy Prime Minister and Home Minister Sardar Patel and others before, as Mountbatten said, "All 564 'apples' fell into the basket."[4] The new government's task was also to fix the external boundaries of India, a task that was by and large completed during the 1950s for all the land boundaries, except those with China and in Jammu and Kashmir, while the maritime boundaries were established by the 1980s.

~

As formal successor to the Raj, India took over 672 treaties, conventions, and agreements as well as membership in fifty-one international organizations in 1947. But independent India's apparatus to formulate and implement foreign policy was very limited and had largely to be built from scratch. The Department of External Affairs, along with the higher staffing of the Intelligence Bureau, was the least Indianized part of the British government of India. The Indian Political Service within the elite Indian Civil Service handled India's relations with Britain's protectorates on the subcontinent, managed the diplomatic affairs of the Raj, and administered frontier areas. It was divided into two main departments, both directly under the viceroy until the very end of the Raj: the Political Department, which dealt with the princely states and protectorates and the Foreign Department, which handled diplomacy and the frontiers. In the early 1930s the Foreign Department was renamed the Department of External Affairs. While the Indian Civil Service had been opened up to Indians in 1860, Indians were specifically excluded from the Indian Political Service.[5] The first Indian to be taken into the Political Service was K. P. S. Menon in 1925, but it remained overwhelmingly British and was never truly Indianized until independence. When it became clear during World War II that Britain would be leaving India, a deputy secretary in the Department of External Affairs, S. B. S. Shah, who later played a prominent role in Pakistan, suggested the 50 percent Indianization of the department. Despite Foreign Secretary Caroe and Viceroy Wavell's support for the proposal, London's Whitehall took a dim view, and no real expansion of Indian numbers occurred in the External Affairs Department until the interim government headed by Nehru in 1946. In July 1947 the new Ministry of External Affairs inherited only seventeen Indians from among the 124 officers of the erstwhile Indian Political Service of the Raj. In foreign policy therefore the new Indian state was less well resourced than in internal affairs and defense, where the police and the Indian Army were overwhelmingly staffed by Indians and the civil service had been considerably Indianized.

Harcourt Butler once said, "We want lean and keen men on the frontier and fat and good-natured men in the states."[6] Under the Raj, candidates for the Political Service had to be army officers under the age of twenty-six or civilians with five years' experience. They were required to be unmarried at the time and to pass a not-very-difficult exam. There is some truth in the claim that the Political Department consisted of soldiers with brains and civilians who could ride and shoot. Unhampered by the Civil Service commissioners in London, the Political Department could adopt a more practical approach in selecting the right men to fill the various posts of consul, diplomat, resident, or frontier officer. Curzon paid the ultimate compliment to the Political Service after leaving India when he said, "There is no more varied or responsible service in the world than that of the Political Department of the GOI."

In 1900 more than 650 "native states" made up British India, containing roughly 63 million people in an area of about 700,000 square miles. No one could be precise about the statistics, since there was no clarity on whether to include Nepal or tiny statelets in Kathiawar. Excluding these, the total was about 630 states with huge variations in their powers and practices. Five of the largest were in direct political relations with the government of India: Kashmir, Hyderabad, Mysore, Nepal, and (from 1876) Baroda, all of which were dealt with by the Foreign Office and its Political Department. The historic Rajput kingdoms such as Jaipur and Udaipur were grouped under the Agent to the Governor General (AGG) in Rajputana; and Maratha principalities Gwalior and Indore were placed with 146 other states under the AGG in Central India. Most of the remainder came under the control of provincial governments including the Sikh states in the Punjab, Travancore and Cochin in Madras, Rampur in the North West Province, and Sikkim and Cooch Behar in Bengal. The majority of all the "native states" of India, over 350 of them, were regulated by the Political Department of Bombay presidency. Nepal was the most autonomous of all the states in the subcontinent (other than Afghanistan after 1880), whose foreign relations were conducted by the government of India. While Calcutta did not interfere in Nepal's internal administration, it controlled Nepal's import of weapons and refused to let it fight Sikkim or any other state. "Divide and rule" was rampant within the subcontinent in the complex arrangements that the British made to deal with all these entities.

The major states and all those under the AGGs came within the orbit of the Political Department of the Foreign Office. The foreign secretary in India was a civil servant who, unlike other government secretaries, was not responsible to a member of the viceroy's council but to the viceroy himself. (There are shades of this practice today in the direct interest that Indian prime ministers take in the Ministry of External Affairs.) The foreign secretary ran the Political Department, dealt with "native chiefs," and administered the foreign relations of the government of India. His arc of responsibility stretched from Aden to Bushire, up to Kashgar and to Tibet. Foreign Office posts included a resident in "Turkish Arabia," another in Bushire in the Persian Gulf, and a consul general in Kashgar in Chinese Turkestan, each considered significant for the Great Game or protecting the sea route to India. In the hierarchy of politicals, the top posts were the residents of Hyderabad and Mysore who each received salaries of 48,000 rupees, the same as high court judges, the AGGs, and the foreign secretary himself.

In Victoria's empire, three-fourths of civilians on active service were stationed in the regulation provinces (Bengal, Bombay, Madras, and the North-Western provinces); one-tenth, or some ninety, civilians worked at desks in Calcutta, Simla, and provincial capitals; and the rest were distributed among the native states serving as residents and political agents in the political departments and the non-regulation provinces, where they worked as administrators in Burma, Assam, the Punjab, and central provinces. In all places outside regulation provinces administrative posts were shared between Indian Army officers and the Indian Civil Service. In 1856 Governor-General Dalhousie insisted that places in non-regulation provinces be divided equally between the army and civil service. In 1867 the civilian element was increased to two-thirds and the military role was gradually eroded. By 1903 army officers were no longer employed in the Punjab. In 1907 they were excluded from Assam and confined to Burma and the North-West Frontier. In the Political Department, however, they retained their ascendancy, consistently outnumbering civilians by a ratio of 7 to 3.[7] Notice the landward bias. The sea was a purely British concern, dealt with by London through the Royal Navy. Some of this bias carried over into Indian institutional thinking after independence, making the new republic sea-blind for a few decades.

The new government of independent India did not inherit a cadre of people versed in foreign policy and strategy. There were a few individual Indians who had been in the Political Service, some of whom became familiar with foreign and security policy because of Caroe and others—personages such as K. P. S. Menon, Girija Shankar Bajpai, and S. B. S. Shah. But actual experience of handling foreign relations was limited and the new India had to build a diplomatic service and foreign office of its own. Despite this inheritance, the government of free India was often assumed to have inherited the institutional embodiment of "subimperial diplomacy," or have adopted the British view of themselves as being at the center of a vast sphere of influence controlled from the mountain-top capital of Simla.[8] Instead, the new leaders of India had a very different view of the function of diplomacy and an instinctive mistrust of the instruments of the Raj that they had struggled against to attain India's freedom.

Nehru built a very different Foreign Office and sought to imbue it with a new spirit. He staffed it with Indians drawn from public life, academia, and the freedom movement, from War Service Commission officers who had enlisted to fight in World War II when the armed forces were among the few respectable careers open to educated Indians, and from the former princely classes. He tried to shape this miscellaneous group into a Foreign Office to serve new India's interests, imparting his ideas and setting in place practices and habits of intellectual curiosity, pluralism, patriotism tinged with internationalism, and independent thinking, which for many years enabled India to punch above its realpolitik weight in the world.

Speaking to a young Y. D. Gundevia, a future foreign secretary of India, in his South Block office in 1948, Nehru pointed to spots on the world map and excitedly told the young officer, "We will have forty embassies! We will have forty missions!" That was achieved in five years.[9] Today India has the twelfth largest diplomatic contingent the world, with 181 diplomatic posts of which 124 are embassies or high commissions, 48 are consulates, 5 are permanent missions, and 4 are other representations. India has come a long way.

～

The government of independent India had its hands full at independence at home and in the subcontinent. But the world doesn't wait at your convenience, allowing you to sort out your internal order before challenging you. Before the new government could catch its breath, two events pointed out independent India's geopolitical future as different from that of any previous regime or state on the subcontinent—the creation of Pakistan and China's entry into Tibet.

In addition, at this same juncture the world was being divided into two camps, one led by the United States and a second by the Soviet Union. On March 5, 1946, at a college in Fulton, Missouri, with U.S. President Harry Truman present, former British prime minister Winston Churchill spoke of an iron curtain descending on Europe "from Stettin in the Baltic to Trieste in the Adriatic." Churchill went on to speak of the "special relationship" of the United

States and Britain, of the "sinews of peace," of "Communist fifth columns," and that there must be no appeasement of Stalin and the Soviet Union—all the main themes of future Cold Warriors in the West.

Different views pervaded the Indian leadership, of course, on how to transform India, on the priorities, and on how to address poverty and inequality. Opinions ranged from the communists, the second largest party in India's first parliament, some of whose comrades were leading an armed uprising in Telangana, to the extreme right who saw a capitalist road as the only answer, with others through all points in between. Each group was reflected in the ruling Congress Party itself, and each had a foreign policy line of its own. The communists sought an alliance with the Soviet Union, while rightists saw alliance with Britain and the United States as the way forward. Clear differences of opinion ranged from how India should approach its strategic tasks, on its international role, to how to harness the world to India's economic development.

For Nehru, India's independence marked the rise of Asia. As he had said in the Tryst speech: "Those dreams are for India, but they are also for the world, for all the nations and peoples are too closely knit together today for any one of them to imagine that it can live apart." As early as 1928 the Calcutta Congress resolution had spoken of an "Asia whose fate is tied together" and sought a conference on Asia in 1930. One of the first tasks Nehru undertook was to organize the Asian Relations Conference in Delhi in March 1947, inviting not just the states of Asia but also those who were still colonized or not yet free. For Nehru it was through a larger "community of peace" and through political, economic, and cultural ties and solidarity that Asia would overcome its deficit of power and prosperity and find security.

On the other hand, K. M. Panikkar, along with C. Rajagopalachari, T. T. Krishnamachari, and others, was akin to the British in seeing India's centrality in what they called the near and far east. They especially saw an advantage in maintaining close association with Great Britain. Panikkar had advocated as early as 1919 to "knit India to England and England to India in free partnership."[10] In 1943 he saw India as a security provider and key economic power for the region because of its "geographic position, size, resources, manpower and industrial potential."[11] He quoted President Quezon of the Philippines as declaring that "without a free India no nation in south-east Asia can be free." Panikkar was not alone in his suggestions. T. T. Krishnamachari advocated a regional organization from Suez to Australia with a defense council, all centered on India and in association with Britain. Others such as Iqbal Singh and P. N. Kirpal advocated similar views. Within the Congress Party itself, there were differences. Patel too seemed sometimes to suggest that he believed that India's rightful place was as a Western ally opposed to totalitarian Communist regimes.

Perhaps the clearest expression of Panikkar's views was in 1946 when he wrote, in words that echoed Caroe: "The Indian Ocean area together with Afghanistan, Sinkiang and Tibet as the outer northern ring constitute the real security of India. Geographically also this is one strategic unit, with India as its great air land center and as the base and arsenal of its naval power. From the central triangle of India the whole area can be controlled and defended."[12]

This is a very different view of India's role in Asia's geopolitics from Nehru's sense of an Asian renaissance based on decolonization and an equal association of free states in opposition to imperialism and bloc politics that he called the "area of peace." Panikkar and Patel prioritized the fight against communism and saw a role for India as a security provider in southeast Asia. Nehru, instead, prioritized decolonization as a means to enable pan-Asian solidarity, leading to joint actions to preserve peace, in contrast to the traditional power politics of the United States and western powers that he blamed for India's and Asia's condition. Where Nehru and Panikkar agreed was that the Cold War had established a new global strategic order—an extension of a European-dominated system that would ultimately be transient.

There was also a "Hindu" alternative to the debate in the Congress, often called Hindu nationalism, although Hindus were involved in all sides of the discussion. Swami Vivekananda had argued at the end of the nineteenth century that reformed Hinduism based on the early Vedas could liberate India and free the world from "fanaticism and religious wars." This, he believed, would involve *karma-yoga*, making Indians physically strong and rebuilding Indian civilization using modern ideas. Once India mastered science and became a "European society with Indian religion," it would conquer its former conquerors, Muslim and Western, by spiritual rather than by military power. The idea that India's security could be achieved by universal acknowledgment of the truths of Hindu *sanatana dharma* (roughly, the true, eternal way) also later drove the thinking of Vinayak Damodar Savarkar, president of the right-wing Hindu Mahasabha political party, and M. S. Golwalkar, who led the Rashtriya Swayamsevak Sangh (or National Volunteer Organisation) from 1940 to 1973. This idea is also reflected in current prime minister Narendra Modi's professed goal for India as a *vishwaguru*, or world teacher. Savarkar and Golwalkar both argued that Hinduism is destined to bring world peace, but that *sanatana dharma* would only be taken seriously when India is a "self-confident, resurgent and mighty nation." Both men had a Hobbesian view of an anarchic world composed of "selfish individuals and parochially minded communities" where war was inevitable. For them national power came from exclusionary religious nationalism and a strong martial national identity. Cosmopolitanism was nether desirable nor necessary for Savarkar. Alliances were to be based on self-interest rather than ideals for Golwalkar: "Nations change their friends and foes as it suits their self-interest."[13] Theirs was, at that time, a small voice without influence on power and was focused by its leaders on eliminating "internal threats"—Muslims, Christians, and communists—in the pursuit of which they were ready to work with the colonial power while admiring the European fascists.

The Indian Communists too had their own internal debate on foreign policy because not all were willing to blindly follow the Comintern or Soviet line. They differed on whether India was ripe for armed revolution, and since Soviet policy under Stalin had shifted on this question (depending on Stalin's need for Britain during the war and his rather dim view of peasant revolutions in China and India), the Comintern line kept shifting too. Those Indian communists not flexible enough to follow the shifts and who thought for themselves soon found themselves outside the party and even less effective than before in shaping newly independent India's policy. It was only after they broke free of outside direction and tutelage and began thinking as Indians in the 1960s that the communists began to have some influence on India's foreign policy.

At independence all sides of the debate were, in a sense, anticipating events, and all were ultimately blindsided by what actually transpired. India's independence came well before most of southeast Asia was free. Ideas of a greater Indian role in southeast Asia, whether as a leader of pan-Asianism or as a security provider along with Britain, ignored the resentment and hostility aroused by India's role as the gendarme of colonialism in Asia in the nineteenth and early twentieth centuries and the Indian Army's significant contribution to restoring colonialism in Indonesia, Malaya, and Indochina after World War II. It was the Indian Army that actually defeated the Japanese Army in land warfare on the Asian continent. In the last months of 1945, troops of the British empire, most of them from the Indian Army, had reconstituted the great crescent of land that Britain had occupied before 1941 and had then fanned out beyond it, from Bengal through Burma and Thailand and on to Singapore. By 1946 the British military empire stretched wider still, from the Persian railhead at Zahedan to New Guinea and the Australian seas—an arc of control from Suez to Sydney. For a while Indian troops occupied half of French Indochina and large parts of Indonesia and were part of occupation forces in Japan.[14]

It was this use of the Indian Army as an instrument of the British empire that Nehru and the Congress objected to. One of the first things that the interim government under Nehru did after coming to power in September 1946 was to ask for and secure the withdrawal of Indian Army units from Japan, Annam, and other points, but it was only in 1947 that all Indian Army units were finally withdrawn from southeast Asia.

Panikkar's ideas of India working in partnership with Britain as a security provider in postwar Asia were not practical policy after Partition. The internal security duties the army had to perform and the war in Jammu and Kashmir of 1947–1948 severely limited what the army could do. India lacked the maritime dominance in the Indian Ocean and Arabian Sea of the Royal Navy before 1941, and had lost its access to west Asia with Partition. Nor did the situation in southeast Asia permit India to play the sort of role that Panikkar envisaged. Patel's death in December 1950 removed the last powerful advocate of such thinking within government. And perceived British perfidy at the United Nations on Kashmir in 1948 made argument for continued close association with Britain more difficult. This did not extend to Nehru, who saw value in finding a way for India to remain in the Commonwealth as a republic, without owing allegiance to the British sovereign as had been the case. It also says something for Nehru's catholicity of outlook and tolerance, and perhaps of the paucity of Indian experience and talent, that despite differences in approach, he appointed K. M. Panikkar as his second ambassador to China and, after 1951, Egypt, whose leader Nasser was Nehru's friend and partner in building the idea of nonalignment.

Whatever their differences on how to engage with the world, all sides in the debate were agreed on an active Indian role abroad. Nehru not only summoned an Asian Relations Conference in New Delhi in March 1947, but thereafter played an active role mediating conflicts in Korea and Indochina and pushed for decolonization in Asia. The high point of pan-Asianism was probably the Bandung conference of Afro-Asian countries in 1955. Thereafter, the Cold War and preoccupations with decolonization made options of working with the West much less likely and attractive.

In other words, while there were differing conceptions within the Indian leadership of India's role in the geopolitics of Asia initially, no view was fully in consonance with the reality of the situation in Asia or with India's capabilities, further constrained by the consequences of Partition. Most Indian leaders deferred to Nehru's greater knowledge of the world in matters external to India. In any case, Nehru's stress on decolonization and pan-Asianism—a prevailing view up to Bandung in 1955—was soon eclipsed by the Cold War and the great powers.

~

Nehru, as we have seen, had a grander, more expansive, and more ambitious view of India's role in Asia than other Indians who thought of these issues. Nehru sought nothing less than a radical and complete reworking or remaking of Asian and global geopolitics. Three overarching causes impelled him to do so: the first was the need to transform India. The second was the threat of nuclear annihilation after the atom bomb gave nations the power to destroy human civilization. And the third was the need to free Asia and Africa from the colonial yoke. Nehru saw these as interlinked and as warranting an area of peace, or a concert of peace-loving peoples and countries, which would lead ultimately to One World. Almost all his international initiatives through the early 1950s were intended to further these goals.

In March 1947, with India's independence a few months away, Nehru convened a conference at the foot of the Old Fort in Delhi of twenty-eight Asian countries that were independent or still colonies. In his inaugural address he spoke of pan-Asianism not as a turning away from the West but of Asia taking its rightful place in the world. "Asia, after a long period of quiescence, has suddenly become important again in world affairs," he said. "For too long have we of Asia been petitioners in Western courts and chancelleries. That story must now belong to the past. We propose to stand on our legs, and to co-operate with all others who are prepared to co-operate with us. We do not intend to be the playthings of others." Brave and strong words that still inspire. He also said that

in this work there are no leaders and no followers. . . . Apart from the fact that India herself is emerging into freedom and independence, she is that natural center and focal point of the many forces at work in Asia. Geography is a compelling factor, and geographically she is so situated as to be the meeting point of Western and Northern and Eastern and South-East Asia. Because of this, the history of India is a long history of her relations with the other countries of Asia.[15]

Was Nehru reasonable to seek such grand goals? For Nehru that was a secondary question. He saw that power, military and economic, was not enough without legitimacy. He was also realist enough not to underestimate the difficulty of what he was trying to achieve. To those who thought he should concentrate on India's internal development and not the world, he would answer that world peace was essential for India's development. Besides, he believed strongly that India, with her civilizational legacy, was the natural thought leader of global processes despite her limitations of hard power.

One must admire the boldness of Nehru's worldview, unlike those of Panikkar and others whose thinking was somewhat derivative and shifted with the fashion of the day. But Nehru's ideas, prioritizing legitimacy over power, also led him to ignore real threats and ultimately to failures, as in his dealings with China.

However, three of Nehru's goals were actually achieved in large measure, although not by the means he envisaged or entirely by Indian agency. First, India's and Asia's economies today have been transformed beyond expectations, but not following Nehru's chosen economic path. Second, a nuclear holocaust has been averted, thus far. Third, Asia and Africa have been decolonized. In little more than fifteen years following India's independence, the regional international system was transformed from one dominated by empires to one populated by sovereign states. Decolonization in the Indian Ocean region was a far more fundamental shift than even the end of the Cold War. Rather than just a shift in alliances or a change in power distribution, or the entrance and departure of new states, it changed beliefs about the legitimacy of empire and replaced empire with sovereign states. For the first time in centuries the constituents of the regional Asian order were essentially identical in the Indian Ocean, maritime Asia, Europe, and the rest of the world.[16] Whether this was due to the better side of our natures asserting themselves or because of the operation of balance of power politics dear to realists, or other reasons, is something that will always be contested. Ironically, Nehru's ultimate goals of Asian solidarity and One World have become the slogans of a nation he might not have expected, China.

It is easy in hindsight to criticize Nehru for his advocacy of One World in a Cold War world. We forget that this was not just an Indian idea and that it had wider attraction. U.S. president Franklin D. Roosevelt was among the leaders who had spoken of the idea. In India the Quit India resolution of the Bombay Congress in 1942 championed the cause of world federation: "The future peace, security and ordered progress of the world demand a world federation of free nations, as on no other basis can the problems of the modern world be solved." Even in 1942 this was not a new sentiment for Nehru and the Congress. Earlier resolutions on foreign affairs, from 1921 onward, had spoken of "an Asia whose fate is tied together" and sought a conference on Asia in 1930. It was hardly surprising that India was therefore one of the most enthusiastic supporters of the UN at its inception.

The role that India played in these processes of decolonization, Asian solidarity, and peace building in the 1950s was truly remarkable, given its lack of capability and domestic preoccupations and the increasingly unpropitious international situation. But in the end Nehru's attempt to remake Asian geopolitics came up against the state of the world in the Cold War, Asia's own divisions, and events.

~

In the aftermath of another world war, the world that the new Indian state was born into in 1947 was still in flux and dominated by U.S. economic, military, and political power. The United States faced only the Soviet Union as a potential but far weaker competitor. Despite Churchill's "iron curtain" speech, the Cold War was not yet set in stone.

India was among the first colonies to achieve freedom. Nehru's first instincts were to seek good relations with all. He visited the United States relatively early in 1949 and again in 1956, but by then, the lines of U.S. policy had already hardened. A McCarthyite United States was judging the world through a yes or no test: communist or not communist. The newly empowered country seemed to be searching for scapegoats to blame for the loss of China to the communists. In India's case this was ameliorated somewhat by the U.S. hope that democratic India could be won to the anticommunist cause, having just fought off an armed Communist uprising in Telangana, by an appreciation of India's potential as a market, and by India's potential as a partner against communist China. But Nehru's three-week visit from October 11 to November 4, 1949, did not go well. Nehru's sympathies were with American progressives such as W. E. B. Du Bois, who was a persona non grata to the State Department. Nehru added three days to his stay to meet with friends on the left, such as actor and activist Paul Robeson, and with the NAACP and others fighting segregation in the country. As U.S. politics moved away from Franklin D. Roosevelt's New Deal and into Cold War ideology under Truman, Nehru was increasingly out of tune with U.S. policy. Nehru was certainly not anti-Western, but his idea of the West diverged from the direction in which the United States and Europe were evolving. Ironically, this occurred just as the United States was gaining an increasing role in Asia, independent of Britain and the declining European colonial powers, and when neither the Soviet Union nor China could match the United States in Asia. Asia's politics and economy throughout Nehru's lifetime were largely determined by the actions of the United States and its allies and the reactions they provoked. At no stage could the Soviet Union build alliances or a military and economic presence in Asia to challenge the United States.

Nehru also tried to reach out to the Soviet Union, which he had visited in 1927, but until Stalin's death in 1953, nothing significant occurred. Stalin reportedly did not once meet the first Indian ambassador, Nehru's sister, Vijaya Lakshmi Pandit, although he did meet two of her successors. In part, both Stalin and China's Mao, his ally, were skeptical of India as a former part of the British empire. It took some time for both to accept Indian independence as genuine. Stalin may have revised his view of India, however, after seeing India's neutral approach and attempts at mediation during the Korean War, leading to his pulling back on support for communist revolution in India.

As the Cold War hardened in Asia in the mid- to late 1950s, it affected and limited the geopolitical space available to India. While the United States approached others with a for-or-against-communism attitude, a more isolated Soviet Union saw any country that was not an enemy as a friend. The United States organized SEATO in 1954 and CENTO in 1955, further hardening Cold War positions. Pakistan was a founder member of both.[17] The Soviet Union, on the other hand, lacked allies or a treaty presence in Asia apart from North Korea and its difficult partner, China. The Soviets therefore befriended countries that could be neutral like India. As U.S.-Soviet relations intensified in the mid-1950s through various crises, and as Sino-Soviet antagonism worsened after Khrushchev's denunciation of Stalin in 1956, Indo-Soviet ties warmed through the late 1950s, surviving despite Nehru's public criticism of the Soviets during the Hungarian uprising of 1956 and in 1958.

As noted above, Nehru preferred a nonpartisan role for India during the Cold War, one free of the entanglement of alliances. He had learned a valuable lesson from World War II, when the country had been dragged into the conflict by its British overlords. "We propose, so far as possible, to keep away from the power politics of groups aligned against one another, which have led in the past to world wars and which may again lead to disasters on an even vaster scale," Nehru said in September 1946. An early sign of this policy was the decision by the new government of independent India to forgo war reparations from Japan after World War II and not to sign the San Francisco Peace Treaty, which Nehru considered victor's justice. Instead India signed a separate peace treaty with Japan and sought to facilitate Japan's reentry into the international community.

For Nehru nonalignment was as much pragmatism as principle, an instrument as much as a policy. It was, he said, "not a wise policy to put all our eggs in one basket . . . purely from the point of view of opportunism . . . an independent policy is the best."[18] He always said that nonalignment was best judged by its results and outcomes in practice. He was temperamentally opposed to any attempt to raise it to credo or to institutionalize it. Nehru therefore successfully resisted attempts by China at Bandung and by Indonesia's Sukarno and others later to organize the nonaligned countries into a regular system of meetings with a secretariat. For Nehru it made no sense to oppose the Cold War blocs only to form another bloc of the nonaligned. Such institutionalization as did occur, and even the nomenclature of a Non-Aligned Movement, only became current and was adopted as his influence waned, particularly after the war with China in 1962. When China tried and failed with Sukarno and others to create an alternate bloc of Afro-Asian countries after 1962, it became clear that Nehru's looser conception of nonalignment, which allowed countries to use the policy for their own ends rather than be led by a bloc or its leaders, was much more practical and appealed to many more countries.

$\sim$

Nehru's grand conception of India's place in the world was chiefly circumscribed by geopolitical changes that followed the partition of India and the Chinese occupation of Tibet. Both Pakistan and China limited Nehru's attempt to remake Asian geopolitics. As Olaf Caroe noted, partition had turned the subcontinent in on itself, and in his eyes the events of 1947 were tantamount to the "negation of India's power.[19]

The new government of India was faced at birth with outright war and a series of Pakistan-related crises, the most significant of which involved Jammu and Kashmir in 1948, 1950, and 1951. Those had been preceded by Junagadh and Hyderabad and by bilateral crises over water, property, refugees, and other issues.

The details of Kashmir's accession to India and the war of 1947–1948 are well known. Less well known, probably because it was a lingering and long-lasting crisis, was the continued suffering caused by migration between what was then East Pakistan and India. In 1950 violence against minorities in East Pakistan triggered the movement of a large number of refugees to India, leading

again to the brink of war. War was only averted by Nehru using military mobilization to coerce Pakistan into accepting his proposals for steps to restore
confidence in the minorities. Nehru and Pakistan prime minister Liaquat Ali
Khan did so in the April Nehru-Liaquat pact in Delhi. Several factors im-
pinged simultaneously on the government of India's responses and actions vis
à vis Pakistan thanks to the constant overlay of other events on the running
Jammu and Kashmir crises, such as the effects of Pakistan policy on integration of states like Hyderabad with recalcitrant rulers seeking independence, the
communal situation in India, and broader international ramifications. For instance, the decision to move militarily into Hyderabad on September 13, 1948,
was hastened by the storm in Jammu and Kashmir. It is this interrelationship
between events that drives decisionmakers' minds and that historians miss if
they consider each issue in isolation. Initially, Patel was open to the possibility
of Kashmir joining Pakistan. In the Constituent Assembly he was skeptical of
giving Kashmir special status through the device of Article 370. But once war
broke out, and he saw the ramifications of Kashmir acceding to Pakistan on
other states like Hyderabad, he changed his mind.

The creation of Pakistan had one immediate geopolitical consequence—
India now had a hostile neighbor in the west, with claims on Indian territory,
which had won independence from India, not from Britain as India had done,
and whose fragile sense of identity was built from the beginning in opposition
to India. The story is told that when Zia-ul-Haq, president of Pakistan, was
asked in 1987 why he had introduced *nizam-e-mustafa* (literally, rule by the
prophet) to Islamize Pakistan, he replied: "If an Egyptian stops being a muslim
he is still an Egyptian, if a Turk stops being a muslim he is still a Turk, but if a
Pakistani stops being a muslim he becomes an Indian." Even if apocryphal, the
story reveals a truth that Pakistan's rulers are conscious of—the fragility of the
Pakistani sense of identity.

The international situation was also not helpful to India when Pakistan
first sent tribal raiders followed by the Pakistan Army into Kashmir in an attempt to force the Maharajah to accede to Pakistan and then to take it by force.
India, after Jammu and Kashmir's accession to India on October 26, 1947,
sent in troops and complained to the UN Security Council about Pakistani
aggression. There was no doubt and ample proof of Pakistani aggression. But
for their own purposes, to use Pakistan and to insert themselves into the issue,
the United Kingdom led the United States into treating the matter as a dispute
between two states over the status of Jammu and Kashmir rather than as a case
of aggression that must be vacated. The prevarication and diplomacy involved is

well described in Chandrashekhar Dasgupta's book both as a description of the issue and of how power politics is played. The United Kingdom worked consciously for a solution to Jammu and Kashmir that was satisfactory to Pakistan. The United States was persuaded to go along with British policy on Jammu and Kashmir in the UN in 1948.[20] That these parties could find no solution to the dilemma of Jammu and Kashmir was due to India's coercive strategy and willingness to go it alone and reject what was pushed onto the country through the UN.

There has been much second guessing of the Indian decision to take the Kashmir issue to the United Nations, and of the conduct of the war, including the decision to accept a UN-sponsored ceasefire in December 1948. Patel, for one, questioned Nehru's promising the UN a plebiscite or referendum to determine the future of Kashmir. Hindsight is a wonderful thing, clear and certain and never available to the participants. For me, what stands out is how limited were the instruments available to India at the time. The first commanders-in-chief of both the Indian and Pakistani armies were British and reported more extensively to their own diplomats and their compatriots in Pakistan or India than to their nominal political masters in India. In India there were even occasions when the British commander-in-chief of the Indian Army, General Roy Bucher, did not carry out direct orders from his Indian masters. When a key moment arrived regarding the prosecution of the war in Jammu and Kashmir, it was the considered advice of the Indian and British military commanders to Nehru that India could not carry the war to a victorious conclusion and that India accept a ceasefire.

India rejected the UN resolution of April 1948 but accepted the resolution of August 1948 with conditions. Pakistan refused to implement critical parts of the resolutions, such as the withdrawal from Jammu and Kashmir of Pakistani forces and tribal forces, but later began to use the resolutions for propaganda. Once a ceasefire took effect on December 31, 1948, the ceasefire line was delimited within six months. None of the subsequent steps envisaged by the UN resolutions or agreed to by both India and Pakistan, albeit with conditions, such as the truce agreement, plebiscite, and others, were ever implemented, and they were soon made irrelevant by developments on the ground. All in all, however, in practice India's core interests were preserved in Jammu and Kashmir.

As a result of India's actions to secure Kashmir and the country's further mobilization in 1950 and successful use of coercive strategies, Pakistan concluded that it could not take Kashmir from India by conventional war. Thus, formal peace was maintained for several years, while Pakistan concentrated on covert means and sought to destabilize Jammu and Kashmir and India itself, a policy that continues today.[21]

There are some who blame India's coercion and success in thwarting Pakistan in Kashmir for the outsize political role of the Pakistan Army in Pakistan's politics. This puts the cart before the horse. One of the Pakistan Army's calculations in starting the war in Kashmir may well have been that hostility toward India would help the army gain power within Pakistan. Besides, *jihad* in Kashmir gave the Pakistan Army allies among the religious right in Pakistan.[22] Responsibility for that can hardly be laid at India's door.

As noted earlier, the 1948 war over Kashmir made Pakistan available as a Western partner as the Cold War began. Olaf Caroe argued in the late 1940s that control of the oilfields of southwestern Asia were critical, that in the contest between the West and the Soviet Union, control of India (and Pakistan after Partition) would ensure control of the Gulf region, that stability in the Middle East depended on British control of undivided India, and that with India's breakup Pakistan would have to take over the role of enabling control of the oil fields.[23] After Partition, the West found a ready client in Pakistan. The United States and the United Kingdom worked to create a Western-oriented South Asia in order to serve their Cold War interest in containing the Soviet Union and China. When the war in Jammu and Kashmir made it clear that India-Pakistan hostility made it impossible to have both India and Pakistan as allies and forced a choice between the two, Caroe's arguments about Pakistan's utility prevailed in Western counsels. The United Kingdom argued that having created Israel and alienated Muslim opinion throughout the Middle East, it and the United States would be seen letting down Pakistan, an untenable position to the Arabs, if they did not support Pakistan in Kashmir. Besides, India's neutrality in Korea and on other issues made that country an unlikely partner.

From a Pakistani point of view, the serial Kashmir crises were proof of its need to obtain arms and external security guarantees. Prime Minister Liaquat Ali Khan sought weapons from the United States in a letter to Secretary of State Dean Acheson on October 25, 1951. Two weeks later the United States sought discussions with Pakistan on the defense of the Middle East.

The 1948 war had another effect with lasting consequences. It transformed the Indian Army, previously viewed as an imperial instrument of British India, into the national army of India in the popular mind and in the minds of the leaders of the freedom movement. The war also clarified Indian attitudes as to force and its use. Gandhi, the apostle of nonviolence, himself justified this war because Indian territorial integrity was threatened.[24] As far back as 1928

Gandhi had written, "If there was a national government, whilst I should not take any direct part in any war, I can conceive of occasions when it would be my duty to vote for the military training of those who wish to take it. . . . It is not possible to make a person or society non-violent by compulsion." At a prayer meeting on September 26, 1947, Gandhi spoke of his long opposition to all warfare, but added that if all other avenues had failed to secure justice, war was the only alternative left to the government. Faced with tribal raiders sent by Pakistan into Kashmir in October 1947, Gandhi said that it was right to save Srinagar (capital of Jammu and Kashmir) by rushing troops there. He added that he would rather that the defenders be wiped out to the last man to clear Kashmir's soil of the raiders than to submit.

~

On October 7, 1950, 40,000 troops from two divisions of the Peoples Liberation Army (PLA) crossed the Sino-Tibetan border at three points. On the same day China announced its military support for the beleaguered North Koreans who had bitten off more than they could chew by invading South Korea and provoking American-led intervention.

The creation of the People's Republic of China in 1949 and its occupation of Tibet in 1950 marked the second major geopolitical shift that accompanied the birth of the modern Indian state. Tibet was to be central to India-China relations in the 1950s and to have long-term consequences for Indian policy long after the fate of Tibet itself as a political entity had been decided.

It had been clear for some years that China intended to occupy Tibet, as it figured into Mao's 1936 list of territories lost to China, which also included Nepal and Bhutan. While waiting in the western hills outside Beijing, from April to September 1949, he had noted the "liberation of Taiwan and Tibet" among the first tasks of his new government.[25] Nehru and his officials were aware that this would create problems along India's borders. They therefore initiated contacts in 1947 with the Tibetan government of the Dalai Lama to see what might be done, and the military options were examined internally from 1948 on. An Indian Army major, Zorawar Chand (Zoru) Bakshi, later called "India's most decorated general," was sent into Tibet by Foreign Secretary K. P. S. Menon to report on the situation and its possibilities. The Tibetans themselves were divided on what to do and the fourteenth Dalai Lama was still a minor. Apart from Finance Minister Tsepon Wangchuk Deden Shakabpa and Head of the Mint Tsarong Dzasa, the rest of the Kashag, or Tibetan cabinet, did not want to risk provoking the Chinese with a military buildup. When the cabinet did finally ask for arms from India and sent a delegation to canvas the world in 1948, it was too little too late. India supplied some weapons in June 1949 and attempted training, but as Chief of Army Staff General Cariappa told Nehru in October 1950, the Tibetans had no military capacity to withstand the battle-hardened PLA, which had just driven the nationalist Chinese troops off the Chinese mainland. Cariappa added that the Indian Army itself, engaged in war in Kashmir and internal security duties, could at best spare one battalion of troops for Tibet. They would not be acclimatized and deployment would be limited to Yatung in the Chumbi Valley or, at the limit, no further than Gyantse and then not for long. In effect, India had no real military options in Tibet.

Nehru therefore had no choice but to use nonmilitary means such as diplomacy and persuasion. And in that, too, he was inhibited both by what the British had done to promote and recognize Chinese suzerainty over Tibet (in order to keep the Russian bogeyman out) and by the Tibetan desire to negotiate directly with China. The British had consistently refused to arm the Tibetans in the past, and a 1940 British Foreign Office note opined, presciently, that "China is bound to absorb Tibet after the war if not before and we can do nothing to prevent it." Once the Chinese moved in, the United States encouraged the Dalai Lama to go into exile in Thailand or Sri Lanka, but he chose not to accept the offer. Mao had offered better terms and abandoning his people in Tibet must have seemed wrong.[26]

Nehru is sometimes accused of "losing" Tibet in 1950, but he had little choice but to choose non-intervention. In effect, India had no military options and little diplomatic play. On November 18, 1950, Nehru wrote: "It must be remembered that neither the UK nor the United States, nor indeed any other power, is particularly interested in Tibet or the future of that country. What they are interested in is embarrassing China." Sadly, this is arguably as true today as when Nehru wrote those words. When the Tibetans appealed to the United Nations on November 7, 1950, they received no support.

The signing of the 17 Point Agreement for the Peaceful Liberation of Tibet on May 23, 1951, between the Tibetan authorities and the People's Republic of China, further limited India's options. The agreement has since been repudiated by the Dalai Lama. Incidentally, this remains the only such agreement in the People's Republic's history, and its signing implicitly recognizes de facto Tibetan independence before 1950 and that Tibet's status is different from that of the rest of China.

Deputy Prime Minister Vallabhbhai Patel had written to Nehru early in November 1950 bitterly criticizing Chinese actions in Tibet and warning against the dangers this posed to India. Nehru answered the note on November 18 and scheduled a discussion of the issues raised by Patel in cabinet, but Patel died on December 15, 1950. The conventional wisdom is that Patel's concerns were ignored. In actual fact, much of what he advocated was put into practice both before and after he had written of his concerns. While Patel may have died, the real author of Patel's note, Sir Girija Shankar Bajpai, remained in government as secretary general in the Ministry of External Affairs and then governor of Bombay and continued to advise and be consulted by Nehru.

Nehru's realism is evident in the actions he took when it was clear that China would occupy Tibet. He moved quickly to fasten the Himalayan states to India and to ensure the security of the North East Frontier Agency (NEFA). The treaties with Nepal (July 31, 1950), Sikkim (December 15, 1950), and Bhutan (August 8, 1949) bound their security to India's. The Chinese reacted to the treaty with Bhutan but not the others, saying that India had no right to make Bhutan a protectorate. On November 20, 1950, Nehru declared in parliament that the McMahon Line is India's boundary "map or no map," and that "we stand by that boundary and will not allow anyone to come across that boundary." A North and North East Border Defense Committee was set up under Deputy Defense Minister Major General Himmatsinhji to advise on measures to secure the entire India-China border, particularly the eastern sector. NEFA was formed and detached from Assam to be put under direct central government administration. The Sixth Schedule of the Constitution came into effect on January 26, 1950, for the administration of NEFA. Normal administration was introduced into the zone between the boundary and the inner frontiers left by the British in the northeast. In 1956 the Indian Frontier Administrative Service was formed. On February 12, 1950, Major R. (Bob) Khathing arrived in Tawang to extend Indian administration and expelled Tibetan ecclesiastical officials. (The Monpa tribes in this area, now the Kameng division of Arunachal Pradesh, are all of non-Tibetan origin.)

However, one must question some other steps that the government of India took in that period. For instance, on November 1, 1950, defense expenditure was pegged by the government at 1 percent of GNP, the Army was reduced by 50,000 men, and capital expenditure on defense was capped at 350 million rupees. The pre-Partition Indian Army of half a million had already been reduced by Partition to 280,000 and by 1951–1952 only numbered 230,000. The defense budget of 1.65 billion rupees was cut in 1952–1953 to 1.6 billion rupees.

India's subsequent actions in relation to Tibet can also be called into question. In 1954 India gave up the privileges and rights that it had inherited from

British India in an Agreement on Trade and Intercourse between India and the Tibet Region of China. Under the agreement India agreed to dismantle its wireless, telegraph, military detachments, and posts in Tibet and to effectively limit Indian presence and trade in Tibet. India even permitted the Chinese to feed their troops in Tibet with grain from India, and for the first few years Chinese supplies to Lhasa went through India! When an agreement with China was first being considered in 1951, Girija Shankar Bajpai, K. P. S. Menon, and others urged Nehru to make the agreement conditional on a clear understanding of where the India-China boundary lay and to negotiate that simultaneously. The ambassador to China, K. M. Panikkar, on the other hand, opposed the linkage to the boundary or even raising the issue. Nehru chose to listen to Panikkar.

By 1956 when the Dalai Lama and the Panchen Lama came to India on November 24 for the 2,500th anniversary of the Buddha's enlightenment, eastern Tibet or Kham was in full-fledged revolt against the Chinese.[27] The Dalai Lama told Nehru that he did not wish to return to Tibet. Chinese concern over the Dalai Lama's new position is evident from Premier Zhou Enlai's three visits to India—between November 1956 and January 1957—until he managed to persuade Nehru and the Dalai Lama to drop the idea. Nehru always regretted this decision. In 1959, however, India readily granted asylum when the Dalai Lama escaped Tibet, and asylum continues to be assured in India—partly perhaps to ameliorate Nehru's guilt at having asked the Dalai Lama to believe Chinese assurances in 1956.

Tibet, and China's determination not to lose Tibet, was to be central to India-China relations in the 1950s and 1960s, ultimately leading to war in 1962. In the early 1950s, China's pretext for occupying Tibet was to protect it from an Indian takeover. This was also the argument used by Mao to justify the 1962 decision to attack India.

The Tibet issue had other long-term consequences for Indian foreign and security policy. India and the United States kept their relations on an even keel through the 1950s despite U.S. Secretary of State John Foster Dulles' charge that nonalignment was "immoral." This was in part because the two countries agreed on Tibet. Such congruence was expressed in clandestine cooperation with and support for the Tibetan guerrilla resistance, begun as early as 1956 when China began consolidating its hold over the Khampas in eastern Tibet and settling Tibetan nomads in Szechuan prefectures.

Another consequence is still working itself out today, even when Tibet should no longer cause China neuralgia, now that Chinese power makes it unlikely that China will lose her physical grip on Tibet. After 1956, convinced that India was using the Tibetan refugees and the Dalai Lama to separate Tibet from China, China looked for other levers to pressure India. One that was close at hand was Pakistan, with its inveterate hostility to India, which was and remains the cement in the relationship between these two dissimilar allies.

Significantly, widespread sympathy for the Tibetan refugees and the Dalai Lama in India led to public opinion, the media, and the Indian parliament becoming increasingly hostile to China through the 1950s. China's brutal treatment of peaceful Buddhist Tibetans who represent no threat still arouses widespread indignation in India. This effectively limited the Indian government's options in dealing with China and the boundary question. There was no realistic prospect of rolling back the Chinese occupation of Tibet or of securing international recognition of Tibet as a country. Nor was there a meaningful possibility of working with the Chinese, as Nehru tried briefly in 1954–1956, to make Tibetan lives better and to preserve their autonomy, their links with India, and India's role and presence in Tibet. Especially after 1959, given Chinese paranoia about Tibet, there were few good options for India's Tibet policy.

⁓

Although a lack of hard power may have limited India's options vis à vis China during this period, it did not inhibit dealings with the rest of the subcontinent. A stark contrast exists between Nehru's methods in Nepal and Bhutan in 1947–1951 and those of China in Tibet. Nehru was quick to seek to stabilize relations with the Himalayan kingdoms and did not hesitate to use India's dominance to influence their internal affairs, drawing on the legacy of British India but preferring minimal coercion and interference in the subcontinent's affairs, unlike his less restrained daughter, Indira Gandhi.[28] Under Nehru, India assumed responsibilities that had previously been managed by British India in the Himalayan kingdoms in the treaties signed with Nepal, Sikkim, and Bhutan soon after independence. All three had been part of the inner ring of the Raj. In 1940 the Foreign Department had described Nepal as "a state with very special relationship with His Majesty's Government." The status of Bhutan and Sikkim was never clearly defined. As a nationalist, Nehru saw advantage in reorganizing their existing rights and international personality, ambiguous as those were. As a realist, however, he was wary of changes that might affect Indian security or the ability of the subcontinent to be a cohesive geopolitical unit.

Like all subsequent governments of India, Nehru's government treated south Asia as the core of India's security sphere. From the point of view of India's smaller neighbors, India was an influential presence in their economies, polities, societies, and culture. India's predominance in south Asia—with 75 percent of the population, 79 percent of GDP, and 75 percent of land area of south Asia narrowly defined, without Afghanistan and Myanmar—is compounded by its geographic centrality to the subcontinent. All other south Asian countries border India but none border one another, except Pakistan-Afghanistan and Bangladesh-Myanmar. It is natural for other states in the subcontinent to hedge against Indian dominance and push back, while at the same time drawing cultural, political, and other influences from India. And with sizeable ethnicities across each of India's borders, the internal stability of its neighbors directly affects India's security and vice versa.

From the 1950s these same affinities—crossborder ethnicities, social commonalities of language, religion, and culture, and economic integration, as well as porous borders within the subcontinent—have affected India's security. Indian reactions to developments in the subcontinent are not a colonial Raj reflex or a regional hegemon's policy. Instead those reactions constitute a neighborhood policy that flows from geography and history.[29] What India sees as defensive reactions to developments is sometimes seen differently by others. India is not helped by the fact that official and political India has adopted a very different and idealistic way of presenting its actions in the subcontinent as purely benevolent and altruistic. Particularly in its neighborhood policy, this sets up a false binary between values and interests, between the demands of realpolitik and stated principles like non-interference and sovereign equality. In most cases, the demands of both are or can be reconciled. Where they cannot, India has invariably chosen realpolitik over declaratory consistency.

Take, for instance, Nepal. In 1950–1951 India actively assisted King Tribhuvan and democratic forces led by the Nepali National Congress, which had been formed in 1947, to bring about the fall of the Rana autocracy. King Tribhuvan sought refuge in India in November 1950, and a pro-democracy rebellion by the Nepali Congress succeeded in February 1951. India strongly supported democratization then and during the rest of the decade. When I. K. Singh led a rebel faction of the Nepali Congress into revolt in January 1952, India provided military assistance to support the democratic regime forcing him to flee to exile in Tibet. But when the royal coup of 1960 ended Nepal's first experiment with democracy, returning the kingdom to royal autocratic rule, India chose to work with the resulting regime of King Mahendra.

In Burma, as well, India worked closely first with General Aung San's interim government and then, after he and his interim cabinet were assassinated in July

1947, with Prime Minister U Nu's democratic government. India even provided military assistance for U Nu to fend off a communist rebellion in 1948. When Burma became free on January 4, 1948, there were 12,000 Kuomintang troops in northern Burma, and Karen ethnic insurgents were fighting the government with the full support of the Communist Party of Burma and the Chinese communists. Nehru provided the embattled government of Burma with weapons, ammunition, and six Dakota aircraft. U Nu later said, "Without the prompt support in arms and ammunition from India, Burma might have suffered the worst fate imaginable."[30] Burma had pleaded with the United States to prevail on the Kuomintang on Taiwan to withdraw their troops from Burma, but to no avail. India and Burma then took the issue to the UN Security Council in April 1953. This was part of a policy of working with the governments of neighbors to stabilize the periphery and build the larger Asian area of peace, as Nehru called it, rather than an ideological call. Later, when the 1962 military coup ended fourteen years of multiparty democracy in Burma, India again worked with the new regime. In both these cases, the changed external environment, particularly with China, and an assessment of the internal stability of the new dispensations led to a pragmatic policy choice rather than a futile attempt to export India's preferred liberal democratic values.

India's active commitment to Indonesia's freedom was also evident even before the country was fully independent. Nehru had met Mohammed Hatta in Brussels in 1927. Between 1946 and 1949, with the Indonesian struggle for freedom at its peak, the Indian National Congress under Nehru did its level best to support the struggle. Earlier Nehru had been firm in opposing ideas in the Congress of sending a brigade to Vietnam to assist Ho Chi Minh in his armed struggle against the French. But he was ready to extend all other kinds of support to General Aung San's effort in Burma and to Sukarno and Hatta in Indonesia. On July 22, 1947, Indian politician Biju Patnaik, who had flown Hatta back to Indonesia, piloted a Dakota to help Indonesia's prime minister, Sutan Sjahrir, escape the Dutch. India also raised the Indonesian issue in the UN Security Council on July 30, 1947, and with U.S. support resolutions were passed calling on Holland to stop its brutal crackdown. The Dutch, however, were not deterred. In early January 1949 Nehru convened an eighteen-nation conference on Indonesia in Delhi, and its conclusions were soon reflected in UNSC resolutions on January 28, 1949, recognizing the Republic of Indonesia. Sukarno visited India within weeks of assuming office on January 1, 1950, and was the chief guest at India's first republic day on January 26, 1950.

India soon overcame a mixed reputation and legacy it had inherited at independence by strongly committing to decolonization, supporting national movements in southeast Asia, and working with established governments and democrats in the subcontinent. India had proven that it was no longer a colonial state. India also had to overcome the fact that some Indians had worked with the Japanese occupiers, which some nationalists in southeast Asia found repugnant. To overcome this legacy was truly an achievement for India.

Nehru is sometimes accused of neglecting the subcontinent in his pursuit of peace in Asia and the world, but this view is unfair. He perceived south Asia—a term popularized in the 1970s by U.S. social scientists and limiting in its scope—as deeply part of Asia. In this he was probably right. The subcontinent's problems of poverty, security, and development, and of a peaceful international environment, were no different from those in the rest of Asia. Indeed, he practiced activism in the subcontinent and attempted to make the subcontinent as a whole a part of his larger conception of an Asian "area of peace."[31]

Early actions by India in the late 1940s and 1950s in the subcontinent suggest an instinctive consolidation of the periphery by India through the renewal or renegotiation of treaty commitments, the coordination of foreign policies, and economic and social integration with immediate neighbors, the two largest excepted, China and Pakistan. The initial focus was on the neighbors with whom India shared a land boundary. The land boundaries were by and large agreed in principle in the 1950s, though demarcation on the ground was to take several years, again except for Pakistan in Jammu and Kashmir and with China. The initial sea-blindness was soon overcome in the next two decades when maritime boundaries with Indonesia, Malaysia, and others were agreed, and the Indian Ocean region and neighbors such as Singapore began to play a growing role in Indian thinking.

~

The other geopolitical consequence of the creation of Pakistan was that India was cut off from central Asia, and its dealings with west Asia were now limited to the sea route, a route that India no longer dominated or controlled. The role that British India had played in west Asian security was no longer possible for India without extraordinary effort and diversion of resources. In any case, developments in the region itself minimized any role India could play because of the mix of new Arab nationalist and pro-Western regimes installed in west Asia after World War II. The creation of Israel in 1948 had further polarized west Asia and the Muslim world, which fed into India's difficult relationship with Pakistan and the communal situation at home. This required particular effort by India to balance and manage its relations with countries in west Asia.

~

All in all, India successfully managed the rapid shifts in her geopolitical situation in the early years, before the Korean War hardened Cold War positions into alliances like CENTO and SEATO in the mid-1950s. However, events did limit India's options. The choice of nonalignment, the best policy at the time, was limited in its effect on others. In a broader sense, India was on the side of history on the big questions of the time—decolonization, nuclear disarmament, and expanding the zone of peace, as Nehru called it. But that did not make short-term choices any easier or the environment any less challenging as Pakistan and China showed, while successive Cold War crises limited India's political space.

3

Cold War Asia

The preoccupations of independence, of Partition, and of China's occupation of Tibet placed the new republic of India in an unprecedented geopolitical situation. From the 1950s through the early 1960s, until Nehru's death in May 1964, the Cold War further complicated India's situation. The Cold War also enabled India to play a role in Korea and Indochina that hard-power calculations alone would not have predicted. Overall, however, the Cold War influenced but did not determine everything in Asia.

As a contest for global political and military dominance and supremacy between the United States and the Soviet Union, the Cold War was also an ideological contest between two opposing systems of organizing life. Nothing like it had ever been seen before in history. Such a global contest was only possible after European hegemony had knitted the world economy together in the late nineteenth and early twentieth centuries, and after technologies such as the radio, telegraph, railways, and steam navigation made geographical barriers and boundaries permeable, effectively reducing distance to a calculation rather than an obstacle.

In their histories, origins, and behaviors, the United States and Russia were similar in more respects than they cared to acknowledge. Both were offshoots at the wings of Europe's great expansion in the late nineteenth century. While nineteenth-century United States expanded westward to the Pacific, Russia raced even faster eastward to the Pacific, at a rate of six miles a day, building a bigger empire and arousing British fears about its empire and its jewel, India. In the early twentieth century both countries almost simultaneously adopted internationalist ideologies that saw themselves as models for other countries— Wilsonian idealism and communist internationalism. The difference was that while the United States always saw itself and was seen by others as the future, Russia was primarily conservative and backward looking until communism became its ideology. In both cases their actual behavior was guided by a strong nationalist sense of manifest destiny and exceptionalism. The United States was secure behind a moat of two of the greatest oceans on earth and could retreat into isolationism, as it did in what W. H. Auden called the "low, dishonest decade" of the 1930s. Continental Russia, on the other hand, was a land power conscious of being surrounded by enemies and of having been invaded repeatedly in history.

In geopolitical terms, the Cold War constituted a system in that the world's leading powers all based their foreign policies on some relationship to it.[1] It was never the only game in town and did not decide everything but it influenced most things.

What makes it unique in history is that it was bipolar. Most world orders tend to be multipolar with many different powers contending for mastery. The bipolar exceptions are few and rare—eleventh-century China between the Song and the Liao; fifteenth- to seventeenth-century western Europe with Spain versus England; and ancient Greece where Athens and Sparta contended. All these bipolar systems except the Cold War ended in war and catastrophe—the collapse of the Liao in China, the Thirty Years War in Europe, and the Peloponnesian War between Athens and Sparta.

In the late nineteenth century for the first time in history, one continent, Europe, and its offshoots, the United States and Russia, dominated the world. This unique development led some Europeans to believe that they could take control of the whole world's future through the ideas and technologies that they had developed—an idea that lives on through communism and the American sense of being the "City on the Hill." We hear echoes of it in triumphant Chinese commentary since 2012 and in Xi Jinping speaking at the October 2017 Nineteenth Party Congress of a Chinese model as the way forward for other countries. Parts of Europe—Britain, France, and the low countries—had been militarily predominant on a world scale since the late eighteenth century. They were also economically predominant globally in terms of innovation and trade. By the late nineteenth century, the United States and Russia, both very special kinds of empire, were catching up and in some areas were overtaking Europe. The U.S. share of world GDP rose from 9 percent in 1870 to 28 percent in 1950 to about 25 percent today.

During the Cold War, there was never a perfect balance of power between the two superpowers. The advantage in economic and military power was always greatly in favor of the United States. That was why the United States could afford to follow Kennan's[2] strategy: contain the Soviet Union and wait it out, forcing the USSR into a ruinous arms race and into overextended military commitments, such as in Afghanistan, ultimately, to prevail. The Soviets countered by specializing in the weapons of the weak—espionage, insurgency, sabotage, and propaganda. The Soviets also resorted to much tighter control over their allies, in ways for which there was no equivalent in the West.

Soviet strengths were in some forms of military power, geographical location, which gave it control of Eurasia, and the global appeal of communism, particularly after the two disastrous world wars, widely seen, not just by Nehru, as having been brought about by unfettered capitalism and empire. By 1985, 38 percent of the world's population lived under communist regimes. In postwar Asia that appeal was buttressed by the congruence between nationalism and communism in China (thanks to the Japanese invasion in the thirties), Vietnam (where the Viet Minh under Ho Chi Minh were the only effective resistance to French colonialists), and elsewhere in decolonizing Asia where the communists offered another way of organizing economy and society different from the past and from the "free" markets of the colonizers. But in terms of effective military power or alliances and presence on the ground or influence in local economies, Soviet influence in Asia could never match that of America. It was the United States that determined Asian geopolitics, in the 1950s and 1960s, not the Soviets.

There is a Cold War foundational myth in the West that persists today of the United States setting up a "liberal rule-based order" after World War II to which is ascribed much of the good that followed such as the long postwar economic boom and the peace between the superpowers. But this Cold War world was neither liberal nor orderly nor rule-based for most of Asia's inhabitants.[3] Great power behavior in the Cold War and thereafter was driven by the pursuit of their interests and not of some mythical order.

In fact, U.S. commitments to rescue Britain financially after the Second World War and to rebuild Western Europe were far from popular in the United States in 1946. As the then U.S. ambassador to the Soviet Union, Averell Harriman, noted, Americans "wanted to settle all our differences with Russia and then go to the movies and drink Coke." In a repeating story, true again today, U.S. policy elites believed in a Western international order of free trade, multilateral institutions, and a global U.S. military presence. But popular and political support for it in the United States only came when such an order was seen as part of an existential struggle with the Soviets. Something similar may be happening with U.S.-China relations today. The so-called liberal rule-based order was slow in the making and evolved gradually, not necessarily in response to a Soviet threat, which hardly existed, but in piecemeal U.S. responses to situations designed to contain Soviet power and protect itself. The Bretton Woods institutions were established while World War II was on. The United States supported pro-Western governments in Turkey and Greece in 1947, the Marshall Plan was unveiled in 1948, NATO was created in 1949, the U.S.-led military coalition began fighting in Korea in 1950, and the final piece in the order, the new security treaty with Japan, was only signed in 1960.[4]

The Cold War helped to cement a world dominated by superpowers, a world in which might and violence, or the threat of violence, were the yardsticks of international relations, and where beliefs tended toward the absolute. Only one's own system was good. The other system was inherently evil. The Chinese and North Korean regimes still claim authoritarian forms of legitimacy going back to the Cold War.

It is remarkable that the Cold War between the superpowers ended peacefully. It was less successful in keeping the peace. John Lewis Gaddis calls it "the long peace,"[5] a description that ignores the violence at all levels below the superpowers and the great powers. During the Cold War, an average of more than 1,200 people died in wars of one type or another every day for forty-five years. While the primary focus of the Cold War was in Europe, the Cold War's emphasis shifted steadily to Asia, and the most violent confrontations were between the Mediterranean and the Pacific, where most battle deaths linked to the Cold War occurred in what Chamberlin calls the Cold War's killing fields.[6] Seven of ten people killed in violent conflict between 1945 and 1990 died in rimland Asia, in the almost contiguous belt of territory from the Manchurian plain, through Korea, Indochina, and west across central and west Asia, which formed the front lines of the Cold War. Here, along Asia's southern rim, more than 14 million people were killed in warfare. The superpowers flooded the area with foreign aid, sending 80 percent of it to the "Third World" here.[7] The Cold War also solidified the partitions of India, Korea, Palestine, Indochina, and Germany, often by local wars. Historian John Lewis Gaddis explains the long peace as follows: "The nations of the post-war era lucked into a system of international relations that, because it has been based upon realities of power, has served the cause of order—if not justice—better than one might have expected."[8] To my mind, the great powers enjoyed a "long peace" after World War II as a result of the balance of power and nuclear deterrence rather than any widely accepted or enforced "order," and by exporting contention and violence to the so-called Third World. If the Cold War did not turn hot between the superpowers, some credit is definitely due to the awesome power and destructive capacity of nuclear weapons. We have since learned to live with the bomb but in the 1950s nuclear annihilation was still a new and terrifying thought, particularly after the Castle Bravo test of March 1, 1954, which at fifteen megatons turned out to be 250 percent more powerful than predicted by the physicists.

Because superpower dominance was neither total nor uniform, there was space in the Cold War world for other, weaker actors to take the initiative. Superpower rivalry made nonaligned politics possible. Even allies and client states could actually take the initiative and lead their powerful patrons onto paths that they did not wish to take, as the wars in Korea and Indochina show.

~

Originally neither Joseph Stalin nor Harry Truman considered Korea particularly important or worth defending. Like Germany, Korea was jointly occupied by the United States and Soviet Union at the end of the war in Asia in 1945. (It had formally been part of the Japanese empire since 1910 and occupied since 1885.) The allied powers had set the 38th parallel as the demarcation line splitting the peninsula in half, the north under a communist regime led by Kim Il-sung and the south under a U.S. ally with authoritarian tendencies, Syngman Rhee. Both Rhee and Kim wanted their patrons to let them reunify the peninsula, but neither was encouraged to do so. In fact, the United States withdrew troops from Korea in 1948–1949 and decided to only defend some island strongpoints in Asia, namely, Japan, Okinawa, and the Philippines, and not Korea or Taiwan. This was announced by Secretary of State Dean Acheson on January 12, 1950, when he described the U.S. defense perimeter in a speech expanding on remarks by President Truman. Promptly, Mao and Kim saw an opportunity to persuade Stalin to permit Kim to reunify the peninsula by force. Kim maintained that the war could be won in three days. With this, Stalin saw an opportunity to compensate for his losses in Europe in Greece and Turkey and to open a second front against the United States in Asia, where the United States had not intervened to save the Kuomintang (KMT) on mainland China or on Taiwan. North Korea invaded the south and drove South Korean troops almost off the peninsula, until the United States intervened, authorized by a UN Security Council resolution that passed in the absence of the Soviets. The Soviets were boycotting the council because of the U.S. refusal to seat Beijing in place of Taiwan in the Chinese Security Council seat. MacArthur landed troops at Inchon near Seoul in mid-September, trapped North Korean forces south of the 38th parallel, and marched victoriously toward the Chinese border.

China watched this turnabout with dismay and sent warnings to the United States through Ambassador Panikkar in Beijing and others that the United States should stay away from China's land borders or China would intervene militarily in Korea. When these were ignored by MacArthur, China formally sent 300,000 troops across the Yalu River, its boundary with North Korea, on November 26, 1950, and chased U.S. and South Korean troops to the 38th parallel in some of the most brutal weather and fighting in history. China had prepared the ground for its military intervention by infiltrating soldiers into Korea from October. By spring 1951 the Chinese People's Volunteers, as they were euphemistically called, had outrun their supply lines. Chinese troops in Korea included Mao's son, Mao Anying, who was killed in November 1950. The following two years of appalling fighting devastated the peninsula, killed 36,568 American troops, about 400,000 Chinese troops, and over 2 million Koreans. Finally, in July 1953, after Stalin's death on the night of March 1–2, 1953, and with Truman replaced by Eisenhower in January 1953, an armistice was signed, leaving the boundary where it was when the war began.

India played a role in Korea even before the Korean war. In late 1947 the United Nations created a UN Commission on Korea to oversee troop withdrawals as part of a UN General Assembly agreement to Korean independence. K. P. S. Menon, India's first foreign secretary, chaired the commission to advise the UN on political arrangements in Korea. The commission recommended that the UN restore the unity of Korea and warned in its 1948 report that if the unity of Korea was not restored, "Korea may blow up and that may be the beginning of a vast cataclysm in Asia and the world." Two years later Menon's prophecy came true. Soon after the report was presented, the United States introduced a resolution to establish a sovereign state in south Korea called the Republic of Korea, thus going against the recommendations of the commission. India voted for this resolution, in a turnaround, unlike the two other members of the commission, Canada and Australia.[9] Given its painful experience of being partitioned in 1947, it was not surprising that India instinctively opposed the partition or attempts to make permanent the division of Korea, Palestine (to create Israel), Germany, and Indochina. However, in each case India was quick to accept the emerging reality and to deal pragmatically with both Koreas, Israel, and the regimes or states that emerged from internationally accepted partitions.

When the Korean war broke out, India sent an army medical unit as part of UN forces, carried messages from the Chinese to the United States even though

Truman did not want to hear them, and insisted from the very beginning on an end to war and a withdrawal to the 38th parallel. India also subsequently played a role in the prisoner of war issue: China and North Korea wanted all soldiers repatriated; South Korea and the United States would only repatriate those who were willing to return. India headed the commission that ascertained the prisoners' preferences and negotiated a way forward after Rhee, to prove his point and get his way, released all the prisoners of war who didn't want to return to China and North Korea. India was not particularly effective in Washington, D.C., initially. Truman had a blind spot about India and Nehru. "He just doesn't like white men," Truman complained after meeting Nehru for the first time. He also blamed India for the United States not winning in Korea. Nehru's efforts had convinced Truman that "Nehru has sold us down the Hudson. His attitude has been responsible for us losing the war in Korea." President Eisenhower, on the other hand, after his 1953 inauguration, signaled an interest in the comprehensive Indian proposals for a ceasefire. What was finally agreed in the armistice was very close to what India had proposed two and a half years before, which had been so resisted initially by whichever side thought it was winning the war. It had taken the death of Stalin, the election of a general as U.S. president, and a huge cost in human lives and suffering to secure agreement on the Indian ideas.

For Nehru, India's activism in Korea was a result of his conviction that unless Asia were to be made into an area of peace, the world risked real disaster. He therefore persevered in attempting to expand what he saw as the space for reason and diplomacy between the warring great powers and to moderate the conflict so that it did not result in a global conflagration, a role as peacemaker that peaked in the early 1950s. His successors, such as Lal Bahadur Shastri and Indira Gandhi, did not share his views, with their narrower sense of the priority and exclusivity of India's security interests in the subcontinent over Asian and global peace.[10] Nehru's broader conception of India's role continued to guide Indian policy in the next few years in Indochina, during the 1955–1956 Formosa strait crisis, in the Tibet trade agreement with China in 1954, and in the diplomacy leading up to and around the Bandung Conference of Afro-Asian countries in 1955. For Nehru, these events were linked and part of India's key role as a peacemaker. Both superpowers found this role useful in 1954–1955, and even encouraged it, as was apparent when First Secretary Nikita Khrushchev and Premier Nikolai Bulganin visited India in 1955 and President Eisenhower changed U.S. policy from treating nonalignment as hostile to U.S.

interests to being potentially useful. In the brief period of superpower detente that resulted in Austrian neutrality and the Big Four agreement on Indochina and other issues in the mid-1950s, India helped to ameliorate tensions in Asia.

The Korean war was the first-large scale conventional war fought after the deployment of nuclear weapons. It proved that bloody and protracted armed conflict could involve countries with nuclear weapons and take place in conditions of nuclear asymmetry, when one combatant and not the other had nuclear weapons. It was the only instance, we now know, of actual combat between Soviet and American armed forces as Soviet pilots flew fighter missions in Korea against the U.S. Air Force.

It also showed how the Cold War embroiled superpowers even in issues that were not direct threats to them. Faced with worries about "losing" China, Truman had to react to the Korean scenario even though that region was not critical to U.S. security. The Korean war made Japan an important U.S. ally. In other words, if China made Korea important, Korea made Japan important to the United States. This logic led to President Eisenhower speaking in 1954 of the "dominoes" that would fall if the United States did not defend its allies in Asia and would later justify U.S. involvement in the quagmire of the Vietnam War. A peace treaty was signed with Japan in San Francisco soon after the Korean War broke out, as Japan had become central to U.S. military planning.[11] The United States began to work with Japanese politicians and leaders associated with militaristic Japanese governments of the 1930s, such as Kishi Nobusuke, a future Japanese prime minister. In Pakistan as well, the Pakistan Army and the anticommunist religious right wing were the beneficiaries of the U.S. search for local allies. If the Cold War strengthened the right-wing and polarized politics in Asia, it did so within the United States as well. Korea sent the anticommunist paroxysms of Senator Joseph McCarthy into overdrive and toughened the roots of an emerging and fervently anticommunist U.S. foreign policy establishment.

~

A similar pattern was repeated elsewhere in Asia, where India was active in building peace and where the logic of the Cold War created superpower involvement in local issues and disputes even when a superpower's security was not directly affected.

When World War II ended, Ho Chi Minh declared Vietnam independent in August 1945, establishing the Democratic Republic of Vietnam (DRV), and Sukarno proclaimed a new sovereign state of Indonesia. By January 1947 Aung

San had also negotiated the withdrawal of the British from Burma. Like Subhash Chandra Bose, who formed the Indian National Army from Indian prisoners of war taken by the Japanese, both Aung San and Sukarno had worked with the Japanese during their occupation, on the promise of freedom. In turn, the Japanese also had promised India independence, whereas the British under Churchill had only guaranteed autonomy as the Japanese readied for an invasion of India in 1944. U.S. president Franklin D. Roosevelt rightly feared that reimposing colonialism in southeast Asia after World War II would drive nationalists into communist arms, as proved to be the case in Indochina, but the European colonial powers—Britain, France, Holland, and Portugal—were determined to restore their empires. In 1947, when the Communist Party of Indonesia revolted openly, the United States intervened politically, forced the Dutch to leave, and worked with India to get the UN to recognize Sukarno's republic. India under Nehru actively assisted Sukarno in Indonesia and Aung San in Burma to shed the colonial yoke, offering political and some military and logistical support. It was clearly in independent India's interest to expand the area of free and like-minded countries in its periphery. However, given the limited resources available, and the determination of the colonial powers, unopposed by the United States before 1947, the British were able to reimpose their hold on Malaya, though at the cost of more than a decade of communist insurgency.

The French return to Indochina after World War II was harder than the British restoration of empire in southeast Asia, France having been knocked out of the war at the very start and French colonial authorities having collaborated with Japanese occupying forces under Vichy. When Roosevelt, Stalin, and Churchill met at Potsdam in July 1945 they did not even consult de Gaulle in deciding that Britain would occupy and accept the Japanese surrender in Indochina south of the 16th parallel and the Republic of China would do the same to its north. The British, worried about preserving their own empire in Asia, allowed the French to take control of southern Vietnam, using Indian Gorkha troops to establish order while Japanese troops joined the French in combat against the Vietnamese in September–October 1945.[12]

Over the next decade France attempted to isolate Ho Chi Minh's Democratic Republic of Vietnam and to send troops north of the 16th parallel. The French hold over territory in the north was sporadic and weak. For both sides, it was only with the evolution of the international situation, the founding of the People's Republic of China in October 1949, and the onset of the Cold War that the French and Ho Chi Minh began to get meaningful international backing. The French had hoped to create a French protectorate by installing three monarchies in Laos, Cambodia, and Vietnam and uniting them in an "Associated States of Indochina." The United States recognized the Associated States in 1950 and began sending military advisers and supplies to the French as the Cold War hardened. Stalin and Mao recognized Ho's Democratic Republic of Vietnam in January 1950 and began to send military and other aid in significant quantities, in an attempt to shore up one of the People's Republic of China's vulnerable flanks, the other being Kim in Korea. When the Korean war intensified after 1950, so did Chinese and U.S. involvement in Vietnam. In the initial stages, both China and the United States refused to enter Vietnam militarily but sent advisers and weapons, politically supporting their allies, the Democratic Republic and the Associated States, respectively.

But France was losing the full-blown colonial war on the ground against Ho's Vietnam, and the war ended in spectacular defeat for France at Dien Bien Phu in May 1954. The Democratic Republic of Vietnam engaged and defeated the Western colonizer in a set-piece battle, in which President Eisenhower refused to intervene. The battle was epic in its impact: militarily in Vietnam, politically within France. Most important, it led to the international negotiating table. From Ho Chi Minh's point of view, the victory at Dien Bien Phu was perfectly timed politically. International developments had been moving in the direction of detente between the great powers with the armistice in Korea in mid-1953. A new Soviet leadership under Khrushchev and Bulganin needed time to consolidate its domestic position, and the United States under a new president, Eisenhower, was weary after the Korean war. In September 1953 the Soviets proposed a conference of the United States, United Kingdom, France, and the Soviet Union to reduce international tensions in Germany, Korea, and Indochina. Germany was discussed by the powers in Berlin in January–February 1954. On May 8, 1954, the day after Dien Bien Phu fell, the conference took up the question of Indochina in Geneva.

The United States was not prepared to recognize or sit at a table as equals with the People's Republic of China or the Democratic Republic of Vietnam. It was at Geneva that Secretary of State John Foster Dulles famously refused to shake the outstretched hand of Zhou Enlai, a slight that Richard Nixon righted at Beijing airport in 1972 and that the Chinese still mention today. The practical solution in Geneva was to allow each of the Big Four—the United States, Soviet Union, United Kingdom, and France—to bring a guest, and China attended as a guest of the Soviet Union. The main Indochina parties joined the "Four Powers plus China," namely, the Associated States of Indochina—Vietnam,

Laos, and Cambodia—and the Democratic Republic of Vietnam (DRV). The dynamic at the conference was interesting. The United States did not wish to get involved in another hard and long Asian ground war. The Soviets wanted to concentrate at home and in Europe where they saw a real threat. China wanted to keep the United States from replacing France on its southern flank. China and the Soviet Union were pursuing peaceful coexistence with India and other noncommunist Asian states to neutralize U.S. collective security arrangements in Asia. (The United States had signed the Mutual Cooperation and Security Treaty with Japan on March 8, 1954, and later would agree to a mutual defense treaty with Chiang Kai-shek's Republic of China on Taiwan on December 2, 1954.) Indeed, Zhou Enlai visited Burma and India in the midst of the Geneva Conference to sign the Five Principles of Peaceful Coexistence with India and Burma.

Before and during the Geneva Conference, Nehru told Zhou quite clearly that communist efforts to create states under communist parties—the Pathet Lao in Laos and the Khmer Issarak in Cambodia—were hardly neutral acts, that they would only arouse fear among other states keen on peaceful coexistence in postcolonial Asia and would justify U.S. attempts to organize an anticommunist bloc. The Soviets and China wanted to convince other Asians such as India that there was no communist threat to them that justified direct U.S. military intervention in Asia or that required them to join U.S. security arrangements. China and its Soviet allies therefore rolled back Ho and Vietnamese communist expectations, getting the DRV to withdraw Vietnamese troops from Laos and Cambodia and to agree to a partition at the 17th parallel, which meant the communists vacating considerable strategic territory. In return the Vietnamese were promised elections throughout Vietnam in mid-1956 to decide whether Vietnam would be unified under the Democratic Republic or the State of Vietnam. A ceasefire was initialed by France and the Democratic Republic of Vietnam on July 21, 1954. The first Indochina war had come to an end. In effect, Vietnam was partitioned at the 17th parallel between two authoritarian regimes: a communist north under Ho and a capitalist south under Ngo Dinh Diem, who had been named prime minister of the state of Vietnam by Head of State Bao Dai in 1954.

Again, like Korea, the war in Indochina had ended with an armistice and a declaration but no formal peace agreement. The Geneva accords could not stop the Vietnamese from warring against each other, nor could they stop indirect military involvement from the United States in Indochina becoming direct over time. The Geneva Conference did achieve a ceasefire. Both Korea and Indochina were stalemated and frozen conflicts for a while. Once the Cold War and great power dynamics shifted in Asia with the Sino-Soviet split and normal geopolitical factors began to operate, the trajectories of Korea and Indochina diverged. In Indochina the stalemate did not last long, and the issue was settled in Vietnam when North Vietnam prevailed militarily in 1975 after prolonged resistance to the U.S. military and its South Vietnamese allies. Ironically, after 1975, the same North Vietnam was opposed by China and the United States in the rest of Indochina. In Korea the long military stalemate continues and has now been further entrenched by North Korea's nuclear weapons.

India was not invited to the Geneva conference, though, like others, it was an interested party present on the margins. But the role that India played was significant. India was important during and after the conference in helping to arrive at an agreement and in implementing it. India had chosen not to recognize either the Associated States of Indochina or the Democratic Republic of Vietnam, preferring to steer a neutral course between communists and colonialists and their superpower sponsors. In Geneva Krishna Menon had about 200 interviews in three weeks with various heads of delegation and others, playing a bridging role. It was a measure of the significance of India's role that Zhou Enlai visited India in the midst of the conference at the end of June. In India, Zhou reaffirmed India's peacemaker role and endorsed the logic of the peace area. Nehru prevailed upon him and the Soviets to reassure Asian countries worried by their export of communism to accept a compromise in Vietnam. For China, the threat of U.S. military bases and presence in Indochina, when still dealing with the aftermath of the Korean War on its eastern flank, was a powerful spur to compromise. China saw neutralizing Indochina and preventing its becoming a springboard for the United States against China as the goal. Nehru's motivation throughout was not to pursue narrow balance of power security but to seek to stabilize the geopolitical status quo by promoting an area of agreement in contested zones around India.[13] The simultaneous negotiation of the 1954 Panchsheel Agreement with China and normalization with China was also designed to limit the effects of the Cold War around India following the November 1953 military supply and defense agreement between Pakistan and the United States.

The Geneva conference set up an International Control Commission for Vietnam, Laos, and Cambodia, of which India was a member with Canada and Poland, to supervise the peace and implementation of the Geneva accords.

While this was recognition of India's acceptability to all sides of the conflict and proof of its nonalignment, in practical terms the elections and other steps were stymied from the outset by the disinclination of the powers and their clients to compromise or share power in Vietnam. No unified elections were ever held, and the war soon resumed, first as a civil war and then, in the 1960s, with increasing direct U.S. military involvement in the fighting.

~

India played a similar bridging role, and indeed can be said to have averted U.S.-China clashes, in the Formosa or Offshore Islands crisis. From September 1954 to August 1955 China, on the one hand, and the United States and Taiwan, on the other, indulged in brinkmanship over several islands spread along nearly 400 miles of China's eastern seaboard. In August 1954 Chiang Kai-shek moved 58,000 troops to Quemoy, an island two miles away from PRC-held Amoy, and 12,000 troops to Matsu, off Fujian. On September 3 the People's Liberation Army began to barrage Quemoy, which was met by KMT air attacks on Amoy. When the United States strengthened 7th Fleet deployments and increased reconnaissance over China, a U.S. aircraft was shot down and fifteen U.S. airmen were taken prisoner by China. By November 23 the United States and Taiwan had agreed to the terms of their defense alliance under which the United States was committed to defend Taiwan but not the offshore islands, and their defense treaty was signed on December 12, 1954. By March 15, 1955, Dulles was warning publicly that a major communist move to capture Taiwan would be met by U.S. intervention of "sea and air forces equipped with small and precise nuclear weapons." The threat was repeated by President Eisenhower the next day, in words reminiscent of U.S. nuclear threats prior to the French defeat at Dien Bien Phu in March 1954.

The United States and China were mutually antagonistic and suspicious with no proper direct communication channels. Indian diplomacy concentrated on carrying messages between them, with Krishna Menon traveling between Beijing and Washington, which finally led to the establishment of an ambassador-level channel in Geneva between the United States and China, and the release of U.S. prisoners by China. Nehru spent considerable time at Bandung persuading Zhou to recognize the impossibility of taking Taiwan by military means. Zhou's dramatic offer on April 24, 1955, of direct bilateral talks with the United States was a reflection of India's role. At the National People's Congress in Beijing on May 13, 1955, Zhou, at Krishna Menon's urging, said that "the Chinese people have two possible means of liberating Taiwan—namely, by war or by peaceful means. The Chinese people are willing to strive for the liberation of Taiwan by peaceful means, as far as this is possible."[14]

Largely as a result of Indian diplomacy, the U.S. airmen were released by China on August 1, the day on which U.S.-China talks at the ambassadorial level began in Geneva. In effect, Nehru was engaged in each of these cases in a quest for a polycentric world softening the impact and confrontation between the hard security blocs of the superpowers and their allies.

~

If weaker allies like Kim, Rhee, and Ho could maneuver superpowers to do what they wanted, how much more so powers that stayed neutral and kept their links to both sides of the Cold War? That was the realist basis of India's non-aligned policy, which later morphed into the nonaligned movement in 1961. The convergence of their interest in expanding autonomy by encouraging neutrality and resisting superpower hegemony brought Nehru, Tito, Nasser, Sukarno, and, initially, Zhou Enlai together and led to the Bandung Afro-Asian Conference in April 1955.

The conference had a long pan-Asian pedigree and was attended by twenty-nine countries and many more nationalist parties and liberation movements. Participants included India, Indonesia, Egypt, and China, and also Japan, Iran, Iraq, and Turkey, who attacked anti-American views. In effect Bandung showed that a third way other than joining a superpower camp was possible. Nehru was keen that this should not be seen as a third camp or bloc but as an alternative policy, which permitted working with the superpowers for decolonization, disarmament, and development, and against racism and apartheid. In the 1960s, particularly after decolonization in Africa, an economic development agenda and south-south cooperation came center stage in the movement. Zhou proposed at Bandung that the Afro-Asian powers institutionalize their cooperation in the form of a "Liaison Office" or "Joint Secretariat" for future conferences. To Nehru this smacked too much of another bloc, precisely what he was opposing. Nehru therefore was not receptive to such ideas, and indeed his opposition to future conferences led to a rift between him and Sukarno. Nehru opposed nonalignment being formalized into a movement until 1961 in Belgrade, when the Congo crisis had shown that something more was needed than occasional words and meetings or informal coalitions on issues. Though still opposed to the idea of an institutionalized movement, Nehru felt by 1961 that he had no choice but to go along with its creation. The Belgrade meeting set up regular conferences and arrangements for what was later known as the Non-Aligned Movement. By then the Congo crisis had also shown Soviet weakness in the Soviet inability to save Lumumba and the Belgrade meeting therefore sought to challenge the Cold War system through new forms of international cooperation.

The sheer number of countries, including allies of the superpowers, who wished to join nonaligned summits and the movement is proof of the utility, independence, and wide appeal of nonalignment, despite everything that the United States and the West have done to give it a bad name, and all that the Soviet Union did to coopt the movement and make it appear one with the socialist bloc. Nonalignment did achieve most of its early goals in the 1950s such as decolonization, the partial test ban treaty, and international boycotts of apartheid South Africa. It was less successful when it came to economic issues, as this cut to the heart of the dominance of established powerholders in the international system. Nonalignment was also a useful buffer and channel between the superpowers, as Korea and Indochina showed. But this did not work in all cases—in 1956 the United States left popular uprisings in Hungary and Poland to be dealt with by the superpower patron of east Europe, the Soviet Union, and nonaligned countries including India were largely silent spectators.

∿

The other post-Bandung test of the high principles espoused by so many at the conference was the Suez crisis of 1956.

In 1956 Nasser nationalized the Suez Canal. Israeli forces went into action against Egypt on October 29, 1956, just as the Hungarian crisis reached its peak. French and British forces invaded Egypt on November 5. While military victory was theirs, the ultimate resolution of the crisis was not in their favor. A furious President Eisenhower forced them to withdraw. "How could we possibly support Britain and France if in doing so we lose the whole Arab world?," Eisenhower said. It became clear that Britain and France could no longer act independently against the American will and that public opinion in the post-colonial world counted when it worked with the hard power of one of the superpowers. The real winners were Nasser and the United States. Egypt kept the canal, humiliated the colonialists, and balanced the Cold War superpowers one against the other. This secured Nasser's position as the undisputed leader of Arab nationalism. But leaders like Nasser, Ben Bella of Algeria, and Nelson Mandela of South Africa were unhappy with India's position in favor of negotiations during the Suez crisis and its lack of military support to African liberation movements at the time. And in the manner of its resolution, the Suez crisis showed that in a Cold War world, ultimately it was the superpowers who counted and determined outcomes, not the old imperial European powers or the larger numbers of the nonaligned countries.

Nehru told the Lok Sabha on November 20, 1956, that "The use of armed forces by the big countries . . . has really shown its inability to deal with the situation. . . . The greatest danger the world is suffering from is this Cold War business. It is because the Cold War creates a bigger mental barrier than the Iron Curtain or brick wall. . . . It creates barriers of the mind which refuses to understand the other person's position, which divides the world into devils and angels."

～

Bandung was not the only attempt to organize Asia and the newly decolonized states. In 1956 Premier Kishi of Japan proposed to India and the southeast Asian countries an economic confederation through trade opening and investment in industrial development. Kishi's proposals stemmed from his desire to open space for Japan to function internationally. While his appeal fell on receptive ears in southeast Asia, it did not in India where its political motivation was suspect, and it was seen as a stalking horse for U.S. attempts to keep out socialist and communist ideas. The proposal came just as India passed an industrial policy resolution and the country had embarked on autarchic development with strong socialist characteristics with the Second Five Year Plan espousing ambitious industrial goals. Interestingly, this state-led import substitution strategy of industrialization was enabled by cheap grain imports from the United States, which kept prices and wages down. In retrospect, one wonders where the road not taken might have led India, a road that India was to choose three decades later in very different circumstances. In any event, India's per capita GDP grew slowly, at roughly 1.47 percent a year from the late 1940s to about 1980. Indexes of health and literacy were also weak with illiteracy declining just 11 percent from 1960 to 1977 and life expectancy rising only from 43 to 52 years. The population shot up, however, between 1951 and 1981 by 89 percent in India (and 78 percent in China).

It is an iron law of strategy that actions have reactions, though not always equal or precisely opposite. The real reaction to the visible success of the third way that Bandung and nonalignment represented was the consolidation of two U.S.-centered alliances in Asia, SEATO and CENTO. The South East Asian Collective Defense Treaty (SEATO), or Manila Pact, was signed on September

8, 1954, with eight members (Australia, France, New Zealand, Pakistan, the Philippines, Thailand, the United States, and the United Kingdom), more outsiders than Asians, and was headquartered in Bangkok until it was dissolved in 1979. CENTO, or formally the Middle East Treaty Organization, was formed on February 24, 1955, by Iran, Iraq, Pakistan, Turkey, and the United Kingdom. Dulles's explanation for the United States not participating was the "pro-Israel lobby" and the difficulty of obtaining approval of the U.S. Congress. CENTO was headquartered in Baghdad, and later Ankara, until it was dissolved in 1979. Neither treaty achieved much, apart from providing bases for the United States to operate from, nor were members ever called on to exercise collective defense. Pakistan, for instance, provided Peshawar for U-2 reconnaissance flights over the Soviet Union and China, and obtained U.S. weapons and fighter aircraft as an ally. But what the treaties signified was the next step in institutionalizing the polarization that the Cold War brought to Asia. They also revealed the relative Soviet weakness in Asia where it was unable to match the United States, as it had done in Europe with the Warsaw Pact in reply to NATO. Instead, the Soviets had to work with neutral Asian partners like India, Indonesia, and others. In 1955 Khrushchev and Bulganin visited India, supported India on Jammu and Kashmir, supported Goa's reversion to India, and promised and delivered aid. By 1961 the Soviet Union was ready to supply weapons to India despite India-China tensions over the boundary. If the U.S. attitude was "if you are not with me you are against me" until the second Eisenhower administration, Soviet weakness led them to "if you are not with my enemy, I am with you."

In many ways 1954–1955 was the high point of Nehru's peacemaking efforts in Asia, when his influence was at its height, coming off diplomatic success in Korea, Indochina, and the Offshore Islands crisis, the normalization of relations with China in the 1954 Agreement, his successful opening to the Soviet Union, and acceptance by President Eisenhower of an Indian role in Asia. The "Nehruvian" impulse in India's foreign policy was at its height. Thereafter, events, domestic politics and changing external circumstances would play an increasing role in restricting India's policy choices.

The SEATO and CENTO treaties were the high point of the classical binary Cold War in Asia which made Nehru's peacemaking diplomacy possible. This was when the binary Soviet-U.S. Cold War was at its most intense in Asia. Soon thereafter the Sino-Soviet split and other developments in Asia meant that the Cold War became only one driver of events, much less so than in Europe.

On February 25, 1956, Khrushchev spoke at the 20th Party Congress of the CPSU and denounced Stalin. The shock in the communist world was extreme. Polish Communist Party leader Bierut actually had a heart attack and died when he read Khrushchev's speech. For Mao the speech had several implications; that his model Stalin could be attacked meant that he could be too. And space had now opened up for him to bid for leadership of the international communist movement replacing the Soviets. Before long there were Sino-Soviet differences on peaceful coexistence, on the degree of militancy in the opposition to the United States, on their attitude to the use of nuclear weapons, and on leadership of the international communist movement. The unity of one of the two Cold War blocs was broken, and broken in Asia, never to be repaired until the end of the Cold War when the Soviet Union collapsed. Nehru was one of the first to recognize the Sino-Soviet dispute for what it was, a clash of nationalisms and ideological tendencies. Indeed, he had predicted it, or indicated that he thought it inevitable, as early as his first meeting with Truman on October 13, 1949, when he suggested that actions be taken to create a wedge between the two. The United States, particularly Dulles, thought the signs of a split were an elaborate deception by the communists. The geopolitical effect of the split was to complicate binary Cold War calculations in Asia. In Vietnam, for instance, competition between Russia and China gave Ho Chi Minh the means to carry on his war against impossible odds, to the extent of Chinese fighter pilots flying missions over Vietnam against the U.S. Air Force in the sixties. But its broader effect was to limit the scope and effectiveness of the sort of peacemaking that Nehru had undertaken in the first half of the fifties.

~

While the Cold War had by 1956 become more complicated in Asia, it still provided the basic international framework for addressing major issues of the day. Significantly, India and other countries were still able to play an active role in multilateral diplomacy on issues of wider interest. Take disarmament, for instance. The awesome power of nuclear weapons made it clear to everyone, even in the absence of common language, ideology, or other interests, that they shared a stake in each other's survival, given the tiger they themselves had created but now had to learn to live with. Many of the ideas that resulted in the Partial Test Ban Treaty, the Treaty on the Non-Proliferation of Nuclear Weapons, and other nonproliferation efforts grew from serious discussions of nuclear disarmament initiated by India and other nonaligned or neutral countries in the 1950s and 1960s. India worked with both camps and both superpowers.

It was always clear that nuclear disarmament was one of the hardest areas to negotiate and the least likely to succeed because no superpower would relinquish such hard-core power. But mankind's survival justified the effort. In 1957 Indian was a founding member of the International Atomic Energy Agency, which provided a forum to separate nuclear weapons competition from peaceful uses of atomic energy. Nothing in the multilateral negotiations, however, could address countries' security concerns until bilateral and other bloc arrangements had first been put in place by NATO and the Warsaw Pact, as well as the protection extended by the nuclear weapon states to their allies. Multilateral negotiations on nuclear disarmament certainly mitigated the risk of nuclear conflict and helped to limit the spread of nuclear weapons to many more states, even though the goal of general and complete disarmament remained distant as the two superpowers accumulated thousands of nuclear weapons.

Unlike disarmament and nuclear weapons, decolonization was not a Cold War issue. Neither the United States nor the Soviet Union was interested in maintaining Europe's colonial empires unless each nation's own interests were affected. By 1954, with Eisenhower's domino theory and direct U.S. bilateral commitments to defend treaty partners influencing American foreign policy, the United States was supporting local authoritarians around the world rather than the former colonial masters. Nor were the colonizers in any condition to carry on with their empires after World War II. The spirit may have been willing, but their flesh was weak. Decolonization accelerated in the decade and a half after India's independence, and the UN's considerable role was key to that process.

The weakest link in the Bandung and nonaligned program was economic development. The world economy was dominated by the West led by the United States. The West was the source of capital, technology, and markets to which all developing countries aspired. Throughout the Cold War, the Soviet Union was unable to provide a successful economic alternative to the Western capitalist economy, except in the most government-controlled sector of all, weapons. Very little of the economic development agenda put forward by India and the nonaligned was ever agreed multilaterally or implemented in practice.

In sum, the Cold War influenced everything but did not determine everything in Asia. It polarized and divided Asia and heightened the significance and impact of local conflicts as in Korea and Vietnam, and permitted some benign effects, as in decolonization. The direction of internal politics in several east Asian and southeast Asian states was directly determined by their involvement in the Cold War between the superpowers and the hot war in Korea. India and southern Asia were fortunate to be largely left alone to their own devices as they were marginal to the central conflicts of the Cold War in Europe and east and southeast Asia.

Did India have a good Cold War? Not really. Nonalignment made the best of a difficult situation. Essentially the Cold War system broke Asia into sub-regions and treated it as one more arena and therefore a sideshow to the confrontations of the two superpowers. While India can be said to have managed its effects on her policies through nonalignment and other mitigating means, the Cold War was certainly a complicating and limiting factor in Indian policy-making. Bipolar systems can be cruel on middle powers unwilling to be allies or clients of the superpowers. The Cold War exacerbated many of India's tactical policy failures. This was most apparent in its dealings with China and Pakistan which both found external sponsors and were willing to ally with the superpowers to further their aims vis à vis India.

～

The India-China boundary is a good example of both the Cold War's influence on events and policies around the world and of its limited effect when strong national interests and emotions were involved.

India has consistently maintained that there is a traditional customary boundary between India and China, one that is formalized by legal agreements for most of its length. When the Chinese People's Liberation Army (PLA) moved into Tibet in 1950, the central Chinese government had a permanent military presence on the border with India for the first time in history. It was settled imperial Chinese policy to refrain from sending supplies, funds, or troops and to avoid entanglement, as was made clear in repeated edicts by successive Qing dynasty emperors when approached for help by Gorkha rulers in Nepal against rising British power in India in the eighteenth century.[15]

After 1950, when India made its view on the boundary clear, the Chinese did not demur. Nehru had told Parliament in 1950 that the McMahon Line was India's boundary, map or no map. In 1954 and 1956 Nehru raised the matter of Chinese activity on what was considered the Indian side of the boundary and of incorrect Chinese maps, and Premier Zhou Enlai responded that those were old Kuomintang maps and that the Chinese were looking into the matter. Zhou assured Nehru that China had no claims on Indian territory. Indeed, the 1954 Agreement on Trade and Intercourse between India and the Tibet Region of China included specific mention of several passes that would be used for border

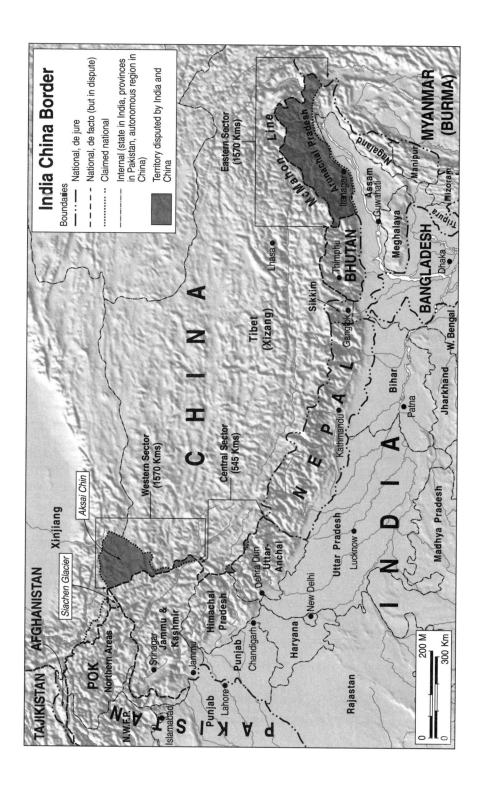

India China Border

Boundaries
- — · — National, de jure
- — — — National, de facto (but in dispute)
- ········· Claimed national
- ——— Internal (state in India, provinces in Pakistan, autonomous region in China)

Territory disputed by India and China

TAJIKISTAN

AFGHANISTAN

Xinjiang

Siachen Glacier

Aksai Chin

Western Sector (1570 Kms)

C H I N A

Central Sector (545 Kms)

Eastern Sector (1570 Kms)

McMahon Line

Tibet (Xizang)

Lhasa

POK

Northern Areas

N.W.F.P.

Srinagar

Jammu & Kashmir

Islamabad

Jammu

P A K I S T A N

Lahore

Punjab

Punjab

Chandigarh

Himachal Pradesh

Dehra Dun

Uttar-Anchal

Haryana

New Delhi

Rajastan

Uttar Pradesh

Lucknow

Madhya Pradesh

I N D I A

N E P A L

Kathmandu

Sikkim

Gangtok

BHUTAN

Thimphu

Itanagare

Arunachal Pradesh

Assam

Guwahati

Nagaland

Manipur

Meghalaya

Mizoram

Tripura

BANGLADESH

Dhaka

W. Bengal

Jharkhand

Bihar

Patna

MYANMAR (BURMA)

200 M

300 Km

0

0

trade, which seemed to confirm the Indian view. (It was only in 1960 that China argued that mentioning mountain passes for border trade did not mean that they were actually boundary passes.) That agreement, whose wisdom has been debated ever since in India, is hard to explain given Nehru's misgivings and doubts about Chinese behavior. It can perhaps only be explained as aimed at shaping a new Asian order and containing the Cold War which had come to India's doorstep when the United States agreed in November 1953 to supply arms to Pakistan. By normalizing relations with China and proactively shaping outcomes in Indochina, Nehru sought to counteract the emergence of new military alliances and to enlarge what he liked to call the area of peace.

Between 1950 and 1954 China concentrated on strengthening its hold on Tibet and India too was integrating border areas into the new republic. On September 27, 1951, Premier Zhou Enlai told Panikkar that "there was no territorial dispute or controversy between India and China."[16] But Nehru was unconvinced, despite the 1954 trade and border agreement. He wrote to Secretary General N. R. Pillai in the Ministry of External Affairs on June 18, 1954: "No country can ultimately rely upon the permanent goodwill or bonafides of another country. . . . It is certainly conceivable that our relations with China might worsen. . . . Therefore we have always to keep in mind the possibility of change and cannot be taken unawares. Adequate precautions have to be taken."

In 1954 a Chinese map showed Bhutan, Nepal, and India's Sikkim and North-East Frontier Agency as parts of China. Despite knowing this, Nehru did not raise the boundary question with Zhou Enlai on Zhou's first visit to India in June 1954. Soon thereafter Nehru decided to firm up India's position. Survey of India maps between 1889 and 1936 did not depict a precise boundary in the western sector but showed Aksai Chin as part of India. The 1945 Survey of India map showed India's present alignment in the western sector but marked it "boundary undefined," as did Indian maps of 1950, 1951, and 1952. They showed Aksai Chin with the same color wash as the North West Frontier Province, which was now in Pakistan. On July 1, 1954, Nehru instructed that the old maps be reexamined and withdrawn if necessary. New maps were printed with a firm and definite frontier without qualifications.

Nehru visited China, the first noncommunist head of government to do so, later that year in October, meeting twice with Mao Zedong. He left those meetings deeply disturbed by Mao's willingness to see the atom bomb used. He said later that he had been ushered in as if to see an emperor. Nehru could not bring himself to do the customary courtesy of inviting Mao to visit India. Nehru did not raise the boundary issue with Mao but did so with Zhou Enlai and told him that "our boundaries were clear and not a matter for argument." Zhou side-stepped the issue saying that these were old Kuomintang maps, according to Nehru's record of the conversation. The Chinese record is different, with Zhou saying that there was a "problem inherited from history," which would be dis-cussed with the neighbor in the future. When Zhou suggested issuing a joint communique at the end of the visit, Nehru demurred. In retrospect, would a negotiated communique have clarified and limited the extent of the boundary issue before it was set in stone and hard to solve? On his return to India Nehru told senior MEA officials Secretary-General N. R. Pillai and Foreign Secretary Subimal Dutt that he had "received the powerful impact of China's arrogant nationalism," and that "sooner or later this nationalism would assert itself and when that happened China would prove a problem for the whole of Asia." But if Nehru was so worried by what he saw in China, why did he not do more to prepare the country militarily and diplomatically and prepare the public for potential trouble with China? The records suggest that China's internal preoc-cupations in Tibet and elsewhere, and Nehru's sense of the Sino-Soviet split and U.S. pressure on China, made Nehru confident that relations between India and China would not deteriorate beyond a point, or, at the least, that India had time.

Zhou Enlai visited India again from December 1956 to January 1957 and raised the issue of the MacMahon line with Nehru. A telegram from the Indian mission in Beijing warned Nehru that Zhou had earlier told Burmese leader U Nu that the MacMahon line was "immoral" and based on an "unequal treaty," but that China would accept it as a de facto border for the sake of an agreement. After meeting Zhou Nehru wrote that Zhou had said that China proposed to recognize the MacMahon line with India just as Zhou had mentioned to U Nu. Zhou did not mention the western sector at all. When the Sino-Burmese boundary agreement was signed on January 4, 1961, it confirmed the MacMa-hon line alignment for the 192 kilometers in Burma, which had been part of India when the Simla Agreement was signed in 1914. On Foreign Secretary Dutt's advice, Nehru did not give Zhou the map he had prepared to show In-dia's borders, because, as Dutt wrote, "We should not be impolite to our guests." This advice from Dutt is all the more surprising because four months after the 1954 Agreement on Tibet, the Chinese PLA had intruded across the bound-ary for the first time, in Barahoti in the middle sector across Tunjunla, where there had long been a local dispute over grazing lands. On July 17, 1954, China protested an Indian intrusion in Barahoti, which was southeast of Niti pass, one of those mentioned in the 1954 agreement for border trade. Other intrusions followed in the middle sector, at Nilang and Shipki. As the situation in Tibet worsened for the Chinese and resistance grew more widespread, border incidents became more frequent and Tibetan refugees began to flow into India. Two Indian patrols sent out in 1958 to check on the Aksai Chin Highway were detained by the Chinese.

Through the late 1950s, the Cold War and the Sino-Soviet dispute sharpened India-China differences, especially after a 1955 visit to India by Khrushchev and delivery of Soviet aid. As Soviet relations with India improved, Sino-Soviet relations deteriorated. Khrushchev finally withdrew all Soviet advisers from China in 1958. The internal situation in China also became acute as a result of Mao's grandiose Great Leap Forward and communization in 1958. Over 30 million people died in the resulting famine and China's GDP dropped by as much as 27 percent in 1961. On April 27, 1959, Mao was replaced as president by Liu Shaochi. Equally, Nehru's 1956 visit to meet with Eisenhower in the United States, during which he spent fourteen hours in talks, was much warmer and more congenial than his earlier visit with Truman. Eisenhower did not think that India's nonalignment was against U.S. interests. A National Security Council document of January 10, 1957, reflected that shift, noting a respect for "India's choice of an independent foreign policy" and that inevitable disagreements should not come in the way of U.S. aid to India.

~

The year 1959 was a pivotal one for India and China in several respects, an *annus horribilis* when several developments led to a road to war without easy off ramps for the two nations.

On January 23, 1959, Zhou Enlai made it clear in writing for the first time that China disputed the fact that there was a legal India-China boundary. China wanted to negotiate the entire line.[17] Zhou did not dispute Nehru's version of the 1956 talks but laid out the full Chinese claim and repudiated all previous agreements. This was taken in India as Chinese duplicity and proof that India, which had acted in good faith, had been deceived by China. To be fair to Zhou, he had never said that he disagreed with the alignment of the boundary on the old Kuomintang maps or that he agreed with the alignment on Indian maps. He had simply said that he was willing to discuss the issue later. India chose not to. Nehru told the upper house of parliament at the end of 1959 that he had felt India should hold its position, that the lapse of time and events would confirm the boundary, and that when the challenge came India could be in a much stronger position to face it.

Mao's suspicion of Nehru as working with the United States against China seems to have become conviction in 1959. The United States moved quickly once the dispute was out in the open, with Eisenhower writing to Nehru and stepping up cooperation, not just in Tibet. Tibet was in outright revolt and large portions of Kham were outside Chinese control, at precisely the time when China itself was undergoing famine and turmoil caused by Mao's Great Leap forward. Mao, always given to conspiracy theories, was fighting to retain political power in the Communist Party after his policies had failed. In this beleaguered state of mind, Mao's conviction that India sought to detach Tibet from China was further strengthened when the Dalai Lama fled Tibet and entered India on March 31, 1959. The Dalai Lama was granted asylum while being treated as a head of state. Soon thereafter *People's Daily* vitriolically attacked Nehru in person, publishing two long articles—"On Nehru's Reactionary Philosophy" (May 6, 1959) and "More on Nehru's Reactionary Philosophy"—articles probably written by Chen Boda, Mao's amanuensis, which were certainly extensively revised by Mao himself.

Tibet and the Dalai Lama's exile in India were major factors in Chinese hostility, in the aggravation of the boundary question, and finally in the Chinese decision to wage war against India. The Chinese deny this, not wishing to advertise their weakness. On April 21, 1960, Zhou told Home Minister G. B. Pant that China did not object to India granting asylum to the Dalai Lama but to his "anti-China" activities. In 1960 a delegation from the Communist Party of India traveling to China asked Nehru what message he might have. He suggested they ask Mao how much of the border trouble was because of the Dalai Lama obtaining asylum in India. They did so, as an afterthought at the end of their meeting with Mao who sat down again and thought for a while. The answer from Mao, whether dissimulating or honest, was surprising: "Better that he sit in friendly India than in the imperialist US." But in 1964 Mao told a Nepalese delegation that "the main problem between India and China was not the MacMahon line but the Tibetan question. In the opinion of the Indian government Tibet is theirs." The immediate Chinese reaction to the Dalai Lama's escape was to crack down in Tibet and to "seal" the India-Tibet border, as the Military Affairs Commission decided on April 23, 1959. Internal PLA documents show 87,000 Tibetans killed between March 1959 and September 1960.

On May 16, 1959, Chinese Ambassador Pan Tsuli made a demarche to Foreign Secretary Subimal Dutt, which is worth reading in detail:

> The enemy of the Chinese people lies in the East—the US imperial-
> ists have many military bases in Taiwan, South Korea, Japan and in the
> Philippines—which are all directed against China. China's main atten-
> tion and policy of struggle are directed to the east, to the western Pacific
> regions, to the vicious and aggressive US imperialism and not to India.
> . . . India is not an opponent but a friend of our country. China will not
> be so foolish as to antagonise the US in the east and again to antagonise
> India in the west. . . . The putting down of the rebellion in Tibet will not
> in the least endanger India. . . . It seems to us that you too cannot have
> two fronts. . . . Is this not so? If it is, here lies the meeting point of our
> two sides. Will you please think it over?

This is a remarkably clear statement for a diplomatic communication. It
formally echoes and spells out what Mao had said privately to Nehru in Beijing in 1954 about fights between friends. It puts India-China relations in the
larger international context, presages China's opening to Pakistan, and offers
a realist modus vivendi. As an example of realpolitik logic, it is hard to better
this demarche, which resonates today. By saying that neither India nor China
can afford two fronts is Pan hinting that India can do what it likes on the western front if it understands China's concerns with the eastern front and does
not support the revolt in Tibet? We will never know. Incredibly, no analysis of
the demarche itself is on file. Nor is there an indication that any attempt was
made to use China's isolation in the international system to fashion a broader
response to this Chinese overture.

India's reaction to Pan's proposal on May 23, 1959, in a harsh note drafted
by Nehru was to reject the approach as "objectionable," "discourteous," and not
in accord with diplomatic niceties. This was a time when China-Pakistan relations were at a low ebb,[18] when China had broken with the Soviet Union, when
China's confrontation with the United States was at its height, and its internal
situation was at its worst under a divided leadership. India's rejection only made
the Chinese leadership even more wary of Nehru and his plans for Tibet and
his clandestine support for the Tibetan guerrillas and led them to suspect the
worst about Indian plans.

For the first time, on August 25, 1959, there was firing on the border
at Longju, which was clearly south of the MacMahon line and had been

acknowledged as such by China earlier in the year.[19] A neutral TASS news agency statement on September 9 convinced Mao that the Soviets were on India's side, and he had a furious exchange with Khrushchev who had come to Beijing on October 20 for the tenth anniversary of the People's Republic.

Soon thereafter, the Chinese softened their approach to India, probably recognizing their isolation and vulnerability in Tibet. On September 8, 1959, the politburo approved an effort to seek a negotiated settlement with India— offering India the proposition that both sides should maintain the status quo before negotiations began. Also approved was Zhou's September 8, 1959, letter to Nehru that made these offers.

In the meantime, opinion in India had hardened considerably, in sympathy with what was happening to Tibetans in Tibet and in response to what was seen as Chinese duplicity when the full scope of the boundary dispute came to light. On September 7, 1959, Nehru placed in Parliament volume I of White Papers detailing the entire exchange of correspondence with China.[20] Now there was no going back. Room for negotiation was further limited and public opinion was even more inflamed. In October five Indian policemen were shot dead by the Chinese at Kongka pass in the western sector. Their bodies were handed over by the Chinese on November 14, Nehru's birthday. Nehru was incensed and henceforth adamant. An aroused Parliament and media were baying for blood. One wonders why Chinese diplomacy in this period was so maladroit. The personal attacks on Nehru, the escalating violence in border incidents, and the choice of date to return the bodies were hardly calculated to lead to an amicable settlement of issues. It is quite possible that a divided Chinese leadership, and a PLA with its own agenda and loyal to Mao, led to the steady hardening of China's approach. The real driver and decider of China's road to war with India, by subsequent Chinese accounts, seems to have been Mao Zedong himself.

One final element in that pivotal year of 1959 bears mention. That is the resignation in India of Chief of Army Staff General Thimayya on August 31, 1959, after a running dispute with Defense Minister V. K. Krishna Menon over China policy, where Nehru took Menon's side. Thimayya argued, rightly, that India needed a major military effort if it was to recover areas in Ladakh that the Chinese had occupied. He also felt that Aksai Chin was a "strategic liability" rather than an asset and that the actual MacMahon line was militarily indefensible. This may have been sound military advice and judgment as events proved in 1962, but it was hardly a politically acceptable course of action in the fervid atmosphere of 1959. Instead of resolving these issues within government and using professional military opinion to educate the public and political classes,

Nehru and Menon encouraged Thimayya to resign. In their view, Thimayya
had strayed into issues outside his authority by advocating accepting the ideas
of Pakistan's president, Muhammad Ayub Khan, on Indo-Pakistani joint defense. Thimayya's departure left the serious issues he had raised unaddressed
and India undefended. This was not an auspicious augury for the handling of
civil-military relations by the new republic.

By the end of 1959 Nehru's China policy was in tatters. He had little room
for maneuver and no hard power either. China was hardly in a better position.
At least Nehru had friends in the United States and Russia and among the
nonaligned. China, on the other hand was isolated, partly by its own poor diplomacy, was internally in chaos, had made an enemy of India, and faced a real
prospect of losing its hold on Tibet. If there was ever a time when India had
a Tibet card, it was 1959, not 1950 or later. But India chose not to use it effectively. China was to use the next three years overcoming or mitigating the
impact of a precarious situation in order to gain leverage over the border with
India. From 1959 until the war in October 1962 China and India attempted
to find a way out on the boundary question without, however, understanding
the adversary's compulsions. Both operated on false assumptions: Nehru that
China would never resort to large-scale military conflict; China that India was
determined to detach Tibet and was in alliance with China's two main foes, the
United States and the Soviet Union.

⁓

Perhaps the last real opportunity to find a way to address differences on the
boundary and arrest the march to war was when Zhou Enlai came to Delhi in
April 1960. He met Nehru seven times during that visit and the leaders were
alone except for interpreters for over twenty hours. Nehru tried to explain his
domestic constraints to Zhou and sent him off to see his ministers and leaders like G. B. Pant, Morarji Desai, and S. Radhakrishnan. The intention was
to convince Zhou that Nehru had very limited room for compromise. Instead
the meetings were a disaster and left Zhou suspecting that he had been set up
by Nehru to be humiliated in an orchestrated series of conversations and in-
sults, as they would have been if the situation had been reversed and it had been
Nehru visiting China and encountering leaders telling him off.

Zhou tried to get Nehru to agree to six common points on the boundary
but India had trouble with the first three points themselves: that there exists
a boundary dispute, that there exists a line of actual control, and that a settlement should take into account the national feelings of the two peoples toward

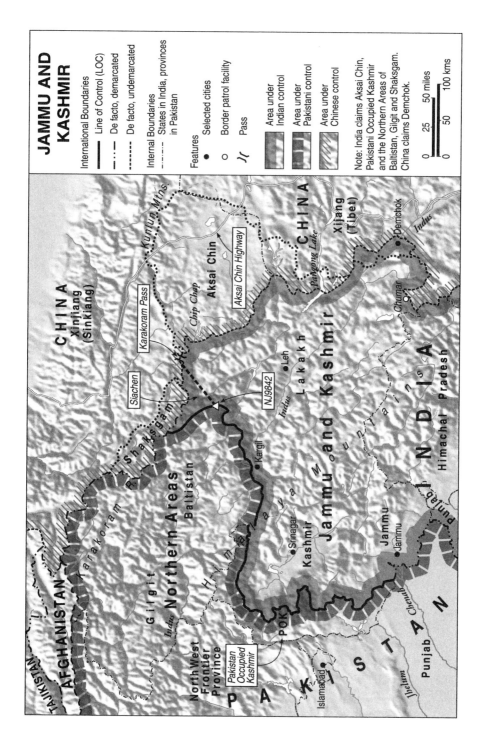

JAMMU AND KASHMIR

International Boundaries
- ——— Line of Control (LOC)
- —··—·· De facto, demarcated
- ·········· De facto, undemarcated

Internal Boundaries
- —·—·— States in India, provinces in Pakistan

Features
- • Selected cities
- ○ Border patrol facility
-)(Pass

- Area under Indian control
- Area under Pakistani control
- Area under Chinese control

Note: India claims Aksai Chin, Pakistani Occupied Kashmir and the Northern Areas of Baltistan, Gilgit and Shaksgam. China claims Demchok.

0   25   50 miles
0   50   100 kms

the Himalayas and the Karakoram mountains. Did Zhou suggest a "package deal" to Nehru, namely, that China might accept the MacMahon Line as the boundary in the east if India accepted the status quo created in the west by China moving forward into Aksai Chin during the 1950s? The Chinese record says that in his first meeting with Nehru, Zhou said that China would be "practical" on the area south of the MacMahon line. In his fifth meeting, Zhou said that the Line of Actual Control could be treated as the basis for a settlement. And in the sixth meeting, Zhou said that if India would recognize the line up to which Chinese administration had reached, China would recognize the Indian administrative line in the eastern sector. The Indian record, however, is ambivalent. S. Gopal, Nehru's biographer, says that no deal was offered. On the other hand, N. R. Pillai, secretary general in the MEA, told the British high commissioner that a deal was offered. In any case, China was never tested on the offer. The entire Indian cabinet was united in opposition to any "barter deal."

Nehru and Indian public opinion were outraged that China was effectively taking over Indian territory through cartographic aggression and by changing facts on the ground militarily, building the Aksai Chin Road from Sinkiang to Tibet, and garrisoning the area in the mid-1950s. To the Chinese, the timing of India's rejection of their offer, after India had given asylum to the Dalai Lama in March 1959, seemed to confirm their belief that India had designs on Tibet, which was in full-fledged revolt against Beijing's rule. The Chinese were convinced that the guerrilla war in Tibet from the mid-1950s to the early 1970s was aided and made possible by the Central Intelligence Agency in the United States and Indian agencies. For India, it was bad enough that the British empire for imperial considerations had sacrificed Indian interests in Tibet at the 1914 Simla Conference, including agreeing to the McMahon Line and handing over Tibet to China to keep the Russians out. Now the Chinese were demanding even more than the gift of territory given them by the British.

The only substantive result of Zhou's 1960 visit, apart from convincing each side of the other's obtuseness, was an agreement to hold talks between officials to examine evidence for their alignment of the boundary. Three rounds of talks in 1960 were held: Beijing, June 15–July 25; Delhi, August 19–October 5; and Rangoon, November 7–December 12. There was no meeting of minds, only a listing of evidence, of which India had much more. On February 7, 1961, Nehru tabled the report of the officials in Parliament, without consulting China about making it public, further inflaming opinion and reducing his room for maneuver.

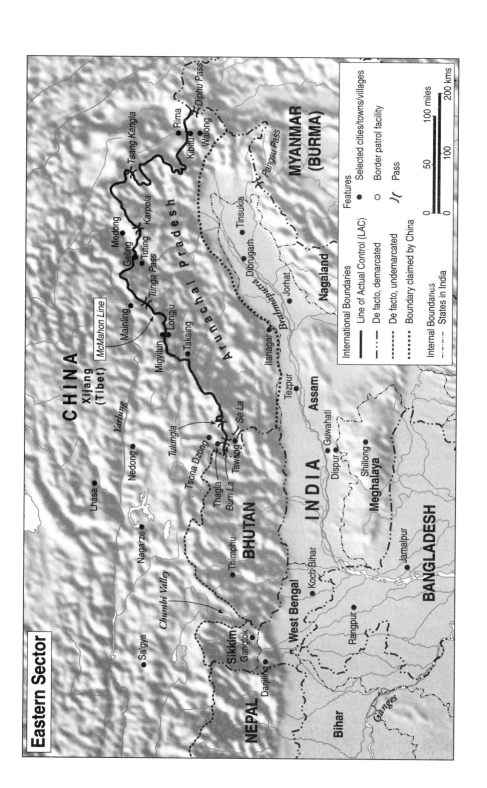

Eastern Sector

CHINA
Xijiang (Tibet)

Yarlung

- Lhasa
- Nedong
- Nagarze
- Sa'gya

Chumbi Valley

- Thimphu
- Tsona Dzong
- Tulungla

Thagla
Bum La
Se La
- Tawang
- Taksing
- Migyitun
- Longju
- Mainling
- Geling
- Medong

Tunga Pass
Longju
Tunga Pass
Karpola
- Tuting
Tsang Kangla
- Rima
- Kibitu
- Walong
Diphu Pass

McMahon Line

A r u n a c h a l   P r a d e s h

Brahmaputra

Pangsu Pass

MYANMAR (BURMA)

Nagaland

- Tinsukia
- Dibrugarh
- Jorhat
- Tezpur
- Itanagar

Assam

- Guwahati
- Dispur
- Shillong

Meghalaya

- Jamalpur

BANGLADESH

INDIA

- Koch Bihar
West Bengal
- Rangpur

Ganges

Bihar

NEPAL
- Darjiling
Sikkim
- Gangtok

BHUTAN

International Boundaries
———	Line of Actual Control (LAC)
—··—	De facto, demarcated
— — —	De facto, undemarcated
·········	Boundary claimed by China

Internal Boundaries
—·—·—	States in India

Features
●	Selected cities/towns/villages
○	Border patrol facility
)(	Pass

Scale:
0   50   100 miles
0   100   200 kms

~

By mid-1960, India and China had in place two elements essential for conflict—the world's biggest boundary dispute and the sense that the other was inveterately hostile. After Zhou's 1960 visit two additional factors entered into the equation. One was domestic developments in China which made war inevitable. The other was superpower contention in the Cold War which determined the timing of the war.

After 1959 Mao steadily lost power following the disasters that his policies and the Great Leap Forward and communization had brought to China. As he later complained, the politburo and Deng treated him like an ancestor, giving him respect and his say but then going off and doing what they wished, which to Mao looked like Soviet revisionism. On the foreign policy front, the head of the International Liaison Department of the Chinese Communist Party, Wang Jiaxiang, argued for "three harmonies and one reduction," namely, less hostility to India, the Soviet Union, and the United States and reduction in support for revolution abroad. In other words, he advocated that China not take on the whole world at the same time. Mao's counterattack to regain power started with foreign affairs, attacking and neutralizing Wang Jiaxiang in summer 1962, and replacing him with Kang Sheng at the Lushan plenum in September 1962. By all accounts, India unknowingly became one of the issues in China's domestic leadership struggle, a stick for Mao to beat his moderate opponents with. Mao pushed for strong action against India to teach India a lesson.

From the start Mao and Zhou had realized that this was not just an India-China matter. Mao had said, "Our struggle against India is a complicated international issue. It is not only an India issue because the imperialists and the revisionists are supporting India." China needed to neutralize the superpowers. And she managed them both well, extracting promises of neutrality from them in the summer of 1962. As a result, when the United States and Soviet Union were distracted by the Cuban Missile Crisis, China had a short period of opportunity when she had a free hand to deal with India.

How China extracted what she considered promises of neutrality from the United States and Soviets in 1962 is an object lesson in diplomacy. On May 29, 1962, Foreign Minister Chen Yi announced publicly that China expected a U.S.-supported Taiwanese invasion. This was the first the United States had heard of this, though Chiang Kai-shek had spoken vaguely of 1962 as a year of decision. The United States rushed to reassure China. On June 23, 1962, when

Wang Bingnan repeated the charge to the U.S. ambassador in Warsaw in the covert U.S.-China channel maintained throughout the Cold War, John Cabot told him, on instructions from home, that the "U.S. government has no intention of supporting a GRC (Taiwan) attack on the mainland in existing circumstances." Wang's memoir says that he could not believe his ears and asked Cabot to repeat his statement, which he did. Wang said later that this played a big part in China's decisionmaking on the war with India because China would not need to worry about the eastern flank. The Chinese may have been wrong to expect U.S. neutrality, but they acted on that conviction.

The Soviet Union was easier. On October 8, 1962, China informed the Soviet ambassador that India was planning a large-scale attack on China. On October 13 and 14, Chinese Ambassador Liu Xiao got guarantees from Khrushchev that if India attacked China, the Soviet Union would stand with China.[21] Indeed the initial Soviet reaction to the war was to tilt in favor of "fraternal" China and against "friendly" India, as we shall see.

In June 1962 the rules of engagement for the PLA were changed in Tibet. The Chinese army began moving beyond the 1956 line that Zhou had indicated in his December 17, 1959, letter to Nehru. Incidents and firing resulted in the Chip Chap valley. The final decision to attack India was taken at a military affairs commission meeting of October 6, 1962, presided over by Mao, but preparations, and the building of POW camps, had long been completed.

In 1962 war broke out in the high Himalayas. On October 20 China attacked isolated Indian posts in both eastern and western sectors that had been established to show the flag and prevent further Chinese incursions into Indian territory. The war was fought in two phases, in October and November. In effect, the Chinese were held at Walong near the Myanmar tri-junction. Near Tawang, beside the eastern tri-junction with Bhutan, the Chinese PLA inflicted a psychologically damaging and politically traumatic rout of Indian forces. In the western sector fighting was fierce at Rezang La, near Chushul, in Jammu and Kashmir state. Chinese troops cleared all Indian posts on what they considered their side of the Line of Actual Control in the Chip Chap River valley, Galwan River valley, and Pangong Lake areas. On November 20, 1962, China declared a unilateral ceasefire and a withdrawal to twenty kilometers behind what it described as the Line of Actual Control of November 7, 1959. During the course of the conflict, India had lost 1,383 soldiers, 1,047 wounded, 1,696 missing, and 3,968 taken prisoner; Chinese losses were 722 killed and 1,697 wounded. Only two Indian divisions had been in theater when the conflict broke out. In Namkachu, one Indian battalion faced three Chinese regiments alone, with predictably disastrous results.

There is an almost perfect chronological correspondence in 1962 between the India-China War and the Cuban Missile Crisis, which is too perfect to be coincidence:

September 11   China encircles Indian posts at Namkachu.
               The United States calls up reservists because of Soviet missiles in Cuba.

October 20   China launches a massive simultaneous attack.
               John F. Kennedy announces the quarantine of Cuba.

October 24   Tawang falls, and Zhou makes three-point proposal.
               Soviets decide to back off on Cuba.

November 20   China announces unilateral ceasefire and withdrawal.
               Cuba quarantine ends.

China had used superpower preoccupation with the Cuban Missile Crisis to do its work. China had also used the Cuban Missile Crisis to get Soviet support when needed at the outset of the crisis. Fearing a clash with the United States over Cuba, the Soviets supported China in October. Khrushchev offered to suspend the MIG 21 deal with India and to issue a declaration supporting China. On November 3, 1962, Chervonenko gave Zhang Hanfu copies of Nehru's correspondence with Khrushchev and Indian materials concerning China.

The United States, on the other hand, was quick to support India. On October 26 the United States announced that it recognized the MacMahon line as the border. In response to two panicky November 19 letters from Nehru, the United States had put 4 U.S. Air Force squadrons, 300 transport planes, and 14,000 troops on forty-eight-hour alert and dispatched a carrier group led by the U.S.S. *Enterprise* to the Bay of Bengal to indicate a willingness to intervene with air power if China continued to advance.

The war was an outright military victory for China and did great damage to India's reputation and role in Asia and the world, particularly to its status among the nonaligned. China's net gain in territory was about 2,000 square kilometers of desert in Ladakh. But the ceasefire was a mixed blessing for China. It solved nothing. China managed, thanks to the war, to pacify the border with India for several years and now could impose its will in Tibet. In effect, China had imposed by military force the border with India that it failed to obtain through Zhou Enlai's diplomacy. The Chinese had undermined Nehru's commitment to nonalignment, humbled India, and secured their immediate territorial objectives. But China certainly underestimated the war's long-term negative impact on Indian opinion and damage to India-China relations. Mao predicted to the politburo that India would forget about the war after thirty years. That might be Chinese psychology, but it certainly is not Indian psychology. Even today, fifty-eight years after the war, its trauma is keenly felt in India. One casualty of the war was the Communist Party of India, which had been the second largest party in India's first two parliaments. After the war it not only split into pro-Soviet and pro-Chinese wings but steadily lost vote share until it was marginalized into a regional party in two states. Indian politics shifted to the right as a consequence of the war.

~

In 1959 southeast Asian countries except North Vietnam joined India in condemning Chinese actions in Tibet. Indonesia remained silent, perhaps because Nehru had publicly restrained Sukarno from using force to take back West Irian, one-third of Indonesia's total territory that the Dutch had chipped away at independence. Three years later, in 1962, however, almost all of southeast Asia with the exception of Malaya had mixed reactions of disbelief about the India-China War and were publicly reserved in their comment. Indonesia and Burma were noncommittal. Tunku Abdul Rehman in Malaya was most supportive, raising a "Save Democracy Fund" and contributing one million rupees to India. India had suffered a loss in reputation and credibility in Asia that was to take several years to repair. In the longer term, the combination of the 1962 war, the course of the Vietnam War, and China's export of communist revolution in the 1960s convinced most noncommunist leaders in southeast Asia that their security could not be entrusted to a third path separate from the dominant power in the region, the United States. The Bandung spirit or Nehruvian area of peace was no longer viable or attractive. To that extent, the 1962 India-China war contributed to the formation of Association of Southeast Asian Nations (ASEAN) and the consolidation of the U.S.-led alliance structure in Asia.

The year 1962 was a disaster for China's third-world relationships. Most nonaligned countries, by and large, stood by India, and were convinced that India had been attacked, despite Chinese protestations. The Colombo Powers tried to mediate and produced proposals sympathetic to India. India accepted them in toto. China had two caveats, indicating from the start that the proposals would never be implemented. The net effect was to further isolate a bellicose China, seen as the aggressive party. When Zhou tried through an African safari to several countries in 1963–1964 to organize GANEFO games or an Afro-Asian organization and summit he failed. China was soon overtaken by the greater convulsions of the Great Proletarian Cultural Revolution. The war left China with enemies on all its borders and further isolated her.

The worsening India-China boundary situation, along with growing Sino-Soviet estrangement after 1958, made India increasingly aware of the Soviet Union's growing strategic value to India. During the war itself, the Soviets initially tilted toward China, needing China's support in the concurrent Cuban Missile Crisis and concerned that support for India further damage the Sino-Soviet relationship. But later, the Soviet Union sought to hedge its bets. As soon as the Cuban crisis was over, Khrushchev reassured the Indian ambassador in November 1962 that while the Soviets would not supply arms to either side, all existing commitments would be honored, including the supply of Antonov-12 military transport aircraft, MiG-21 fighter aircraft, and a MiG-21 factory to India—all committed before the war.

President Kennedy, on the other hand, airdropped weapons for India during the war. The United States immediately responded to Indian appeals for military assistance and supplied equipment and began training the Indian Air Force (IAF) and Indian Army. The United States enhanced the intelligence links that were already in existence. Each of these efforts continued after the war. The United States did not accede to Nehru's appeal for American combat aircraft to be sent to India, not wanting to risk drawing the West into an aerial war with China over the subcontinent. British and American officials told the Indian government that deploying the IAF to attack the PLA would be militarily ineffective in mountainous jungle. Instead, Britain offered surface-to-air missiles for sale, while the United States supplied radar, technical assistance, and Sidewinder air-to-air missiles to the IAF. By placing a fiscal burden on the government the war also increased India's dependence on Western aid.

Nehru was never the same after the war. He had been compelled to ask for U.S. and Soviet intervention for help against another Asian country. This was a huge blow to his prestige and policy. And India itself had forgotten the first rule of politics. The essential condition of a nonaligned policy was the ability to accumulate enough power to defend one's core interests, starting with territorial integrity. It was a lesson never to be forgotten. Meanwhile, failure in the 1962 war with China opened up India to superpower competition and pressure on a new scale.

～

As India's relations with China deteriorated after 1959, the international space for Indian diplomacy began to shrink. Worsening India-China relations put the Soviet Union in a difficult position of choosing between a fraternal China and a neutral India. But this gave the West an opportunity to move India toward the its own camp. The second Eisenhower administration was ready to help India, seeking to wean it away from the Soviet Union and to instill fear of China. The formation of the Aid India Consortium and the commencement of heavily subsidized grain supplies to India in 1958 reflected an increasing U.S. commitment. And in 1959 Eisenhower became the first U.S. president to visit the subcontinent when he spent forty hours in Pakistan and five days in India, to a rapturous popular welcome that surprised both the Americans and the government of India.

The British, ever sensitive to the effect of closer India-U.S. relations on Pakistan, believed that to square the circle of increased Western support to India with Pakistan's lynchpin role in the Western alliance system, a necessary condition was better India-Pakistan relations. They persuaded their American counterparts that drawing India into the Western camp required a thaw between India and Pakistan, which Pakistan would only consider if its issue of Kashmir were addressed. Pakistan's location placed it within striking distance of China, the Soviet Union, and the oil fields of the Persian Gulf. The Pentagon and State Department therefore laid great store by their listening posts and bases at Badaber, Peshawar, and Lahore in Pakistan, whatever presidents Eisenhower and Kennedy's appreciation of India's utility to U.S. strategy. Indeed, Pakistan had reacted in 1959 to improving relations between India and the United States by agreeing with Moscow to jointly search for oil near Attock and had declared its intention to enter into negotiations with the People's Republic of China to demarcate the boundary between Pakistan occupied Kashmir and Xinjiang, China.

A "package plan" was presented to the Indian and Pakistani governments on May 16, 1958, by British and American officials. The plan bundled together the Indus Waters dispute, Kashmir, and India-Pakistan defense cooperation. As anticipated, it was welcomed by Pakistan, which wished to change the regional status quo, while India effectively vetoed it, seeing no advantage or gain in the plan. The United States, working through the World Bank, then exerted considerable effort on the Indus waters dispute, a technical issue more amenable to solutions. The fruit of this effort was the Indus Waters Treaty, brokered by the World Bank and signed in 1960 by Prime Minister Nehru, of India, and President Ayub Khan of Pakistan. The treaty divided rights to use the waters of the rivers of the Punjab in an arrangement that has since survived wars and repeated breakdowns in relations. Ayub was also encouraged to propose to India that India and Pakistan should enter into loose joint defense arrangements for the subcontinent, which he did in May 1959, but was brushed aside by Nehru telling Parliament, "We do not propose to have a military alliance with any country, come what may." Nor was Nehru willing to discuss a Kashmir solution when he met Ayub in Murree in 1960 during his visit to Pakistan for the signing of the Indus Waters Treaty.[22]

In 1963, under intense encouragement from the United States and United Kingdom, a series of talks were held by Swaran Singh, then railway minister, and Zulfiqar Ali Bhutto, the foreign minister of Pakistan. The talks went nowhere because Pakistan overestimated what it could get. And an enfeebled Indian government was in no condition to make the far-reaching concessions that Bhutto was seeking.[23]

Nehru made one last effort on Kashmir in 1964, sending the Kashmiri leader Sheikh Abdullah to meet Ayub and find a solution. He was willing to consider various forms of autonomy and linkages between the two sides of Kashmir and seemed ready to accept the status quo. Sheikh Abdullah was hopeful and thought he might have a deal, but on the day before he returned to Delhi, Nehru died on May 27, 1964.

The failure of Western efforts to broker a settlement of India-Pakistan issues meant that the long-term legacy of the 1962 war was to confirm Pakistan's turn to China, which had begun with worsening India-China relations in the late 1950s. The alacrity with which Pakistan's ally, the United States, had come to India's aid prompted Pakistan to secure alternate allies and to benefit from India's discomfiture. By March 1963 Pakistan had signed a boundary agreement with China, ceding Kashmiri territory in the Shaksgam valley to China. This had its own complications because only in Pakistani-occupied Kashmiri territory does Pakistan share a border with China. The Pakistanis had begun a strategic relationship with China that has grown steadily ever since.

For India, a combination of the defeat in 1962, President Kennedy's death in 1963, and President Johnson's domestic priorities reversed the process of India-U.S. rapprochement begun under President Eisenhower and diminished the central role that India had enjoyed in U.S. strategic planning in Asia as a counterweight to China.[24]

4

The Sixties

The period from independence—the long 1950s—to Nehru's death in May 1964 was followed by the short 1960s, when India's geopolitical situation changed again in several respects. The world was in turmoil in the mid-1960s. All the major powers underwent significant domestic unrest and change, and India was no exception. It was a difficult decade all around.

It was not only in India that domestic politics entered new territory and that fresh leadership was tested. In the United States, the Vietnam War and President Lyndon Johnson's courage in granting civil rights to African Americans and building a Great Society led to a fundamental questioning of the political system, to antiwar riots and to polarized politics. In Europe, 1968 was the year of student protests and rising left idealism. Political violence and terrorism reared its head again in settled Western societies and Japan, as also in west Asia where the Palestinian Liberation Organization invented politically inspired aircraft hijackings and killed Israeli athletes at the Munich Olympics in 1972. In the Soviet Union new leadership under Leonid Brezhnev and Alexei Kosygin eased Nikita Khrushchev out and began the long slide into internal stasis and the artery hardening that ultimately killed the Soviet Union. And China went through the self-inflicted disaster of the Great Proletarian Cultural Revolution from 1966 to 1976, turning its back on the world.

For India this was a decade of domestic preoccupations, of the short prime ministry of Lal Bahadur Shastri, followed by the steady but difficult consolidation under Indira Gandhi's rule. J. N. Dixit calls the period from 1964 to 1977 "the Indo-centric phase" of India's foreign policy.[1] It was a time when domestic preoccupations often overwhelmed the country's capacity for independent action abroad.

Nehru's successor, Lal Bahadur Shastri, was prime minister for a little less than two years but faced multiple challenges. He was very different from his predecessor, with no international ideologies or European experience to draw on and no familiarity with foreign policy. A committed Gandhian of the old school whose personal rectitude was matched by his belief in values in politics, he had big shoes to fill, rivals in the party to see off, and a difficult internal political situation when he became prime minister on June 9, 1964. He inherited a country in low spirits after the trauma and humiliation of 1962. Within four months of Shastri taking over, China conducted its first atomic test in October 1964. In 1965 Pakistan, sensing opportunity in what it took for Indian weakness, tried to take Kashmir by force. On the Asian stage, the United States was increasingly entangled in the Vietnam War, and India had to deal with the multiple consequences of that war for Asian geopolitics.

~

Shastri's greatest test was the 1965 war launched by Pakistan. Pakistan's Muhammad Ayub Khan misread India's apparent internal fragility in the aftermath of the 1962 war with China and underestimated the character of this short but resolute man.

In his search for a solution to the Kashmir question, Nehru had released Sheikh Abdullah from house arrest in Kodaikanal in April 1964. Abdullah was then in touch with the U.S. Central Intelligence Agency (CIA) and Pakistan, seeking peace in Kashmir and between India and Pakistan, and likely also exploring whether Jammu and Kashmir's accession to India could be reversed. Sheikh Abdullah visited Paris, Saudi Arabia, and Pakistan after his release. In Saudi Arabia he told Duane Claridge, a CIA officer who had been in Delhi earlier, that Pakistan would infiltrate small groups of guerrillas from Pakistan-occupied Kashmir into Jammu and Kashmir to create an insurgency, and thereafter send in the Pakistan Army to finish the job.[2] The Pakistanis were encouraged in their bravado by two things. First, they had misread Shastri, a physically small but mentally strong leader with firm convictions and a sense of right and wrong. Second, Ayub and his advisers thought that they had U.S. support because of earlier assurances given them when India had appealed for arms to fight China in 1962. When responding to Nehru's appeal, the United States had assured Pakistan that the security guarantees they had given Pakistan in 1959 against communist aggression would also apply to India. The Pakistani military buildup in 1963–1965 with Patton tanks and F-104 Phantom and Sabre fighter jets from the United States led them to conclude that they could count on U.S. support once infiltrators had done their job and provoked India into attacking Pakistan. But, in fact, President Johnson's conviction that his predecessors had exaggerated the subcontinent's importance in the Cold War had seen a process of U.S. disengagement, which accelerated in the autumn of 1965.[3]

Ayub may have also thought that he had a window of opportunity before the full implementation of India's defense modernization plan after the China war. The plan was for a doubling of Indian Army force levels to one million and for a forty-five-squadron air force. India's defense budget grew from 2.1 percent of GDP in 1961–1962 to 4 percent in 1963–1964. In 1965 the Indian Army had 870,000 men in sixteen infantry divisions, of which ten divisions were ranged against Pakistan. Pakistan had all seven of its divisions against India. Pakistan also had near parity in armor numbers, and the qualitative advantage was believed to be with the Pakistan Army and Air Force.

The Pakistan Army's misreading of Shastri and India was strengthened by the manner in which the short sharp conflict in the Rann of Kutch in April-May 1965 was resolved. Pakistan had contested the boundary in southern Sindh after independence and there had been several border incidents in the area. In 1956 India took control of the Rann.

In 1964 Ayub decided to test India's military preparedness through Operation Desert Hawk in the Rann before attempting his main move in Kashmir, Operation Gibraltar, which was to infiltrate troops disguised as civilians to raise an insurgency in Kashmir. Ayub moved a brigade—later up to a division—to the Rann and started patrolling in Indian territory in January 1965. Ayub was testing the new Indian government's political and military reactions and international responses. Indian intelligence failed to pick up the Pakistani concentration. On April 8 Pakistani troops attacked Indian posts in the Rann. The Pakistan Army did well in the fighting, validated its use of Patton tanks, and held its ground as international diplomacy took over. Under pressure from British Prime Minister Harold Wilson, Pakistan pulled back and accepted a truce and ceasefire on June 6, 1965. The ceasefire was a composite one, with India returning Kargil Heights that it had taken in April. It was also agreed that an international tribunal would rule on the dispute if no settlement had been negotiated by India and Pakistan in two months. (When the tribunal gave its verdict in 1968, it awarded Pakistan 350 square miles against their original claim of 3,500 square miles.) Pakistan concluded that India was in no mood to expand conflict. Ayub was reassured that international mediation and intervention would be available to Pakistan, an ally of the West. He was also convinced of India's lack of political will under the Shastri government and its lack of military preparedness. He told his commanders in his directive for

Operation Gibraltar: "As a general rule Hindu morale would not stand more than a couple of hard blows delivered at the right time and place."[4]

From August 5 onward 4,000 to 5,000 infiltrators were pushed into the Kashmir valley, drawn from Mujahid battalions and Pakistan Army regulars. With no support from the populace, 1,200 were captured by August 12. By August 21 they were routed, killed, or had retreated back into Pakistan-occupied Kashmir. Operation Gibraltar turned into a resounding Indian victory and a jolt to Ayub and his fire-brand foreign minister, Z. A. Bhutto. Had Gibraltar worked, it was to be followed by Operation Grand Slam, an armored thrust to capture Akhnoor and cut the Pathankot-Jammu Highway, isolating Jammu and Kashmir from the rest of the country. Needing to save face, Ayub decided to go through with Grand Slam anyway on September 1, 1965. When Pakistan captured Akhnoor and the Chicken's Neck, cutting off Jammu and Kashmir briefly, Shastri responded decisively. He expanded the war to the Punjab and threatened the Pakistani cities of Sialkot and Lahore. This forced the Pakistanis to move forces from Kashmir. Shastri did not attack East Pakistan to preclude Chinese intervention which Bhutto had promised Ayub, but which never materialized. The war see-sawed one way and another and saw the greatest tank battles since Kursk in World War II at Pillaur and Chawinda, Khem Karan and Assal Uttar, but ended in a stalemate. Pakistan had failed to achieve any of its objectives; India had barely held the line. On September 23 a ceasefire led both sides to pull back to the August 5, 1965, positions by February 26, 1966. India had captured about 700 square kilometers of Pakistani territory in Sialkot and Lahore, while Pakistan had captured about 400 square kilometers of Indian territory around Khem Karan and Chamb, southeast of Lahore.

The peace was negotiated in Tashkent in the Soviet Union in early January 1966 under the auspices of a new Soviet premier, Alexei Kosygin. The Soviets and the United States had worked closely together in the UN Security Council and thereafter on the ceasefire in September to make Tashkent a success. The Tashkent Declaration, finally accepted by India and Pakistan under Soviet and U.S. prodding, provided for both sides to restore the prewar status quo; restore diplomatic relations; abide by previous treaty obligations; and meet to discuss all other issues. Shastri gave up Haji Pir and other strategic gains, much to the dismay of the Indian Army, which was returning this to Pakistan for the second time. Shastri did not get any assurance from Pakistan not to indulge in infiltration and guerrilla warfare, nor a renunciation of war, which led to strong criticism of the agreement in India. In Pakistan public euphoria over what Ayub's government had presented as a great military victory over India was shattered by the shock of the Tashkent Declaration. His own foreign minister, Bhutto, attacked Ayub for losing at the negotiating table what the valiant Pakistan Army had won, a myth that the army was happy to spread. Bhutto was dismissed and formed the Pakistan People's Party. Ayub's political decline had begun.

In many ways the war marked a decisive watershed in the West's association with the subcontinent. It saw the end of the old "special relationship" between Pakistan and the United States. Pakistan felt betrayed by the United States. The United States had refused to mediate and President Johnson essentially said, "Let the Soviets have at it," only getting involved in the ceasefire diplomacy at the UN in the later stages of the war when Chinese statements became belligerent. India was clearly more comfortable with the Soviets than with United States or UN offers to mediate. The United States and United Kingdom imposed an arms embargo on both India and Pakistan at the onset of war, but Pakistan was able to circumvent the suspension by taking delivery of U.S. arms from allies Turkey and Iran. For India, which through the 1950s and early 1960s was dependent primarily on British weapons, this was further incentive to turn to the Soviet Union, which soon replaced Britain as chief source of India's weapons platforms.

The war revealed a growing China-Pakistan nexus and its limits. During the war, on September 8, 1965, China accused India of violating the "Sikkim-China border." On September 16, China accused India of maintaining 56 military installations on the Tibetan side and demanded their immediate dismantling, claimed that 13 representations about 300 Indian incursions had been ignored, and accused India of abducting 59 Chinese yaks. Despite these obvious Chinese efforts to pressure India, and the mobilization of Chinese troops in the western sector of the India-China border, no clashes took place on the India-China border, nor were there other signs of Chinese military preparation for actual intervention. When India and China entered into real sanguinary clashes in 1967, it was for their own reasons on the Sikkim border, where the Indian Army gave as good as it got, or better, in a series of clashes involving casualties on both sides.[5] The India-China border was by and large peaceful for several years after that.

The day after signing the Tashkent Declaration with Ayub Khan, Lal Bahadur Shastri died of a massive heart attack in Tashkent in the early morning hours of January 11, 1966.

~

The Congress Party chose Indira Gandhi as Shastri's successor, or, to be precise, the "Syndicate" of old party bosses—S. Nijalingappa, K. Kamaraj, N. Sanjiva Reddy, Atulya Ghosh, and S. K. Patil—chose her because they thought that she was a *goongi gudiya*, or dumb doll and easy to manipulate, and because her name and pedigree as Nehru's daughter would attract the vote. They were right about the latter but so, oh so, wrong about the former.

The India she inherited was not in good shape. By Nehru's death in 1964 the shortcomings of his planning model were apparent. India was increasingly dependent on foreign aid, especially food imports, most of which came from the United States on highly concessional terms. Between 1950 and 1980 India's share of world GDP shrank from 4.2 percent to 3.2 percent. The compounded rate of growth in per capita income in India in 1964–1980 was as low as 0.84 percent. (East Asia's rate in the same period was 3.44 percent.) The economic impact of the wars of 1962 and 1965 with China and Pakistan was magnified by the failure of two consecutive monsoons in 1965 and 1966, and large parts of the country were on the verge of starvation. As Indira Gandhi wrote to P. N. Haksar in late February 1966, "We are at the beginning of a new dark age. The food situation is precarious, industries are closing. There is no direction, no policy on any matter. . . . As a child I wanted to be like Joan of Arc—I may yet be burnt at the stake."

Politically as well, India was changing. Voting numbers had doubled between 1952 and 1967. (The 1935 electorate, on the basis of a property franchise, involved only about 30 million electors. The electorate had grown with universal suffrage to over 173 million in 1952.) In the 1967 elections the Congress Party's vote share dropped 4 percent, seats in Parliament dropped to 283 in a house of 520, and the party lost power in eight major north Indian states and in Tamil Nadu. The Syndicate, or old Congress Party bosses, were trounced in their own constituencies and Indira Gandhi took control of the party, moving left on policy, allying with the pro-Soviet faction of the Communist Party of India, formed after its 1964 split. Mrs. Gandhi nationalized banks, abolished privy purses to former princes, restricted large businesses with the Monopolies and Restrictive Trade Practices Act and Foreign Exchange Regulation Act, nationalized insurance and coal, and introduced agricultural subsidies and other measures. In late 1969 the Congress Party itself split, and she called for elections in March 1971, one year early, breaking the link between national and local elections. Her platform during the elections was *Garibi Hatao*, or "Banish Poverty," against a grand alliance with the slogan *Indira Hatao*," or "Banish

Indira." She won handily with a margin that exceeded her father's best performance, by 352 out of 518 seats. The next largest party had just 25 seats in Parliament.

~

Given the precarious economy and dependence on imported grain to feed India, Indira Gandhi had little choice but to turn to the United States and to seek an improvement in relations. At the same time her socialist turn in domestic policy, alliance with the Communist Party of India, and her need to build up the armed forces after the two wars meant that she also relied on the Soviet Union, particularly for weapons. The United States had imposed an arms embargo on both India and Pakistan when the 1965 war broke out. Indira Gandhi therefore attempted to "walk on two legs," as it were, working on relations with both the superpowers, balancing the emerging China-Pakistan axis and her dependence on the Soviet Union by attempting to improve relations with the United States.

Within two months of taking office, she visited the United States in 1966 from March 27 to April 2. India's food imports had escalated from 4 million tons to 10 million tons a year. President Johnson was friendly and charmed—her opponents in the U.S. administration claimed that she "vamped" him. Johnson said that he would ensure that "no harm comes to this girl." Gandhi said in public that "India understands America's agony over Vietnam." The United States pledged a general aid package and food aid.

However, the thawing ice soon froze over again. The United States insisted that India abandon cooperative farming and try technology-intensive agriculture, which later came to be known as the Green Revolution. The World Bank demanded that India liberalize imports and relax industrial licensing controls, while the International Monetary Fund and the United States pushed for a steep devaluation of the rupee. On her return to India, Gandhi carried out the devaluation, which was severely attacked in India by all sides of the political spectrum. But the rest of the U.S. aid package failed to materialize, due to Johnson's frustration with India's economic policies and position on Vietnam, and for other congressional and fiscal factors that had little to do with India, which were used by U.S. officials like Walt Rostow and Philip Talbot who saw Pakistan as a valuable ally, even when Johnson did not. Indira Gandhi put the rest of the agreed economic reforms on hold. That experience reinforced her belief in U.S. unreliability and her conviction that self-reliance and independence were the only policy for India. Johnson, who had insisted on the Green Revolution for food aid, would only release grain for one month at a time while monitoring agricultural reform, and India was living "ship to mouth." This was deeply resented by Indira Gandhi. She, nonetheless, fully backed C. Subramaniam and M. S. Swaminathan in the Green Revolution that made India self-sufficient in food by the use of improved seeds and the provision of inputs like fertilizer and irrigation to farmers. Wheat production in India doubled from 1965–1966 to 1971–1972. Rice, India's largest grain crop, saw a significant if smaller rise in output. The gains were, however, unevenly spread and largely concentrated in Punjab, Haryana, and western Uttar Pradesh, where the new middle peasantry who rose moved away from the Congress Party with its dependence on an alliance of upper and lower castes. In 1967 Charan Singh, representing these farmers and beneficiaries of the Green Revolution, defected from the Congress Party, formed his own party, and became the first non-Congress chief minister of Uttar Pradesh.

There were other irritants in the relationship with the United States as well—U.S. arms supplies to Pakistan, U.S. pressure on India to settle Jammu and Kashmir, the Non-Proliferation Treaty negotiations, the Vietnam War, and U.S. objections to Mrs. Gandhi's socialist policies—which would probably have prevented a significant improvement in the relationship, whatever President Johnson and Indira Gandhi may have wanted.

~

Indira Gandhi's outreach to the Soviet Union was more successful, although it too had its complications. The U.S. arms embargo on both India and Pakistan after the 1965 war left India with the Soviet Union as the only source for the weapons that she needed. But a Soviet Union overconfident after its role in brokering the Tashkent Agreement, and concerned with its deteriorating relationship with China, attempted to mend fences with Pakistan at the same time as making peace between India and Pakistan. Premier Kosygin overreached when he wrote to Indira Gandhi in July 1968 about normalizing relations with Pakistan. Gandhi held firm, telling Kosygin that there was no room for third-party mediation and asking that Kosygin "exercise your growing influence with Pakistan and persuade them to start discussions with us."[6]

Keen to bind India closer as the price for military supplies and political support, the Soviets proposed and negotiated a Treaty of Friendship with India in 1968–1969. But Indira Gandhi decided not to sign. It was only after the Nixon visit to China had been announced and when the Bangladesh crisis was under way that she agreed to enter into the treaty in August 1971.

The bombshell, however, was a Russian announcement of military sales to Pakistan, which occasioned a very strong backlash in India. The result was a tentative approach to China by India driven by the logic that if our friends could cut deals with Pakistan, we could try the same with Pakistan's friends. In early 1969 Gandhi publicly expressed a willingness to talk to China without preconditions and hoped that the boundary dispute could be settled. A Beijing in the throes of the Cultural Revolution rebuffed the statement as "hypocritical," but on May 1, 1970, on the Tiananmen rostrum, Mao Zedong smiled at the Indian *chargé d'affaires*, Brajesh Mishra, and said, "We cannot keep on quarrelling like this. We must try and be friends again. . . . We will be friends again some day. We are ready to do it today." Delhi's slow and tepid response, the Bangladesh crisis, and other developments put paid to these first shoots of rapprochement between India and China.

Mrs Gandhi's consolidation of her domestic hold and her outreach to both the Soviet Union and the United States, though less than fully successful, were sufficient for India's GDP to grow 6 percent per year from 1967–1968 to 1970–1971, and for the balance of payments to stabilize. What stands out are the overwhelming domestic preoccupations of Indira Gandhi in this period and how foreign policy was driven by domestic needs at this difficult time.

$\sim$

During her sixteen years in power, between 1966 and 1977, and again from 1980 to 1984, Indira Gandhi was a strong leader and a realist. She took the world as it was. She did not share Nehru's benign view of human nature or of nation-states. Instead she sought a strong and self-reliant India.

As Zorawar Daulet Singh points out, both Nehru and Indira Gandhi "embodied a kind of critical geopolitics in that both sought a distinct, secure, and disassociated space for a nonaligned India from the Cold War system. . . . For Nehru it was about developing an alternative regional philosophy of inter-state relations where security dilemmas could be muted in both Asia and India's immediate vicinity; whereas Indira Gandhi aimed to develop an Indo-centric subregional order where external involvement could be restrained and Indian leadership asserted. India's centrality in southern Asia and the geography did not change."[7]

During the 1960s, she faced several difficult challenges from fighting for control of her party and balancing populist domestic policies such as bank nationalization to managing India's dependence on the United States and the Soviet Union. While convinced of the value of the Soviet connection, she was embittered by her early experience with the United States, and this was not improved in the 1970s. But she managed to steady the ship of state when the Cold War was at its peak, when Sino-Soviet differences and Sino-Pak collaboration were affecting India, when China had become a nuclear weapon state in 1964, and when Asia was becoming polarized.

She did so not only by handling relations with the superpowers. She was the one who began the search for tighter relations with subcontinental neighbors other than Pakistan—with Afghanistan (which had expressed some sympathy for Pakistan in the 1965 war), Nepal, Bhutan, Burma, Sri Lanka, and the Maldives. She made a special effort with Iran, which had granted sanctuary to Pakistan Air Force fighter aircraft during the 1965 war.

Relations with southeast Asia were more complex. While Malaya immediately supported India in the 1962 war and most southeast Asian countries were neutral in the 1965 war, Indonesia under Sukarno was positively hostile. In September 1965 thousands of Indonesians demonstrated outside the Indian and U.S. embassies accusing them of waging war against Pakistan, an Islamic country, and on September 9 the protesters ransacked the Indian embassy, tore down the flag, and gave it to Foreign Minister Subandrio who "appreciated the actions of Jakarta youth." Indian shops were looted. Indonesia offered military support to Pakistan, Sukarno sent his chief of staff to Beijing to get spare parts for eight MIG-19 fighters he was preparing to give Pakistan without the approval of the original supplier, the Soviet Union. The commander of the Indonesian Navy threatened a blockade of the Andaman and Nicobar Islands and claimed that they were an extension of Indonesian territory in Sumatra. Much of this was personal to Sukarno. He was in the midst of *Konfrontasi*, or confrontation, with newly independent Malaya, whose freedom India welcomed. India had turned down his idea of a second Bandung Conference, and his hold on domestic politics in Indonesia was weakening. Once Sukarno lost power later in 1965, relations were soon restored to normal.

To Indira Gandhi must go the credit of settling India's remaining boundaries wherever she could. These included the land boundary with Burma in December 1967 and India's maritime boundaries with Sri Lanka (June 1974), Indonesia (August 1974), the Maldives (December 1976), Thailand (June 1978), and Burma (December 1986).

She also decided that India, with the world's third largest Muslim population, should be a founder member of the Organization of Islamic States (OIC). India was invited to the inaugural OIC summit at Rabat in Morocco in 1969, but Pakistani efforts aided by Saudi Arabia effectively disinvited India. They objected to India being represented by Gurbachan Singh, a Sikh and ambassador to Morocco. The damage had been done by the time India sent Fakhruddin Ali Ahmed as representative, and India had no choice but to stay away when offered second-class treatment at the summit by the hosts.

Indira Gandhi's search for balancing arrangements extended to India's becoming a founding member of the United Nations Conference on Trade and Development and the G-77 and to active participation in the nonaligned movement. For her there was no issue that was too remote for the country, which as a significant power had or would have global interests. She was the only head of government apart from the host to attend the June 1972 Stockholm Summit on the Human Environment, the first global conference on the environment, and she took a personal interest in ecological issues in India and abroad, long before they had become fashionable. She personally insisted on India's active role in the Law of the Sea conferences between 1973 and 1982, which produced the UN Convention on the Law of the Sea, and in COPUOS, the UN Committee for the Peaceful Uses of Outer Space, and in the development of space law.

～

In retrospect, if there was a weakness in her understanding of India's place in the world, it was in her approach to southeast Asia, although here she was sowing in infertile soil.

The Cold War had made southeast Asia an ideological battleground in the mid-1950s. The post-World War II alliance of modernity, nationalism, and social awakening with communism and socialism in the region provoked a countervailing coalition with former colonial powers of traditional elites who had prospered under colonial rule. Former colonial powers and traditional elites were united by their fear of losing power to new democratic dispositions, and by worries that their opponents would seek retribution and equality. The Cold War brought in the United States on their side to oppose the spread of communism. Military-led and authoritarian regimes were bankrolled by the West in southeast and east Asia in the name of fighting communism. Democracy ended in Burma in 1962; in Indonesia a communist-backed coup was ruthlessly and bloodily quelled by the military in 1965, and Sukarno was effectively overthrown; in Singapore Lee Kuan Yew decimated the communists after gaining power in a united front with them; the Cambodian Army under Lon Nol deposed Sihanouk in 1970; and in Thailand the military squashed waves of left-wing protest in the 1970s. With strong leaders and popular demagogues like Marcos in the Philippines and Mahathir Mohamad in Malaysia, authoritarian rule was the norm in southeast Asia by the mid-1980s.[8]

In Vietnam, once the French had been defeated at Dien Bien Phu in 1954 and negotiated their withdrawal at the Geneva Conference, the United States spent more than twenty years to prevent a communist victory and prop up a government in South Vietnam. In this attempt, the United States spread the war to Laos and Cambodia and dropped three times as many tons of bombs on Indochina as all the Allies had dropped during Second World War. America gained nothing for its efforts in Vietnam, but it did change Asia's direction.

The 1960s were a time of great geopolitical flux in Asia caused by the Sino-Soviet split, the Vietnam War, or, more accurately, the war in Indochina, the rise of Japan, and changes in Cold War alliances on both sides. Southeast Asia was a conflict zone and one main fault line of the Cold War ran through it. "Where the winds end" was also where great power interests intersected. In 1965 Johnson upped the ante in the Vietnam War by bombing North Vietnam. A China in the turmoil of a Cultural Revolution of its own was exporting revolution throughout Asia. Every noncommunist country in southeast Asia faced communist insurgency supported by China and most had sizeable Chinese minorities whose loyalty the People's Republic of China claimed. Malaysia and Singapore were still fighting a communist insurgency in the mid-1960s. Indonesia was in violent *konfrontasi* with Malaysia and with Singapore 1963–1966. The Philippines claimed Sabah. Brunei, with British help, had suppressed an internal rebellion backed by Indonesia. There were strong irredentist pressures on the borders between western Malaysia and Thailand and between the Philippines and Indonesia.

This period also saw an economic boom in southeast Asia, helped by the Vietnam War. Southeast Asian economies were pulled along by Japan's phenomenal economic rise in a "flying geese" pattern, as the Japanese economist and politician Saburo Okita called it. Turmoil in Hong Kong and Taiwan caused by the spillover of the Cultural Revolution gave Malaysia, Thailand, and Singapore entry into the textile industry, and they later moved on into semiconductors and other manufacturing. The newly industrializing economies included Hong Kong, South Korea, and Taiwan. In the 1970s they were joined by the southeast Asian "tigers," Malaysia, Indonesia and Thailand, in the 1980s by China, and in the 1990s by India and Vietnam.

In 1964 Japan had floated the idea of an Asia South Pacific Cooperation (ASPAC) Forum in order to contain China and the Soviet Union. Shastri was unresponsive, unaware of the extent of Japan's economic resurgence in the late 1950s and early 1960s. Japan began to concentrate its investment, manufacturing, and trading effort on noncommunist southeast Asia, building the linkages that were to evolve into the global supply chains of today and working with countries that were politically more responsive and accepting and ready to pragmatically work with Japan despite memories of World War II.

With the United States embroiled in the Vietnam War, pro-Western regimes in southeast Asia sought to organize and strengthen themselves into a new bloc. In Indonesia, Suharto had just come to power; Malaysia had gained independence in 1963; Singapore had just separated from Malaysia in 1965; Thailand was a frontline monarchy with communist neighbors that were its traditional rivals; and, the Philippines, a former U.S. colony and ally in SEATO, was a major base for the prosecution of the Vietnam War. On August 8, 1967, ASEAN was founded by four countries and one city-state: Indonesia, Malaysia, the Philippines, Thailand, and Singapore. The *Peking Review* of August 18, 1967, immediately labelled it an "alliance of American stooges." From 1967 to 1989 ASEAN worked closely with the United States, and when the U.S.-China strategic alliance was strong in the 1980s, with them both. In 1967 British and Australian forces and their naval base in Singapore were formally brought within ANZUS, the 1951 defense arrangement between Britain, Australia, New Zealand, and the United States for the western Pacific.

There are different versions on whether or not India was invited to be a member of ASEAN. According to Dixit, Suharto originally wanted India as a full member. He was rebuffed, however, because Indian policy was driven by a limited view of the Cold War, dislike of the Vietnam War, and suspicion of the United States. Minister of State for External Affairs Dinesh Singh is said to have responded that India would not get involved with a group that was part of the U.S. scheme of things.[9] If so, this was a significant misjudgment. The United States cultivated ASEAN but certainly did not see it as a U.S.-led entity. Other accounts suggest that initially Foreign Minister M. C. Chagla made it clear that India would be happy to join ASEAN if the other members were agreeable. Chagla visited Indonesia, Malaya, and Singapore in early 1967. While Singapore and Malaya were in favor of India's membership, Indonesia had reservations, which were shared by Thailand and the Philippines.

Then at the Ministry of External Affairs desk handling southeast Asia, Chandrashekhar Dasgupta recalled things differently. He remembered that India sounded out Indonesia on the question of India's joining the association during Foreign Minister Chagla's visit to Jakarta in 1967, a few months before

ASEAN was launched. The Indonesians indicated very politely that India lay outside the geographical region intended to be covered by the association. Dasgupta was a member of the delegation and formed the impression that the hosts did not want a larger country in the incipient grouping.[10]

ASEAN was formed in August 1967 without India. Sri Lanka was invited but chose not to join. It took more than twenty-three years for India to revive direct contacts with ASEAN as a group and become a partial sectoral dialogue partner in 1992.

In fact, India's reluctance to be drawn into security commitments in southeast Asia ran deep in the 1960s. Several southeast Asian states asked India to join collective security and defense arrangements against Chinese communist subversion amid fears of a "power vacuum" following the British withdrawal east of Suez. India repeatedly declined such invitations.[11]

In any case, neither of the two major trends in southeast Asian politics, toward authoritarian and military rule internally, and toward an anticommunist alliance with the United States externally, held resonance for an internally preoccupied India whose government worked closely with the Communist Party of India and the Soviet Union. India was also too engrossed in its own troubles with China and Pakistan on the immediate periphery. Pakistan's alliance with the United States made other U.S. allies suspect in Delhi's eyes. In 1965 when Lee Kuan Yew approached India and Egypt to help build up Singapore's armed forces, neither deigned to reply. Why would they antagonize Malaysia for Singapore? The Israelis, on the other hand, flew in officials and officers who came in posing as Mexicans, and they were soon followed by New Zealand and British trainers. As the minister of state for external affairs told the Indian Parliament in April 1968 when asked about India taking on security obligations in southeast Asia: "If there were a defence arrangement, it would only mean India committing her manpower to the defence of areas which is [sic] beyond our capacity at present. We have enough troubles of our own. Our security forces are fully committed to the defence of our own borders and some of our immediate neighbours."[12]

~

The other test of India's will to power and readiness to defend its interests in this period was when China tested an atom bomb on October 1, 1964, and the international community negotiated the Nuclear Non-Proliferation Treaty (NPT).

Nehru had been convinced by his physicist friend, Homi J. Bhabha, before independence of the contribution that atomic energy could make to India's development. Bhabha's ideas fitted well with Nehru's inclination to use science to develop India. The use of atomic energy was, however, complicated by its dual uses: producing energy for development and making the most destructive weapons known to man, with the potential to obliterate human civilization. Nehru followed a two-track policy of working internationally for nuclear disarmament while ensuring that India mastered all the necessary technologies, including those with military uses. There is an urban legend that Nehru opposed nuclear weapons for India. Instead, Nehru actually restrained Bhabha when his enthusiasm for disarmament and superpower promises led him to suggest steps by India that might close India's options. I have seen a letter from Nehru telling "Bhai," as they addressed each other in their correspondence, "You take care of the science and leave the politics to me," or words to that effect. Nehru consistently ensured that India entered into no legal commitments that could prevent it from developing its own nuclear weapons, unless the nuclear powers were willing to disarm too.

Together Nehru and Bhabha maintained an Indian position that permitted the peaceful uses of the atom for India's development, cooperating with the United States, Canada, the United Kingdom, and others, while laying the practical foundations for a weapons program, should that become necessary in the future. India was in the forefront of international efforts to negotiate nuclear disarmament. India was instrumental in pushing the superpowers into the Partial Test Ban Treaty of 1963, which prohibited nuclear tests in the atmosphere. India also demanded a Comprehensive Test Ban and a Non-Proliferation Treaty banning both "vertical" and "horizontal" proliferation, phrases coined by Bhabha, and seeking real nuclear disarmament by the great powers.

China's test of an atom bomb on October 1, 1964, two years after the India-China war, changed India's security calculus. The test had been anticipated, and Bhabha had pushed for an earlier or simultaneous Indian test. The Indian plutonium plant was opened in 1964, making it clear that India was a latent nuclear weapon state and could have nuclear weapons if it chose. Opinion in the Indian establishment was, however, divided on the best response to the Chinese test and on whether India should build nuclear weapons. Prime Minister Shastri opted to send his principal secretary, L. K. Jha, to the Soviet Union and the United States seeking a nuclear umbrella, a guarantee of protection and retaliation against a nuclear attack on India. The superpowers were not ready to extend such a guarantee to India. And India complicated the issue by seeking a joint guarantee from the two superpowers. In December 1964 British

Prime Minister Wilson had suggested to Shastri that the three "major" nuclear powers, Britain, the United States, and the Soviet Union, provide a nuclear umbrella to protect non-nuclear states from blackmail by third parties. It was soon clear that with the Vietnam War souring East-West relations, the Soviets would not join Washington and London in nuclear guarantees to India directed at a fellow communist country. For Shastri, a guarantee was only acceptable if Russia joined too.[13] To my mind this was in any case a fool's quest. Why would a superpower put its population at risk for India's or any other country's sake, particularly a non-ally? This is the fundamental credibility problem with extended deterrence and nuclear umbrellas. Despite Bhabha's urgings, Shastri was not ready to abandon his Gandhian commitment to nonviolence and to authorize the atomic energy establishment to work on a bomb or an explosive device. By a coincidence that has fed numerous conspiracy theories, Bhabha died in the crash on Mont Blanc of Air India flight 101 on January 24, 1966, just days after Shastri's death in Tashkent on January 11. Bhabha's death stilled the strongest voice for early weaponization of India's nuclear program in the 1960s. But before his death Bhabha had created and led a program that gave India mastery of the full fuel cycle and a nuclear weapons option, should it choose to exercise it, something that few other countries had managed.

The first Chinese test of 1964 provoked the UN Disarmament Commission to entrust the Eighteen-Nation Committee on Disarmament to study and negotiate a treaty to limit the proliferation of nuclear weapons.[14] Those negotiations lasted from 1965 to 1968. In the initial phase the two superpowers sorted out their own issues. The Soviets objected to the Atlantic Nuclear Force Project proposed by the United States, which would have transferred nuclear weapons to Germany. A Rusk-Gromyko compromise at the end of 1966 saw the United States abandoning the Atlantic Nuclear Force Project and the Soviet Union accepting the status quo—U.S. nuclear weapons on the territory of allies so long as the weapons were under U.S. control and their use was subject to consultation with allies. The establishment of the NATO Nuclear Planning Committee essentially met these conditions and showed the increasing rapport between the United States and Soviets after the Cuban Missile Crisis, despite the Vietnam War. The two superpowers were then ready to face the others unitedly, both the developing countries, which wanted access to nuclear technology and real disarmament, and industrialized countries, which wanted to protect their industrial secrets and maintain their commercial competitiveness. The two superpowers finally brought out a text in 1968 acceptable to seventeen members of the Eighteen-Nation Committee on Disarmament. The UN

General Assembly voted on it on June 12, 1968, with twenty abstentions (including India, Brazil, Spain, Argentina, and France). One week later a U.S., Soviet, and U.K. declaration in the UN Security Council pledged assistance to any non-nuclear state party to the treaty in the event that it was subject to attack or threat of attack with nuclear weapons. The treaty was opened for signature on July 1, 1968, and came into force on March 5, 1970, when three nuclear weapon states, the United Kingdom, United States, and Soviet Union, and forty non-nuclear weapon states, had signed and ratified it.

As it finally emerged, the treaty divided the world into two camps: those nations with nuclear weapon and those without them. It provided for a binding commitment by non-nuclear weapon states, verified by International Atomic Energy Agency safeguards, not to develop nuclear weapons or other explosive devices, while the nuclear weapon states made an unverified commitment to undertake good faith negotiations on nuclear disarmament. In other words, the non-nuclear weapon states accepted IAEA safeguards on all their nuclear activities to verify that there was no diversion to "nuclear weapons or other explosive devices." No matching binding commitment was made of nuclear weapon states. This was a treaty to disarm the unarmed. There was also no definition of a nuclear weapon in the treaty, and it consequently effectively prevented several peaceful uses that might be construed as weapons related. Peaceful nuclear explosions, for instance, had already been carried out by the Soviets and were permitted by Article IV of the NPT and the Treaty of Tlatelolco that preceded the NPT in Latin America. But the implementation of the NPT has ensured that only nuclear weapon states have carried them out.

There were long and heated debates in several countries about the value of the NPT, of nuclear weapons, of superpower patron guarantees, and of extended deterrence. In effect the non-nuclear weapon states were being asked to trust the nuclear weapon states and to leave the nuclear part of the conflict spectrum to their wisdom, and to accept the existing adverse balance of power. Japan and Germany were particularly concerned about industrial espionage through inspections and only ratified the treaty in 1976 and 1975, respectively. The treaty recognized as nuclear weapon states those that had conducted explosions before 1968, thus shutting the legal door to the most exclusive club on earth, letting China in but not India.

Not surprisingly opinion in India was sharply divided on the NPT. Facing an adversarial nuclear-armed China and possessing the ability to build a bomb but not having exercised the nuclear weapon option, India was in a unique position. Most Indian political opinion saw the treaty as discriminatory, as a form of "nuclear apartheid," as Jaswant Singh described it. But there were also Gandhian and civil society voices calling for India to sign the NPT, arguing that this was not the time to be isolated, that India should not abandon its commitment to nonviolence, and that joining the nuclear weapons race was to participate in madness and collective suicide. Like the political leadership, the Ministry of External Affairs was divided at the very top.[15]

Indira Gandhi finally decided not to sign the NPT. She was encouraged in this choice by the opposition in Parliament but not by her own senior colleagues such as Morarji Desai.[16] She also asked Homi Sethna, Raja Ramanna, and Vikram Sarabhai of the atomic energy establishment to do the work necessary to make India nuclear weapon and missile capable. The NPT was the clincher in India's internal debate on whether or not to become a nuclear weapon state. India, an original and vigorous proponent of disarmament, had been pushed by the Chinese test, by superpower unwillingness to disarm, and by the "nuclear apartheid" of the NPT into nuclear self-reliance. Facing a Chinese threat and persistent Pakistani hostility, Indira Gandhi continued to hedge her public statements while preparing for nuclear explosions. Sarabhai's death in 1971 removed a significant opponent to weaponization within the establishment. In September 1972 Gandhi formally approved the test of an Indian nuclear explosive device, which was carried out on May 18, 1974. India had taken a decisive and necessary step toward declaring itself a nuclear weapon state by showing it had the scientific and technical wherewithal to build and the political will to test a nuclear explosive device.

There is a story with a long half-life that when China carried out her first atomic test in 1964 U.S. officials suggested to Dr. Bhabha that India should become a nuclear weapon state with U.S. help, but that Nehru turned this down when it was reported to him by Bhabha. Dixit mentions this version.[17] If this was more than an individual initiative or a probe to test Indian intentions, it did not enter the formal record of exchanges between the two sides, as it should have when we were in daily contact with the United States at multiple levels. The United States was building the first nuclear power plant in Asia in India at Tarapur. I personally find the story hard to credit for it goes against the thrust of U.S. policy as revealed in the drafting of the NPT.

The NPT was a major success for the United States and the Soviet Union, "a nuclear Yalta," as Bertrand Goldschmidt, one of the fathers of the French atom bomb and the only Frenchman to have worked on the Manhattan Project, called it. It divided the world into nuclear haves and have-nots. "This ambition, unprecedented on such a scale, runs counter to the course of history, and the first demonstration of this, the Indian explosion of May 1974, was not long in coming."[18] The NPT also brought home to us in India how the interests of India diverged from those of both superpowers in a crucial sphere.

~

Looking back at the 1960s, India's domestic situation impacted and limited its foreign policy choices, reduced options and clouded its vision, as dealings with southeast Asia showed. This period also displayed the perils of weakness, or of being seen to be weak, which led to the 1965 war. However, despite weakness and constraints, when it mattered, as in exercising the nuclear option, India was able to preserve its strategic autonomy and build capacity, even at a time when the international situation and balance of power were so clearly against the nation, and its internal weakness was evident to friend and foe.

To some extent India was able to adapt because the international system itself was changing in ways that gave India leverage. Both alliance systems faced internal divisions and tensions. The communist movement was no longer a monolith led by the Soviet Union after the Sino-Soviet split. Soviet allies or satellites were restive, as Czechoslovakia proved in 1968 when Brezhnev had to send in the tanks. For the United States, entanglement in Vietnam made it dependent on allies to a much greater extent, something that Japan and the founding members of ASEAN used to their benefit in terms of extracting from the Americans defense and deterrence commitments, aid, and market access. For the first time U.S. and Soviet strategic focus was on Asia, equally with their primary confrontation in Europe. But in Asia the lines were less clear, complicated by China's emergence as an independent actor and India's nonalignment. How that dynamic played out became clearer in the 1970s.

Once the Sino-Soviet split was out in the open in the mid-1960s, and until Nixon's opening to China in 1972, while Moscow and Washington remained Cold War rivals, their strategic objectives in southern Asia of building a strong and stable India and limiting Sino-Pakistan ties were much the same. The sixties therefore showed the two superpowers working together during the 1965 war and on the nuclear issue, limiting the space available for India to pursue her own interests independently but enabling India to survive very difficult economic years in the late sixties. The Cold War did not prevent superpower collusion; indeed, it encouraged it. It is easy to underestimate the degree of common interest that the superpowers shared in maintaining the Cold War system and their places in it compared to other nations.

Indira Gandhi's foreign policy essentially falls into two distinct phases, depending on the nature of the geopolitical situation around India. Even though Pakistan had used the U.S. alliance to strengthen herself militarily, doubling her military capacity by Indian estimates between 1965 and 1969, the Asian situation was in flux, with the United States embroiled in the Vietnam War. China and the Soviet Union engaged in bitter polemics and a border dispute and clashes, and China and Pakistan faced internal political turmoil. Because of these dynamics, Indira Gandhi and her advisers were able to use the geopolitical space that this opened up for India to remake the political geography of the subcontinent when opportunity presented itself in Bangladesh, Sikkim, and elsewhere. But that space soon closed up again, once the United States and China entered into a tacit alliance, brokered by Pakistan, in the early 1970s, China emerged from the Cultural Revolution and the United States withdrew from continental Asia.

In the next decade, geopolitics around India changed again with Nixon's visit to China and the Bangladesh war.

5

Coming of Age

The 1970s began with a double bang: Bangladesh was born, and the United States and China entered into a tacit alliance against the Soviet Union. Both events were linked, and they changed the geopolitics of the subcontinent, Asia, and ultimately the world in ways that still affect us today. The period saw India shaking off some of the external hesitations that its internal preoccupations had caused the previous decade. Not that internal politics were tranquil—for this was the decade of the "Emergency" and its aftermath. But internal developments soon had less direct impact on an India under Indira Gandhi who was more willing to assert Indian interests in the neighborhood while actively entering into the geopolitics of Asia. This is the story of India's decade of the 1970s when Sikkim acceded to India, and India resumed diplomatic dialogue with China—against a background of a new Bangladesh and U.S.-China rapprochement.

~

The story of Bangladesh's birth is often told as though it were pre-ordained or long foretold. Neither is true, as Srinath Raghavan's global history of the event makes clear. Not only was it not inevitable, but it was the result of "conjuncture and contingency, choice and chance."[1]

Pakistan had been created with two distinct wings, east and west Pakistan, separated by a thousand miles of Indian territory. East Bengal and the western provinces of Pakistan had been cobbled together into one state despite their different cultures, languages, politics, and economies, solely on the basis of a common religion. While the majority of Pakistan's citizens lived in the east, political power was in the western part. Salman Rushdie described united Pakistan as "that fantastic bird of a place, two Wings without a body, sundered by the land-mass of its greatest foe, joined by nothing but God."[2]

The politics and economics of Pakistan created the kindling leading to the movement for Bangladeshi independence. But even so, neither West Pakistan's economic exploitation of East Pakistan, nor the initial refusal by a Bengali prime minister of Pakistan to accept Bengali as the second official language of Pakistan, nor the nature of the Pakistani state with its outsize role for a Punjabi army with some Pakhtuns made an independent Bangladesh inevitable. These factors could have as easily led to a federal structure or just greater autonomy for East Pakistan, which Mujibur Rehman, his Awami League, and most others in East Pakistan were demanding through the 1950s and 1960s. It was Pakistani folly, Indian policy reactions, and the impact of global and regional geopolitics that made the birth of Bangladesh possible, through a short and intense war, December 4–16, 1971.

The international context had evolved just before the crisis struck Pakistan. During the late 1960s, both superpowers were evidently disinclined to get involved in India-Pakistan issues and sought to be neutral. U.S. President Lyndon Johnson, embroiled in the Vietnam War, had adopted a plague-on-both-your-houses attitude to the 1965 Indo-Pakistan War, imposed an arms embargo on both countries, and left it to the Soviets to broker the peace at Tashkent. Moscow, which had watched with concern as China drew closer to Pakistan after the India-China war of 1962, had invited Field Marshall Muhammad Ayub Khan to visit in April 1965, the first such Pakistani visit to Russia. When Lal Bahadur Shastri visited Russia seeking Russian support on the Rann of Kutch, General Secretary Leonid Brezhnev observed that, "every question, like a medal, has two sides to it." After war broke out in Kashmir in September of that year, the Soviets asked both sides to stop hostilities, and even before a ceasefire Kosygin offered his good offices to mediate, to forestall the United States and prevent a deepening of China-Pakistan relations, he told India. By 1969 the Soviets decided to begin arms shipments to Pakistan, much to India's annoyance.

By 1971, however, Richard Nixon was the American president, holding considerable negative baggage about India, and Henry Kissinger, with the brains to feed and use his boss's insecurities, was his national security adviser.[3] They were determined to remake U.S. policy in Asia toward China and others. The Cold War context in 1971 was no longer the simple bipolar conflict of the 1950s and early 1960s. Both alliances were splintering. The Soviet Union had to send troops into Czechoslovakia in 1968 to crush the Prague Spring, and the Sino-Soviet split had resulted in armed confrontation and clashes between China and the Soviet Union. Nixon's decision to go off the gold standard had hurt his allies, and the United States was obsessing about a Japanese economic threat.

The Bangladesh crisis started as an internal one in both wings of Pakistan to the east and west of India when Ayub Khan stepped down as president on March 25, 1969, and students began demonstrating for democracy inspired by student demonstrations around the world in 1968. It was natural that demonstrators in East Pakistan should also demand autonomy with democracy. The Eleven Point Program demanded by the East Pakistan Students Action Committee in January 1969 was already ahead of political parties such as the Awami League. Apart from democracy and autonomy, the students also demanded an abrogation of Cold War alliances in Asia and Pakistan's departure from U.S. military pacts, as well as formulation of a nonaligned foreign policy. As the movement progressed, the Pakistan Army and West Pakistani opinion hardened against autonomy, and the students grew increasingly radicalized. The final straw was West Pakistan's tepid response to two catastrophic natural events: the July 1970 floods in eleven districts of East Pakistan and the November 12 cyclone and 20-to-30-foot-high tidal bore that killed hundreds of thousands in the worst natural disaster of the twentieth century in East Pakistan. Not a single West Pakistan politician of note even bothered to visit East Pakistan in the wake of the tragedy.

Faced with continuing and growing domestic unrest through 1970, the Pakistan Army under Ayub's successor, General Yahya Khan, called national elections on December 8, 1970. The army expected a hung parliament and fragmented polity, which it could manipulate to keep power in its own hands and to legitimize Yahya Khan as president. The results were a shock. Mujibur Rehman's Awami League won 160 out of 162 seats in East Pakistan and an overall majority in the national Parliament. In West Pakistan, Zulfikar Ali Bhutto's Pakistan People's Party won 81 out of a total of 138 seats—62 of 82 in Punjab, 18 of 27 in Sindh, and 1 in 25 in the North West Frontier Province (NWFP). After a show of negotiating with Mujibur Rehman, whose Awami League now had a majority in the new national assembly, Yahya Khan adjourned the never-summoned Assembly sine die. In response, Mujib spoke at a public meeting in Dhaka, saying "Our struggle this time is a struggle for independence," and made four core demands: revoke martial law, return troops to the barracks, inquire into the firings that had killed several civilians, and immediately transfer power to the people's representatives. None of these were accepted by Yahya Khan. On March 21–22 at midnight Mujib was arrested and flown to West

Pakistan. Confident that West Pakistan would remain calm because of his understanding with Bhutto, Yahya Khan carried out long-laid plans for a military
crackdown on the Bengalis, concentrating on the Awami League, student leaders, intellectuals, and the large Hindu minority, seeking to impose control over
the province through murder, intimidation, and military force.

Operation Searchlight began late on March 25, 1971. It was a genocidal
attack on its own people by the Pakistan Army. The army had lists of those
sought as it went through Dhaka University and towns, hunting and killing
its opponents and seeking to kill, drive out, or terrorize into submission the 10
million Hindus in Bangladesh. Partition in Bengal had not been a single sweep
of thorough ethnic cleansing as in the Punjab in 1947–1948. In the east, successive bouts of communal violence led to fresh waves of migration into India
through the 1950s. Hence there were repeated Indo-Pakistan crises between
1950 and 1964 caused by communal violence and sudden influxes of refugees
from East Pakistan. Some of this was explained by the differing social composition of the minority. In west Punjab, Sikhs and Hindus were largely well-off
traders and landowners or professionals. In east Bengal, Hindus were mostly
tenant farmers or landless labor.

By end-March 1971 Dhaka was under Pakistan Army control, but not yet
the entire country. The disarming of the East Bengal Regiment and the East
Pakistan Regiment had been botched. They had mutinied with their weapons and held territory, particularly in Chittagong. Many of Mujibur Rehman's
senior colleagues had managed to avoid the Pakistan Army dragnet and escape
to India. On March 28, 1971, they constituted the provisional government of
Bangladesh. On April 11 the Independent Bengal Broadcasting Centre broadcast Awami League leader Tajuddin Ahmad's speech about the formation of a
"mighty army" to liberate Bangladesh. On April 17 the government of Bangladesh was formally proclaimed in East Pakistan's Baidyanath Tala, subsequently
renamed Mujibnagar.

~

India watched the deteriorating situation in Pakistan with growing concern,
worried that the Pakistan Army would try to divert attention from its internal
travails and actions by starting something with India. Tension between India
and Pakistan had risen. In late January 1971 Pakistani agents and Kashmiri
terrorists hijacked an Indian Airlines flight to Lahore and destroyed it on the
tarmac. In retaliation, India suspended overflights of all Pakistani aircraft, civil

and military, thus forcing Pakistan to use the long route via Sri Lanka to reach its own province in the east.

India was initially cautious in its response to the building crisis in East Pakistan. When Mujibur Rehman first asked for help through Deputy High Commissioner Sen Gupta in Dhaka on March 14, 1971, the response only offered Indian support in the most general terms for several reasons. For one, the preferred Indian option was an Awami League government in power in Pakistan—this was seen as the best hope of normalizing relations with Pakistan. The prospect of an independent Bangladesh aroused fears of "Greater Bengal" secessionist movements in the Indian provinces of West Bengal, Tripura, and Assam. There was also worry that a free Bangladesh would fall increasingly under communist influence with Maoists hijacking the movement, giving China another point of entry into the subcontinent. Besides, India was distracted by national elections which Indira Gandhi had called for March 1971.

After the March crackdown, opinion was divided within the Indian government. Ministry of External Affairs officials wanted early recognition of the Bangladesh government. India's best-known strategic thinker K. Subrahmaniam pushed for a quick and full-fledged military campaign in east Bengal, a four- to five-day blitzkrieg, writing that "intervention on a decisive scale sooner than later is to be preferred." But Foreign Minister Swaran Singh, Prime Minister Gandhi, and her office headed by Principal Secretary P. N. Haksar were much more circumspect and followed the advice of R. N. Kao, external intelligence chief, and Asoke Ray, who had been deputy high commissioner in Dhaka in touch with Mujibur Rehman. They preferred to follow an incremental and phased strategy. On April 12, 1971, Indira Gandhi approved Operation Jackpot, a proxy war to degrade the Pakistan Army to precede military intervention by India to create Bangladesh. An April 25 Cabinet meeting approved the strategy and explicitly ruled out early military intervention.[4]

Indira Gandhi was alert to the possibility of Chinese intervention, and to the fact that Pakistan's military strength had been considerably strengthened over the past few years—in fact, internal assessments had shown it had doubled since 1965. From the outset Gandhi chose to go along with what her external intelligence chief advised, namely, to support an Awami League-led guerrilla movement in East Pakistan. "West Pakistani elements will find their Dien Bien Phu in East Bengal," as her close adviser D. P. Dhar put it. The Research & Analysis Wing (R&AW), formed as recently as 1968, was tasked to organize India's covert support to the Bangladesh liberation movement and to build its strength. This was R&AW's first real test, which they passed with flying colors.

By the third week of May most liberated areas in East Pakistan had fallen to the Pakistanis. But the flow of refugees to India only grew. Between April 17 and June 26, 1971, 6.5 million refugees entered India, more than the 5.1 million refugees who had entered India from East Pakistan in the entire period from 1947 to August 1970. By December 1971 the total was to swell to over 10 million refugees. Indira Gandhi therefore chose first to focus on the refugees and insisted in Parliament on May 24, 1971, that conditions must be created to stop any further influx of refugees and to ensure their early return under safe conditions. "If the world does not take heed, we shall be constrained to take all measures as may be necessary to ensure our own security," she said. India's hectic diplomatic efforts at this stage were therefore focused on persuading the international community to bring Pakistan to heel.

⁓

The world, however, was not to be swayed into action until later—and then not in the way that India wanted.

The key drivers of U.S. policy in the subcontinent after 1965 were the worsening war in Vietnam and the experience of the 1965 Indo-Pakistan War in which Pakistan, a U.S. ally, did so unexpectedly badly against India. The United States had little appetite to get involved in regional disputes, and India was happy to see a new U.S. neutrality in the subcontinent in the late 1960s. When President Richard Nixon visited India in summer 1969, he assured India of U.S. economic aid and said, "We will go to Mars together." The only Indian concern was a possible resumption of U.S. arms aid to Pakistan, then under review. As Foreign Secretary T. N. Kaul told the visiting Americans, "Each side has military needs, but India is facing China. What is the threat to Pakistan?" "Don't repeat the mistake of 1954," he added gratuitously. But in end-September 1970 the United States told India that it would make a "one-time-exception" and sell arms to Pakistan—$500 million worth of replacement aircraft and 300 armored personnel carriers. Later in September Indira Gandhi told Secretary of State William P. Rogers of India's great concern about China-Pakistan collusion. Rogers said, "You have no concern about China." Mrs. Gandhi, however, forcefully disagreed and alleged foreign interference in India. "in my father's time and it is so now." By early 1971 India-U.S. relations "had achieved a state of exasperatedly strained cordiality, like a couple that can neither separate nor get along," in Kissinger's words.

U.S. support for Pakistan played against a larger global picture, one with the American opening to China, a rebalancing of the superpowers' global influence (including rising Soviet activism in Eastern Europe and the Third World), the Sino-Soviet split, and U.S. domestic upheavals involving civil rights for black Americans and the Vietnam War. Kissinger had argued that the U.S.-Soviet balance was tilting toward the Soviets and wished to bring China into the balance on the U.S. side. Nixon and his secretary of state, Henry Kissinger, wanted a rapprochement with China to facilitate an honorable exit from Vietnam, as well to preserve America's wider global interests. Nixon mentioned his interest in a new relationship with China during his meetings in India in July 1969. But the actual opening with China was facilitated by Pakistan and Romania acting as secret communication channels. The arms supplies were an incentive to Pakistan.

U.S. support for Pakistan after the genocidal crackdown by the Pakistani military on the people of East Pakistan in March 1971 was also of a piece with broader U.S. actions in south and southeast Asia through the Cold War, supporting authoritarian regimes when seen as necessary for the struggle against communism. The United States was neither the initiator nor a major player on the ground, but dealt with the situation from the point of view of her larger interests.

The United States was convinced that an independent East Pakistan would not be in the U.S. interest and decided to do nothing once the crisis erupted, despite U.S. Consul General Archer Blood's cables from Dhaka detailing the terror and "selective genocide."[5] America's main concerns were the China opening, and what Nixon and Kissinger perceived as the need to maintain credibility by standing by an ally. They were unwilling to use economic leverage on Pakistan as suggested by the State Department, and thus effectively buttressed Pakistan President Yahya Khan's intransigence. U.S. aid was critical to Pakistan: China and the Soviet Union provided only 2 percent and 3 percent of Pakistan's total aid receipts at that time. East Pakistan's jute-based exports had accounted for 43 percent of Pakistan's export earnings just before the crisis. On April 24, 1971, Pakistan declared a moratorium on its debt repayments. The Aid Pakistan Consortium meeting on June 21 of countries and international financial institutions that aided Pakistan was therefore critical to Pakistan's future and ability to sustain the hardline and crackdown in East Pakistan. The United States was the only one to speak up for Pakistan at the meeting, and U.S. pressure won a continuation of existing aid but could get nothing new for Pakistan except for some food aid to East Pakistan. This was the first crack in the united Western front on the issue. Britain and France were also much more forthcoming later, abstaining on UN resolutions that India found difficult to accept.

In retrospect, Richard Nixon and Henry Kissinger's preoccupation with seeing through and protecting the China opening could well have tipped the outcome and made an independent Bangladesh possible. The U.S. tilt toward Pakistan drove India away from the United States and into taking independent action. His confident faith in U.S. support made Yahya Khan even more intransigent with his own people and created false Pakistani hopes of Chinese intervention. In other words, Nixon and Kissinger's policy produced exactly the result they wished to avoid. An independent Bangladesh was the unintended consequence of a U.S. policy designed to prevent it. Throughout the crisis, Nixon and Kissinger came under intense domestic criticism for their Bangladesh policy, including leaks to the columnist Jack Anderson that were massively embarrassing to the administration. It can plausibly be argued that if the United States were not engaged in secretly negotiating the opening to China, it would not have backed Pakistan's crackdown to the hilt and may not have misled Yahya into overreacting, thus encouraging a negotiated settlement with greater autonomy for East Pakistan, which was what the Awami League and others actually sought until late 1970.

On July 15, 1971, Richard Nixon announced the opening to China and that he would be visiting early in 1972.

When Kissinger was secretly in Beijing, July 10–11, 1971, Zhou Enlai told him that Pakistan would not provoke India militarily because it was too weak but that "if they [the Indians] are bent on provoking such a situation, then we cannot sit idly by." He went on, "Please tell Yahya Khan that if India commits aggression, we will support Pakistan." Kissinger thought that China was testing the United States—after all Zhou could tell Yahya this directly through his own ambassador—and that U.S. credibility was on the line if it stood aside, damaging U.S.-China prospects. For me this was Zhou manipulating Kissinger's psychology and sense of importance to get the United States to do what he wanted. When speaking to the Pakistanis, on the other hand, Zhou was telling them as late as November 5 that they should try for a political settlement internally and made no promises about intervention or commitments to Pakistan's territorial integrity, merely promising them the military supplies that they sought. Bhutto, Yahya Khan's special envoy, dispatched to China to obtain Chinese guarantees of intervention, returned home most disappointed.

On his return to Washington from China, Kissinger told Indian

Ambassador L. K. Jha on July 17 that if war broke out and if China were involved on the Pakistani side, "we would be unable to help you against China." Kissinger may have thought he was conveying a warning. What India heard and believed was Kissinger saying that the Americans would not intervene in any India-Pakistani conflict even if China did so. India already saw U.S.-China rapprochement as being "at the expense of India and some others. A strong India is certainly not in their scheme of things" in Foreign Secretary T. N. Kaul's assessment.[6] Kissinger had just pushed India into looking elsewhere for a deterrent against China.

On August 9, 1971, the foreign ministers of India and the Soviet Union signed a Treaty of Peace, Friendship and Cooperation valid for twenty years, which provided in Article IX: "In the event of either party being subjected to attack or a threat thereof, the High Contracting Parties shall immediately enter into mutual consultations in order to remove the threat and to take appropriate effective measures to ensure peace and the security of their countries." The treaty had been finalized at Soviet insistence in most respects in 1969, but Indira Gandhi was reluctant to sign it. It took the U.S.-China opening and the Bangladesh crisis to make the treaty attractive to India. For India it was insurance against Chinese intervention. For Russia it was insurance against a war breaking out. The treaty is often portrayed as setting the stage for India's armed intervention in Bangladesh. It is not clear that it was seen as such by either party at that time. What was common to both Russia and India was that they were responding to what they both saw as an adverse development, the U.S. alliance with China.

The treaty was, of course, a clear commitment by the Soviet Union to India. Soviet Defense Minister Marshal Andrei Grechko had been provoked by departing Ambassador D. P. Dhar on his farewell call into saying that "India should not be worried by Pakistan but by the unpredictable enemy from the North." If China started "to use aggression, the USSR would not hesitate to use its force and strength in repelling it." Grechko had added that it was "vital" to "fix" the Indo-Soviet relationship in a "treaty of mutual help" as the Soviet Union and Egypt had done. Grechko twice said that he saw the treaty as deterrent against aggression by China and Pakistan. For Russia the treaty was a stabilizer; for India it was a source of support.

While the two superpowers reacted to the Bangladesh crisis in terms of their contention, most other countries saw the crisis as threatening to legitimize secession by a portion of a country. Since many faced similar demands from among their own people, the overwhelming majority of states were initially strongly opposed to the idea of an independent Bangladesh. Strong sentiment against separatism among member states meant that the UN was not available to India as an instrument in the crisis. Foreign Minister Swaran Singh told the heads of Indian missions in Western Europe in June 1971, "I am fully convinced of the total ineffectiveness of the UN organisations whether they are political, social or human rights. They talk and talk and do nothing." India had come a long way from its faith in multilateral institutions in the 1950s.

From October 25 to November 12, 1971, Indira Gandhi toured Brussels, Vienna, London, Washington, Paris, and Bonn to explain her case and to stress that it was "no longer realistic to expect east and west Pakistan to remain together." Nixon's response to her was that "the American people would not understand it if India were to initiate military action against Pakistan." In their private conversations Nixon and Kissinger thought "the bitch" was leading them on, and that the "Indian bastards are starting a war." This was the visit when Gandhi famously told Nixon, "I have not come here to talk about the weather" when he tried to make small talk at the beginning of their conversation.

The international media, on the other hand, was much more responsive, playing up the plight of the refugees and causing governments like France and Britain to break from the United States on the issue in the UN. Japan was most understanding on the refugee issue. And Willy Brandt's Federal Republic of Germany was active on both the refugee and Pakistan fronts. Prime Minister Sirimavo Bandaranaike of Sri Lanka tried to mediate between India and Pakistan but Mrs. Gandhi took exception to this and quickly put a stop to it. Having just helped Mrs. Bandaranaike quell a Marxist-Leninist insurrection by the Janatha Vimukthi Peramuna (JVP), Mrs. Gandhi felt particularly aggrieved at the implicit equation of India with Pakistan. In late August Foreign Minister Swaran Singh asked Mrs. Bandaranaike to stop the transit of Pakistani military aircraft through Sri Lanka as India would otherwise have no choice but to intercept them. Sri Lanka did so.

Bangladesh was India's first crisis and war in which the publicity front played a very important role, compensating for state indifference or worse in other countries. What India was unable to achieve with states and governments due to their strong aversion to separatism was achieved with public opinion in the West. Beatle George Harrison's Concert for Bangladesh at Madison Square Garden on August 1, 1971, at maestro Ravi Shankar's suggestion, was the first ever such effort in the world and was an outstanding success. With Eric Clapton, Bob Dylan, and other stars playing, it raised about US$250,000 for refugee relief, well above the $25,000 Harrison had expected. Nongovernmental organizations' such as Oxfam shamed governments and helped to raise public awareness, setting a pattern for the future. For the first time an international crisis and war was also fought in the transnational global space that new technology like TV and satellite communications and the youth revolution of the late 1960s had opened up. International media was generally positive and moved by the plight of the refugees. The Ministry of External Affairs established an XP (or external publicity) Division, appointed an official spokesman, and started daily media briefings. Outreach to NGOs and public opinion was a major factor in making possible the positive outcome of the crisis and in neutralizing the strong bias against secession among governments, in international law, and in multilateral organizations founded with sovereign states as constituent units.

India's traditional friends among the nonaligned, most of whom had secessionists of their own to worry about, were not very helpful—neither Tito of Yugoslavia, who stayed mum, nor Sadat of Egypt, who made several pro-Pakistani statements. Nor was Indian diplomacy any more successful with the smaller Europeans. Instead, India turned to Israel for weapons to arm the Bangladeshi resistance and liberation army, the Mukti Bahini.

~

The tempo of covert operations against East Pakistan had been gradually stepped up from the beginning of the crisis and escalated in August 1971. On her return to Delhi from the United States and Europe, Mrs. Gandhi further increased support to the Bangladeshis. From early October the Indian Army supported Mukti Bahini attacks on Pakistani posts in East Pakistan, first with artillery and then with Indian troops. Mukti Bahini offensives led to an eventual full-fledged military intervention. On November 21 three Pakistani aircraft were downed in the fighting and thereafter Indian troops stayed on East Pakistan territory. In the last week of November Mrs. Gandhi approved a full-scale attack on East Pakistan and D-day was set for December 4.

Pakistan too was simultaneously preparing to attack India. Faced with escalating attacks in the east, General Gul Hassan, chief of general staff of the Pakistan Army, sought Yahya Khan's permission to attack India on the western front. On November 29 Yahya Khan tentatively decided to open the western front, and formalized the decision the next day, setting D-day for December 3, 1971. That evening the Pakistan Air Force attempted preemptive strikes on

Indian airfields. The strikes had been expected. That night Gandhi declared hostilities with Pakistan, and on December 6 she recognized the independent state of Bangladesh.

When the war began, Kissinger tried hard to get China to intervene or at least to threaten India militarily. On December 10 he sent a message from Nixon to Zhou through Huang Hua, the Chinese UN representative: "If the People's Republic were to consider the situation on the Indian subcontinent a threat to its security, and if it took measures to protect its security, the U.S. would oppose the efforts of others to interfere with the People's Republic." When Huang was noncommittal, Kissinger spelled it out, saying that if China attacked India, the United States would ensure that Russia did not enter the fray.[7] According to some reports, Kissinger also shared some intelligence of dubious value about Indian troop movements to encourage preemptive Chinese military intervention. On December 12 the Chinese replied that the UN Security Council should reconvene and made no mention of moving against India. Mrs. Gandhi too had been in touch with China, writing to Zhou Enlai on December 11 saying that India sought friendship and describing the Indian position. Several possible reasons could explain why China did not to respond to Kissinger's invitation to intervene. China had its own civil-military issues, and Zhou later told Kissinger that China believed that military intervention would be futile. Simultaneously Kissinger also pressed the Soviets to lean on India and dispatched the U.S.S. *Enterprise* into the Bay of Bengal "to convince India the thing is going to escalate."[8] The Soviets reportedly sent a submarine to shadow the aircraft carrier.

In the UN Security Council, the Soviets stood by India and vetoed any condemnation of India. But by December 10, the Soviets began to consult India on the elements of a resolution calling for a ceasefire. India went along, on the understanding that the resolution would be introduced by another nation so that the Soviets could make any subsequent changes India wanted. India's need for Soviet support meant that it could not directly oppose Soviet efforts. To India's surprise, however, the resolution was introduced by Poland, which meant that the changes sought would now be impossible. The USSR could hardly amend or veto an ally's text. The Soviets were effectively telling India that they wanted an end to the war but not necessarily on India's terms. India was saved embarrassment, however, when Pakistani Foreign Minister Bhutto, despite contrary instructions from his president Yahya Khan, tore up the text and stormed out of the Security Council chamber. Yahya Khan told Bhutto on the phone to support the Polish resolution, but Bhutto kept saying, "What?"

Finally, the exasperated operator intervened and said there was nothing wrong with the line, Bhutto told her to shut up! Bhutto probably did so to ensure a complete collapse and surrender by the army in East Pakistan, knowing that this would clear his way to power. To the Indians involved, it was clear that the Russians were increasingly uncomfortable, and that the military task had to be completed as soon as possible.

While the UN Security Council could not act due to the threat of a Soviet veto, and China stayed out of the conflict, the war itself went better and faster than expected for India. At 4 p.m. Indian Standard Time on December 16, 1971, Pakistani forces in East Pakistan surrendered unconditionally. India had freed East Pakistan, captured 93,000 Pakistani POWs, and was in occupation of Pakistani territory in Punjab and Sindh too. India declared a unilateral ceasefire on the western front later the same day.

In Pakistan, Yahya Khan's government fell and Bhutto became president and chief martial law administrator on the basis of the December 1970 elections. Mujibur Rehman was released and returned home via London and a rapturous Delhi on January 10, 1972, to become president of Bangladesh. In March 1972, India and Bangladesh signed a Treaty of Peace, Friendship, and Cooperation. By March 17, 1972, all Indian troops had been withdrawn from Bangladesh.

~

India had won a great victory with resounding consequences. Indira Gandhi was hailed as the "Empress of India" by *The Economist* and as Shakti and Durga[9] in Parliament by the opposition. It was her political high point. She had faced down the United States, carried along a hesitant Soviet Union, and helped to create a new state, the first after Israel in 1948, over the opposition of the superpowers. As Srinath Raghavan says, all in all, by creating the large and populous state of Bangladesh from East Pakistan, the 1971 war was the most significant geopolitical event in the subcontinent since the partition of 1947 and tilted the balance of power in the subcontinent between India and Pakistan in India's favor.

But there remains a feeling in India that India lost at the peace table what she had won in war. In July 1972 Mrs. Gandhi and Bhutto, who had become prime minister of Pakistan, met in Simla to discuss the peace. The Simla Agreement of July 2, 1972, provided for India to vacate all West Pakistan territories occupied during the war and to release all Pakistani prisoners of war. Both sides agreed to redraw and adjust the ceasefire line of 1948 in Kashmir and to call the new line the "Line of Control."[10] According to some accounts, Mrs. Gandhi was keen to settle the Kashmir issue and agreed with Bhutto that the problem be resolved by Pakistan keeping what was west of the Line of Control and India the rest of Jammu and Kashmir. Bhutto said that he could not reflect this in a formal agreement for fear of the reaction at home from the Pakistan Army to what would be called an abject surrender. The private understanding on a future settlement of Jammu and Kashmir was therefore left to be formalized publicly later. India was greatly influenced by the sense that an imposed peace like the Versailles peace that ended World War I would only create resentment, unite Pakistan, and sow the seeds for another war, as P. N. Haksar, Mrs. Gandhi's influential principal secretary, argued forcefully in notes to her. What realism dictated came to pass fairly soon. Bhutto backed out of the verbal agreement on Kashmir soon after returning to Pakistan. In any case, by 1975 neither Mrs. Gandhi nor Bhutto had the political capital at home to make the Line of Control the permanent international boundary between India and Pakistan.[11]

On balance, it is hard to see how a settlement of Jammu and Kashmir legalizing the status quo would have been politically accepted in either country—in a Pakistan smarting from defeat, when large portions of the populace and army sought revenge from India, or in a triumphal India. It is also moot whether such a settlement would have lasted, since it would have left both sides dissatisfied and would have soon fallen victim to the fractious turn that domestic politics took in India and Pakistan within a few years. But this is speculation. What is certain is that, on balance, the Simla Agreement brought stability and helped to avert a conventional war in the subcontinent for many years.

The subcontinent continues to this day to live with some baleful consequences of the 1971 war. Pakistan's realization that it could not take Jammu and Kashmir by conventional war led to a pursuit of nuclear weapons and to increasing reliance on terrorism and other asymmetric means to slake its desire for revenge on India for breaking up Pakistan. Bhutto and the Pakistan Army decided at Multan in 1972 to build nuclear weapons, "even if we have to eat grass," as Bhutto said. Bhutto also turned to the Islamic world for support, holding the second Islamic Summit in Lahore in 1974, giving impetus to a process of Islamicizing Pakistan's society and polity that was to reach fruition in the 1980s under Zia-ul-Haq during the war against the Soviets in Afghanistan. The conflicts over Siachen and Kargil are legacies of the Line of Control drawn after the 1971 war. Pakistan's stoking of insurgency in Kashmir and other parts of India and Bangladesh's deep political divides and fissures are among the legacies of the war with which we are still coming to terms.

The U.S. opening to China affected India's conduct in the Bangladesh crisis and subcontinental geopolitics. But Sino-U.S. rapprochement also changed the nature of the Cold War and affected the broader geopolitics of Asia, fundamentally transforming the environment for Indian foreign policy.

China and the United States had been adversaries in Asia since the communists came to power in China in 1949. The Korean War was ended by an armistice, not a peace treaty, and in Vietnam at least 320,000 Chinese soldiers served against the U.S. Army.[12] At the same time Zhou and others had signaled to the United States that the war was Vietnam's and not China's. On April 2, 1965, Zhou told Ayub Khan, the president of Pakistan who was planning a visit to Washington, that China would not provoke a broader conflict unless it was attacked. Only an American ground invasion of North Vietnam, the collapse of the North Vietnamese government, or a direct assault on China would pull Beijing directly into the fight, he said, in words that were clearly meant to be relayed to Washington. China was telling the Americans that it was not looking for another Korean War. In any event, it was to become deeply involved, sending troops and aircraft with Chinese pilots flying missions in the Vietnam War, but not formally confronting the United States militarily, unlike Korea. Unlike during the 1950s, it was not India that was carrying Chinese messages to Washington, but Pakistan.

The October 16, 1964, Chinese atom bomb test was a major factor in Johnson escalating U.S. operations in Vietnam. India, which had just fought a war with China, sought a U.S. nuclear umbrella. China, instead, had struck out on its own. The test therefore also changed China's status in U.S. eyes and convinced the American establishment that the Sino-Soviet split was real. On July 12, 1966, Johnson became the first U.S. president to speak of communist China in conciliatory terms. "Cooperation not hostility," "reconciliation," and the "free flow of ideas, people and goods" with China were his goals, President Johnson said in a nationally televised address. As India-U.S. relations cooled in the late 1960s, the ground was shifting between the United States and China. By calling the capital Peking instead of Peiping, shifting from the old Nationalist name meaning "northern peace" to the Ming dynasty and communist usage of "northern capital," the United States signaled an implicit acceptance of the city as the capital. By such small signs does diplomacy signal major shifts.

In October 1967, while out of office, Richard Nixon wrote a remarkable piece for *Foreign Affairs* titled "Asia after Vietnam," demanding that the United

States "come urgently to grips with the reality of China." It was America's duty to bring China back into the "family of nations." Leaving it "to nurture its fantasies, cherish its hates and threaten its neighbors" was too dangerous. "The world cannot be safe until China changes," Nixon argued.

The 1971 opening was thus a bombshell, but a carefully prepared bombshell, and not a great political risk for the United States. America was ready. But the world could not believe that a China in the throes of the Cultural Revolution would come to an understanding with its longstanding enemy. Initially China was not ready, and the shift was probably harder for China, though logic and realism argued for it. China was in the midst of the Great Proletarian Cultural Revolution and the Lin Biao affair, in which the prospect of a thaw with the United States may have figured. China tested its first ballistic missile on October 27, 1966, and an H-bomb on July 17, 1967. Nine days later President Johnson told Romanian President Gheorghe Maurer, who was going to China, that the United States had no intention of changing China or its government but that he wanted to talk to China about nonproliferation and rules for avoiding nuclear war. At that stage China was not ready to respond. Guochang Wang shook his fist at Cabot in Warsaw and called Johnson's outreach "a big lie." It was only in November 1968, just weeks after Nixon had won the White House, that Zhou signaled a willingness to resume the Warsaw talks that China had suspended at the height of the Cultural Revolution in 1967.

U.S. motives in seeking an opening to China were simple. At the geostrategic level the United States wanted to counter the Soviets and to extract itself from the quagmire of Vietnam with some honor. Nixon also wanted to "cultivate China" to ensure it would not turn into "the most formidable enemy that ever existed in the history of the world." (Ironically, that could well be the result in practice of an overlong continuation of Nixon and Kissinger's policies toward China.) Nixon and Kissinger had convinced themselves that the balance with the Soviets was tilting against them. Kissinger's enthusiasm also arose from the administration's need for a foreign policy win after years of dead ends in Indochina, the Middle East, and East Europe.

The opening to China required a rebalancing of the United States' presence around China and a readjustment of other relationships in Asia. Beginning in July 1969 Nixon began drawing down U.S. forces in South Korea, ordered the 7th Fleet to stop patrolling the Taiwan Strait, and began moving U.S. soldiers out of Taiwan. Although the April 1970 U.S. invasion of Cambodia caused a blip, by June 18, 1970, U.S. troops were out of Cambodia. The U.S. military threat to China had been reduced and ping-pong diplomacy could proceed.

The story of Kissinger's secret visit to Beijing July 9–11 from Islamabad, where it was put out that he had an upset stomach after his Delhi visit, and the drama of the Nixon visit in February 1972, have been told often and well elsewhere.

What are worth reading are the transcripts of Kissinger's conversations with Zhou.[13] They are an object lesson in how not to negotiate. Kissinger made outsize promises, belittled U.S. allies like Japan, implied that the United States was eager to dump Chiang Kai-shek, and tried to get Zhou to commit to acting against India and for Pakistan during the Bangladesh crisis. He gave Zhou what China wanted up front while accepting postdated cheques on U.S. demands, which were never cashed. He provided intelligence on Soviet troop deployments on the Chinese border, bringing gifts without asking for anything in return. He made a series of astounding statements and promises: he announced a U.S. intention of retreating from the western Pacific; he committed the United States to withdrawing from Taiwan; U.S. forces in Korea would also wind down before the end of Nixon's second term; the United States would not assist Chiang in any assault on the mainland; and the U.S. alliance with Japan was to prevent Japan from turning to war again. Zhou said that when the United States pulled out of Taiwan, reunification could be expected. Kissinger agreed. He never mentioned the decades long U.S. insistence on "peaceful reunification." He also gave Zhou a detailed road map for China's entry into the UN. They both agreed that Nixon would visit China before May 1972. When Mao heard of Kissinger's promise to withdraw U.S. troops from Taiwan, he said that it would take some time for a monkey to evolve into a human being. The Americans, he said, were now at the ape stage, "with a tail, though a much shorter one, on his back."

Nixon's conditions for his visit, as he told Kissinger before the negotiations, were the release of all Americans in Chinese custody; China to lean on Vietnam to agree to a peace deal; and Nixon to be the first U.S. statesman to visit China—he did not want Senator Ted Kennedy or Senator George McGovern to beat him. There were some releases of ex-CIA operatives captured by China during the Korean War, and the Chinese also refrained from receiving any other U.S. political leader before Nixon. The United States probably overestimated how far China was willing or able to pressure Vietnam when Vietnam could also turn to the Soviet Union.

China went into the discussions with a more meaningful set of demands but a far more demanding domestic situation in which to carry out the opening. At that point, China's leadership needed the United States far more than the reverse for reasons ranging from geostrategy to the very basic imperative of survival. But one would never believe that from the Chinese telling, nor would you from Kissinger's accounts of the opening.

The internal chaos of the Cultural Revolution (Great Proletarian Cultural Revolution) and turmoil within the People's Liberation Army after the Lin Biao affair meant that Mao had few or no cards to play. He had asked the four marshals—Chen Yi, Ye Jianying, Xu Xiangqian, and Nie Rongzhen—to study two questions: Who was China's main enemy and was war likely? In a series of reports from June to September 1969, the marshals answered that the Soviet Union was China's main enemy and that war with the Soviets was a real possibility. On repeated prodding by Mao and Zhou, they finally suggested that to avoid Soviet harassment China should seek accommodation with the United States and drop its long-standing condition that the United States first withdraw from Taiwan.

In March 1969 Sino-Soviet relations had turned from tense to deadly with clashes on the Ussuri River between Manchuria and Siberia, resulting in hundreds of casualties. These were followed by credible reports that the Soviets were planning a surgical strike on Chinese nuclear facilities. In August 1969, a KGB officer sounded out a U.S. diplomat about President John F. Kennedy's original idea of a surgical strike on China. This time the United States balked. On September 9, 1969, the U.S. under secretary of state said in public that the United States would not "let Soviet apprehensions prevent us from bringing China out of its angry, alienated shell"—the first time that Americans had publicly warned the Soviets against bullying China.

China was isolated internationally, in terrible economic shape, had no hope of unifying Taiwan, and was threatened by the Soviet Union. Chinese Communist Party leaders had been trying to solve each of these four problems for decades, and the United States held the key to each of them.

In the end, China gained on all four fronts as a result of the opening, with American assurances based only on China's promise to help extract the United States from Vietnam. China's isolation ended in 1971 when it assumed the permanent seat in the UN Security Council that had been held by Taiwan. China's development received a major boost from access to Western technology, capital, and markets. The Soviets were indeed deterred from attacking China, and China got invaluable military intelligence in what amounted to a tacit military alliance. In addition, Kissinger indicated that the United States would remove its troops and would turn a blind eye if China were to forcibly unify Taiwan.

This turned out to be a promise too far. An alarmed Congress reacted by pass-ing the Taiwan Relations Act after President Jimmy Carter extended diplo-matic recognition to China in 1978. The act committed the United States to providing arms for Taiwan's self-defense and other measures.

However, Kissinger's promises had raised Chinese expectations, which sub-sequently the United States was unable to meet. This undermined U.S. cred-ibility and sowed the seeds of distrust in China, Taiwan, Japan, and the rest of Asia. On February 17, 1973, Mao received Kissinger and proposed an alliance with the United States to contain the Soviet threat. "We were enemies in the past but now we are friends," Mao declared. The United States and China were "in the same trench," he pointed out. "We should draw a horizontal line — the U.S., Japan, Pakistan, Iran, Turkey and Europe." "And we can work together to commonly deal with the bastard," Mao said.[14] This time it was the United States that was reluctant, wanting to protect equities with the Soviet Union with SALT-I, which was about to be signed during Brezhnev's June 1973 visit. As Kissinger said later, "The U.S. wanted to continue to have our mao-tai and drink our vodka." Mao too dropped the idea as he was disappointed by the slow pace of normalization and diplomatic relations. And soon he had second thoughts, gathering Zhou and other officials on November 17, 1973, and warn-ing them to be wary of the Americans, forcing Zhou, who had been diagnosed with cancer, to make a self-criticism before the Politbureau, getting his wife Jiang Qing to attack Zhou for "humiliating the country," and rehabilitating Deng Xiaoping, an obvious alternative to Zhou. By February 1974 Mao was getting Deng to proclaim his Three Worlds Theory to the UN and running a campaign in China to "criticize Lin Biao and Confucius," a thinly disguised attack on Zhou—all this for following Mao's policy initiatives faithfully.

In 1976 Mao and Zhou died. The older Communist Party leadership soon got rid of Mao's chosen successor, Hua Guofeng, and the Gang of Four left-ist followers of Mao including his wife Jiang Qing. China entered a new phase under Deng Xiaoping's leadership, concentrating on building the economy, using markets and foreign trade, and taking advantage of the access to world forums to transform itself—all made possible by the U.S.-China opening in 1971. Nixon and Kissinger believed that the geopolitical implications of their gambit with China trumped everything else. But, ultimately, they helped to create a peer competitor to the United States itself.

Under Deng Xiaoping, China and the United States built a de facto alliance. The United States provided China with military equipment and intelligence.

When the Shah of Iran was overthrown on January 29, 1979, the United States lost listening posts in Iran on the Soviet border. China stepped in to offer the Americans posts in Xinjiang to monitor Soviet nuclear tests and communications in Operation Chestnut. The U.S.-China alliance grew from strength to strength in the 1980s, on Vietnam, in Cambodia, and in Afghanistan.

The opening converted the U.S. bilateral contest with the Soviet Union into a three-cornered relationship with the United States as the only one that had ties with both the other parties. It was not until the mid-1980s that the Soviet Union under Mikhail Gorbachev was able to reach out to China to even out the triangle. In the meantime, Leonid Brezhnev, who had resisted invitations to a disarmament summit with Nixon in 1970, soon scheduled meetings and entered into the Anti-Ballistic Missile and SALT-1 treaties in 1972. Kissinger and Nixon were right in assuming that the opening would help the United States to better manage its relations with the Soviets.

They were less acute in their judgment of the opening's effect on Asian geopolitics. The immediate impact on U.S. allies in Asia was severe. Japanese Prime Minister Eisaku Sato, who had been given only a few hours' notice of Nixon's announcement, was reduced to tears and told Gough Whitlam, the Australian Labor leader, "I did everything the Americans asked and yet they let me down." The Japanese problem was how to build bridges with China now that the United States had done so first. In talking to Zhou, Kissinger had used Japan's alleged militarism to justify keeping U.S. troops in Asia, adding insult to injury. Left and right in Japan were united in wanting better ties with China, seeing them as giving Japan independence from an unreliable United States. Yet with the strength of U.S.-Japan ties and economic interdependence so strong, the Japan-U.S. security relationship survived the "China shock." What was true of Japan was also true of other U.S. allies in Asia, like the Association of Southeast Asian Nations (ASEAN), all of whom had been blindsided and now rushed to develop direct ties with China. China too adjusted her policies to fit the new alliance with the United States, cutting back support for communist revolutions in southeast Asia and concentrating on economic benefits from her diaspora. ASEAN came to terms with China and joined the process of integrating China into global manufacturing and value-added chains. With great power politics out of the way, southeast Asians were free to concentrate single-mindedly on building their economies, which they did with great success.

In January 1973 the United States and North Vietnam formally ended the Vietnam War, removing 100,000 U.S. combat troops. from China's vicinity. In

April 1975 Saigon fell to North Vietnamese troops and Vietnam was reunified. In a rapid turnabout, unified Vietnam allied with the Soviet Union and began to consolidate its periphery in Indochina, thus uniting the United States, ASEAN, and China in opposition to this new direction. Ten days after Sino-U.S. normalization, Vietnam invaded Cambodia and overthrew Pol Pot. Eight weeks after normalization, China invaded Vietnam to "teach Vietnam a lesson" in a war that was disastrous for the PLA.

Pakistan, which had provided the first test of the U.S.-China alliance in the Bangladesh crisis, was to figure even more actively in it when the Soviet Union ended the decade by invading Afghanistan on Christmas Day 1979, and the United States, China, and Pakistan worked together to turn Afghanistan into Russia's Vietnam quagmire.

~

For India, the U.S.-China alliance was clearly a limiting factor, by backing a hostile Pakistan. That support probably contributed to Bhutto reneging on the promises he made at Simla in July 1972. It also left China without an immediate incentive to follow up on the initiative by Mao to improve relations with India in 1970.

As India's geopolitical space tightened, conditions were also worsening within India. Less than four years after her magnificent victory in the 1971 war, Indira Gandhi felt compelled to declare a state of internal emergency and delay elections to stay in power. How and why she did so is outside the scope of this book. But the fact is that proven Indian capabilities in war and diplomacy were not matched by the country's internal economy or administration. By the mid-1970s most of the promises that independent India had held out to its own people had been belied in the popular mind. The cost of the 1971 war, the United States stopping aid that same year, the burden of 10 million Bangladeshi refugees, and a renewed failure of the monsoon rains saw a precipitous decline in the Indian economy. The economy suffered double-digit inflation after the 1973 oil shock when an OPEC oil embargo led to oil prices quadrupling in less than a year from $3 to $12 dollars per barrel. From mid-1973 to mid-1974 inflation in India was at 33 percent and there was a rapid deterioration in the balance of payments. Several developing countries had forged ahead of India, lowering India's status in the world. Under this worsening scenario Mrs. Gandhi's economic policies took a dramatic turn: she now sought a more open and market-friendly model. The trigger was a botched attempt to nationalize the wheat trade in 1973, and she turned to industrialist J. R. D. Tata and others for economic advice. As a consequence, from 1975 to 1978 the Indian economy grew at an average of 6 percent, but a second oil shock in 1979 saw it contract by 5.2 percent in one year.

Despite domestic preoccupations, Indira Gandhi was behind three significant external initiatives designed to compensate and offset the adverse shifts in Asian geopolitics. One was the nuclear explosion of 1974. The others were the integration of Sikkim into the Indian republic and the resumption of ambassador-level relations with China. In addition, efforts began to consolidate India's immediate periphery in the subcontinent, intervening actively in the neighborhood. In sum, Mrs. Gandhi's reaction to the constriction of India's geopolitical space in Asia as a consequence of the U.S.-China rapprochement was to undertake measures to strengthen India's deterrence and to consolidate the immediate periphery in the subcontinent.

∼

In the aftermath of the 1971 war over Bangladesh, Nixon's tilt to Pakistan, and his visit to China, it was clear that India's external environment had deteriorated. China's nuclear weapons program was moving forward from an atom bomb to missile and hydrogen bomb tests in the late 1960s. In response, India had built up the technical capabilities and separated plutonium that could be used for a bomb. The superpowers were unwilling to extend a nuclear umbrella to India when Prime Minister Shastri sought one in 1964. But so long as both the Soviet Union and the United States had adversarial relations with China, the uncertainty about their response added some deterrence should China threaten India with her nuclear weapons. In any case, China's nuclear weapons were still being built into an effective force and China was convulsed by the Cultural Revolution. Indian planners therefore did not see the Chinese threat as imminent or urgent in the mid-to-late 1960s. But that situation changed after the Nixon visit to China and the Bangladesh war. By sending a nuclear-powered aircraft carrier into the Bay of Bengal to coerce India into stopping the 1971 war, the United States had implicitly issued a nuclear threat. Soon after the war, Mrs. Gandhi asked the department of atomic energy to prepare to test a nuclear device. On May 18, 1974, "Buddha smiled," according to the coded message sent to inform the prime minister of the test's success. Given India's economic difficulties and need for outside support and aid, the test was described as a peaceful nuclear explosion, something that was provided for in the Nuclear Non-Proliferation Treaty (NPT). Nor did India proceed immediately to build the infrastructure needed for a full-fledged nuclear weapons program, which would require a significant commitment of national resources, as P. N. Haksar, Mrs. Gandhi's principal secretary, pointed out in a note to her at that time.[15]

The world, however, saw the test for what it was—a demonstration of India's ability to manufacture an atom bomb. And the United States, Canada, and other Western powers reacted with sanctions on technology transfers to India, formed a cartel of nuclear suppliers called the Zangger committee, which later evolved into the Nuclear Supplier Group, to define and restrict dual-use nuclear supplies to non-weapon states, and cut off nuclear cooperation with India. The exceptions were Russia, France, and some non-NPT states like Brazil and Argentina, which were willing to continue cooperating with India in peaceful uses of nuclear energy. India's "nuclear apartheid" had begun, and the country was forced onto a path of self-reliant development, which was a useful spur to autonomy in the long run, although it did involve economic pain for some time. India had broken no law or commitment with the nuclear explosion. And now India had shown a determination to deal in the currency of twentieth-century power and was a latent nuclear weapon state.

It is often said, particularly by Pakistanis, that the Pakistan bomb is a response to India's 1974 explosion. This is not factually true and is belied by chronology. In January 1972, one month after taking power in Pakistan and six months before pledging peace to Mrs. Gandhi in Simla, Bhutto called his scientists and closest advisers to a meeting in Multan where he decided to pursue a Pakistani bomb at any cost. The rest of the story is well known, personified by A. Q. Khan, who led Pakistan's clandestine quest for the bomb, with Chinese assistance for the weapons and their delivery systems. A. Q. Khan stole European enrichment technology and brought it to Pakistan. In May 1976 Bhutto obtained assurances of help for his nuclear weapons program from Mao. Chinese cooperation grew over time, with Deng authorizing the transfer of an early Chinese A-bomb design and enriched uranium for two bombs to Pakistan, and China's testing a Pakistani device in 1991 in Xinjiang. China-Pakistan nuclear cooperation continues to this day. The China-U.S. alliance and their need for Pakistan in Afghanistan through the 1980s led the United States to turn a blind eye to Pakistan's nuclear program and to the unprecedented Chinese proliferation of nuclear weapons to another state. A straight line runs from that China-Pak cooperation to the nuclear weapons programs in North Korea, Libya, and Iran that today so bother the world, and that should worry China.

As the international environment turned hostile, India was consolidating its periphery, and not just through its actions in the Bangladesh crisis.

In April–May 1971, Sirimavo Bandaranaike, prime minister of Sri Lanka, asked for Indian military assistance against an armed insurrection by the Janatha Vimukthi Peramuna, an extreme left-wing group that was backed by North Korea and China. India promptly sent naval ships and troops. By May 25 Bandaranaike was thanking Indira Gandhi for the successful intervention.

Located strategically on the border with Tibet, Sikkim was a princely state of British India in 1947, unlike the other two Himalayan kingdoms, Nepal and Bhutan. In Sikkim the Political Officer sent to Gangtok by Delhi had supervisory rights over the internal administration. The Government of India Act of 1935 had listed Sikkim as an Indian princely state. In December 1947 the Sikkim State Congress Party had sought accession to India, which was rejected by Nehru who chose to treat Sikkim as a buffer state. In December 1948 the Indian Army restored order in the state for the administration. Soon after the establishment of the People's Republic of China in 1949, a new agreement was signed by India with the Himalayan kingdom where sovereignty rested with India, and some enhanced powers were delegated to the local prince or Maharaja. But Sikkim's internal politics were unstable. In 1950, Sikkim's population of 150,000 was 80 percent Nepalese, 15 percent Bhutias of Tibetan origin, and 5 percent Lepcha, the original inhabitants. The Maharajas were Bhutias and ruled with the support of the minorities represented by the Sikkim National Party, while the Nepalese represented by the Sikkim Congress founded in December 1947 sought democracy and closer integration with India. Internal politics in Sikkim boiled up periodically. By 1973 there were anti-monarchy riots in Sikkim. At the same time the Maharaja was seeking more independence, thinking after 1962 that he could play international politics with the United States and others, and sidelining the Indian-appointed Dewan who ran the administration.

In late December 1972, Mrs. Gandhi asked her external intelligence chief and trusted principal secretary whether India could do anything about Sikkim. A fortnight later an operational plan was worked out, which was also backed by the new foreign secretary, Kewal Singh, who, unlike his predecessor, T. N. Kaul, was not inclined to give in to the Chogyal's escalating demands.[16] Delhi was naturally worried about instability in a state bordering Tibet and the possibilities that this might open up for China to link up with Naxalite or Maoist insurgents in eastern India. Besides, Sikkim is positioned just north of the twenty-two-kilometer-wide Siliguri corridor, the so-called chicken's neck, the rest of India's only land link to the northeastern states.

Matters in Sikkim came to a head with the state becoming ungovernable by the Chogyal after a democratic upsurge from 1973 onward. Elections in April 1974 resulted in the first steps toward democratization and real power being given to elected officials. In response to a demand by the elected Assembly, on September 14, 1974, the Lok Sabha passed the 36th Amendment to the Constitution changing Sikkim from a protectorate to Associate State status with political representation in the Indian Union. A referendum was held in the state, which overwhelmingly voted to merge the state with India. But the Chogyal remained unreconciled. In February 1975 he visited Nepal and, in an act of defiance, met with the Pakistan ambassador and a Chinese vice-premier. At a Kathmandu press conference, he also spoke of "leaving no stone unturned to preserve Sikkim's separate identity and status." That was the last straw and was opposed by his own people and Assembly. On May 16, 1975, Sikkim merged with the Indian Union as its twenty-second state.

China, which had sporadically objected to India speaking or negotiating on Sikkim's behalf, protested vociferously at what it described as the annexation of Sikkim but made no military moves, and the border remained quiet. China's attempt to canvass support at the UN met with little interest. It was only in 2003 that China accepted that Sikkim was part of India and now shows it as such in its maps. The United States avoided official comment. Mrs. Gandhi's willingness to impose India's will on its periphery, in contrast to Nehru's reluctance to do so, is stark in the case of Sikkim.

~

Another part of Mrs. Gandhi's response was an attempted opening to China in the mid-1970s.

China posed a conundrum. Before tying up the opening to the United States, Mao had signaled a willingness to improve relations with India. Eight years after the war of 1962 on the India-China boundary, on May 1, 1970, Mao made it a point to speak to the Indian *chargé d'affaires*, Brajesh Mishra, on the Tiananmen rostrum in front of the entire diplomatic corps, gathered to watch the May Day fireworks with the Chinese leadership. Mao said, "We cannot keep quarrelling like this. We should try and be friends again. India is a great country. The Indian people are good people. We will be friends again someday." When Mishra replied that India was ready to do it today, Mao said, "Please convey my best wishes to your President and your Prime Minister." This was the "Mao smile," a premeditated gesture that caused considerable perturbation in Delhi. Despite the *chargé's* advice that India should respond by sending an ambassador to China, having withdrawn the ambassador first in 1961, Indira Gandhi's advisers, P. N. Haksar and G. Parthasarathi, were negative and skepticism prevailed in Delhi. "Probe" and "keep the ball rolling" were the instructions to Mishra, though Mrs. Gandhi gave Mishra the clear impression that she was in favor of reciprocating the gesture and seeking a new opening in the relationship with China. It is hard to say whether Mao's public gambit was genuine or meant to prod the United States into being more forthcoming. China was certainly seeking options to avoid a two-front war and looking for a way out of its difficult situation. Whatever the Chinese motives, this episode of the Mao smile, when India failed to respond meaningfully to China in 1970, must go down in the books as an opportunity unexplored, perhaps missed.

China was on Mrs. Gandhi's mind even as she dealt with the Pakistan crisis and the consequences of Nixon's opening to China in 1971. The eternal pragmatist, she was more open-minded on China than her closest advisers. On August 12, 1971, three days after the signing of the Indo-Soviet Treaty, Mrs. Gandhi sent a slip to P. N. Haksar, her principal secretary and closest adviser, that read, "should we not indicate to Mishra that the Indo-Soviet Treaty does not preclude a similar treaty with China?" Haksar took a week to send back a long note detailing reasons why this should not be done.[17] In July, after Kissinger's visit to India, Gandhi wrote a note to Premier Zhou Enlai expressing willingness to have a dialogue at any level on bilateral issues. There was no Chinese response. By now the United States and China were working on their own initiative and China had other options.

Mrs. Gandhi's next attempt was in the mid-1970s when the international situation prompted and her internal emergency enabled her to attempt an opening to China. In 1975–1976 the government negotiated the return of ambassadors to Delhi and Beijing. K. R. Narayanan presented credentials in Beijing in July 1976, on the same day as K. S. Bajpai did in Islamabad, restoring ambassadorial relations with Pakistan for the first time after the 1971 war. By choosing that date, the Chinese were making the point that they had not abandoned Pakistan or moved ahead of their friend in dealing with India.

In February 1979 Atal Behari Vajpayee, foreign minister in the coalition Janata Party government between 1977 and 1979, visited China, the first such visit ever. This began the long trek back to normalcy after the 1962 war with decisions to reopen trade and other links, to restart pilgrimages to Kailash and

Manasarovar, and to resume discussions on a boundary settlement and improved relations. Within a year Foreign Minister Huang Hua was in Delhi, and it was formally announced that officials would begin negotiations on the boundary. India-China relations were still tense, dominated by the boundary and overshadowed by differences on Sikkim, by Chinese support to Indian Maoist groups and to insurgents in northeast India, and by China's commitment to Pakistan. But relations were better than they had been when Mrs. Gandhi first came to power.

~

Both Jawaharlal Nehru, the father, and India Gandhi, the daughter, enjoyed a favorable balance of power in the subcontinent, though each worked it differently. Mrs. Gandhi was much less inhibited about intervening in India's periphery. But the broader canvas, once the bipolar world was consolidated in the mid-1950s, made it harder for Nehru to follow his quest to build an area of peace in Asia and open a third way. For Mrs. Gandhi the broader situation was initially favorable in the late 1960s and early 1970s when the global balance of power and alignments opened options for Indian activism in Sri Lanka, Bangladesh, and Sikkim, making the subcontinental balance of forces usable. Especially after 1969, the international situation cracked open enabling India to exploit its inherent advantages in the subcontinent. But the global and Asian window closed in the mid-1970s with the China-U.S. alliance and other shifts, as it had for her father in his later years. The international situation was trying for Mrs. Gandhi in the later years of her prime ministership. This might help to explain the marked differences in approach between Nehru the peacemaker and Indira Gandhi the security seeker and the much more hard-headed politics of Indira Gandhi. Both, however, sought a separate space for a nonaligned India in the Cold War system. While this was Asian and global for Nehru, for Indira Gandhi it was an Indocentric subregional order. For both of them, Indian centrality was a given.[18]

In retrospect, the 1970s, which began with such promise with the birth of Bangladesh, saw the country's domestic failings and the Sino-U.S. alliance close off India's external options. By the end of the decade, India was dependent on the Soviet Union for weapons and political support, Pakistan was under military rule again, Bangladesh was under a military dictator who sought to build his country's nationalism in opposition to India, and southeast Asia was increasingly polarized against a Vietnam dominant in Indochina. An economic boom in southeast Asia was passing India by.

But despite adverse changes in the external situation, India had, in the face of U.S. and Chinese opposition, remade the neighborhood, won a great military victory, broken up Pakistan, and weathered an economic storm. India was behaving as a realist power, carrying out a nuclear test, using force, and deploying the instruments of state for its own interests. That it still had insufficient power to transform India or to determine developments in the broader periphery does not diminish the evolution in India's behavior and its increasing agency. Like a young adult, India was on its own and had to make its own way in the world. India had come of age.

The next decade was to see a determined effort by India to break out of these constraints, despite difficult political choices when the Soviet Union invaded Afghanistan, Vietnam invaded Cambodia, and China invaded Vietnam.

6

Hard Times

The 1980s were an eventful and crowded decade: the external constraints that held India back in the previous decade reached their peak, and internal ones began to be overcome. India experienced economic and foreign policy adjustments and built capabilities that would serve the country in good stead when the Soviet Union collapsed at the end of the decade, leading to the most fundamental change in Asian geopolitics since decolonization. But the decade marked transformation, shifts and changes in Asia that tested Indian policy, its realism, flexibility, and judgment during Indira Gandhi's second term from 1980 to 1984, and even more so when her son, Rajiv Gandhi, was prime minister in the second half of the decade.

For India the 1980s were preceded by three significant events in 1979. In January the Iranian Revolution overthrew the Shah of Iran, a U.S. and Pakistani ally, who was replaced by a theocracy headed by a supreme leader, Ayatollah Khomeini, opposed to the United States and the West and much more open to India. The next month, China attacked Vietnam and was defeated by the newly unified Vietnamese; this military defeat became, in the end, a diplomatic and economic victory for China in Indochina with U.S. help. Last, the Soviet Union invaded Afghanistan in December. Each of these events still reverberates today.

∼

The Iranian Revolution remade the geopolitics of west Asia. The post–World War II order in the region had contained the regional powers, Egypt, Iran, Israel, and Turkey, within a bipolar Cold War framework, despite efforts by Egypt's Nasser to break out of it. Through the late-sixties and seventies, as relative Soviet capacity diminished, Arab nationalist regimes were replaced in

Egypt and elsewhere by autocrats or military regimes, and west Asia became an unstable component in a primarily Western-led order with a major role for Israel.

The oil boycott in 1973 was the first event that struck at the core of the Western belief that it could count on countries in the Middle East and especially the Organization of Petroleum Exporting Counties (OPEC). The Iranian Revolution of 1979, however, marked a significant shift, with the dominant regional power opting out of the Western-led order. Within Iran, the revolution enjoyed mass support because it was seen as a political quest for sovereignty, rather than simply a religious takeover as portrayed in the West. The Iranians were ridding themselves of an imperialism shadowed by American hegemony and an organized coup, in 1953, that had been organized by the Central Intelligence Agency and had set up the Shah. Indeed, the Iranian episode was the last of the great successful revolutions in the postcolonial world, in an Islamic form.[1] The course the revolutionary Iranian regime chose was the most anti-American of any state since China in the 1960s, symbolized by making hostages of diplomats in the U.S. embassy in Tehran. The consequences for west Asia were momentous. One reaction was the Iran-Iraq War, September 22, 1980–August 20, 1988, which set an Iraq armed and supported by the United States and Saudi Arabia to contain Iran and to prevent the contagion of her radical politics spreading to Western allies in the Gulf and Levant. Pitted against the Iranian revolutionaries was Saudi Wahhabism, a most retrograde form of political Islam, using secular Baathist Iraq as its instrument and marking an intensification of the political uses of Islam, for which the Soviets' Afghan war was to create new and deadly instruments in the same decade. The Iran-Iraq War ended in a stalemate, leaving deep divisions and several issues critical to the future of the region undecided. West Asia now saw Shia-Sunni, Arab-Persian splits compounded by geopolitical pushback against Iran. And the aftermath was also a quest for nuclear weapons by several parties: Iran, Iraq, and Libya. All three justified themselves by pointing to the open secret that Israel already possessed nuclear weapons.

The Iranian Revolution posed no direct threat to India so long as it was not exported east. Indeed, the threats within India were actually from Sunni groups funded by Saudi Arabia and some Emirates in the Persian Gulf. The Shia in India are a minority within a minority who often feel most threatened by their coreligionists and have therefore traditionally worked with the secular authorities. By the time of the Iranian Revolution, India had a significant diaspora of about 2 million Indians living and working in the Persian Gulf states, depended on the region for its energy supplies, and sought to deny adversaries like Pakistan use of the resources and religious authorities in west Asia against India. With the passing of the Shah and the coming of the revolutionary regime, India and Iran began to find strategic congruence in Afghanistan and in opposition to the radical reinterpretation of Sunni Islam promoted by Saudi Arabia, Pakistan, and Western sponsors of Wahhabism and mujahideen jihadism in Afghanistan against the Soviets. For India, Iran has been a steady source of energy and an economic and political partner in the western periphery, and has given India access to Afghanistan and Central Asia. From an Indian point of view, the revolutionary regime in Iran has overall been easier to work with than its predecessor.

~

On Christmas Eve 1979 the Soviet Politburo headed by Leonid Brezhnev approved the deployment of the Soviet 40th Army into Afghanistan between December 27–29, 1979. That decision was preceded by long-term instability in Afghanistan's internal affairs marked by rivalries and jockeying among the outside powers, each working with allies within the country. In 1973 Prince Daud Khan had overthrown his cousin King Zahir Shah and converted Afghanistan into a republic. The Saur Revolution of 1978 saw the communist People's Democratic Party of Afghanistan (PDPA) stage a coup, seize power, install Nur Mohammad Taraki as president, and begin a radical program of social engineering with Soviet support. The internal opposition to the communist regime was led by religious parties and ethnic leaders and was assisted externally by Pakistan and Saudi Arabia backed by the United States. The PDPA itself was far from united and divided into Khalq and Parcham factions. In September 1979 Taraki's own foreign minister, Hafizullah Amin, had him killed. Amin reached out to the United States and Pakistan for support. Hafizullah Amin and Pakistan's Zia-ul-Haq attempted to address the hoary issues of the Durand Line and of Pashtun aspirations and unrest in both countries.

The Soviet Union had considerable stakes to protect in Afghanistan, which was the outer ring of the Soviet periphery in the Cold War, protecting the largely Muslim central Asian republics from the Cold War alliance of CENTO, from the more recent U.S.-China anti-Soviet alliance, and, in 1979, from the threat of Islamic radicalism, which seemed to have found a new home in Iran, Afghanistan's neighbor. And the Soviets also had considerable influence in

Afghanistan, not just through the PDPA. By 1978, the Soviet Union accounted for 64 percent of Afghanistan's total imports and 34 percent of its total exports. Total Soviet credits to Afghanistan had reached US$1.26 billion (compared to US$470 million from the United States).[2]

In 1979 what the Soviets saw in Afghanistan was a deteriorating situation, the growing influence of their enemies, and their friendly communist government in danger. When the Soviet Army invaded, it took Kabul, killed Amin, and installed Babrak Karmal of the Parcham faction of the PDPA in his place. The Soviet intervention put an end to Zia-ul-Haq's overtures to Amin. Zia opposed the Soviet invasion publicly and began his two-track policy of providing clandestine military assistance to Afghan insurgents while appearing to work in public through the UN for peace and a Soviet withdrawal. The Soviet invasion of Afghanistan brought Afghanistan, Pakistan, and the subcontinent to the center of the Cold War contest between the superpowers.

Afghanistan mattered deeply to India, and had always been intertwined with Indian history, as the old silk routes brought invaders like Alexander and traders and poets like Amir Khusro to the rich plains of the Punjab. And yet, independent India had been a cautious participant in Afghan affairs. During the 1950s and 1960s India had not supported Afghanistan on the Pashtunistan issue or on the revision of the Durand Line drawn up in 1893. Nehru refused to comment during the 1961 Pakistan-Afghanistan crisis. Nor was King Zahir Shah supportive of India in its wars with Pakistan in 1947–1948, 1965, or 1971. He equivocated in public on the Kashmir issue. Afghanistan's difficulties with Pakistan on the Durand Line and Pashtunistan issues, which led to its refusing to join the Baghdad Pact and to the Afghan tilt toward the Soviet Union when Pakistan became a critical element in U.S. Cold War strategy, had not necessarily translated into tighter India-Afghan relations.

When the Soviets invaded Afghanistan, the Soviet ambassador in Delhi, Yuli Vorontsov, sought a meeting with India's caretaker prime minister, Charan Singh. Charan Singh was not immediately available, so Vorontsov met with Foreign Secretary R. D. Sathe at midnight on December 29 seeking Indian support and understanding for the Soviet invasion. Sathe merely promised to convey what Vorontsov had said to the prime minister. When Vorontsov finally met Singh, the prime minister told him with a cold and stern expression that India could not endorse the intervention, and that the military invasion of a nonaligned country that was India's neighbor was unacceptable no matter the circumstances. Charan Singh also advised that Soviet troops should be withdrawn as soon as possible. In public as well, the Charan Singh government described the act as "unacceptable" and urged the withdrawal of Soviet troops. But this policy did not last more than a fortnight. Indira Gandhi was waiting in the wings to take power and formed her government in mid-January. A December 28, 1979, Ministry of External Affairs statement attempted a balancing act: "India has always opposed outside interference in internal affairs. . . . [It is our] earnest hope that no country or external power would take steps which might aggravate the situation." These mealy-mouthed sentiments satisfied no one. On December 30 the ministry spokesman said: "We are not supporting or opposing anyone. We are still assessing whether the Soviet assessment that they extended their help and assistance on the request of the duly constituted authorities in Kabul is right or wrong. . . . We have, however, taken note of the justification given by the Soviet Union." The shift away from condemning the invasion was evident.

On January 12, 1980, in the first statement approved by Mrs. Gandhi's advisers, even before her government was sworn in, India's permanent representative to the UN, Brajesh Mishra, told the UN General Assembly that India had no reason to disbelieve the Soviet commitment to withdraw troops when asked to do so by the government in Kabul; that India hoped that the Soviet Union would respect the independence of Afghanistan by not keeping its troops a day longer than necessary; and, that India was gravely concerned over the response of Pakistan, China, the United States and others in arming Afghan rebels and expanding naval activities in the Indian Ocean, all of which intensified the Cold War and posed a threat to India. The Indian speech and abstention on the resolution condemning the Soviet invasion, which was carried by 104 to 18 with 18 abstentions, caused surprise and dismay among nonaligned circles. India was isolated and this isolation was exploited by Pakistan. The average Afghan and the non-PDPA elite in Afghanistan nursed a sense of betrayal by India. From then on, the West and Islamic countries marginalized India in international processes dealing with the Afghan crisis.

Mrs. Gandhi's approach was determined not just by India's need for the Soviet Union or by the fact of U.S. support for Pakistan but also by the sense that the PDPA and the Soviets were attempting to create a modern, secular, democratic Afghanistan, rather than one based on religious identity as Pakistan and Saudi Arabia sought. Such an Afghanistan would clearly be the best possible outcome from India's point of view as it would likely fight extremism and follow a nonaligned foreign policy. That did not mean that Indira Gandhi approved of the intervention. In fact, she repeatedly made her opposition clear in private conversations with Soviet leaders such as Andrei Kosygin, where she pressed for withdrawals and timetables or a political solution.

In public, however, Mrs. Gandhi temporized right through 1980. Behind the scenes a more nuanced response was evident. Foreign Secretary Ram Sathe was sent to Islamabad in February 1980 to ascertain Pakistani thinking. He was told by the Pakistani foreign secretary, "We have different perceptions." Later that month when Gromyko was visiting Delhi, Afghanistan was barely mentioned in the joint communiqué. It was the same during a trip to Moscow in June by External Affairs Minister Narasimha Rao and when Brezhnev came to India in December. Privately, India urged the Soviets on each occasion to begin with a token withdrawal and to specify a time frame publicly for withdrawal of the bulk of troops. In retrospect, this approach led the world to believe that India supported the Soviet Union, progressively making India less of a factor in the negotiations and on the ground.

On the ground, Pakistan funded, armed, and supported the Afghan resistance to the Soviet-backed Kabul regime with help from the United States, Saudi Arabia, the United Arab Emirates, and others. The United States saw a chance to embroil the Soviets in the quagmire of a guerrilla war as payback for Vietnam. Pakistan, the reliable rear base for the resistance, insisted on channeling all U.S. assistance through its Inter-Services Intelligence (ISI) to the seven mujahideen groups based in Peshawar. Among those groups, the ISI, Pakistan's premier intelligence agency, favored Gulbuddin Hekmatyar's Hizb-e-Islami and forced other groups to work with the Hizb.[3] Led by General Akhtar Abdul Rehman Khan, Zia's director general of ISI from 1980 to 1987, the attempt pioneered several methods of clandestine warfare that are now common place.[4] Moderate Islamist leaders were sidelined and the mujahideen were made steadily more lethal. They were brutally successful in making it impossible for the Kabul regime to rule Afghanistan and extracted a toll of Soviet lives of around 15,000 dead and 35,000 injured by 1989. Estimates for Afghan civilian casualties from this phase of the Afghan wars run from 562,000 to 2 million people. Over 3.5 million refugees fled Afghanistan for Pakistan and over 1 million went to Iran.

The Soviet invasion of Afghanistan rescued U.S.-Pakistan relations. Just six months before the Soviet invasion, the U.S. embassy in Islamabad had been burned by a Pakistani mob while the police stood by and watched and president Zia-ul-Haq refused to take U.S. telephone calls. On April 6, 1979, President Jimmy Carter imposed economic sanctions on Pakistan to halt its nuclear weapon program, used U.S. influence to block World Bank loans, and pressured France and others not to sell nuclear technology to Pakistan. But when the Soviets invaded Afghanistan, U.S. National Security Adviser Zbigniew Brzezinski argued in a December 28 memo to Carter that Pakistan was the perfect conduit to increase clandestine assistance to mujahideen groups. This, he wrote, "will require a review of our policy toward Pakistan, more guarantees to it, more arms aid, and, alas, a decision that our security policy toward Pakistan cannot be dictated by our non-proliferation policy." Carter agreed, lifted sanctions on Pakistan, and added US$400 million in economic and military aid to Pakistan. The door was open for Pakistan to make its atom bomb. The U.S. sense of Pakistan's utility in the anti-Soviet war in Afghanistan was so great that the United States chose to turn a blind eye throughout the 1980s to Pakistan's determined quest for a nuclear weapon, aided as it was by the other ally in the Afghan fight, China. China supplied over US$2 billion worth of small arms and weapons to the mujahideen through Pakistan's ISI, paid for by the United States. Pakistan also passed along U.S. Sidewinder missiles and launchers—shoulder-fired anti-aircraft weapons—to the mujahideen directly. As A. Q. Khan said in a TV interview in 2009, the Afghan war against the Soviets "provided us with space to enhance our nuclear capability. Given the U.S. and European pressure on our program, it is true that had the Afghan war not taken place at that time, we would not have been able to make the bomb as early as we did."

"Proximity talks," or indirect Pakistan-Afghanistan negotiations, began under UN oversight in Geneva in June 1982. By 1988 as a result of war weariness and its internal slide toward collapse, the Soviet Union agreed to withdraw from Afghanistan. The Geneva Accords of April 14, 1988, incorporated four separate agreements: a bilateral Afghanistan-Pakistan Agreement on Principles of Mutual Relations in particular over Non-Interference and Non-Intervention; a Declaration of International Guarantees by the United States and the Soviet Union; a Bilateral Afghanistan-Pakistan Agreement on Repatriation of Refugees; and an Agreement on the Interrelationships for the Settlement of the Situation relating to Afghanistan and Pakistan witnessed by the United States and Soviet Union. A schedule for Soviet troop withdrawals was also laid down.

By February 15, 1989, Soviet troop withdrawals from Afghanistan were complete. Two years later the Soviet Union itself was history, and the central Asian republics became independent.

When the Soviets withdrew and the United States disengaged, Afghanistan was left with no legitimate state structures, no national leadership, multiple armed groups in every locality, a devastated economy, and a people dispersed throughout the region. Despite that, much to everyone's surprise, President Mohammed Najibullah Ahmedzai's PDPA government in Kabul survived the Soviet troop withdrawal and showed surprising resilience for three years. Major mujahideen offensives and attempts to take towns like Jalalabad in 1989 failed. The ISI and Saudi Arabia cajoled the Peshawar groups into a *shura*, or council of reconciliation, which chose an interim Islamic government for Afghanistan. Reportedly US$26 million was spent on this exercise and US$1 million a month thereafter to maintain the Islamic government.

India strongly supported Najibullah, his policy of national reconciliation, and his abandonment of the radical PDPA social agenda in the countryside, sending food, medicine, and other assistance. But once the Soviet Union fell and Soviet assistance and support ceased, the Najibullah government collapsed in April 1992. In the aftermath, the government's own supporters rushed to curry favor with the mujahideen. This was driven home to India when Dostum, the Uzbek warlord who controlled Kabul airport, prevented Najibullah from seeking asylum in India on April 17, 1992. His family had already been granted asylum in India and prime minister Narasimha Rao had promised Najibullah safety. The UN humanitarian chief, Sevan, was sitting in an aircraft on the Kabul airport tarmac waiting to accompany Najibullah to India. But Dostum was doing deals with the advancing mujahideen forces, splitting the PDPA between Pashtun and non-Pashtun factions. Dostum sealed Najibullah's fate and did not let him board the aircraft. Najibullah subsequently sought protection in the UN compound in Kabul.

In 1992 Kabul passed to Ahmed Shah Masood, the Tajik leader from the Panjshir. On October 26, 1992, the mujahideen factions meeting in Pakistan concluded the Peshawar Accord on a rotational arrangement and proclaimed the Islamic Republic of Afghanistan. This was recognized by several countries including India even though, as a wag put it, it may have been Islamic, but it was hardly a state and certainly did not rule Afghanistan. The mujahideen leaders had agreed to rotate the leadership, but when Burhanuddin Rabbani of the Jamaat-i-Islami took over, he decided to carry on himself, would not hand over, and ruled, shakily, from 1992 to 1996, challenged by Pakistan and his own prime minister, Gulbuddin Hekmatyar, the ISI favorite.

By this time the collapse of the Soviet Union had buttressed regional and ethnic identities in central Asian republics and Afghanistan as well. Afghan ethnic groups, such as Tajiks, Uzbeks, and Turkmen, now had their own supporters abroad and countries to look to for funding, bases, and help.

Major General Naseerullah Babar, Benazir Bhutto's interior minister, was exploring an overland route to Central Asia from Quetta to Turkmenistan through Kandahar and Herat in autumn 1994. His interests coincided with those of U.S. firms like the Union Oil Company of California, or Unocal, to access the oil, gas, and natural resources of Tajikistan and other new states, and with a broader Western desire to weaken Central Asia's links with Russia. Unocal wanted to build a Trans-Afghan Pipeline to run from the Caspian Sea through Afghanistan and Pakistan to the Indian Ocean. When Babar took six Western ambassadors, including the U.S. ambassador, to see the route and demonstrate its viability while seeking funding for the project, security was provided by a small band of madrassa students, the Taliban. This was the seed from which Babar and the ISI built up a fighting organization. The Pakistan Army provided them with unified command and control, firepower, training, mobility, and communications. Building on Pashtun resentment of non-Pashtun control of Kabul, the Taliban, stiffened by Pakistan Army regulars, overcame local warlords and captured Spin Boldak, Kandahar, and Herat in 1995 and Kabul in September 1996. One of their first acts in Kabul was to drag Najibullah out of the UN compound where he had holed up since 1992 and to execute him brutally. Eleven years later, in 2007, you could still see the lamppost on which his tortured and abused corpse was strung up.

The creation and use of the Taliban by Pakistan was supported by Saudi Arabia and the United Arab Emirates, and by the United States on the pretext of isolating Iran and stopping the flow of drugs out of Afghanistan. The Taliban never fought the Soviet Union and were only created in the mid-1990s. Pakistan's goal was Pashtun predominance in Afghanistan—or at least to prevent the emergence of a transnational Pashtun movement that would threaten Pakistan's hold west of the Indus. The Taliban's ferocity, extremism, and intolerance, however, dismayed many nations. Only three countries formally extended diplomatic recognition to the Taliban's Islamic Emirate of Afghanistan—Pakistan, Saudi Arabia, and the UAE—all of whom had midwifed the outfit. India, Iran, Russia, and all the central Asian republics except Turkmenistan were alarmed enough by the Taliban into working together in support of Ahmed Shah Masood and his Northern Alliance, a grouping of anti-Taliban forces.

India had very limited relations with the Rabbani government from 1992 to

1996. Elements in the Taliban initially reached out to India but their brutality against Afghan Hindus and Sikhs soon ended that. Their training of Kashmiri, Pakistani, and foreign militants in Afghanistan in preparation for a jihad in Jammu and Kashmir was soon apparent. In 1992–1993, under Indian pressure, the United States came close to declaring Pakistan a state sponsor of terror. Pakistan consequently moved many Kashmiri terrorist group bases to eastern Afghanistan.[5] Pakistan was paying the Jalalabad *shura* and later the Taliban to take Kashmiri militants under their protection. Bin Laden was encouraged to join the Taliban in 1996 by Pakistan as he too was sponsoring bases for Kashmiri terrorists in Khost. In 1998 Mullah Omar, the one-eyed leader of the Taliban, spoke publicly, "We support the jihad in Kashmir." This was when the insurgency in J&K was still strong. The effects of the deteriorating situation in Afghanistan were brought vividly home to all of India by the hijacking of Indian Airlines flight IC-814 to Kandahar on December 24, 1999, which only ended with the release of three Pakistani terrorists from Indian jails. The Taliban exploited the Kashmir jihad knowing that Pakistan could refuse them nothing so long as they provided bases for Pakistani and Kashmiri militants. The Afghan Taliban, however, were resistant to some Pakistani interests and never recognized the Durand Line, something no Afghan government has found possible.

Events in Afghanistan in the 1980s and 1990s still reverberate today. The tools of Islamic extremism and terrorism were forged, found bases, and gained strength there, as did various counterinsurgency and counterterrorism strategies. The 9/11 attacks in the United States and the continuing U.S. war in Afghanistan since 2001, the longest military engagement in American history, are direct legacies of the Afghan war of the 1980s. Each of the states that sponsored the Taliban—Pakistan, the United States, Saudi Arabia, and United Arab Emirates—has suffered direct harm from the forces unleashed.

The Talibanization of Pakistani politics is a long-term phenomenon that seems unlikely to be reversed in the foreseeable future. The effect on states in the region, particularly Pakistan and Afghanistan, weakening already fragile state structures, has been baleful and long lasting. If Soviet decline was a fact even before the war in Afghanistan, the defeat in Afghanistan certainly hastened its collapse. The greatest victim of the terrorism spawned by the Afghan war was, of course, west Asia where radical ideologies and terrorist groups have spread.

Afghanistan poisoned U.S.-Iran relations. The U.S. reliance on Saudi Arabia and hardline Sunni elements, whom President Reagan welcomed to the White House as "freedom fighters," gave Iran another reason to oppose the United States. Despite brief periods of cooperation in Afghanistan after 9/11 to topple the Taliban's Islamic emirate, the United States and Iran are still unable to overcome their deep-rooted hostility playing itself out on Iran's periphery in Afghanistan, Iraq, the Persian Gulf, and the Levant.

The war showed once again why India cannot be and is not politically neutral to what happens in Afghanistan. Among the drivers of India's Afghan policy are the balance between Afghanistan and Pakistan, its effect on the evolving international political environment, and the evolution of Afghan politics.[6] In the immediate aftermath of the Soviet invasion, India's relations with Pakistan took a turn for the worse as Pakistan continued to pursue a nuclear weapons program and to apply the same covert warfare methods in Punjab and Jammu and Kashmir in India. In addition, the Karakoram Highway between Pakistan and China through Khunjerab Pass was inaugurated in 1979. Indira Gandhi returned to power within fifteen days of Zia-ul-Haq's restoring strategic equations with the United States. India's reticence in criticizing the Soviet invasion and support for Babrak Karmal's government in Afghanistan naturally created strains between India and Pakistan and increased the distance between them.

The war against the Soviets in Afghanistan further solidified the alliance between the United States, Pakistan, China, and some Islamic countries. And that emboldened Pakistan vis-à-vis India. In 1984 Zia-ul-Haq approved a move by the Pakistan Army into the Siachen glacier area, attempting to capture salients toward the Karakoram pass, to link up with the Chinese People's Liberation Army (PLA), in an attempt to revive the Kashmir issue. He chose his moment with care, just after India had to send troops into the holiest Sikh shrine to clear the Golden Temple in Amritsar of terrorists in Operation Blue Star in June 1984. Mrs. Gandhi and Defense Minister R. Venkataraman neutralized the Pakistani effort in northern Jammu and Kashmir. Acting swiftly and decisively, they sent Indian troops to the Siachen glacier first, which India has held ever since—the highest battlefield in the world, more than 18,000 feet above mean sea level.

An Afghanistan under the Taliban was first a refuge, then a base, and finally a launch pad for Islamist extremists and terrorists from around the world, including Al Qaeda and Osama bin Laden, who planned and launched the September 11, 2001, attack from his base there. In many ways Afghanistan was the model or archetype for what we see of Islamic terrorism in Central Africa, west Asia, possibly central Asia, and on a smaller scale in southern Thailand and the

Philippines. It was terrorists funded, armed, and trained by Pakistan and aided by the United States, who ultimately nurtured and gave sanctuary to those who bit the hands that fed them and have made Pakistan what it is today, a dysfunctional society with an outsize army, a feeble state backing terrorist armies and organizations as part of daily life.

Pakistanis in authority like to portray themselves as victims of terrorism. There is no denying the price in lives, in the corrosion of society, and in state fragility that Pakistan's use of terrorism as an instrument of state policy has exacted. Even so, Pakistan is more fundamentally a victim of its own flawed strategic vision and the actions of its own intelligence agencies than of the terrorists who were their chosen instruments. Pakistan's consistent twin motives in its Afghan policy have been to develop "strategic depth" against India and to prevent the emergence of a strong movement for a unified Pashtunistan. A strong Pashtun movement in either Pakistan or in Afghanistan would threaten its hold on the North-West Frontier Province (now called Khyber-Pakhtunkhwa) and the tribal areas east of the Durand Line and west of the Indus river, whose population has more in common with fellow Pashtuns across the Durand Line than with the rest of Pakistan. Neither of these Pakistani goals was achieved or now seems attainable. Instead, an unstable area is overshadowed by a multipronged power sharing among tribes, extremist and terrorist groups, and the Pakistan Army. If anything, the situation is worse than the ambiguous but relatively stable frontier constructed by the Raj, where Indian law extended up to the Indus, Indian power extended to the Durand Line, and Indian influence enjoyed periods of strength in Afghanistan. The scholar and writer Ahmed Rashid says that Zia had dreamed like a Mogul emperor of recreating a Sunni Muslim space between infidel "Hindustan," heretic (because it is Shia) Iran, and "Christian" Russia. Zia believed the message of the Afghan mujahideen would spread to central Asia, revive Islam, and create a new Pakistan-led Islamic bloc of nations. What Zia never considered was what his legacy would do to Pakistan."[7]

Taking the longer view, in history Afghanistan developed as a buffer state between competing empires—the Russian and British and, briefly, the Chinese—and then, during the Cold War between competing alliance systems, the Soviet and the American. Regional instability and escalating Cold War tensions tore the state apart from the 1970s onward, when it moved from being a buffer state to a battleground, the arena of superpower contention. The Soviet invasion and the fragmentation of society when communists attempted massive social change in Afghanistan broke state structures and tribal loyalties. Soviet counterinsurgency strategy, the way Pakistan channeled U.S. and Saudi aid to its favorites in the seven religious resistance bands, weakening and undermining secular and nationalist Afghan leaders, and Iran's policy of arming Shia groups intensified divisions and contributed to the fragmentation of Afghanistan's society, polity, and sovereignty.[8]

Today, the question is how a fragmented and divided Afghanistan will fit into the larger consolidation of the Eurasian landmass that China is attempting through projects like the Belt and Road Initiative. Russia and China are today working together with Pakistan in Afghanistan and are persuading the Americans that the Taliban should be brought in from the cold into government. A tired America wants a face-saving way out of its very long Afghan commitment. Whether the Taliban are ready to be domesticated or to be junior partners in an Afghan government is another matter, and one does not know what price they are willing to pay to see the United States depart. U.S. patience will probably run out before the Taliban's. Clearly, peace in Afghanistan requires including in the government the widest and most representative coalition possible, including the Taliban. But the terms on which this might be done remain unclear. While Pakistan's goals in Afghanistan remain the same, the endless dance of the neighbors and great powers, using local partners and proxies, continues. And Afghanistan and its people continue to pay the price.

∼

If the Afghan war limited India's space for maneuver to the west, developments in Indochina constrained and closed India's options to the east. Cambodia and Indochina were where the U.S.-China-Japan-ASEAN alignment was most visible and operationalized.

When North Vietnamese troops took the presidential palace in Saigon in April 1975, Vietnam was reunified. Two days later on April 17, 1975, Phnom Penh fell to the Khmer Rouge and for the first time all of Indochina was communist. There were now eight independent states in southeast Asia, and this sharpened the Association of Southeast Asian Nation's (ASEAN) awareness of their shared interests and of their differences with the three communist states in Indochina—Vietnam, Cambodia, and Laos. ASEAN, which had been united by the common fight against communist insurgencies in each country, reacted to the communist victories in Indochina by convening the first ASEAN leaders summit in 1976. What no one foresaw in those heady days was how the Sino-Soviet split would interact with the Vietnamese-Cambodian alliance, historical animosities, and ethnic tensions in Indochina to change the course of the Cold War in southeast Asia and China's trajectory.

Vietnam's unification was the culmination of a long history of fierce struggle, effective organization, and military success reflecting political cohesion in the north. In Cambodia, however, war's end saw the murderous Khmer Rouge in power, under whose rule over 2 million Cambodians were killed, about one-third of the total population, with between half to 1 million of them likely executed.[9]

China-Vietnam relations had been complex even before the Sino-U.S. rapprochement of 1971. After the U.S. opening, China stayed neutral, leveraging Vietnam's resistance on the ground, and, in the U.S.-North Vietnam talks in Paris, to obtain bilateral advantage from the Americans for itself. From the Vietnamese point of view, the February 1972 Nixon visit to China was a disaster that could not have come at a worse time, and Nixon was able to obtain the 1973 ceasefire agreement from the isolated North Vietnamese, allowing him to withdraw U.S. ground troops from Vietnam with a modicum of honor. On the other hand, to prevent Hanoi from leaning toward China, Moscow gave North Vietnam what General Vo Nguyen Giap needed to launch his offensives. Competition among the Soviets, Americans, and Chinese squeezed Vietnam's options. The Chinese were the hardest to please because of fear of encirclement by the Soviets; they saw a Vietnamese tilt toward the Soviet Union in most actions. The Soviets pushed back against the Sino-U.S. alliance by intensifying their relationship with Vietnam and consolidating relations in the region. This polarization between ASEAN and Vietnam and between the Soviet Union and China presented India with difficult choices.

In order to obtain an early ceasefire agreement with North Vietnam in 1973, Kissinger and Nixon had widened the war to the rest of Indochina, bombing Cambodia and thus buying a couple of years for South Vietnam and permitting a "decent interval" between U.S. disengagement and the final North Vietnamese victory over South Vietnam in April 1975. That bombing and support for the Lon Nol regime also energized the malign Khmer Rouge under Pol Pot, who came to power in the chaos generated by the United States in Cambodia.

The Khmer Rouge ignited the kindling in Indochina in September 1977 by attacking and attempting to control areas in southern Vietnam. Caught off guard, Vietnam asked China to rein in Pol Pot. But China, fearing that Vietnam was taking over all of Indochina and handing it over to the Soviets, continued to support the Khmer Rouge. Hanoi was convinced that China was using the Khmer Rouge to encircle her, a fear heightened by the security treaty that China signed with Laos at the same time. Vietnam expelled Chinese living in Vietnam, creating the "boat people." The Khmer Rouge massacred Vietnamese living in Cambodia. Later in 1977 Vietnam sent the People's Army of Vietnam deep into Cambodia in a clear warning to the Khmer Rouge to stop attacks and as a signal to the new leadership under Deng in China. In response, China stopped economic and military cooperation with Vietnam. And the United States played the China card, announcing the normalization of relations with China on December 15, 1978. Isolated, Hanoi signed a Treaty of Peace, Friendship, and Cooperation with the Soviet Union in November 1978 providing for mutual defense before moving against the Khmer Rouge. This only confirmed Beijing's worst fears and dragged Indochina further into the Sino-Soviet dispute and U.S.-Soviet rivalry. Deng visited the United States in January 1979 and appears to have obtained President Jimmy Carter's tacit blessing for his promise to "teach Vietnam a lesson," the same justification that China had used to attack India in 1962. As a historian put it, "All the actors were now on the way to transforming their worst fears—many of them pure fantasies at the start—into deadly and destabilising realities."[10]

On December 25, 1978, the Vietnamese Army entered Cambodia, easily overthrew the Khmer Rouge, installed Heng Samrin's regime, and ended the genocide. Over 200,000 refugees and the Khmer Rouge leadership fled to the Thai-Cambodian border. The Soviet Union supported Vietnam. Against them were lined up China, the United States, and ASEAN, supporting Pol Pot's Khmer Rouge as the legitimate government of Cambodia. Bases were established on the Thai-Cambodian border to prosecute a war against the Heng Samrin regime.

Indira Gandhi's government recognized the Heng Samrin regime on July 7, 1980—one of the promises in her election manifesto. This put India at odds with China, the United States, and ASEAN, which wanted to isolate and condemn Hanoi and the Heng Samrin regime in Phnom Penh. While ASEAN saw a link between the Soviet invasion of Afghanistan and the Vietnamese invasion of Cambodia, India did not, following a traditional policy course. India had not been ready to join regional defense agreements in southeast Asia against China in the 1960s. It had enough problems of its own and its forces were fully stretched.[11] Now that China and ASEAN were together with the United States, India again found itself on the other side. India was on her own, and this was starkly evident on February 17, 1979, when China attacked Vietnam while Foreign Minister A. B. Vajpayee was in China on the first-ever visit by an Indian foreign minister to China, restoring ministerial visits after a gap of over seventeen years. An embarrassed Vajpayee cut short his visit and returned home to considerable criticism.

The Chinese had attacked Vietnam with five PLA divisions, using satellite imagery provided by the Americans, and this also reassured them that the Soviets would not attack from the north, involving them in a two-front war. But the PLA suffered heavy losses and were militarily defeated by second rank People's Army of Vietnam units and militia. The PLA were up against one of the best trained, equipped, experienced, and motivated armies in the world. General Vo Nguyen Giap had defeated in succession the French, the Americans, and now the Chinese. For the Chinese leadership this was a wake-up call that set in motion the comprehensive modernization of the Chinese military, the results of which we see and feel today.

But China salvaged a diplomatic and economic victory from the ashes of military defeat against Vietnam. It managed to isolate Vietnam politically and internationally with U.S. and ASEAN support, kept the murderous Khmer Rouge alive in camps on the Thai-Cambodian border, and prevented the Heng Samrin regime from occupying Cambodia's seat at the UN. China owed the satisfactory political outcome in Indochina to its alliance with the United States and to ASEAN's steady backing. In return, China dialed back its advocacy of the rights of the prosperous overseas Chinese diaspora in southeast Asia and reduced, but did not yet fully stop, its support to communist insurgencies in that part of Asia. China had been a long-term supporter of the Burmese Communist Party in its war against the Burmese Army, which ended in 1989. The Malayan Communist Party in the jungles of southern Thailand surrendered the same year. Thailand was told that China would withdraw support from the Communist Party of Thailand if Thailand turned a blind eye to China's arming the Khmer Rouge. They did so.

Prime Minister Rajiv Gandhi tried to mediate on the Cambodia issue in 1987–1988, sending Minister of State for External Affairs Natwar Singh to Vietnam and the ASEAN countries as special envoy. Vietnam had informed Natwar Singh in January 1987 that it was ready to withdraw from Cambodia in 1989 and was willing to accept any government in Cambodia so long as Pol Pot was not part of it. When Natwar Singh attempted the equivalent of shuttle diplomacy, he met with a cold shoulder from ASEAN, which refused to believe the Vietnamese offer was genuine. While the results of Indian diplomacy fed into the August 1989 Paris Conference on Cambodia, the context was shifting every day with Sino-Soviet normalization, Rajiv Gandhi's visit to China, and other developments. India may have attempted to engage but was hardly decisive or even significant, and frankly, was a marginal player. In September 1989 Vietnam withdrew its troops from Cambodia, and the 1991 Paris Conference saw the signing of the Paris Peace Accord, which gave the UN a role in conducting elections and installing a Kampuchean government.

It was great power politics that determined Indochina's fate. With the Cold War over in both Asia and Europe, all the major players in the war supported the UN-backed peace conference in Paris in October 1991 that ended almost fifty years of war in Indochina. A UN peacekeeping mission brokered and enforced a ceasefire in Cambodia and a Vietnamese withdrawal. UN-supervised elections followed in 1993 to create a coalition Royal Cambodian Government. In 1995 Vietnam became a full member of ASEAN. Myanmar (Burma) joined in 1997. In 1998 Pol Pot died and the Khmer Rouge was disbanded. Unlike the arrangements for peace and international supervision in Indochina in the 1950s, India played no role.

The end of the Indochina wars and the repair of Sino-Soviet relations were primarily the work of Mikhail Gorbachev. Seeking peace for Russia's reform and economic development he remade Russian foreign policy and negotiated an end to the Cold War with Reagan. He also accepted Deng's three conditions for normalizing Sino-Russian relations: reduction of Soviet troops on the border with China; Soviet troop withdrawal from Afghanistan; and a Vietnamese pullout from Cambodia. Soviet aid to Vietnam fell 63 percent in 1990. From 1989 on communist regimes in east Europe imploded one after the other, and China entered its own crisis leading to the Tiananmen Square massacre. The Socialist Republic of Vietnam, isolated diplomatically, negotiated a political settlement to end the war in Cambodia, and swallowed its pride and improved relations with China, following the Soviet lead.

The Soviet collapse and U.S. preoccupations at home and in the Middle East left the field open for the steady growth of Chinese influence in Indochina and southeast Asia in the 1990s. The spectacular economic results from Deng Xiaoping's reforms and the accretion of hard power, China's more moderate policy toward overseas Chinese communities, and China's common cause with ASEAN against the Vietnamese occupation of Cambodia, had presaged growing southeast Asian political closeness and economic integration with China.

India had much a harder row to hoe. The third Indochina war had left India with few openings to the east.

~

And in her second term, 1980 to 1984, Indira Gandhi found her foreign policy overshadowed by the aftermath of the Soviet war in Afghanistan and Pakistan's destabilization efforts in the Punjab and Jammu and Kashmir.

India supported Vietnam in the Cambodian conflict right through the Vietnamese occupation of Cambodia from 1979 to 1989. This caused misgivings and even animosity among other east and southeast Asian neighbors. The rapidly growing Asian tigers' export driven growth, while the Indian economy remained relatively slow and closed, added to the estrangement and sense of drift. India remained outside east Asian production networks that benefited from massive flows of Japanese investment in the 1980s and 1990s. India was also excluded from Asia-Pacific regional organizations emerging at this time. The Asia-Pacific Economic Cooperation (APEC) was formed in 1989 and the ASEAN Regional Forum (ARF) in 1994. India joined the latter after two years and is still not a member of the former. India's political and economic trajectories began to converge with ASEAN's only after Prime Minister Narasimha Rao's "Look East" policy in 1992 recognized the new realities and sought to use them for India's development.

It can be argued that in southeast Asia the Cold War ended in 1979, a full decade before the fall of the Berlin wall in Europe. The Cold War dynamic shifted in the 1980s after the U.S. withdrawal from Vietnam. The main Asian fault line was now Sino-Soviet, not U.S.-Soviet as in the Cold War; ideology, a basic feature of the Cold War, was irrelevant in Asia now. The United States let SEATO die a quiet death in 1977. If Sino-Soviet contention, with the United States on China's side, was now the primary contradiction in Asia, it was fought out in Afghanistan (through Pakistan) and Indochina (through the Khmer Rouge). This limited India's options. India was progressively excluded by the China-U.S. alliance from both international negotiations and actual affairs on the ground in Afghanistan and Indochina. At the same time, Indian discontent with Soviet policies in Afghanistan and their deleterious consequences for India were tangible and strong.

Faced with a China-Pakistan-U.S. alliance, a moribund Soviet Union, and a deteriorating neighborhood, India sought to break out of encirclement with direct approaches to Pakistan, the United States, and China. The approach to Pakistan only lasted months. The seeds for a future transformation of relations with the United States were planted, but many ups and downs were yet to come. Of the three, it was the opening toward China that was sustained through the

1980s and into the next century. Both China and India saw the benefits of a stable relationship. By the early 1990s, when the U.S.-Soviet Cold War ended in Europe and the Soviet Union collapsed, the slow but steady normalization of India-China relations began to bear real fruit in the Border Peace and Tranquility Agreement of 1993.

Mrs. Gandhi's initial response to the closing strategic space and limiting of India's options as she began her second term in 1980 was to attack what she saw as the root of the problem by improving relations with the United States. The U.S. decision to supply US$2.5 billion dollars' worth of arms to Pakistan in June 1981, including F-16 fighters that were of no use in Afghanistan, stymied her initial attempts through special envoys to Washington. It was not until she met President Ronald Reagan at Cancun in October 1981 at a conference to consider global economic issues that India-U.S. relations began to improve. The United States agreed to France supplying enriched uranium for Tarapur, the first nuclear power station in India. Mrs. Gandhi visited Washington in July 1982, before she went to Moscow, a measure of her dissatisfaction with the USSR and her domestic turn to the right on the economy. The visit also saw the first discussion in years on U.S. defense supplies to India. But a scrum of difficult issues remained between the two countries that required more drastic actions by the two governments before relations could improve significantly. An accumulation of Indian positions adverse to the United States, particularly at the UN, many of them involving no direct Indian interest, had poisoned the well. The true transformation of India-U.S. relations had to await the opening up of the Indian economy and the post–Cold War world in the 1990s.

Mrs. Gandhi's other response was to send her adviser G. Parthasarathi to China to explore improving relations and a boundary settlement. Parthasarathi's conversations with Deng Xiaoping, when Deng reiterated Zhou Enlai's 1960 "package deal" on the boundary, was the public tip of the iceberg. She also authorized Foreign Secretary Ram Sathe to begin an exercise in MEA in 1981–1982 to look at options for a boundary settlement. Ambassador Venkateswaran in Beijing was authorized to explore issues with the International Liaison Department of the Chinese Communist Party. The ministry's work advanced to the level of establishing the legality of a boundary settlement with China in light of previous Supreme Court judgments and the 1962 Parliament Resolution pledging to recover every inch of Indian territory from China. Options for a boundary settlement were presented to Indira Gandhi and even approved by her. It is not clear from the official record why this attempt petered out.

With Russia relations stagnated or even regressed during Mrs. Gandhi's second term, Foreign Secretary J. N. Dixit mentions a controversial and still-born Soviet suggestion in the second half of 1982 that India take advantage of the Soviet presence in Afghanistan and assume control of the whole state of Jammu and Kashmir across the Line of Control, which was still under Pakistani occupation.[12] In the absence of any Soviet troop presence in the Wakhan corridor where Kashmir borders on Afghanistan, but with Chinese troops in western Tibet who could interdict Soviet pressure on Pakistan, Delhi apparently decided that this was a Soviet attempt to get India embroiled in their Afghan adventure.

By the time she was assassinated on October 31, 1984, Mrs. Gandhi's entire attention was focused on India's immediate periphery in Sri Lanka, Pakistan, and Bangladesh, and at home on the secessionist movement fanned by Pakistan in the Punjab, which ultimately led to her death and to her son, Rajiv Gandhi, being propelled into the prime ministry. In her sixteen years as prime minister, Indira Gandhi had tried to increase India's options and to be more than a tactical politician. She was prescient in 1972 at the Stockholm environment conference, for instance, to declare that the greatest polluter is poverty and that there is no first world or second world or third world. We are all part of one world. But this was getting harder and harder to believe.

~

While India's domestic and south Asian preoccupations grew, Asia to the east was rapidly changing.

For southeast Asia as a whole, the 1980s were a decade of economic growth and increasing prosperity. While average life expectancy in the region in 1950–1955 was forty-one years, by 2016 Cambodia's was seventy-two years, Laos's sixty-eight years, and Thailand's seventy-five years. The 1980s were the start of the steady urbanization of the region, which has led to 74 percent of the population in Malaysia and 66 percent in the Philippines living in cities.

For Japan the 1980s were golden years. The economy was booming, and Japan was on the crest of an industrial wave that threatened to upend the postwar global economic order. In steel, automobiles, and electronics Japan was the world leader. Japan's success had different effects on its most important relationships and on Asia as a whole. For Deng's China, Japan was a model to be emulated, making it worthwhile for China to put aside its traditional disputes and complex history with this troublesome neighbor. For the United States, Japan's rise aroused economic fears just when the opening to China lessened Japan's strategic significance. This was also the decade when Japan led Asia into building global manufacturing and value-added chains and integrated manufacturing across borders, kickstarting globalization in Asia.

As a result of the economic boom of the 1970s, by December 1981 Japan had significant market share in the United States in a wide variety of products.[13] On the other hand, no U.S. product except aircraft, which Japan did not manufacture, had more than a 10 percent share of the Japanese market. U.S.-Japan trade disputes from the early 1980s were also a result of Japan's growing dominance of semiconductors, which worried American national security professionals who, since the Korean War, had traditionally overruled trade and economic negotiators on Japan. By the 1980s, the United States was ideologically committed to the skewed formula of an undiluted mix of markets and democracy. This conveniently ignored crucial ingredients in the U.S. model— publicly funded research labs and military spending. Japan's bureaucratically guided capitalism had led to its outperforming the United States in heavy industry (steel), and in low-wage industry (textiles) and, by Reagan's presidency in 1981, in high-end consumer markets (cars and electronics) and advanced technology (semiconductors and machine tools). The Reagan administration forced "voluntary" export restrictions on Japan, the unintended consequence of which was to convert Japan from an exporter of low-value small cars to an exporter of high-value luxury cars.

For more than two decades beginning in the late 1970s, the United States waged an economic battle against Japan that almost undid pax-Americana in Asia, and that opened economic and political doors for China. That scenario could be seen as a dress rehearsal for U.S.-China economic tensions today.[14] The problem was that, like China today, the real Japanese import barriers were structural, and the United States could not point to formal import tariffs or quotas. Instead it had to target the entire political and economic system of Japan. As with China, the United States accused Japan of a managed economy, manipulated currency, mercantilist trade policies, stealing technology, and bemoaned the weakness of civil society. The United States also identified "devils" who were responsible in Japan and China, namely, Japan's Ministry of International Trade and Industry and the Chinese Communist Party.

The United States presumed that Japan's exchange rate was manipulated to promote Japanese exports and discourage imports. In September 1985 the Plaza Accord was signed by the United States, Japan, Germany, the United Kingdom, and France to empower central banks to effect a huge orderly devaluation of the dollar aimed at stimulating U.S. exports to Japan and Germany. This had only limited and gradual impact. One consequence of the Plaza

Accord is today's stagflation in Japan. In an attempt to offset the impact of a rising currency on exports in the mid-1980s, Japan's central bank flooded the economy with cheap money, which rapidly built up the price of shares and land, an asset bubble that peaked in 1989 and has taken decades to deflate peacefully. When the United States pressed China on its overvalued renminbi from 2006 onward, the Chinese made it clear that they saw the Plaza Accord as something that the Americans had forced on Japan to stymie the threat from Asia to U.S. global dominance and that China would therefore refuse any such arrangement.

By the 1980s, President Ronald Reagan also wanted Japan to increase its military spending as part of his full court press on the Soviet Union. In late 1981 Japanese Prime Minister Suzuki promised Reagan that Japan would take responsibility for the defense of its sea-lanes up to 1,000 nautical miles from the shores of its main islands. In 1982 Prime Minister Nakasone added promises to defend U.S. ships in Japanese territorial waters and to export high technology for defense to the United States.

Meanwhile, Deng's China respected and imitated Japan's economic model in a way that the West was slow to do. Kong Fanjing, an economist in the State Planning Commission, wrote with admiration that Japan "had made foreign policy subordinate to domestic policy and domestic policy subordinate to economics." In October 1978 Deng became the first Chinese leader to visit Japan after more than 2,000 years of contact. During the visit he exchanged instruments of ratification for the Sino-Japanese Peace and Friendship Treaty. Japan had the capital, technology, and management skills to develop China and had shown that it could remain Asian while westernizing and modernizing. A high point of Japan-China economic cooperation followed Deng's visit, and Japan undertook the first wave of infrastructure building in China in the early 1980s. This was also when China, Japan, and the United States were in strategic alignment to counter the Soviet Union. In order to pursue his goals, Deng was prepared to say in public that issues such as the disputed Senkaku/Diaoyutai islands should be left to future generations to solve. He hoped to suppress the demand for Japanese reparations for the war. In 1982 China and Japan, under Nakasone, began exchanging intelligence on Soviet missile deployments in Asia. This was when the United States was opening listening posts in Xinjiang against the Soviets, and the Americans and Chinese were united in Afghanistan. The high point of U.S.-China-Japan intelligence cooperation against the Soviet Union was 1982–1989. The three were aligning on security while splitting apart on trade.

The Chinese approach was, however, not uniformly popular within the

Chinese leadership. Among the charges against Chinese Communist Party General Secretary Hu Yaobang, when he fell from power in December 1986, was that he was too soft on Japan and the Tibetans. When Nakasone visited the Yasukuni shrine with most of his cabinet on August 15, 1985, anti-Japanese riots broke out in China. It was only when Nakasone announced that he would not go there again that demonstrations abated and things returned to normal. This remarkable and abject backing down by Japan may have "taught the dog to piss on the rug," in U.S. diplomat and Secretary of State Lawrence Eagleburger's vivid phrasing, and set a pattern for Chinese responses to perceived slights by Japan in the future. The history wars, and the evolution of Japan with a new generation who were unwilling to apologize for the sins of their forefathers, added to tensions in the twenty-first century as China rose to be a real competitor to Japan and the United States, overtaking Japan as the world's second largest economy.

The other area of disagreement within the Chinese leadership was on Tibet policy. In the immediate wake of reform and the shift to economic priorities in 1978, Deng and the leadership reached out to the Dalai Lama through his brother, Gyalo Thondup, indicating that they were ready to discuss all issues with the Dalai Lama, other than Tibetan independence. Fact-finding delegations were sent from India to Tibet and China by the Dalai Lama in the early 1980s. On March 13, 1981, the Dalai Lama wrote to Deng Xiaoping about negotiating to "solve the problem in accordance with existing realities in a reasonable way," given the "sad conditions" that the delegations found in Tibet.

In July 1981 General Secretary Hu Yaobang announced China's Five-Point Policy toward the Dalai Lama, asking him and his followers to return, promising the same status and living conditions as before 1959, and suggesting he live outside Tibet in China but visit Tibet from time to time. Negotiations between the Dalai Lama's representatives and the Chinese Communist Party United Front Department dragged on through the early 1980s. The Chinese sought to convert this into a negotiation on his return and status and reiterated at each stage that "the most important thing is that the Dalai Lama stop his activities aimed at splitting China." For the Tibetans the negotiations were about their freedom and autonomy and better conditions in Tibet. Popular resentment in Tibet against the Han presence was high and erupted in riots in Lhasa and other Tibetan towns in autumn 1987. With Hu Yaobang no longer in power, and internal tensions in China itself, the Chinese line toward the Tibetans hardened.

The Dalai Lama attempted in his Five Point Plan of 1987 and his Strasbourg

Proposals of 1988 to offer a Middle Path short of independence as a framework for the negotiations, but China was tightening control on the ground in Tibet and hardening its position at the negotiating table. By 1989 China was describing the Dalai Lama as a "wolf in monk's clothing." A beleaguered Chinese leadership saw the Nobel Peace Prize awarded to the Dalai Lama in December 1989 after the Tiananmen killings in June that year as another Western attempt to split China.

Controversy within the Chinese leadership on Tibet policy and on relations with Japan was part of a more fundamental division about the way forward for China, the extent to which it should imitate the market economies of the west and Japan, and whether it was necessary to simultaneously introduce a degree of openness to avoid the mistakes and disasters of Mao's later years. While CCP General Secretary Hu Yaobang agreed with Deng on opening the economy and on the validity of foreign market models, the two disagreed on the degree of openness, on relaxing control by the CCP, and on introducing some inner-party democracy. Where Deng believed in tight ideological and political control, Hu was ready to experiment, as in his approach to Tibet. In December 1986 Hu was replaced as general secretary by Zhao Ziyang after large-scale student demonstrations in major Chinese cities that Deng blamed on Hu.

Under Zhao, economic reform proceeded apace but with unforeseen consequences. Price reform in 1987–1988 led to 27 percent inflation in 1988, and the stresses of change, of "shattering the iron rice bowl," soon divided the Chinese Communist Party itself. When Hu Yaobang died on April 15, 1989, unmourned by the party establishment, university students chose to demonstrate in Beijing in his memory demanding more freedom and democracy. The students protesting soon gained strength and widespread support from other sections of society, including workers, journalists, artists, civil servants, and party members, and occupied Tiananmen Square in the heart of the capital, Beijing. The government and the CCP appeared paralyzed and unresponsive due to differences between the leaders on how to handle the protests and the issues raised by the students. When Gorbachev visited Beijing in May, Deng and the Chinese leadership had to face the embarrassment of not controlling even the square outside the meeting halls in the heart of their capital and smuggled Gorbachev into the meetings through a back door. By the end of May Deng and the old guard had had enough and sent in the PLA to clear the square and regain control of Beijing by force. The result was the June 3–4, 1989, killings in Tiananmen and elsewhere.

The crackdown and purge that followed extended from CCP General

Secretary Zhao, who lost his posts, to the schools and factories that the agitators had come from. For the next two years the fate of economic reform in China hung in the balance. It was only after Deng made a tour through the southern provinces in 1992, strongly supporting the validity of market-oriented reforms in Shenzhen and other places, that reform began again. But the overall impact on Deng and Communist Party thinking of the Tiananmen incident remained. Tiananmen had occurred as communist regimes were cracking in Europe, when the strains of combining perestroika and glasnost in the Soviet Union were becoming apparent, and as the Berlin Wall fell. For Deng it was clear that the United States had prevailed in the Cold War over the Soviet Union, and that China, as the last great communist country standing, might well be the next U.S. target for regime change. He had the causes of Soviet collapse studied by several separate groups and hierarchies, amalgamated their findings, and, learning from them, set in place a series of systemic measures to prevent China from going the same way. Perestroika was out for China, and a foreign policy of staying close to the United States, while building China's strength, was a significant part of Deng's answer.

On June 9, 1989, Deng blamed the "turmoil" on failures of "ideological and political education." This was the start of a tightening of internal ideological and security controls in China that has now climaxed under Xi Jinping. In essence, Deng sought political centralization with economic decentralization. Deng's measures included succession planning and term limits at the top of the Communist Party, patriotic education of youth and party members, a much tighter internal security regime, and a renewed stress on military modernization. The PLA had proved to be the regime and Deng's ultimate strength and savior, enabling the crackdown and the resumption of reform without political liberalization, when the internal security organs had failed. It was clear that the Chinese regime would do all it could to belie Western hopes that China turn into a liberal democracy.

The international reaction to the Tiananmen killings, while full of condemnatory statements, did not really extend to much more than the formalization of steps previously taken by the West in its self-interest, which were now presented as sanctions. For instance, some pending arms sales ceased and limits formally placed on arms sales to China by the West. But Western businesses were untouched, trade and investment were barely affected, and president George H. W. Bush and his national security adviser, Brent Scowcroft, chose to downplay and limit the effect, reaching out privately to Deng by the end of June to minimize the effect of the Tiananmen killings on China-U.S. relations.

They did so both as a result of their personal inclination and for larger reasons of state. They worked to prevent a free-fall in relations with China and prevent the Democrats from using the issue against Bush, a former head of the U.S. Liaison Office in Beijing, the precursor of the embassy. In any case, the Western world was preoccupied with the Soviet collapse, German reunification, and the reordering of Europe. Western politicians would rather celebrate victory in the Cold War than deal with the apparent return of Stalinism in China.

～

For India, the changes in China created opportunity. Through the 1980s China's domestic preoccupations with economic growth and later with the divisions that Tiananmen had shown made it more willing to come to an accommodation with India. So did its worries about the rapid changes in the international situation and the collapse of the Soviet Union. Rajiv Gandhi had visited China just six months before the Tiananmen killings, the first visit by an Indian prime minister since Nehru's 1954 visit. India decided to continue with the first round of foreign secretary-level talks on the boundary within a month of the killings. As the post-Tiananmen waters were tested, it became clear that China's concerns with the United States, domestic turbulence, and the end of the Soviet Union presented an opportunity to stabilize India-China relations. The 1993 Border Peace and Tranquility Agreement was the result.

～

It is easy to forget how mono-focal India-China relations were after the 1962 war. In fact, there was no real relationship. Those of us who served in the Beijing embassy in the mid-1970s spent our time watching China through a glass darkly and trading démarches with the Chinese on Sikkim and the boundary. Trade was minuscule, and visitors few and far between, mostly fellow travelers. External Affairs Minister Vajpayee's visit in 1979 started a slow and desultory process of official talks on the boundary, and the pilgrimage to Mount Kailash and Lake Manasarovar in Tibet, which are holy to Hindus, Buddhists, and other Tibetan religions. The early 1980s saw seven rounds of negotiation between officials on the boundary question. In the July 1986 round, Vice Foreign Minister Liu Shuqing told us that China had resumed patrolling up to the Line of Actual Control. Hints of Chinese flexibility on a boundary settlement—such as the repetition by Deng Xiaoping to G. Parthasarathi in 1982 of a package settlement with both sides keeping what they had—were never repeated in the officials' talks and were soon denied by China in formal conversations.

From 1985 on China upped its demands to include Tawang, a populated city in the eastern sector that had consistently sent representatives to the Indian Parliament. The stalemate in the boundary negotiations was soon followed by trouble on the ground.

In 1986 the Sumdorungchu, or Wangdong, incident occurred, with Chinese troops establishing a permanent presence on the Indian side of the watershed in the sensitive sector near Tawang. India responded immediately, moving troops into the area, and a military stand-off developed with troops facing each other, literally a few meters apart. Later that year India declared statehood for Arunachal Pradesh, which the Chinese vehemently objected to as this was the area that they claimed in the east. Ignoring the boundary issue with China was no longer an option.

Under these circumstances, Rajiv Gandhi's decision to visit China in 1988 was a brave one, befitting a leader who had a view of India's place in the international community unconstrained by legacies of the past. As he reached out to Deng Xiaoping and Premier Li Peng to see what was possible, Gandhi also was attempting through secret diplomacy to reach out to Benazir Bhutto who had just come to power in Pakistan. Apart from his view of India's place in the world, the international situation also prompted the decision to visit China. In July 1986 Mikhail Gorbachev spoke in Vladivostok making it clear that he too wished to improve relations with China. He was to visit China five months after Rajiv Gandhi in the midst of the Tiananmen protests. The United States had established full diplomatic relations with China by then, and the international environment around India was changing. If India was to prepare for the twenty-first century and to deal with its other complex relationships—like Sri Lanka, where Indian troops were engaged, Nepal, where a democratic movement was gathering strength, and Afghanistan, where the Soviet withdrawal was imminent—India needed to open up channels with all the major powers and its neighbors. Rajiv Gandhi's visit to China was therefore part of a larger strategy of situating India in the world through a much more active diplomatic posture.

It became clear in the course of preparing the visit a year earlier that both countries wanted it to be a success. The actual negotiation of the Joint Statement in the Chinese Foreign Office, completed in October 1988, took less than two hours, and that included the time taken for interpretation. The contrast was striking with the long and tedious negotiation of other, much less consequential, joint communiques and statements when the relationship was on a more even keel in subsequent decades.

There is no question that Rajiv Gandhi's visit to China in December 1988 was one of the three most transformative events in India-China relations in the twentieth century, after China's 1950 entry into Tibet and the 1962 war. The primary result of the visit was to put India-China relations on a steady trajectory for two and a half decades. This was truly a remarkable achievement, considering the low-level of the relationship and the breathtaking changes that had taken place in China, India, and, indeed, the world. The crucial decisions taken by the two governments during the visit were to address the boundary question in a joint working group headed by the foreign secretaries; to permit the rest of the relationship to grow and develop without making it contingent on the settlement of the boundary; and to begin working together where possible on the international stage. It was clear to both sides that all of this was only possible if peace and tranquility were maintained on the border with both sides respecting the status quo. This understanding was subsequently elaborated and formalized during Prime Minister Narasimha Rao's visit to China in September 1993 in the Border Peace and Tranquility Agreement.[15]

Every subsequent Indian government, irrespective of its political composition and leanings, has followed the same approach to India-China relations. That attests to the long-term validity of the approach that was worked out through internal debate in India and with the Chinese through the late 1970s and 1980s and was formalized in the December 1988 visit. After the visit the border was generally peaceful, even in the absence of a boundary settlement, and stayed where it was until 2013. In 1988 India did less than US$200 million in trade with China. Now India does more than US$90 billion, and China is its largest trading partner in goods. Over 23,000 Indians study in China today. As a result of that strategic framework or modus vivendi, both countries have been free to develop themselves and to pursue their other interests without being tied down by India-China conflict.

The reaction at home and internationally to the Rajiv Gandhi visit was almost uniformly positive. Critics of the government did not know what to make of it and held their fire. Friends supported the initiative. All of them saw it as a potential game changer, and they were right. Where everyone was wrong was in expecting it to lead to an early resolution of the boundary question. Gandhi himself had spoken to his inner circle of settling the boundary in his second term as prime minister. Fate and the Tamil Tigers, a terrorist group in Sri Lanka, intervened. Rajiv Gandhi was ready to follow through on the promise of the visit, and we went ahead with the first boundary joint working group meeting in Beijing a month after the June 1989 Tiananmen killings, when the rest of the world was hesitating in its dealings with China.

~

The other part of India's reaction to the reordering of Asia in the 1980s and to the Sino-U.S. alliance was to concentrate on the subcontinent, consolidating and managing relations with immediate neighbors.

By the 1980s, the subcontinent was one of the least integrated subregions in the world in terms of formal trade and investment, though it probably had the highest level of ethnic, cultural, linguistic, and religious affinity. Its economies had been hard hit by the 1973 and 1979 oil shocks, and most of them faced recurring balance of payments crises. By most progress indexes, the subcontinent was being left behind by east and southeast Asia.

Bangladesh President Zia-ur Rehman, in 1980, first proposed the creation of a South Asian Association for Regional Cooperation (SAARC), consisting of India, Bangladesh, Pakistan, Nepal, Bhutan, Maldives, and Sri Lanka. India was initially skeptical and reticent about institutionalizing regional cooperation. Its relations with both Bangladesh and Pakistan were difficult at the time, and many Indian officials saw the proposal as an attempt to gang up against India by its smaller neighbors. On the other hand, if India did not join the forum it was certain to acquire that nature or tone. SAARC's proponents in India argued that as the largest country in the region with an interest in promoting stability and economic development, India should see SAARC as an opportunity to overcome the economic consequences of the fragmentation and partition of the subcontinent in 1947. If SAARC were limited to social and economic issues, it would offer an opportunity to reintegrate the subcontinent in important respects. Indira Gandhi finally approved India's participation in the negotiations to establish SAARC, despite what she saw as the risks, and the terms for its formation were almost finalized when she was assassinated on October 31, 1984. Rajiv Gandhi, despite the reservations of much of the Indian foreign policy establishment including External Affairs Minister P. V. Narasimha Rao, was much more willing to take an active leadership role in SAARC, thus denying adversaries a way to marginalize India and using India's economic and other strengths in the neighborhood. SAARC was formed under his watch in 1985. It has had a checkered history since, not for faulty design but for lack of political will among members in making it work.

~

In Sri Lanka as well, Rajiv Gandhi was willing to make commitments and take risks that previous Indian governments had not.

India's difficulty in Sri Lanka arose from the effect on India of tensions between the majority Sinhalese and minority Tamils in that country. The introduction of democracy in independent Ceylon in 1948 had seen Sinhala majoritarianism disadvantage the Tamil minority, which had achieved superior economic status and administrative power under the colonial government. Tensions between the two communities came to a flashpoint with anti-Tamil riots in July 1983. Nearly 300,000 Sri Lankan Tamils fled the Sinhala government-organized pogrom as refugees to India, and there was a groundswell of anger in the Indian state of Tamilnadu, which was soon transmitted to the rest of the country.

Indira Gandhi's initial response to the brewing ethnic crisis in Sri Lanka was to apply overt and covert pressure on the Sri Lankan government, while mediating between the Sri Lankan government and the Tamils. Her compulsions were multiple. The J. R. Jayewardene government in Sri Lanka was oppressive and discriminatory against Tamils and was cultivating links with the United States, Pakistan, and Israel, none of whom was particularly friendly to India at the time. The Afghan and Indochina wars were at their polarizing height. Pakistan was the Americans' main instrument in Afghanistan and the quid pro quo that it demanded and got from the United States was the freedom to pursue its nuclear program and to strengthen itself strategically against India. India-China relations were uneasy. Sri Lanka was just fourteen miles off the Indian coast. And Tamilnadu had been home to a strong separatist movement in the late 1950s and early 1960s. Sri Lankan Tamil militancy received moral and material support from the populace in Tamilnadu and reportedly from India's external intelligence agency to generate pressure on the Sri Lankan government. Tamil militancy was a threat to India. After the July 1983 riots, External Affairs Minister P. V. Narasimha Rao and G. Parthasarathi were sent as special envoys to President J. R. Jayewardene to convey that India did not seek the breakup of Sri Lanka but also could not tolerate policies that created strategic threats to India; India was ready to mediate.

An attempt at mediation almost succeeded. An All-Party Conference agreed on a devolution package fashioned by Parthasarathi in consultation with Jayewardene and the Sri Lankan Tamils, who had all agreed to its contents. However, Jayewardene scuttled it, clandestinely using the Buddhist clergy and the Sri Lankan opposition parties and then claiming that he could not implement the package in the absence of national consensus. He was not known in Sri Lanka as "the silver fox" for nothing. It was at this delicate stage of events in Sri Lanka that Indira Gandhi was assassinated on October 31, 1984, and Rajiv Gandhi assumed office.

Rajiv Gandhi was cut from different cloth. He reoriented Indian policy in several ways. He recognized the ebbing of socialist orientations, saw the changes that Gorbachev was bringing, and thought that the utility of the nonaligned movement had diminished in the new international configuration. With the failure of the All-Party Conference in Sri Lanka, he shifted to a more neutral Indian stance between the Sinhalese and the Tamils, "an Indian rather than a Tamilnadu policy" toward Sri Lanka, as Romesh Bhandari, then foreign secretary, described it.

From March 1985 to December 1986 India tried to persuade both the Tamils and the Sri Lankan government to compromise. Tamil groups were asked to drop their demand for a separate Tamil state (or Eelam), to give up violence and terrorism, and to accept substantial autonomy and devolution in running their own affairs in merged provinces within a united Sri Lanka. Simultaneously the Sri Lankan government was asked to give up its xenophobic ethnic approach and to restructure the polity to meet minority aspirations and isolate extremists. The Sri Lankan government pretended to negotiate while systematically intensifying military operations against the Tamils. The Tamils, with their deep distrust of the Sinhalese and government, insisted that they would only compromise if India guaranteed the arrangement. The Sri Lankan government, however, said that they could not accept India as a guarantor as that would be seen by their people as Indian interference in their internal affairs. By December 1986 Indian mediation was at a dead end. In January 1987 the Sri Lankan government launched a military campaign against the Tamil majority area, Jaffna, and blockaded the northern peninsula, thus confirming the Tamils' worst fears. By now Rajiv Gandhi was convinced of the need to shift Indian policy to apply more direct pressure on the Sri Lankan government to be reasonable with the Tamils who were, after all, Sri Lankans. India opposed the Sri Lankan military action and was now willing to guarantee a compromise.

On June 4, 1987, India intervened directly, breaking the Sri Lankan military blockade of Jaffna and airdropping supplies for the civilian population, when attempts to send the supplies by sea had failed. The Sri Lankan government had been given very short notice of this display of power. Once India displayed firm intent, both the Sri Lankan government and the Tamil militant groups, including the most militant, the Liberation Tigers of Tamil Eelam (LTTE) under Prabhakaran, were willing to compromise, and they all agreed to a set of measures within the framework of a united Sri Lanka to solve the crisis. These included the devolution of powers to the provinces and the merger of the Tamil-speaking areas in the northern and eastern provinces.

On July 27, 1987, the Indo-Sri Lanka Agreement was signed by Rajiv Gandhi and J. R. Jayewardene in Colombo. Simultaneously, Jayewardene announced a devolution package and passed the 13th Amendment to the Sri Lankan constitution devolving power to the provincial governments, merging the two provinces where the Tamils were a majority and reflecting the agreed political compromises. India promised to send troops, in the form of an Indian Peace Keeping Force (IPKF), if requested, which it was asked to do by the Sri Lankan government immediately after the signing of the agreement. Jayewardene left the pacification of the Tamil north to the IPKF, putting that force in direct conflict with the LTTE, while using the Sri Lankan Army to suppress a rebellion by the Marxist-Leninist Janatha Vimukthi Peramuna (JVP) in the Sinhala south. Neither the Sri Lankan government nor the LTTE kept the promises they made in the Indo-Sri Lanka Agreement, in the 13th Amendment, or directly to India. The LTTE broke its promise to disarm while, Jayewardene put off actual implementation of the 13th Amendment based on one pretext or another. Had either Jayewardene or Prabhakaran been sincere in the implementation, the Indo-Sri Lanka Agreement might have brought peace to Sri Lanka. Instead, after a brief lull, Sri Lanka's civil war was to last another twenty-two years.

By 1989 Ranasinghe Premadasa, a Sinhala chauvinist, had replaced Jayewardene and become president of Sri Lanka. Rajiv Gandhi insisted on the IPKF finishing the job and Premadasa went along while Gandhi was in power, but the December 1989 elections in India brought in a government under V. P. Singh who had no stomach to continue the fight against the LTTE, and the IPKF was soon withdrawn. More than 1,500 Indian soldiers had died in an attempt to bring peace and to keep Sri Lanka united in a war fought with one hand tied behind their back. For political reasons they had been pulled out of Sri Lanka without fully achieving their objectives.

On May 21, 1991, Rajiv Gandhi was killed while campaigning in the general election in Tamilnadu by an LTTE suicide bomber.

∼

In the Maldives, unlike Sri Lanka, politics and timing were on India's side. On November 3, 1988, Maumoon Abdul Gayoom was president of the Maldives when a group of Sri Lankan mercenaries belonging to the People's Liberation Organization of Tamil Eelam (PLOTE) attempted a coup in that archipelagic country of about 300,000 people. The group had been funded by a few disgruntled Maldivians abroad led by a businessman named Abdullah Luthufi. An eighty-member-strong team of raiders had landed by speed boat from a freighter, while others had infiltrated as tourists beforehand. Gayoom sent an SOS to several countries, including India, Pakistan, Sri Lanka, and the United States. Before anyone else could react, Rajiv Gandhi sent Indian paratroopers to secure the capital Male, in what was called Operation Cactus. The mission was short and successful and soon restored Gayoom's legitimate civilian government.[16]

～

Nepal was another example of Rajiv Gandhi's more robust approach, and of his willingness to be seen exercising power and using the military instrument in the subcontinent.

India's special relationship with Nepal from the 1950s has included an open border, the treatment of Nepalese in India as Indian citizens for all practical purposes, including employment and their recruitment into the Indian Army, a free trade regime tilted in Nepal's favor, and a security commitment tying India's defenses to the high Himalayan range. To these must be added ties of religion, language, and kinship across the open border, which lead to an intimacy in relations that is probably unequalled by any two sovereign states elsewhere.

That intimacy does not mean that the relationship is without its own excitements, some as a result of occasional Nepalese attempts to use its position between India and China to play one off against the other, some due to Nepal's own internal fragilities, and some when India forgets to respect Nepal's sensibilities about its sovereignty. In 1950 King Tribhuvan had fled to India where he was in exile from November 1950 to February 1951 and was restored to real power with Indian help over the Rana oligarchy, which had ruled Nepal for over a century. As his successors tightened the grip of royal rule in Nepal through the 1960s and 1970s, Nepalese democrats and politicians sought and obtained refuge just across the border in India.

In 1988 these trends in which Nepal sought to balance India and China and the development of a democratic movement created a crisis in India-Nepal relations. Nepal decided to buy weapons from China, delinked her currency from the Indian rupee, and cancelled work permits for Indians. At the same time, popular pressure within Nepal for democracy was growing. India added pressure, including a blockade, which contributed to the success of the surging democracy movement within Nepal. In 1990 Nepal transitioned to a constitutional monarchy and introduced elective democracy. Rajiv Gandhi's willingness in 1988–1990 to act in defense of India's privileged relationship with Nepal and in support of the democracy movement within Nepal was of a piece with the more robust role that India adopted in the internal politics of its neighbors in his time as prime minister.

~

The China visit was Rajiv Gandhi's single biggest foreign policy achievement. But it was not his only one. He did much to consolidate India's relationships within the subcontinent. He rescued relations with the United States from the trough that they were in in the early 1980s and began effective economic diplomacy. His focus on information technology, computers, and biotechnology, and on building an India for the twenty-first century, served India well abroad, changing her image from a closed, backward-looking society dependent on the Soviet connection to a more open, modern, and realistic country. He was not a prisoner of ideology or of the past in his outlook; he had a vision of modern India and was in a hurry to achieve it. He also prepared India for life after the Soviet Union, anticipating the end of the Cold War by his openings to China and the United States. He resumed defense cooperation with the Americans and hosted Caspar Weinburger, the first U.S. defense secretary to visit India. India was the first non-ally to receive a U.S. supercomputer. By giving the green light to the development of nuclear warheads and their delivery systems, his pursuit of the nuclear submarine project, and by signing the Kudankulam nuclear power plant agreement with Gorbachev, he established a framework that served India well in the tumultuous period to come. Domestic preoccupations prevented him from establishing diplomatic relations with Israel as he wished to. His robust responses to the crises in Sri Lanka and Maldives, and his enthusiastic espousal of SAARC, changed the terms of India's engagement with the subcontinent and the near abroad.[17] More fundamentally, his regime's steps toward economic opening began India's thirty-year spurt of over 6 percent GDP growth each year, which accelerated after the big bang reforms of 1991. And that has enabled the subsequent transformation of India and Indian diplomacy.

~

The extended neighborhood was closing in on India in the early 1980s. The Cold War dynamic in Asia had changed with Sino-Soviet contention. The United States was now on China's side on the primary fault lines in southeast and east Asia, though U.S.-Soviet contention remained the driving force in Afghanistan and west Asia, fought out through Pakistan in Afghanistan and the Khmer Rouge in Cambodia. Both Indira Gandhi and Rajiv Gandhi dealt with relative isolation and the difficult Asian situation in the 1980s by concentrating on the immediate neighborhood, by reaching out to erstwhile adversaries, and by adjusting to the new superpower dynamic. Afghanistan and Cambodia changed the nature of the Cold War and brought that war to India's doorstep. History will judge whether India's choices on these two issues were correct. On Afghanistan it is hard to see viable or realistic alternatives that were available to India, and subsequent developments vindicate the Indian approach. But the damage to India's interests from its partisan position on Cambodia and exclusion from regional and global economic integration of southeast and east Asia took a long time to repair.

All in all, India navigated the difficult 1980s and ended the decade in a better position than when it began. By the end of the 1980s, the first wave of globalization, reform in the Soviet Union and China, and shifting great power alignments in Asia left India in need of new foreign and domestic policies. The two Gandhi governments had made some tactical adjustments, most successfully with China, and less so with the United States. But the real change was yet to come. The winding down and shifts in the Cold War order in the 1980s were followed in the 1990s by fundamental changes brought about by the final end of that contest. India had significant choices to make. In the 1990s, it chose not to stay aloof, as in the 1970s and early 1980s, and instead plunged into the world.

7

The Dam Bursts

India was in crisis in 1990–1991. Former Prime Minister Rajiv Gandhi had been killed by a terrorist human bomb while campaigning. The general election brought a minority Congress Party government under P. V. Narasimha Rao to power on June 21, 1991. India was in financial crisis, long-brewing but allowed to assume threatening proportions by the weak V. P. Singh and Chandrashekhar governments. Its primary cause was profligate borrowing by Rajiv Gandhi's government since 1985. The tipping point came when the first Persian Gulf War of 1990–1991 sent oil prices soaring. India had no money to buy oil and nonresident Indian capital began to flee the country. The country's foreign exchange reserves were down to US$1 billion, equivalent to two weeks' imports. India had to send part of its gold reserves to London as collateral for a US$2.2 billion emergency loan from the International Monetary Fund. Prime Minister Rao and his finance minister, Manmohan Singh, devalued the rupee by 20 percent in two steps over the first three days of July, drastically liberalized trade policy, and dismantled the production licensing permit Raj for industry (but not the regulatory inspector Raj, unfortunately). Crisis had driven India forward. Over the next two years, the fiscal deficit dropped from 8.4 percent to 5.7 percent of GDP, foreign exchange reserves shot up from US$1 billion to $20 billion, and inflation declined from 13 percent to 6 percent. Foreign exchange reserves began to double every year from $150 million in 1991 to $3 billion in 1997. Customs duties were slashed from a peak rate of 200 percent to 40 percent by the mid-1990s. India was unbound.[1]

Externally, the collapse of the Soviet Union, the end of the Cold War, and the demise of the bipolar world that it spawned saw the dawning of the United States' moment in history as the sole superpower, its unipolar moment, something that no other power had ever enjoyed—not even the British empire at its height, as Britain had never really dominated European politics and had left much of the world in Latin America and Africa to its own devices. The United States had gone from being the leading global maritime power to the sole un-challenged global power. The 1990s and early 2000s saw American hegemony and the inception of a unipolar world system.[2]

For India the fundamental, disruptive, and ultimately benign change in its external circumstances came just when it was undergoing a domestic economic crisis. Fortunately, Narasimha Rao and Manmohan Singh provided the experi-ence, vision, and will to use the opportunity opened by this conjunction of in-ternal crisis and external change to remake the practice of Indian foreign policy, making new friends and exploring new strategic options.

$\sim$

On December 26, 1991, the Soviet Union was dissolved by a decree of the Su-preme Soviet of the Soviet Union, granting independence to the constituent re-publics and simultaneously creating the Commonwealth of Independent States (CIS). On December 25, 1991, Soviet President Mikhail Gorbachev, eighth and last leader of the Soviet Union, resigned, declared his office nonexistent, and handed over power and the nuclear missile codes to Russian President Boris Yeltsin. This was only the final act of the collapse of the Soviet bloc that had begun in 1989 with the fall of the Berlin Wall. I will not go into the reasons for the collapse, whether it was glasnost or perestroika, or Soviet overreach in an arms race with the United States, or U.S. action, or the economic hollow-ness at the heart of the Soviet system, or suppressed nationalisms in the satellite countries, or some combination of these and other causes. What mattered was that the Cold War was over.

Some victors declared, in an understandable act of hubris, that this marked the end of history, and that the world would now all follow liberal democracy and market economics, although Francis Fukuyama's premise in his article and book of that name was not exactly that message. History does not stand still, of course. But what was recognized at the end of the Cold War was that the United States was the uncontested and sole superpower in the world, the only power with global reach and ambitions. It also meant that what had been the central fault line in international politics, the partition of Europe between the two blocs, was no longer central to world geopolitics. Europe was now a sideshow in international politics. NATO had to find a new role now that its enemy, the Soviet Union no longer existed. At the same time, German reunifi-cation was no longer impossible. The fear of a unified, powerful, and domineer-ing Germany at the heart of Europe, with no defensible geographical borders, which had driven European politics since at least the middle of the nineteenth century, was dissolved in the euphoria of victory in the Cold War.

India had been asleep at the wheel, partly due to domestic crisis. The actual fall of the Soviet Union occurred when the V. P. Singh government was in the saddle. Showing little imagination or professionalism, neither New Delhi nor the mission in Moscow had stayed in touch with leaders or political forces other than Gorbachev and the Communist Party of the Soviet Union for fear of endangering their privileged access and relationship with the Soviet authorities. Their political assessments were, to say the least, unrealistic.

For countries like India, the end of the Cold War meant that we no longer had to choose sides or decide issues bearing in mind the inevitable antagonism among the great or superpowers. It was now possible for India to seek good and constructive relations with all the major powers. Some of us in government had argued in 1988–1989 that world politics was already so multisided and complicated that we could no longer follow a traditional nonaligned policy but should try to work with all the major powers, including former foes like China. How could we be nonaligned when there were no real blocs to be aligned with? I had asked. Told not to use such heretical language, I did find that the idea itself was not opposed at political levels in Delhi if one used neutral terms such as "strategic autonomy."

In effect, the end of the bipolar world in 1989 liberated India's foreign policy, creating space. Of course, as with any great change, not everyone saw this as an opportunity. While most younger Indian diplomats and the top political leadership saw the possibilities, mostly older diplomats saw the changes as a threat to long-established and comfortable ways of dealing with the world. In mid-1986 when we in Beijing pointed to Gorbachev's speech at Vladivostok as marking the end of the Sino-Soviet split, our seniors in Moscow sternly warned us not to indulge our ignorance on issues above our pay grade, or words to that effect. Delhi, however, was more realistic and was willing to listen and to take the necessary steps to prepare for the new world that was coming. And when India simultaneously faced the economic crisis and the end of the Cold War, Prime Minister Rao undertook a reform of Indian foreign policy that was as thorough as the foundations that Nehru had laid in the 1950s for India to cope with the bipolar Cold War world. The difference was that while Nehru enjoyed broad domestic support and wrote on a blank slate, Rao did not. But essentially both dealt with a rapidly changing world by adjusting the rules of engagement and finding a uniquely Indian way to do so. Due to his domestic political constraints, however, Rao presented his changes as continuity. Rao downplayed the radical nature of what he was doing, finding Nehruvian precedent and arguments to justify them. The true measure of his achievement, crafted in the fog of change and turmoil, is that subsequent governments of India—and there have been several of every ideological cast possible—have followed the essential lines of foreign policy that Rao laid down in 1991–1996.

~

When he took office, Rao inherited "an inbox from hell."[3] India's foreign relations needed their own liberation. While this had been realized for some time, and the first tentative steps had been taken by Rajiv Gandhi's government, it was Rao who took them forward and gave the shift concrete, irreversible shape. He stressed economic diplomacy, including a special Look East policy in Japan in 1992.

In essence, Rao opened up India's relationship with the United States. He moved away from the reflexive anti-Americanism widespread in the Indian political class that was increasingly counterbalanced by the admiration of the growing Indian middle class for the United States. As the center of gravity of Indian politics moved from left of center toward the right, a process that continues today, Rao opened up substantive relations with the United States. His economic liberalization, his two visits to Davos, the first Indian prime minister to do so, and his establishment of diplomatic relations with Israel in January 1992 aligned Indian and U.S. postures on issues important to the United States. By the time he visited Washington, D.C., in May 1994, his credentials as a reformer and liberalizer spoke for him. Besides, with the war against the Soviets in Afghanistan over, U.S. interest in supporting Pakistan was now diminished, reducing an old irritant to manageable proportions.

One issue that still clouded the India-U.S. relationship was the nuclear question. India was publicly ambiguous about its own pursuit of nuclear weapons. By the time Rao visited Washington, India had demonstrated its capability to build a bomb in 1974 and had shown the ability to deliver them to Pakistani cities by testing Prithvi missiles in February 1993. Polls in India in the early 1990s showed public support for strategic ambiguity: around 50 percent of the population was for signing the Nuclear Non-Proliferation Treaty (NPT), while 81 percent also were for developing nuclear weapons. The public wished to have their cake and eat it too.

From the American point of view, now was the time to eliminate a possible threat to global stability, namely, nuclear proliferation. In multilateral negotiations, the NPT was extended in perpetuity; an ostensibly equitable

Comprehensive Test Ban Treaty was pushed through and finalized to prevent anyone else from testing nuclear weapons after the nuclear weapon states had already tested well over 2,000 times; and, pressure was applied to cap and roll back the Indian strategic program. The international non-proliferation regime was tightening just when India's security environment was worsening. Pakistan was sponsoring terrorism in Jammu and Kashmir, and had claimed to have nuclear weapons and threatened India with them just before the Rao government came to power.

Rao's response to the shrinking space for ambivalence on India's nuclear weapons was twofold. On the one hand, he authorized a step-by-step full weaponization of the program. On the other, he began a conversation on the subject with the United States, entrusting Chandrashekhar Dasgupta with the task of keeping the talks going. When the United States protested in 1995 at what it saw as preparations for a nuclear weapons test at Pokhran, Rao had done all that was necessary for India to be ready to test its nuclear weapons and had signaled clearly to the United States and others that India had the capability. And by having the United States announce these facts, the message was made all the more credible to India's adversaries.

Two months after visiting the United States, Rao was in Moscow to shore up a relationship that was critical to India's defense and to rebuild political congruence where possible. He also began the process of clearing away the detritus left by the collapse of the Soviet Union, settling the rupee-ruble balances and other legacies. It was a time of confused politics in the former Soviet Union and Russia under Yeltsin, but Rao managed to keep the relationship on an even keel.

With China as well, Rao was quick to use the beneficial effects of shifting geopolitics. For China the collapse of the Soviet Union removed the glue in its alliance with the United States and aroused Chinese fears after Tiananmen that they could be the next target of U.S. attempts to fell communist regimes. China was also reaching out to several Asian countries that had not imposed sanctions after the Tiananmen incident. China was therefore open to Indian suggestions to legalize the status quo on the border, setting in place measures to maintain peace and to undertake military confidence-building measures. The Border Peace and Tranquility Agreement signed during Rao's September 1993 visit to China left both countries free to concentrate on their priorities, namely, internal developments and relations with the United States. At the same time China moved toward a relatively neutral position on India-Pakistan issues, with President Jiang Zemin advising the Pakistan National Assembly in December 1996 to do with India what China had done: discuss difficult bilateral issues but at the same time to cooperate, trade, and practice normal relations. At the 1993 Human Rights Council, China joined Iran in persuading Pakistan not to press its resolution to condemn India for human rights violations in Jammu and Kashmir. And in 1999 China joined others in stressing the sanctity of the Line of Control in Jammu and Kashmir when Pakistan attempted to stealthily occupy territory across that line, provoking a short, sharp war with India.

China was also accommodative on what has always been a core issue, Taiwan. Taiwan had been ready to help India during its financial crisis without asking for any complicated quid pro quo return. This offer was discussed but not acted upon, but contacts continued as part of the economic diplomacy that Rao and Manmohan Singh ushered in. Silent diplomacy on both sides of the Taiwan Strait resulted in India's establishing a non-official presence in Taipei—the only country to do so while maintaining an embassy in Beijing without provoking a political reaction. Today Taiwan's trade with India is over US$7 billion a year and investment, airline and shipping, students, and other connections between India and Taiwan are normal.

In effect, Rao was able to manage an omni-directional foreign policy in a world that was no longer bound by Cold War binaries. The opening to Israel was accomplished without damage to other west Asian relationships and was endorsed publicly by Yasser Arafat of the Palestinian Liberation Organization beforehand. Indeed, Rao, a fluent Persian speaker, simultaneously strengthened the relationship with Iran, which supported India in the UN against Pakistani attempts to raise the Kashmir issue and endorsed India's plural polity after the Babri masjid demolitions.[4]

Rao's emphasis on the economy is clear from the fact that his first visit abroad was to Germany. He was the first Indian prime minister to attend the World Economic Forum at Davos, the epitome of capitalism, and he understood the importance of integrating India with global markets. When reform began in 1991, 15.2 percent of India's GDP was external merchandise trade (compared to China's 38.4 percent). By 2014 this proportion was 49.6 percent, higher than China's 41.5 percent in the same year. As India grew more integrated with the Western liberal globalized order, it also became the greatest beneficiary after China of two decades of open trade and investment flows that followed the end of the Cold War. The Look East policy that Rao first spelled out in Tokyo in April 1992 was part of his attempt to tap into the most dynamic economies in the world, then in southeast Asia and the far east. Rao was the first Indian prime minister to visit South Korea, which was to overtake Japan as an investor and trader with India and was to sign a comprehensive economic partnership agreement with India before Japan. The Look East policy was initially primarily economic in its presentation but has since also acquired political and security overtones as the situation in the Asia-Pacific evolves.

In the subcontinent, the Rao government's emphasis on economic development opened new possibilities for regional and bilateral integration, separating economic integration from the settlement of political differences. It took some time for India's immediate neighbors to see that it was no longer politics as usual in Delhi. Sri Lanka was the first, and a free trade agreement was negotiated through different Indian governments from 1997 onward, even while the civil war was still going on in the late 1990s; the agreement came into effect in 2000. In Nepal, as well, relations were much smoother once it became clear that India and China were dealing cooperatively with each other. After a slight lag, a new realism began to permeate Indian policy toward Myanmar, with a more calibrated engagement with the military regime, thus better serving India's security interests when Indian insurgents find sanctuary in Myanmar and India's only land route to southeast Asia is through that country.

If the new situation opened up space for India, it also did so for other countries. In the wake of the collapse of the Soviet Union and the instability in Afghanistan after the Soviet defeat there, Pakistan attempted to push its proxy, Gulbuddin Hekmatyar, and his Hizb-e-Islami into power in Afghanistan. When it became clear that he could rocket Kabul but not take it, Pakistan created the Taliban and supported them militarily and financially to bring them to power in Afghanistan.

The 1990s were also the years when crossborder terrorism from Pakistan against India was at its height, when Pakistan attempted to take territory near Kargil and to revive the Kashmir issue, and of the hijack to Kandahar of IC-184 in 1999. India, however, did not allow these incidents to divert India from internal transformation, attempting repeatedly to arrive at a framework for coexistence with Pakistan. As early as January 1994 P. V. Narasimha Rao sent Foreign Secretary J. N. Dixit to propose to Pakistan an arrangement similar to the 1993 Border Peace and Tranquility agreement that had been reached with China. Subsequent attempts by Prime Minister A. B. Vajpayee visiting Lahore in 1999 and the Agra Summit in 2001 did not change Pakistani behavior and the string of large-scale terrorist attacks on civilians in India, beginning with Mumbai in 1993 and extending to the attack on the Indian Parliament in December 2001.

In the immediate aftermath of the Soviet withdrawal from Afghanistan, India's Pakistan policy had to cope with exaggerated Pakistani notions of the efficacy of jihad and mujahideen as instruments of state policy. India's responses were essentially indirect and covert, countering terrorism in Jammu and Kashmir and ensuring that Pakistan's traditional supporters did not support its efforts in Kashmir and the UN. This the Rao government was successful in doing, both with the United States and even, to a considerable extent, with China. Pakistan, misreading the international situation, found China, Iran, and the United States working against its attempts to internationalize Jammu and Kashmir during sessions of the UN Human Rights Commission in 1993, and its traditional allies, such as Saudi Arabia, distinctly lukewarm. Pakistan's support for Hekmatyar and the Taliban in Afghanistan, its nuclear weapons program, and the risk it posed to the early rapprochement between India and the United States and India and China had contributed to this outcome. India had sought nothing more at this stage from them than to neutralize support for Pakistan's sponsorship of crossborder terrorism and its attempt to internationalize the Kashmir issue. And those goals were accomplished.

While India had success with the world, Pakistan remained a harder nut to crack over time. It took time and many incidents to convince the Pakistan establishment that it needed to be seen attempting to come to terms with India, while awaiting their moment.

While achieving some success in the new post–Cold War world, India still had a problem refashioning its relationship with a new Europe. From a policy point of view, India continued to look at Europe through an economic lens and did not see it as an independent political actor. Hence, the focus was on economic arrangements and vehicles such as the Broad-based Trade and Investment Agreement, which has still to be concluded.

~

Rao and Manmohan Singh's reforms turned the Indian supertanker's course, when others had tried and failed. If the 1970s and 1980s diminished India's role on the world stage, their reforms of the Indian economy and of foreign policy after 1991 brought India back into the world. This was nothing short of a 180-degree reworking of India's foreign relations, since it dealt with the neighborhood, the United States, China, Russia, Japan, Israel, Taiwan, and others. As leader of a minority government with fractious elements within his own party, Rao chose to downplay his originality and said that he was merely implementing what Nehru had laid down and completing what Rajiv Gandhi had begun. But his reforms clearly differed from what had been done before or even attempted. Acknowledging reality on the China border, accepting the facts of the new global balance of power, and letting economics drive political relations were significant shifts. It is only at the broadest level of the pursuit of strategic autonomy, as in building a nuclear weapons program, and awareness of India's unique situation, that Rao's claims of continuity are true. But he certainly changed the practice of Indian foreign policy and his example has endured. For Rao, the substratum of policy or its ideological underpinnings had not changed, nor had his consciousness that India's was a unique situation, necessitating that India take care of its own security and prosperity, using the external world and shaping it when it could. Rao saw domestic economic liberalization and his striving for strategic autonomy as mutually reinforcing.

To the West, neo-liberalism, the increasingly aggressive turn to free-market capitalism, seemed to have triumphed in 1989 and was presented as the correct way to organize the world. Two prominent accounts advanced in the 1990s were treated as prospectuses for the future rather than as understandings of the present: Francis Fukuyama's 1989 article "The End of History" and Samuel Huntington's article "The Clash of Civilizations?" published in *Foreign Affairs* four years later.[5] Fukuyama saw "the universalization of Western liberal democracy as the final form of human government," thanks to the acceptance of liberal economics by Asia, particularly China. At the end of his article, though, he wrote that "clearly the vast bulk of the Third World remains very much mired in history, and will be a terrain of conflict for many years to come" and that "terrorism and wars of national liberation will continue to be an important item on the national agenda." Huntington was less optimistic than Fukuyama and rebutted him. He predicted not the triumph of Western values but, rather, the rise of "challenger civilizations," especially China and Islam, as part of the relative decline of the West. What he proposed was not a threat to the West from a heartland but, instead, a different geopolitical shaping of the Eurasian question, with the rimland far more problematic than the heartland. Developments after 9/11 saw Huntington's piece translated into thirty-three languages.

From India's point of view, at its stage of underdevelopment, neo-liberalism might have some utility but was hardly a panacea. But it was primarily a neo-liberal world with which India had to come to terms. Manmohan Singh and Rao's prescription was of a "middle path" in global economic growth—where the siren songs of material progress would not drown out the appeals of the less fortunate. Rao made his position clear at the Mecca of the neo-liberal consensus, the Davos World Economic Forum. While parts of the new Russian establishment embraced this ideology—with disastrous domestic results—India, like China, used parts of it, while keeping its hesitations close and preserving domestic policy space and autonomy. This was most evident in India's stance at the Rio Earth Summit in June 1992, which negotiated the UN Framework Convention on Climate Change. Rao was also concerned about the effects of the unilateralist and sectarian course advocated in the UN and elsewhere as part of the neo-liberal consensus under the guise of "preventive diplomacy" or "humanitarian intervention" or "the right to protect." His misgivings led him to urge a note of serious caution bilaterally and in multilateral appearances; in retrospect, his views have been proved correct in north Africa and west Asia.

Rao represented continuity in another important respect, the fundamentally realist view of the world inherited from Prime Minister Indira Gandhi, which was continued by his successors in the first National Democratic Alliance and subsequent United Progressive Alliance governments, particularly Manmohan Singh. None of these leaders was taken in by claims of a "new world order" or expected existing power holders to willingly share power or adjust international institutions to recognize new economic and power realities and accommodate India. That, it was clear, would have to await the accumulation of economic, political, and military power by India and its transformation into a strong, prosperous, and modern country.

On balance, therefore, Rao's reform of Indian foreign policy, like all great and successful reform, was both traditional, as well as inventive and realistic, and reworked tradition to go well beyond it. He pragmatically concentrated on the opportunities opened up by geopolitics while flagging but effectively postponing world order or status issues, such as a seat on the UN Security Council for India. Rao's were a remarkably wise set of choices, despite being made in the fog and confusion of a world in fundamental change. In essence, it was Rao's vision of a reinvigorated India retrieving a place of dignity and worth in a fast-changing, sometimes erratic, often unpredictable world that drove Indian foreign policy until 2014. The foreign policy reforms of the early 1990s are worth studying because they teach us how one country successfully navigated fundamental change in the international system. Today, again, the international system is undergoing a new transformation before our eyes: U.S. hegemony is challenged by a rising China; the globalized world economy is fragmenting and shrinking; and, demagoguery and authoritarianism are on the rise everywhere. The economic optimism and political hope of the early 1990s seems far, far away.

～

The end of the Cold War changed the situation in Asia, both east and west of India.

India had been "missing in action" in the east Asian order since the 1970s. With its "Look East" policy in 1992, India returned to the fray, first economically and then politically and in terms of security cooperation with southeast Asian partners. But the Asia that India returned to was very different from the one it had known earlier.

The Soviet collapse left Afghanistan at the mercy of warring mujahideen factions until the rise of the Taliban in 1995–1996. It also meant that Pakistan's utility to the United States was diminished, as the United States concentrated on Europe and the Middle East, and for the first time in decades there was a chance to de-hyphenate India-U.S. relations from U.S.-Pakistan relations, as Prime Minister Narasimha Rao attempted and Prime Minister A. B. Vajpayee succeeded in doing later in the decade.

The collapse of the Soviet Union left Vietnam with little choice but to make peace and withdraw its troops from Cambodia, come to terms with China, and accept the results of the 1991 Geneva peace conference, which provided for a UN-supervised election in Cambodia. Vietnam entered a period of building up its own economy, and it was now possible for it to turn to the United States, despite lingering doubts on both sides about a power that it had fought a war with only fifteen years before. In effect, Vietnam came to terms with an Asia in which the United States and China had aligned their interests and worked together. This was very different from the Asia-Pacific of the 1950s and 1960s with its Cold War binaries that India was used to working with. It was also a much more economically integrated Asia-Pacific.

Since the 1970s Japan had increasingly integrated southeast Asian economies into regional and later global value and production chains. In what Saburo Okita called the "flying geese" pattern of development, Japan led the four little dragons of east Asia—Taiwan, Korea, Hong Kong, and Singapore—which in turn brought Malaysia, Indonesia, and the Philippines into successive waves of economic integration and prosperity. In 1990 post-Tiananmen China was still an outlier, though open to foreign capital and technology and to Japan undertaking the first wave of infrastructure development in China in the 1980s. Economic success in eastern Asia had also been based on Asian ideas—seen in Singapore, Japan, and others in east Asia as unique Asian development values, which could replace Western values.

Like India, both China and Japan worried about the end of the Cold War, though for different reasons. Japan's fear was that the United States might turn to China, particularly as China offered a tabula rasa for U.S. companies. Japan's economy in 1990 was still three times larger than China's. Even after years of stagnation Japan still accounted for two-thirds of all Asian output. But through the 1990s Japan began to realize that its decline or stagnation was structural and difficult to change. As China began its comeback spurred by Deng Xiaoping's 1992 victory on economic policy, and the United States began a technology-driven resurgence, Japan's insecurities rose. Interestingly, a rising China restored Japan to its central role as a security ally of the United States rather than as a trade foe. The United States and Japan were now starting to focus on their shared interest in managing the great-power challenge from China.

India, "looking east" to Japan as an economic and political partner, was concerned, however, that Japan's uncertainties made it "strategically available" to China through the 1990s. Significant portions of the Japanese elite saw their country's destiny as lying in Asia and linked to China. But China was unable to overcome historical distrust. Japanese politics itself was undergoing a churn and the Liberal Democratic Party, with its commitment to the U.S. security treaty, was soon replaced in power by the Democratic Party of Japan under prime ministers Ichiro Ozawa and Yukio Hatoyama, who believed that Japan must be less dependent on the United States and closer to China. Ozawa's anodyne term for this radical shift was that Japan should become "a normal nation." But China missed the Japan bus.[6] A series of disputes flared up between China and Japan after Deng Xiaoping's death in 1997.

~

For China, the fall of the Soviet Union came at an awkward time and raised worrying possibilities. The year 1989 was the year the Berlin wall fell and also the year of Tiananmen Square, which had revealed the depth of divisions in the Chinese leadership and in Chinese society about how much opening and political change should be permitted. A beleaguered Chinese leadership under Deng sensed that after the breakup of the Soviet Union, China might be the next target of U.S.-induced regime change. It was hardly surprising that a Chinese regime beholden to the People's Liberation Army might hunker down, concentrating on strengthening internal controls rather than economic reform, particularly when faced with Western sanctions. It was only by 1992 that Deng was strong enough internally to kickstart reforms again.

Deng blamed the Tiananmen demonstrations on the Chinese peoples' ignorance of their own history. He therefore launched a campaign stressing the party's role and stepped up "patriotic education," relaunching the history wars and the narrative of a "century of humiliation," blaming foreigners, the West, and especially the Japanese, for bullying and humiliating China. Unlike Mao, who positioned the party and the Chinese people as heroic victors in the class struggle against foreign imperialists, Deng's successors made China the victim with primary enemies in the West. As a corollary, Confucius and China's past, which Mao blamed for China's weakness, were now extolled and glorified, leading to a new wave of Chinese nationalism and chauvinism. The parallels with what is being attempted in India today are striking. The consequences for China and the region have not been good.

Japan was conflicted about its own political stance. When the United States sought active Japanese support in the first Persian Gulf War in 1991, all that Japan could do was to bankroll the U.S. military effort. When the Japanese government offered to send 100 medical volunteers, only ten applied, and they refused to go to any battle zone. Finally, Japan sent a fleet of minesweepers to the Gulf—in spring 1991, two months after the fighting ended. Though Yasuhiro Nakasone had called Japan "a porcupine with rabbit ears," prickly and alert, U.S. diplomats described it as more like a tortoise, making slow and steady progress in a set direction but, when frightened, withdrawing its head into its shell and remaining immobile. In the end Tokyo contributed a massive US$13 billion but got contempt in return. U.S. Defense Secretary Richard Cheney used to boast that "we ended up with a US$60 billion war and only paid US$5 billion." Most of the funding came from Gulf Arab states. With China, on the other hand, the United States was grateful for an abstention in the UN Security Council, for which China extracted a foreign minister's visit to the White House, the first by a senior Chinese official after the 1989 Tiananmen killings.

The shifts and the outlines of politics in eastern Asia during this period were defined by four issues: the South China sea, the North Korean nuclear weapons program, the Taiwan Strait crisis, and attempts to reorganize Asia and build institutions. All were symptomatic of the rise of China, of other powers attempts to come to terms with it, and the new power realities in the region that India was now trying to return to.

~

China's expansive claims in the South China Sea had first been described in an eleven-dash line on maps by the Kuomintang regime in 1947. That line included all the waters and islands in the sea by running alongside the Philippines, Indonesia, and then up past Brunei and Malaysia past the Vietnamese coast to the mainland. The claims had been adopted wholesale by the communist regime, with the dropping of two dashes by Zhou Enlai in a fraternal moment as a gesture to Vietnam during the Vietnam War. In 1974, as that war was winding down, China fought the Vietnamese Navy and ejected them from islets in the Paracels. Other clashes occurred in 1988.

China never clarified whether it claimed only the islands—about six square miles before China's recent island building—or all the waters around them as well, amounting to 1.4 million square miles in total. Either way, its claims contradicted those of several Association of Southeast Asian Nations (ASEAN) members and Taiwan and have effectively been declared illegal by the United Nations Convention on the Law of the Sea tribunal in 2016 when the Philippines brought the issue up. China has, however, preferred to negotiate individually and bilaterally with other claimants, bringing its considerable political and economic weight to bear.

In effect, China first built the capability and then started to assert control over one of the world's most strategic seaways. One-third of the world's shipping carrying about US$3 trillion worth of trade passes through the South China Sea each year, and the area is also the site of major oil and gas deposits. In 2002 China agreed to negotiate a Code of Conduct with ASEAN, but no code has been finalized. Over time China has built up and enlarged several islands, putting military facilities, runways, and fighter aircraft on them. It has used a variety of methods including fishing fleets, fisheries administration, coast guard, and a militia to assert sovereignty and plant its flag. Today, the South China sea is, in practice, a Chinese lake.

China has used the South China Sea issue to make it clear that a distant United States is not a reliable partner for others with claims in the area, nor are international institutions and international law of any benefit. Instead, the message is that parties must deal directly with China. The political effect of this behavior in the South China Sea has been to worsen China's relationship with every country in the region except landlocked Laos and client Kampuchea. Perceptions of China as a bully and an aspiring hegemon have led to significant increases in defense, security, and intelligence cooperation among China's neighbors such as Japan, Vietnam, Australia, Indonesia, Singapore, and India. The idea of the Indo-Pacific as one maritime space is another outcome. At the same time, China's weight and power ensured that ASEAN was unable to issue joint statements on this vital issue for over half a decade and may be coming to terms with accommodating China in the South China Sea.

India has been drilling for oil on Vietnamese concessions in waters disputed by China since 1988, without taking a stand on the sovereignty issues involved. The significance of the South China Sea for India has continued to grow as foreign trade has become ever more important to a globalizing India, and an ever greater portion of India's trade now flows eastward rather than to the west. Freedom of navigation in the South China Sea is therefore an increasingly significant Indian interest. This has occurred just when China has taken steps to enforce her claims, thus creating another irritant in India-China relations.

~

In 1992 International Atomic Energy Agency (IAEA) inspectors first reported discrepancies and gaps in the North Korean accounting of nuclear materials. As a non-weapon state signatory to the NPT, North Korea had an obligation to show that all of its nuclear materials and facilities were being used for peaceful purposes. The IAEA found itself unable to certify that as true. The United States and its allies, sometimes with China, tried in multiple ways to bring the North Korean nuclear weapons program to a verifiable halt. Pyongyang has given ground at times, but never to the point of abandoning its nuclear bombs and their delivery systems. Through the 1990s, the political cover and economic lifeline that China provided North Korea served to harden Japanese opinion against China, while it reminded the United States of China's potential utility. This was a game that China had mastered, and even now plays, of never actually using its influence with North Korea to the point where the issue is resolved, lest its own utility to the United States and others disappears. North Korea, for its part, has shown equal skill in pursuing nuclear weapons while periodically engaging the world in talks to obtain international recognition of its sovereign independence and to prevent Korean unification on South Korean terms. For India, the North Korean nuclear weapons program was a problem because of its links with Pakistan's clandestine quest for nuclear weapons and their delivery systems. A. Q. Khan, the father of the Pakistani bomb, visited North Korea and exchanged nuclear centrifuges and their technology for North Korean missile technology in the 1990s.

In 2003, in what was widely seen as China's coming of age, China convened the Six Party Talks on the North Korean issue with the United States, Japan, Russia, China, and the two Koreas at the table. The talks lasted until 2007. Under the George W. Bush administration, Christopher Hill and Condoleezza Rice aimed to make a grand bargain through the Six Party Talks, persuading North Korea to give up nuclear weapons in return for a peace treaty and finally ending the Korean civil war. They also wanted to turn the Six Party Talks into a permanent security forum for east Asia to sort out disputes. By mid-2008 the United States announced that it would take North Korea off the list of state sponsors of terrorism in return for Pyongyang declaring its nuclear program open to inspection. This, in theory, would have been the first in a series of cascading steps leading to dismantling North Korea's nuclear weapons program. In the end, an ailing Kim Jong Il, who had suffered a stroke, rejected the deal. U.S. intelligence believed that once he fell ill, Kim lost interest in a grand bargain over the nuclear program and used his remaining political capital to ensure that his son, Kim Jong Un, succeeded him. North Korea has tested nuclear weapons several times since 2006. Today, the denuclearization of the Korean peninsula is an ever more remote prospect.

~

Among China's core issues is the status of Taiwan, and in 1996 China faced what has become known as the Taiwan Strait crisis. China had found that despite years of cultivating the Kuomintang (the Chinese Nationalist Party headquartered in Taiwan) and booming trade and investment ties between the mainland and the island of Taiwan, there was a real risk that Lee Teng-hui would be elected the next president of Taiwan. The Kuomintang had so far maintained the fiction that it was the legitimate ruling party of all of China, the Republic of China. However, Lee, who was born on the island, spoke better Japanese than standard Mandarin, and made no secret of his strong Taiwanese identity. China saw him as a potential leader of an independent Taiwan. In March 1996 China began intensive shelling of the waters around Taiwan, just before the first-ever presidential elections on the island. Unarmed Chinese M-9 missile tests targeted shipping lanes at the southern and northern ends of Taiwan. The United States responded. Defense Secretary William Perry, warned the Chinese of "grave consequences" and President Clinton ordered two aircraft carrier battle groups to the waters east of the Taiwan Strait—the largest U.S. naval deployment in Asia since the Vietnam War.

There was little that China could do in response. It had no military options and had to call off the shelling and missile firings to avoid hitting a U.S. navy ship. The Chinese leadership was headed by an ailing Deng Xiaoping. Lee won the election with an overwhelming majority to become the Chinese-speaking world's first elected president, not a model encouraged by mainland China. One lesson that China drew was that trade and investment and contacts with Taiwan had not translated into a rise in the desire for reunification with the mainland. As China became stronger, its ability to seduce its neighbors, as opposed to threatening and coercing them, only seemed to weaken. Lee was succeeded by what from China's point of view was an even worse alternative: Chen Shuibian, who was committed to Taiwan's independence. Since then political relations between the two have worsened, although business ties have flourished.

China suffered an acute loss of face in the 1996 Taiwan Strait crisis. It could not even track American ships a few score nautical miles off the coast. After this experience China began consolidating its claims to and hold on the South China and East China Seas and strengthening its navy and air force. This was a long-term shift from its historical preoccupation with being a continental power, threatened from the north, to a maritime power with the ability to project power and protect maritime interests to the south and east.

From this incident comes much of what we have seen subsequently in the South China Sea, as already alluded to and now subsumed under the Belt and Road Initiative of Xi Jinping. The combination of the North Korean and Taiwan crises in the 1990s accelerated a wholesale strategic shift in China's military efforts. The PLA, whose role was already greater in Chinese decision-making after Tiananmen, was probably even more important now, leading to more assertive Chinese behavior. A focus on advanced technology rather than massed manpower, an effort to dominate the skies with a modern air force, and the development of long-range bomber groups and their integration with the rest of the military were kickstarted by U.S. military displays in the first Persian Gulf War and the Taiwan Strait crisis. China is attempting a historic and unprecedented shift from a continental to a maritime strategy. It is still an open question whether it will be able to make that transition and sustain it.

One month after the PLA's guns fell silent across the Taiwan Strait in April 1996, President Clinton and Japanese Prime Minister Hashimoto signed an agreement that implicitly extended the U.S.-Japan security treaty to Taiwan and the Korean peninsula. Cautiously worded, it referred to "situations that may emerge in the areas surrounding Japan and which will have an important influence on the peace and security of Japan [and] the Asia-Pacific region." The Taiwan crisis had crystallized for Japan that a rising China had become a threat. The United States, however, still sought to balance its relationship between the two nations. In 1998 Clinton decided not to stop in Japan on his way to China, which was buoyed by Clinton's 1998 Three No's policy on Taiwan— no independence, no two Chinas, and no admission of Taiwan to international organizations requiring statehood as a precondition for membership.

China's growing strength and aggressive nationalism was on full display in its opposition to New Delhi and Tokyo's bid for permanent seats in the UN Security Council, the Senkaku island dispute, intimidation of Taiwan, and India's 1998 nuclear tests. The effect of these Chinese actions was to cement the growing understanding between New Delhi and Tokyo. Within Japan the "China school" in the Gaimusho lost control of the relationship, just as the Chinese MFA was supplanted by the PLA and powerful state-owned enterprises like China Petroleum in determining Japan policy. A Chinese nuclear submarine intruded near Okinawa in late 2004, for example. It was noisy, easily spotted, and tracked by the United States and Japan, which may have been the point. Chinese missiles aimed at Taiwan could easily be targeted on China's other neighbors. As China's assertive behavior toward Japan escalated, the U.S.-Japan alliance was extended to Taiwan and Korea, Japan and the United States jointly deployed missile defenses, and constitutional restraints on Japan's military have been gradually removed.

This pattern repeated itself in China's relations with larger neighbors such as India, but not Russia, which consistently saw the West as a greater threat requiring accommodation with China. As China has accumulated hard power in the twenty-first century, a more assertive Chinese nationalism and posture have seen China's neighbors seek other partners to balance China's influence such as the United States. As realist practitioners of realpolitik, the Chinese seem to expect others to behave as they do. China recognized, acquiesced in, and worked with U.S. hegemony as a junior partner in the 1970s, 1980s, and early 1990s. Now that China has acquired power of its own, it expects the others to behave as it did when faced with superior power, acquiescing to it. In this China has been disappointed by her neighbors, who act from very different strategic approaches and cultures. As a result, China finds herself with few friends in her periphery.

~

There has long been a streak in Japanese politics supporting greater Asian solidarity and a lesser U.S. role, both on the right and left. Japan had fluctuated since the Meiji restoration in 1868 between wanting to be Western, pan-Asian, or both. Every few years there was a fresh Japanese initiative to bind Japan closer to Asia. In 1956 Prime Minister Kishi had suggested much closer economic integration of east and southeast Asia but had failed to interest an India that was turning to planning and import substitution for its industrialization. At that time the idea naturally excluded communist China. At one stage in the 1970s it was the creation of a "yen zone." Later in that decade, Japanese and Australian academics proposed a plan for regional economic integration that years later would become APEC, the Asia-Pacific Economic Cooperation forum.

By the 1990s some in east and southeast Asia ascribed the economic success of the region to Asian values of thrift, hard work and social cohesion. In the 1990s Prime Minister Ozawa sought a place for Japan as "a normal nation" and wanted to push Asian values as a means to economic success, replacing Western models. India, as an economic and ideological outlier, having missed the economic boom of the 1980s in southeast and east Asia, was not part of the reincarnation of pan-Asianism in its new guise in the 1990s. In 1997 Prime Minister Mahathir Mohamad of Malaysia proposed an East Asian Caucus, without the United States, Australia, and India—"a caucus without Caucasians," as a local wag described it. In reality, this idea of a purely east and southeast Asian economic community and trading bloc ignored the dependence of east Asian economies, including China, on the American economy through the 1980s and 1990s. It was only after the 2008 global financial crisis, when the world experienced its deepest recession since the 1930s, that ideas of Asian reorganization and pan-Asian solidarity began to get a real hearing, whether in the form of an East Asia Summit, the Brazil-Russia-India-China-South Africa grouping, the New Development Bank, China's Belt and Road Initiative, or the Asian Infrastructure and Investment Bank.

In 2009 Yukio Hatoyama of the Democratic Party of Japan became prime minister of Japan. He was determined to build an autonomous east Asian community of nations as he was convinced that the U.S.-led era of globalization was coming to an end. Hatoyama was a concern for the United States. A popular politician, Hatoyama believed he had a mandate to shift Japan away from the United States toward China. As prime minister in the 1950s his grandfather had wanted to establish ties with China over American objections. In 2009, after the global financial crisis, Hatoyama kept pushing plans for a new Asian community that excluded the United States. He hoped to rebalance the U.S. alliance and bind China tightly into regional forums. But Hatoyama's days in power were numbered. He had taken on too many opponents at the same time—the powerful Japanese bureaucracy, the United States, and the establishment—and resigned in June 2010 after only nine months as prime minister.

Earlier, in the late 1990s, during the Asian financial crisis, Tokyo floated a proposal for a regional monetary fund. The United States crushed that and also came down hard on Japan's Ministry of International Trade and Industry's idea of a regional economic grouping early in the new century. When the annual

East Asia Summit finally got started in 2005, it was initially without the United States. India had begun the 1990s as a bystander to east and southeast Asia's economic progress and outside the institutions for regional integration. By the time the East Asia Summit was formed in 2005, India's Look East policy was bearing fruit. India was a founding member of the new organization, through which the region's leaders meet every year.

The Asian financial crisis of 1997, triggered when southeast Asian countries were forced to devalue their currencies by speculative attacks that led to a widespread loss of confidence in their economies, made it clear to Asian nations that they had to go it alone. The Western response to the crisis—from the United States, World Bank, and International Monetary Fund—was to impose on Asia more pain and monetarist adjustment policies, a prescription that clearly failed when compared to the more Keynesian approaches advocated by Mahathir Mohammad of Malaysia and Premier Zhu Rongji in China. The latter, when adopted, worked and were politically more palatable.

In retrospect, U.S. opposition to Japanese attempts to build economic integration institutions over the years in Asia left institutional gaps and a clear field for China to fill when it was ready to do so in the second decade of the twenty-first century.

~

A dominant thread running through the geopolitics of Asia east of India in the 1990s and the early part of this century was the rise of China and the different reactions to it, a phenomenon that was accentuated by the two financial crises: the Asian financial crisis of 1997–1998 and the global financial crisis of 2008–2009. Today, India's geography and role in post-Cold War interactions, combined with its re-emergence as a "rising" power, gives India a significant but not a dominant place in the Asia-Pacific. China, on the other hand, has emerged as the pre-eminent Asian economic and military power.

In 2010, China overtook Japan as the second largest economy in the world. It had weathered the 2008 global financial crisis better than the West and was basking in the afterglow of hosting the 2008 Beijing Olympics and the sixtieth anniversary of the Chinese Communist Party.

When the 2008 financial crisis hit, China, like the rest of the world, faced the prospect of a recession as its export markets collapsed. But China pushed forward a giant financial stimulus program, equal to the U.S. financial stimulus in an economy one-third the size. Growth picked up in China the next year, while Europe and the United States were still waiting for a recovery. As Chinese

Vice Premier Wang Qishan told Hank Paulson, Bush's treasury secretary who had closely coordinated responses to the crisis with China, "You were my teacher, [but] I look at your system, Hank. We aren't sure we should be learning from you anymore."[7] The shoe was now on the other foot.

Russia's Vladimir Putin had approached Chinese officials during the crisis, suggesting the two countries work together to bring down the U.S. financial system, dumping U.S. Treasury bills, for instance. The Chinese politely declined, since almost 80 percent of China's reserves were in U.S. dollars. Instead they spoke to the United States and set up a direct channel for daily coordination with the U.S. Treasury so as to prevent the collapse of the U.S. dollar.[8]

This was a China where the politburo members had undergone a study session in 2003 on the rise and fall of great powers since the fifteenth century. The session had resulted in a twelve-part TV series on China Central Television and an eight-volume set of books. China was convinced that the future was rightfully hers. Meanwhile, Zheng Bijian, who was running the Central Party School, coined the phrase China's "peaceful rise" to encapsulate the idea of how China could achieve a prominent place among the world powers and reassure those worried by China's rise. The phrase had even been used by premier Wen Jiabao and president Hu Jintao in 2004. But widespread opposition to the phrase led to a replacement: "peaceful development." The PLA did not like "peaceful rise" because it seemed to lower the importance of military modernization. Chinese hawks thought it sent the wrong signal to Taiwan and Japan by restricting China's options to use force. Clearly a larger cast now had a say in Chinese policy with the PLA a significant actor again. The Ministry of Foreign Affairs, on the other hand, lacked relative formal status in the Communist Party, with no representative in the politburo from the early 1990s until 2017, when the external situation was perceived as having turned adverse. The burden of dealing with foreigners for a party that had built its reputation on standing up to them hardly helped the MFA's cause internally. This is a problem for most foreign offices but is particularly acute in the Chinese case.

For China the key to unlocking its great power status was breaking through the "first island chain," the perimeter of islands and sea-lanes that block China's free passage to the Pacific and Indian oceans. PLA commentary has talked for some time of the "C-shaped encirclement" that the United States is believed to have constructed to keep China hemmed in. Anchored in Japan, some Chinese strategists spoke of the barrier as extending all the way to Afghanistan through southeast and southern Asia. India has thus always been seen as potentially a part of the U.S. containment of China, and Pakistan as the answer. As two

PLA Navy colonels put it, "Because of the nature of geography, China can easily be cut off from the sea." One writer's solution was simple: "Vietnam, Japan and the Philippines are America's three 'running dogs' in Asia. We only need to kill one and it will immediately bring the others to heel."[9]

Even accomplished diplomats like Foreign Minister Yang Jiechi betrayed signs of hubris. In July 2010, when U.S. and ASEAN foreign ministers spoke one after another at an ASEAN Regional Forum meeting in Hanoi criticizing China's behavior in the South China Sea, Yang told the meeting angrily that, "China is a big country, and other countries are small countries, and that's just a fact." Yang's outburst came when those in favor of a more assertive Chinese policy departing from Deng's 24-character strategy were probably pressing more cautious status quoists like State Councillor Dai Bingguo. Yang's stance got him Dai's job on the State Council handling foreign affairs in 2013 when Xi Jinping rose to the top.

For China, surpassing Japan's economy in size was "the most significant landmark in Asian history since Japan's defeat of China in the first Sino-Japanese war" in 1894–1895. In short, China was back where it belonged. From that point on China only had eyes for the true great game of global politics pitting China against its sole peer, the United States. Some in the United States too were coming to a similar conclusion, leading president Obama to attempt a pivot to Asia.

∼

West of India the picture was very different and geopolitically much more complex during the 1990s.

West Asia is a region of weak state structures overwhelmed by society, religion, and strong leaders. In history the area had four traditional regional powers—Egypt, Iran, Iraq, and Turkey—divided by religion and historic animosities. To these have been added Israel. Iraq has been largely removed from the equation by the United States through two Gulf wars. State boundaries drawn by colonial powers after World War I did not match ethnic or other divisions, creating artificial states in Lebanon, the Gulf, Saudi Arabia, and Jordan, to maintain imperial control of what had become an economically significant resource, oil. Animosities and differences between sects, tribes, nations, and states in western Asia were exploited by the imperial powers to maintain a tight hold on what Caroe had called the wells of power, the oil that ran the world economy. The imperial powers, and then the superpowers, played local rivalries and used the regional powers to balance each other, not allowing Arab nationalism—particularly its secular or socialist forms such as the Baathists, Nasserites, or the Palestinian Liberation Organization—to unite the Arabs and oppose the control that they exercised through the kingdoms and sheikh-doms athwart the oil in Saudi Arabia and the Gulf.

The geopolitical center weight of the region has long been Iran. Controlling Iran was therefore critical for outside powers wishing to manage the region. Through the twentieth century Iran was managed by outside powers through its occupation, or partition, or by setting up opponents to Iran (as in the 1907 Anglo-Russian division of Iran into spheres of influence, the joint 1943 inva-sion and partition of Iran by Russia and Britain, or the Iran-Iraq War), or even by regime change, as the CIA undertook in 1953 to oust the democratically elected regime of Mossadegh in favor of the Pahlavi dynasty. By the 1990s the Iranian revolution of 1979 had long since removed the West's ally the Shah, and the Iraq-Iran war, when Iraq had been funded and armed by the United States and Saudi Arabia against Iran, was over, leaving a weakened but unbowed Iran. The region was without a local center of gravity and adrift internationally.

∼

The end of the Cold War opened up the situation in west Asia as it did else-where. The end of Soviet support for the Palestinian Liberation Organization (PLO) and Arab nationalism, and poor military prospects against Israel, per-suaded most Arab regimes to go along with a new multilateral Middle East peace process to solve the Palestine question, begun at Oslo and subsequently taken over by the United States to bring peace between Israel and its Arab neighbors such as Jordan, Syria, and the PLO.

Initially the peace process had some success. Egypt under Sadat had already made peace with Israel under Begin at Camp David in 1979. Jordan and Israel, which had long collaborated covertly against the Palestinian majority in Jordan and against terrorism, signed a peace treaty in 1994 as a result of the process. The Oslo Accords of 1993 led to Palestinian acceptance of Israel's right to exist in return for the withdrawal of Israeli forces from the West Bank and Gaza strip. A Declaration of Principles in Interim Self-Government Arrangements signed on the White House lawn in 1993 also gave the Palestinians some autonomy in running their own affairs. On the Palestinian track, a series of interim agree-ments led to an Israeli withdrawal from the West Bank and Gaza, occupied in the 1967 war, and the establishment of the Palestinian National Authority under Yasser Arafat, a quasi-government recognized by most nations.

The Fatah-led Palestine National Authority (PNA) was, however, under attack from both hardline Palestinians and right-wing Israelis and found its room for negotiating increasingly squeezed. Palestinian extremist factions—Hamas, the Popular Front for the Liberation of Palestine, and others—egged on by rejectionist states such as Syria and Iran, cut into PNA support. The Israeli right and religious parties, fed by large-scale immigration from Russia—almost 2 million people in a total population of 6 million—steadily gathered strength and power within Israel through the 1990s, especially after Rabin's assassination in November 1995, and after Bibi Netanyahu of the Likud formed his first government in 1997. With the Likud and religious parties in power in Israel, it became impossible to arrive at a settlement of final status issues on anything like honorable terms that both sides could present as fair to their own people. These final status issues included the right of return of Palestinian refugees, the boundaries of the new state of Palestine, Jewish settlements in the West Bank, terrorism and security issues, and the status of Jerusalem. Opinion on both the Palestinian and Israeli sides has steadily hardened, increasing the gap between the two sides on final status issues until it is well-nigh unbridgeable. On each of these questions Israel has steadily changed facts on the ground, building Jewish settlements in areas occupied in the 1967 war, walling off Palestinian areas, and cleansing Israel's economy of its dependence on Palestinian labor, while making Gaza and large parts of the West Bank virtually unlivable. The unbridgeable gap became clear when President Clinton tried at a Camp David summit in 2000 to bring the two sides together on a two-state solution. Since then, despite Oslo's 2003 road map for peace, indicating a formal willingness of the parties to accept a two-state solution, the Middle East peace process has been marking time. Today, in 2020, even that two-state solution is questioned by the current U.S. and Israeli leaderships.

India recognized the PLO as the sole legitimate representative of the Palestinian people and as a state in 1975 and was one of the first non-Arab countries to do so. India participated in multilateral meetings—the Madrid process—to support and aid the Middle East peace process. That peace process also led Yasser Arafat to support establishing an Indian embassy in Tel Aviv in 1992: he wanted the Israelis to hear an independent, non-Western point of view. When the peace process was moving forward in the early 1990s, it was possible for those of us in the Tel Aviv embassy to handle relations with both the PNA and PLO, on the one hand, and the booming relationship with Israel on the other. Seventeen chief ministers of Indian states and eight cabinet ministers visited Israel while I was there between 1995 and 1997, alongside an Israeli presidential visit to India. By early 1997, however, it was clear that India needed a separate office in Gaza, where the PNA was then located.

India was the only country that simultaneously managed good relationships with all the regional powers in western Asia and Israel from the 1950s onward. Diplomats from other countries often ask how this feat was managed in the midst of rivalries and hostilities among countries of the region. We had little choice. Western Asia accounts for about two-thirds of India's crude oil imports, about 7 million Indians today live and work in the Gulf and Saudi Arabia, and it is an area of extremely high priority for India's security, both for counterterrorism and to prevent Pakistan using its religious affinities and the regional states to pursue its antagonism toward India. We therefore have had no choice but to work with all the major actors in the region. That India was able to do so, unlike most other countries, was also because it stayed out of others' internal politics, was secular itself, never made the mistake of becoming bodyguards for regimes or kings as Pakistan did, and stayed clear and principled in its approach to internecine quarrels among the Arab states and their conflicts with Iran.

The one time that we broke these rules, we lived to rue the consequences.

Saddam Hussein of Iraq, too, saw the end of the Cold War and U.S. preoccupation with Europe and Russia as an opportunity. He had several grouses against Kuwait, not least that Kuwait had not written off the huge debt that he had incurred when fighting Iran in the Iran-Iraq War on Kuwait and Saudi Arabia's behalf in 1980–1988. Iraq also claimed Kuwait as its own territory left over from the Ottoman province of Basra; it resented the British carving out Kuwait to divide the marsh Arabs and make Iraq virtually landlocked.

In August 1990 Saddam invaded and occupied Kuwait, leading to the first Persian Gulf War of January–February 1991. The international reaction to the invasion was immediate and unambiguous. Within hours the UN Security Council passed a resolution calling for an Iraqi withdrawal from Kuwait. A cascading series of resolutions in the Security Council and Arab League imposed sanctions and deadlines on Iraq. Only Iraq and Libya opposed the Arab League call for an Iraqi withdrawal. On November 29, 1990, Security Council Resolution 678 set January 15, 1991, as the deadline for an Iraqi withdrawal and authorized "all necessary measures" to enforce the resolutions, thus permitting the use of military force against Iraq. The United States put together the largest military coalition since World War II of thirty-five countries to fight the war.

India's reaction under the V. P. Singh government with I. K. Gujral as foreign minister was both "ambiguous and pusillanimous," in J. N. Dixit's words.[10]

The Indian government adopted a spuriously neutral stance without recognizing that Iraq had invaded a fellow member of the nonaligned nations. Gujral rushed to both Kuwait and Iraq to concentrate only on getting Indians home without expressing sympathy for the Kuwaitis. In Baghdad he was photographed hugging Saddam Hussein just when the whole world was organizing itself to oppose Hussein. India's credibility plunged among the Arabs, the nonaligned, and at the UN. The Indian mission in Baghdad reported that Saddam's army could withstand U.S. forces and win. The only Indians to emerge with credit from the episode were the diplomats, officials, air and ship crews, and others who arranged one of the largest evacuations of a civilian population ever out of Kuwait by land, sea, and air in a remarkable feat of improvisation and organization.

By the time the United States had got UN Security Council approval, built the coalition, and launched the first Persian Gulf War in January 1991, Chandra Shekhar was prime minister in Delhi, although as a caretaker. Chandra Shekhar eliminated any ambiguities in India's stance, firmly declared India opposed to the invasion of Kuwait, joined the international community in its call for Iraq to vacate aggression, and allowed refueling in India for U.S. military aircraft transiting to the war zone.

The war itself began with a phase of intense aerial and naval bombardment from January 17 onward with 100 hours of land combat on February 24–28. The Iraqis were routed in short order. President George H. W. Bush declared a ceasefire, leaving Saddam Hussein in power but with severe restrictions on his future military activity. Kuwait and Saudi Arabia paid US$32 billion out of the US$61.1 billion total cost of the war.

The war essentially eliminated Iraq from west Asian geopolitics and led to strengthening Iran's hand, an unintended consequence. Iran's hand became firmer after the American invasion of Iraq in 2003 (the second Persian Gulf War, or the Iraq War) when it was thought the country harbored a nuclear arsenal. President George W. Bush sought also to establish democratic institutions in the country and these accorded the Shia majority real political power, thus giving Iran, by proxy, a major say in Iraqi politics. The chaos that resulted from the second Gulf War in Iraq and the Levant in 2003 in general played into the hands of Iran, which worked to build its influence across Iraq, Syria, and Lebanon and later used the Arab Spring in 2011 to also strengthen its links with the Shia majority in Bahrain and the sizeable Shia populations in Yemen and through the Persian Gulf. Iran has influence in a belt of territory westward from its borders all the way to the Mediterranean. In this Iran is assisted to some extent by the Turkish and Russian governments and by the friendly Assad government in Syria. Much of what we see today in western Asia is a rear-guard action by Saudi Arabia and other regimes against Iran and its influence in Lebanon, Yemen, Iraq, Syria, and the Gulf. While all such contests are unpredictable by nature, it does not seem to be going well for the Saudis, which raises questions about the stability of Saudi Arabia itself.

For India, Iran is a critical partner in west Asia: is a source of oil; shares an approach to Afghanistan where each country has worked closely together; provides access to Central Asia and Afghanistan; and shares a border with Pakistan, India's neighbor. India's Muslim population includes a sizeable proportion of Shia adherents, about 20–25 percent of 180 million Muslims, who have been good citizens and a factor for stability. We therefore have good reason, apart from civilizational and historical links, to stay clear of attempts to isolate and contain Iran, particularly since much of the opposition to Iran is from regimes that support extremists and terrorists in India who claim to be Sunni.

Another consequence of the first Gulf War in 1991 was the radicalization of the young Saudis who carried out the 9/11 attack on the United States in 2001; that attack was triggered by the U.S. troop presence in Saudi Arabia after the war. The American reaction to that event—invasions of Afghanistan and Iraq and the resulting turmoil—has bred one extremist group after another, leading ultimately to the most deadly, the Islamic State. There is a direct line that can be drawn from even the earlier wars in Afghanistan in the 1980s, to those in Iraq and again in Afghanistan, and the civil war in Syria today to the deadly malevolence of Islamic State. The world has reaped the whirlwind, and India has paid a heavy price.

For a while, Washington's preoccupation with radical Islam after 9/11 subordinated other issues such as the growing estrangement between China and the United States and, subsequently, post-communist Russia's course as well. Now that the United States is self-sufficient in oil and is a net exporter its need to stabilize and manage the fractious politics of western Asia is not what it was in 1991. It no longer needs to stabilize and manage the politics of west Asia as it did earlier. As the world stands on the brink of an energy revolution in renewables, west Asia's troubles and conflicts will matter less to the West, but more to Asia. India, China, and Japan's reliance on west Asian oil only grows. The West will therefore attempt to confine west Asia's troubles and their effects to that subregion, rather than underwrite security as it used to. Whether Asian powers like China, India, and Japan will step in to guarantee the free flow of energy remains open.

8

The Globalization Decades

I f the Narasimha Rao government seized the opportunity created by the transitions of the early 1990s to reform the economy and to chart a new foreign
policy, the subsequent governments of Atal Behari Vajpayee and Manmohan
Singh explored the advantages of a globalizing world and of an international
order dominated by a single superpower, the United States, until the global
financial crisis of 2008 changed the situation again.

In these years the American neoliberal project, which advocated market
fundamentalism (as opposed to a Keynesian approach) and unfettered financial
markets, coincided with unrivalled American political and military dominance
in the world. This new approach was very different from the post-World War II
economic order built by the United States. The institutions set up at the Bretton Woods meetings such as the World Bank and International Monetary Fund
and the subsequent General Agreement on Trade and Tariffs sought to implement lessons learned from the Great Depression and World War II. Then, it
was understood that unrestrained market forces could generate economic and
social distress. The first postwar order was primarily informed by economist
David Keynes's ideas, embracing but mediating market forces so that individual
states could pursue domestic political and social agendas of their own as they
saw fit. One economist called the approach the "compromise of embedded liberalism." The critique of Keynes came in the form of new classical macroeco-
nomics and the theory of rational expectations championed by economists such
as Robert Lucas and Thomas Sargent. Their theory of rational expectations
implied "policy ineffectiveness," namely, that there was little that governments
can do to influence the economy at all except inefficiently get in the way. From
the anti-Keynesian perspective financial markets always know best and should
be left to supervise themselves.

The second order, instituted after the Cold War, was anti-Keynesian and constituted a financial liberalization project not just for the United States but for all the world. The dismantling of capital controls led to increasing financial instability, as was evident in the Asian financial crisis of 1997–1998, which planted seeds of doubt in Asian minds and ultimately delegitimized the second U.S. order, as did the success of nonmarket economies such as China.

~

India, like China, had domestic political and social reasons not to buy into post–Cold War liberal and market fundamentalism. Narasimha Rao (prime minister 1991–1996), Atal Behari Vajpayee (1998–2004), and Manmohan Singh (2004–2014)—all prime ministers—knew India and economics too well to feel that neoliberal prescriptions could be applied fully in India. Instead, when Rao spoke at the World Economic Forum at Davos in 1992, he urged a middle way in managing economies that also took into account the demands of equity and social justice, in addition to relying on markets for economic growth. That caution did not prevent the governments of India and China from using the opportunities created by the open world trading and investment system. In some areas, such as the provision of welfare, both went further, applying World Bank advice to move from redistributive social justice to targeted interventions to create social security nets for the vulnerable. India benefitted from access to foreign markets, foreign investment, and some technology. But the greatest beneficiary of the globalization decades was, of course, China, although India was among those who emerged from those decades much improved. Between 1995 and 2013, per capita GDP grew 9 percent per annum in China.[1] India's GDP grew at more than 7 percent per annum in real terms, 1993–1994 to 2011–2012.[2]

India had been a significant part of the world economy throughout history. For most of the last two millennia India had been the world's largest economy.[3] The Mughal empire presided over one-quarter of the world's GDP. By 1947, however, the British empire had reduced India to the point where it produced only 4 percent of world GDP. By 2016 India accounted for 7.32 percent of world GDP (in PPP terms). The opening of the economy also invited new risks and exposure. For instance, nearly half of all freely traded shares on Indian stock markets are now owned by foreigners. India now attracts as much foreign investment as China did at the peak of its growth in the mid-2000s.[4]

From 1991 onward India was increasingly integrated into the globalized world economy of the second financial order, although less into global supply chains than with markets. Between 1995 and 1998 India's exports averaged 13.4 percent growth annually, the third best performance in the world after China and Vietnam. At the same time, globalization could also be seen as having made India more dependent on the external world for its growth. There were several causes:

+ a weak manufacturing base compared to China,

+ the presence in the Indian market of already thriving domestic firms, unlike China where multinationals found a blank slate to write on,

+ social stratification and inequality, and

+ the vestiges of a bureaucratically controlled economy.

If the worst of the license-permit Raj was done away with in 1991, inspector Raj continued. Despite these limitations, these were the best decades of growth in history for the Indian economy, and as a result more people were taken out of poverty than in the fifty years after independence. Well over a 100 million people escaped poverty. Poverty declined in India from 37 percent of the population in 2004–2005 to 22 percent in 2011–2012.[5]

The pattern of this growth built a new, young, aspirational India. It also exaggerated existing inequalities in Indian society. By far the greatest portion of India's wealth flowed to the top 1 percent. That top 1 percent of India's population today, in 2020, owns more than half of national wealth, one of the highest rates in the world.[6] The rise of the super-rich is tied to the phenomenon of crony capitalism and corruption in India, as in the rest of the world, and to cycles of financial boom and bust. In the Indian context, where infrastructure and other investment is largely private, banks were left holding bad assets of at least US$150 billion in 2017. Inequality in India today makes it more like Latin American societies than east Asian societies (other than China), which stayed broadly egalitarian by building basic social nets and providing education and health care to all citizens.

It was clear across the Indian political spectrum that the economic transformation of India required at least a working relationship with the global hegemon, the United States, whose order prevailed globally. In reality there was much more to India-U.S. relations than temporary convenience. A growing strategic convergence, the opening of the Indian economy, and a shift to the right of the center of gravity of Indian politics enabled a dramatic improvement in India-U.S. relations. Declining U.S. interest in Pakistan after the Soviet withdrawal in 1989 and the end of the Afghan war, common concerns about the effects of a rising China, a congruence of nonproliferation interests once India declared and the United States was ready to accept in practice that India was a nuclear weapon state, and economic complementarity made for a considerable and growing congruence of interest. India-U.S. relations also benefited from the growing and powerful cohort of Indian Americans, particularly those in and around Silicon Valley, who were involved in the American digital revolution. As India opened its economy to the world, it signed free trade agreements and comprehensive economic cooperation agreements with the Association of Southeast Asian Nations, Japan, and Korea. Its relations with Japan, always good, now became closer, and India's Look East policy saw India's increasing involvement with U.S. allies in the region.

There were limits to India-U.S. convergence, however. When the United States invaded Iraq in 2003 and sought assistance from allies and friends, a considerably body of opinion in India, including Deputy Prime Minister L. K. Advani, External Affairs Minister Jaswant Singh, and others argued for India to send troops to Iraq. In 2003 I chanced to witness Prime Minister Vajpayee, all alone, prevent this in a cabinet committee on security meeting where every single ministerial speaker had previously supported the move. Vajpayee's logic was simple: how would he explain the death of an Indian soldier to that soldier's parents and the people. His caution reflected more an attitude to the use of force than to relations with the United States of which Vajpayee was a strong advocate, describing India and the United States as "natural allies" in his address to a joint session of the U.S. Congress.

Both India and the United States had given the other cause for offense during the Cold War. For India, the U.S. military alliance with Pakistan after 1954 and cooperation with China in Asia through the 1980s had resulted in the two countries' being on opposite sides of the big Asian issues such as Afghanistan and Kampuchea. For the United States, India's close ties with the Soviet Union, willingness to work with China in the 1950s, and organizing the nonaligned in opposition to U.S. purposes were inexplicable and often deeply hurtful. The post–Cold War world, however, gave both sides an opportunity to begin afresh. Common ground began to emerge on fighting terrorism and extremism, the rise of China, on stabilizing west Asia, on maritime security in the Indian Ocean and eastward, and in economic cooperation, once India's economy opened up to the world.

That growing convergence made the transformation of India-U.S. relations a bipartisan political effort in both countries. In the United States, Republicans and Democrats cooperated on India-related issues in Congress, despite an increasingly polarized domestic milieu. In India the Indian National Congress and the Bharatiya Janata Party (BJP), the two major national parties, pursued the transformation while in office, although in 2007 the BJP, then in opposition, chose to decry the India-U.S. civil nuclear cooperation agreement in parliament when it was finalized, even though it only carried forward lines of policy that had begun with the party's previous Vajpayee government. Once in power after 2014, the BJP became strong advocates of the agreement.

By 2008 mutual inhibitions, previous false starts, and a difficult past could no longer prevent India and the United States from consulting and cooperating in the region, while working together on sensitive issues such as intelligence, counterterrorism, and defense. The civil nuclear cooperation agreement signed in 2008 and the Nuclear Supplier Group exemption that it made possible were the most visible symbols of the two sides' success in overcoming the past and remaking the relationship.[7] The fact that the U.S. Federal Bureau of Investigation was on the ground in Mumbai within days of the terrorist attack originating in Pakistan in November 2008, and that it occasioned no public comment or pushback, was practical demonstration of the new stage the relationship had reached. And the fact that real estate developments outside Delhi were being named Palm Beach and Orange County showed how U.S. images resonated with a newly aspirational and young population produced by a reforming India.

~

The post–Cold War world was one of new opportunity and India used globalization well. But it also posed new dangers. It could be plausibly argued that the end of the Cold War reduced the sole superpower's interest or commitment to stability maintenance everywhere and in all cases around the world. A local conflagration such as those in Kosovo or Bosnia in the 1990s would have been inconceivable between 1950 and 1989 for it would have risked a superpower confrontation that could easily have turned nuclear and would therefore have been stamped out much earlier. In a unipolar world, the elimination of that risk meant that the sole superpower did not feel compelled to prevent or get involved in every conflict or civil war or source of instability unless it directly threatened its security or the continuance of its unipolar order.

This was also evident in the nuclear domain, where the Nuclear Non-Proliferation Treaty (NPT) was made permanent in 1995, using legal means rather than relying on direct political intervention by the superpowers, as in the Cold War, to maintain their monopoly of nuclear weapons. During the war against the Soviets in Afghanistan and soon thereafter, Pakistan exploited the opportunity created by U.S. distractions with the fall of the Soviet Union, the reunification of Germany, and the reordering of Europe to speed up its nuclear weapons program. Primary support for Pakistan's nuclear weapons program came from China, with possibly some Saudi financing, and its proliferation activities occurred with the knowledge and connivance of other powers. Through the 1980s the United States and other powers who were in a position to stop it turned a blind eye to Pakistan's pursuit of nuclear weapons so long as she was useful in the war against the Soviets in Afghanistan.[8] Under U.S. law, the United States could not provide aid or arms to non-weapon states seeking to acquire nuclear weapons. Pakistan was exempted in 1981, and when that expired in 1987 Pakistan argued that stopping U.S. arms flows to Pakistan and the mujahideen in Afghanistan would weaken the U.S. bargaining position in Geneva, harden the Soviet position, and forestall success in forcing a negotiated Soviet withdrawal. In December 1987 the U.S. Congress waived restrictions on aid to Pakistan, on the grounds that India was producing nuclear weapons. Effectively, aid and technology to India were restricted, while Pakistan was exempted due to its value to the United States. India was naturally outraged.

Through the 1980s and early 1990s, China continued testing in anticipation of the Comprehensive Nuclear Test-Ban Treaty (CTBT) in the 1990s; and the treaty itself was written in convoluted ways to force India into the straightjacket of becoming a non-nuclear weapon state. The CTBT was drafted unlike any other legal instrument so as to enter into force only if India were to sign it as a non-nuclear weapon state and to accept that it would never test again. Since the nuclear weapon states had already conducted over 2,000 tests, a ban on future testing would effectively prevent others from continuing to develop their nuclear weapon programs while minimally affecting the nuclear weapons states. India naturally rejected the treaty in this discriminatory form.

India had been threatened with nuclear weapons in the past and had complex relations with four of the five nuclear weapon states recognized by the NPT. For India to be without nuclear weapons when both its neighbors, China and Pakistan, had them would have been politically intolerable for any Indian government, no matter how Gandhian.

India had shown nuclear restraint after demonstrating the capability to produce a nuclear weapon in 1974. Despite the Chinese test of October 1964, India's situation on the northern borders ameliorated somewhat in the late 1960s with the development of indigenous military capability, the Sino-Soviet split, and China's domestic chaos in the Great Proletarian Cultural Revolution, with the People's Liberation Army fully committed to internal duties and defense against the Soviet Union. That changed fundamentally after the tacit China-U.S. strategic alliance established under the Nixon administration in 1972, and with Pakistan's determined pursuit of nuclear weapons after the loss of Bangladesh in 1971. Hence the 1974 demonstration of nuclear capability. Throughout the 1970s and 1980s India advocated general and complete nuclear disarmament, as Rajiv Gandhi did most forcefully and comprehensively in the Second UN General Assembly Special Session on Disarmament in 1988 when he called for a world free of nuclear weapons and suggested a pathway to it. But India was also determined to maintain the nuclear option legally and, despite pressure, refused to either sign the NPT or to accept full-scope safeguards on all its nuclear facilities.

Subsequent developments in India's neighborhood and the post–Cold War tightening of the global nuclear order in the name of nonproliferation meant that India had to stay abreast of nuclear weapons technology and delivery systems. When Rajiv Gandhi saw the tepid reaction to his proposals for a nuclear weapon free world, he authorized further work on nuclear weapons and their delivery systems, work that was carried to its logical conclusion by Prime Minister Rao, making it possible for the Vajpayee government to carry out nuclear weapons tests in May 1998 soon after coming to power.

Vajpayee had long advocated that India should have the bomb. Indeed, India's is probably the most democratically discussed nuclear weapons program in the world. The possibility of an Indian nuclear weapon had been debated repeatedly since the 1950s in Parliament, the press, in public, and within government. By the late 1990s it was clear that India's nuclear restraint entailed rising costs and left the nation unable to respond to the rapidly accelerating nuclear weapon program in Pakistan, aided by China, or to the international nuclear order that imposed technological and other sanctions on India. The 1998 tests not only ended ambiguity but also signaled India's intent to deal with global politics in the language of power.[9] The transition to nuclear certainty coincided with India's rise as a political, economic, and military power. In 2008, within ten years of the 1998 tests, the Nuclear Supplier Group's India-specific exemption made India the only non-NPT state with a nuclear weapon program able to undertake civil nuclear cooperation with other willing NSG states.

The 1998 decision by India to declare itself a nuclear weapon state after public tests can be seen as a direct consequence of these geopolitical shifts and the international stakes that India had developed in the 1990s as a result of reform. Those same stakes created by reform also ensured that, unlike the long-lasting sanctions that followed the 1974 explosion, normalcy was restored to most of India's relationships within about two years of the 1998 tests, thanks to initiatives by countries like France and Russia, by former Prime Minister Mori of Japan, and the United States. It was soon largely business as usual for India on the international front, with the additional benefit that the combination of India's remarkable economic performance and the will to power displayed in the bomb tests seemed to have enhanced India's reputation.

Resolving the nuclear issue, which had divided India and the United States since 1974, now became the enabler of their relationship. The 1998 Indian nuclear weapons tests triggered the accelerated transformation of India-U.S. relations that had begun under Prime Minister Vajpayee and seen through by the Manmohan Singh government. The initial Clinton administration's reaction to the surprise of the tests was coordinated with China and included furious condemnation and the imposition of sanctions.[10] Reportedly, the Central Intelligence Agency's first reaction to learning of the tests from the State Department was that only hearing of it from CNN, the news outlet, would have been worse.[11] The tests signaled how seriously India took its own security and that India was willing to go it alone. Since sanctions were clearly insufficient to roll back India's strategic program, the United States began a high-level dialogue on nuclear and security issues with India. This dialogue, between Deputy Secretary of State Strobe Talbott and Vice Chairman of the Planning Commission Jaswant Singh took place over two and a half years in fourteen meetings at ten locations in seven countries on three continents.[12] The dialogue did not find an immediate solution to the nuclear issue, where the United States sought to defend the international nuclear order based on the NPT and to roll back the Indian program, while India sought security, sovereignty, equality, and acceptance of its nuclear weapon program. But the dialogue did establish that these were not entirely incompatible goals and thus made possible the basic understandings that transformed the India-U.S. relationship over the next decade, culminating in the India-U.S. Civil Nuclear Cooperation agreement and the unique NSG exemption in 2008 permitting countries to cooperate with India as though it were a nuclear weapon state in terms of the NPT.

~

The nuclear weapon tests also had consequences for India's relationship with its most vociferous critic, China.

Both the Vajpayee and Manmohan Singh governments had continued Narasimha Rao's live-and-let-live policy toward China, implementing the modus vivendi formalized in the 1988 Rajiv Gandhi visit of discussing the boundary question, not allowing it to impede the development of bilateral relations, and cooperating on the international stage where possible. Peace was generally kept on the border and the status quo was respected in practice, even though there were areas that both sides considered to be on their side of the Line of Actual Control. Routines and standard operating procedures were worked out with the Chinese to prevent face-offs or other encounters from escalating, while capabilities, presence, and infrastructure on the border were steadily built up by both sides. While the balance on the border was still largely in China's favor, India began to catch up. Each side was in a position to embarrass the other. Deterrence and unwillingness to be embroiled in conflict combined to keep the peace.

For its part, until 2006 or so China continued the public neutrality on India-Pakistan issues that President Jiang Zemin had signaled in December 1996 when speaking to the Pakistan National Assembly. In private, China still built Pakistan's military and strategic capabilities, ensuring that Pakistan remained only one step behind India at every stage of the Indian nuclear weapons and missile programs.

The India-China bilateral relationship developed through the 1990s and early 2000s, and trade grew steadily until China became India's largest trading partner in goods, as did India's trade deficit in China's favor. China has significant market share in important Indian markets such as smartphones, power generation equipment, telecom and ICT equipment, steel, and toys. The trade imbalance has grown to the point where it accounts for over 40 percent of India's overall deficit on the trade account, and the deficit is so far not offset by investments or trade in services or Chinese manufacturing in India. This is a serious issue in public discourse in India on the relationship with China.

When Prime Minister Vajpayee visited China in 2003, discussions on the boundary were raised to the level of special representatives appointed by the leaders to take a political and strategic view of the issue and find a solution. The first fruit of their work was the agreement on Guiding Principles and Political Parameters for a Boundary Settlement signed during Premier Wen Jiabao's April 2005 visit to India, three months before the civil nuclear initiative with the United States was announced in Washington. The Guiding Principles were the culmination of the first stage of a work plan that the special representatives had set themselves, namely, to agree to the principles for a boundary settlement, then a more detailed framework for a settlement, and finally to apply the guidelines and framework to produce a boundary line. Subsequently, as talks proceeded it became clear that Chinese demands had grown considerably from those indicated by earlier Chinese leaders such as Zhou Enlai and Deng Xiaoping. The special representatives still made progress toward a framework for a settlement. Over time the channel evolved into an authoritative way for the leaders of India and China to communicate and to review the strategic situation in which the two countries find themselves, thus stabilizing the relationship and successfully managing problems that arose.

~

India was relatively quick to see the rise of China as its greatest strategic challenge and to reorient policy from the early 1990s onward. As a consequence, Prime Ministers Rao, Vajpayee, and Singh were determined to moderate or manage the relationship with Pakistan so as to deny China that lever, to free India from worry about a two-front conflict, and to leave India free to concentrate on what really mattered.

After several false starts, that approach bore fruit between 2003 and 2007. The years from end-2003, when a ceasefire was agreed and respected in practice, to November 2008, when the Mumbai attack took place, saw a decline in cross-border terrorism, the opening up of trade and travel and other links between the two countries, and a back channel dialogue that came close to finding an interim solution to the Kashmir issue. Why it did so then, and the advantages it brought India are relevant today as government struggles to find an effective way to manage the Pakistan Army's institutional hostility, born of its interest in a managed level of hostility with India to guarantee the army's stranglehold on Pakistani politics, the government budget, and the popular Pakistani imagination as guardians of Pakistan.

The period of relative calm was preceded by serial Indian attempts to make peace with Pakistan's civilian leaders. The end of the war against the Soviets in Afghanistan, Chinese neutrality in public, and U.S. disinterest in Pakistan until the 9/11 attacks in 2001 combined with the Pakistan Army's preoccupation with bringing its extremist and terrorist friends in the Taliban to power in Afghanistan had left Pakistan isolated in the 1990s. By the late 1990s, elements in Pakistan, such as Pakistani business and civilian politicians, realized that the way out of Pakistan's isolation was to be seen to be improving relations with India. As its lack of indigenous roots caused the Pakistani-sponsored jihad in Jammu and Kashmir to falter, the civilian government in Pakistan became increasingly receptive to overtures from the Vajpayee government. In a dramatic gesture Prime Minister Vajpayee crossed the border and traveled to Lahore in a bus in 1998, restoring the bus service between the two neighbors. In Lahore he agreed to a set of measures with his civilian counterpart, Prime Minister Nawaz Sharif of Pakistan, which were reflected in a Lahore Declaration. The declaration provided for a composite dialogue on all significant aspects of the relationship. The two leaders also agreed on a discussion on nuclear issues between the two countries that had recently tested nuclear weapons.

The visit and agreements with the civilian prime minister of Pakistan were followed almost immediately by the Pakistan Army's surreptitious attempt to take the heights near Kargil, plotted by Pakistan Chief of Army Staff General Pervez Musharraf. The Pakistan Army covertly launched troops and irregulars to occupy heights on the Indian side of the Line of Control. A brief but sharp war followed when they were discovered in spring 1999, which drove home India's conventional capability to clear its territory. Equally important, Pakistan's traditional friends like China, the United States, and Iran all urged Pakistan to withdraw and stressed the sanctity of the Line of Control. Pakistan's plan to occupy more Indian territory, to spark an uprising in Jammu and Kashmir, and then to seek international intervention on its side had backfired in every respect. Pakistan's gambit had only strengthened the international legitimacy of the Line of Control that it was trying to demolish.

Kargil made it clear that the Pakistan Army's opposition to an improvement in India-Pakistan relations was deep seated and chronic enough to lead to folly. That conclusion was underlined when, in December 1999, an Indian Airlines flight, IC-814, from Kathmandu was hijacked. The hijackers demanded and obtained the release of Masood Azhar and other Pakistani terrorists from Indian jails as the price for releasing the passengers and aircraft, which they had taken to Kandahar in Taliban-controlled Afghanistan. Immediately thereafter the hijackers and released terrorists obtained sanctuary in Pakistan. One of the released terrorists, Masood Azhar, the head of the Jaish-e-Mohammad terrorist group, was even promoted by the Pakistan Army as a mainstream civilian politician in the Pakistani Punjab in the 2018 elections. The hijacking to Kandahar was followed by a series of escalating Pakistan-sponsored or -controlled terrorist attacks on India, in Jammu and Kashmir and on the families of Indian servicemen.

When Musharraf's Kargil plans came undone, he blamed the civilian leadership and engineered a military coup, seizing power himself in October 1999. The Vajpayee government tried to come to terms with General Musharraf, who styled himself the CEO of Pakistan, inviting him to a summit at Agra on July 14–16, 2001, but it became clear from Musharraf's demands and public statements that he was still not yet ready for an improvement in India-Pakistan relations. He would not offer more than vague verbal assurances of peace and would not commit to stopping crossborder terrorism but sought binding Indian commitments on Kashmir. The summit's only real product was Musharraf's assumption of the presidency of Pakistan, using the legitimacy that the Indian invitation to Agra had given him.

Relations deteriorated even further when the Indian parliament was attacked by Pakistan-supported terrorists on December 13, 2001. Musharraf's use of terrorism against India continued. In response, India recalled its representative in Pakistan and mobilized troops on the border, attempting coercive diplomacy. Unlike the Agra summit, the attack on Parliament took place in the post-9/11 world. Musharraf and Pakistan had been posed a stark choice by the United States of continuing to be seen as a sponsor of terrorism with all its consequences, or of supporting the U.S.-led war on terror. Like Zia before him, Musharraf chose a dual policy of publicly working with the United States and doing just enough to avoid sanctions and obtain U.S. aid, while privately giving the Taliban, Al Qaeda, and even Osama bin Laden sanctuary, support, and intelligence in Pakistan. By doing so he hoped to be left alone to continue his jihad against India in Kashmir and elsewhere, just as Zia had cooperated with the Americans in fighting the Soviets in Afghanistan and obtained tacit U.S. acceptance of Pakistan's pursuit of the bomb and jihad in Punjab and Kashmir in the 1980s.

In April 2003 Prime Minister Vajpayee reached out again in a speech in Srinagar promising the Kashmiri people governance based on *insaniyat*, or humanity, and extending a hand of friendship to Pakistan, expressing a willingness to discuss all issues between the two countries and restoring ambassador-level relations, broken after the attack on Parliament. Pakistan and Musharraf responded positively with statements about stopping terrorism and other gestures.

What had changed between the July 2001 Agra summit and April 2003 to evoke a positive Pakistani response? Three things can be surmised to have weighed in Musharraf's decision. For one, the international situation was very different after 9/11 after the United States declared a global war on terror. The United States did not want Pakistan distracted by its eastern borders because the Americans needed Pakistan's help in the west in Afghanistan and the tribal areas.

Nor was China as supportive as in the 1980s. Musharraf sought China's help in December 2001 in the wake of the attack on the Indian Parliament and

Indian troop buildup along the shared border. He wanted China to express support for Pakistan's territorial integrity, raise the issue in the UN Security Council, and postpone Premier Zhu Rongji's January 2002 visit to India. China replied that there was no interest among UN Security Council members in discussing the issue in council, that the defense of Pakistan was the responsibility of the Pakistani government for which China would supply weapons, and that the visit to India was long planned and would go ahead. In effect, China offered Pakistan military supplies and little else. However, when U.S. officials pressed Chinese counterparts to lean on Pakistan to concentrate on the threat from the west and accept that there was no threat from the east, China disagreed and argued that Pakistan's Army had to maintain vigilance against the Indian threat from the east.

Second, Musharraf knew that the insurgency in Jammu and Kashmir was winding down. His Kargil misadventure had also made it clear that Pakistan's conventional military options against India were limited. Last, Musharraf's internal position was not as strong as he liked to claim. He faced two assassination attempts in December 2003 from Jaish-e-Mohammad followers in the Pakistan Air Force—India had warned him about these beforehand. In other words, it took Pakistan's difficult situation after the 9/11 attacks, its economic meltdown, its isolation after the military coup by Musharraf in October 1999, and U.S. pressure to force Pakistan to concentrate on helping U.S. forces in Afghanistan. The same Pakistan Army had to come to a tactical accommodation after 2003 with first the Vajpayee and then the Manmohan Singh governments.

In November 2003 Pakistan responded positively to an Indian proposal for a ceasefire. Not only did the Pakistan Army respect the ceasefire, but it also extended it to Siachen. By January 2004 the situation had improved to the point where Prime Minister Vajpayee could attend the South Asian Association for Regional Cooperation summit in Islamabad when General Musharraf promised in a joint press statement not to permit terrorism in any manner against India. Both sides agreed to resume the composite dialogue, thus getting back on the track for improving relations agreed in 1999 at Lahore. That SAARC summit also agreed and signed the South Asia Free Trade Agreement.

The next three years saw a drop in the number of infiltration attempts by terrorists across the line from Pakistan, a decrease in terrorist incidents in Jammu and Kashmir, and an enduring ceasefire. India-Pakistan contacts, travel, and trade boomed as the governments made them easier. India played a cricket series in Pakistan after eighteen years. Considerable progress was made in back-channel negotiations between S. K. Lambah and Tariq Aziz on behalf of Prime Minister Manmohan Singh and General Musharraf on finding a way to permit trade and travel across the Line of Control and to grant some relief to Kashmiris on both sides of the line, thus moving toward a solution of practical issues in Kashmir without changing borders.[13] Within Jammu and Kashmir, normal political processes and elected governments restored calm to the valley on the Indian side.

By early 2007, however, it was becoming clear that this peace process would not survive the stresses of Pakistan's internal politics and the regular recourse to terrorism in India by the Pakistan Army and its intelligence service (ISI). In any case, Musharraf's hold over his own country and institutions was steadily weakening, eroding his ability and willingness to follow through on his commitments to Vajpayee and Singh. Internal opposition to Musharraf was high, galvanized by his attempt to sack the chief justice. In January 2007, General Musharraf told India's External Affairs Minister Pranab Mukherji that he could not handle several fronts simultaneously and that he would return to finding a Jammu and Kashmir solution once he had sorted out his internal enemies. He never managed to do either. Under American and British pressure, Musharraf came to an understanding with former Pakistani Prime Minister Benazir Bhutto to let her return from exile and promised a free election in return for guarantees of immunity for his actions. But on December 27, 2007, Benazir Bhutto was assassinated while campaigning in Rawalpindi. Musharraf's government, the Pakistani Taliban, and others were among the list of suspects in what remains an unsolved murder despite a UN attempt to investigate the death. Musharraf's position weakened dramatically thereafter and by November 2008 he tendered his resignation to avoid impeachment and went into exile in London.

The attacks on suburban trains in Mumbai on July 11, 2006, made it clear that Pakistan-based terrorists and their handlers were determined to derail the peace process by escalating terrorist attacks in India and that they had support within the Pakistan establishment. In July 2008 Pakistan opened a new front when the Pakistan-sponsored and -based Haqqani group organized the suicide bombing of the Indian Embassy in Kabul killing Indian officials and Afghan visa seekers and passersby. This took the war to another level and another country. By the time of the commando-style terrorist attack on Mumbai on November 26, 2008, carried live on television screens across the world for three days, public opinion in India had naturally turned decisively against Pakistan and a peace process with such a regime. The brutal, spectacular, and horrific nature of the Mumbai attack was compounded by the irrefutable evidence of Pakistan Army and ISI collusion with Lahkar-e-Toiba terrorists. The attack would have been inconceivable without the approval or connivance of the Chief of Army Staff-cum-President, Musharraf. And these preparations had been carried out while peace and normalization initiatives were under way in 2003–2007. The attack made it clearer than ever that the peace process had always been tactical from the Pakistan Army's point of view. By the end of 2008 it was evident that neither Pakistan's internal structures nor Indian public opinion would support an engagement that went beyond the pro forma, the tactical, and the theatre of politics to address fundamental issues in India-Pakistan relations. And that is what we have witnessed in India-Pakistan relations ever since.

From an Indian point of view, the management of our relations with Pakistan in this period helped us to concentrate on our other priorities and to transform India. Pakistan was not allowed to impede our truly consequential relationships with our neighbors, the United States and China. The Vajpayee and Singh approach of engaging Pakistan in dialogue and contacts while building capabilities to counter Pakistani adventurism and asymmetric warfare against India, and working directly with Pakistan's main supporters—China, the United States, and Saudi Arabia—was successful both in its effects within Pakistan, and in isolating the Pakistan problem from the rest of India's foreign and security relations. The policy left India free to pursue much more important goals, which it did.

∼

The other significant feature of Indian policy during the globalization years was the attempt, begun under Vajpayee and accelerated by the Manmohan Singh government, to restore the subcontinent's economic integrity. To this end, they used both bilateral and multilateral means. The free trade agreement with Sri Lanka, negotiated during the Gujral and Vajpayee governments, was the first such arrangement entered into by India since the 1970s and after the 1991 reforms. Signed in December 1998, it did not insist on reciprocity or bilateral exclusivity and enabled trade between the two countries to grow phenomenally. Once the agreement came into effect, Sri Lankan exports to India grew in each year between 2001 and 2006 by 50 percent, 35 percent, 114 percent, 94 percent, and 53 percent. The total volume of trade also grew and the Sri Lankan trade deficit with India shrank.

Multilaterally, India made it possible for the SAARC Summit in Islamabad in January 2004 to agree on the South Asia Free Trade Agreement. Even though Pakistan has since chosen not to implement the agreement in respect of India, it has served its purpose by increasing trade and integrating India with the other subcontinental economies. The Manmohan Singh government effectively reduced duties to zero on all but a few sensitive items, such as liquor and beef, if they came from within the subcontinent, except from Pakistan, which chose to cut itself off from the Indian economy and pin its hopes on the Chinese economy instead.

More significant in the long term were attempts during this period to promote cooperation in previously difficult areas like water resources and flood management, to link the power grids of India, Nepal, and Bangladesh, to sort out long-pending border issues such as the enclaves on the India-Bangladesh border, and to create habits of cooperation in counterterrorism and other sensitive subjects. These were successful in changing the nature of India-Bangladesh relations over a period of years. Where relations were already exemplary, as in the case of Bhutan, they deepened the levels of cooperation considerably. The King of Bhutan himself led operations by the Royal Bhutanese army against Indian insurgents who had found hideouts in southern Bhutan. With Myanmar as well, cooperation against Indian insurgent groups began to bear fruit, forcing insurgent and secessionist groups like Muivah's National Socialist Council of Nagaland (NSCN-IM) to come to the table and seriously negotiate with the government of India.

Nepal is a good measure of the change in the climate of relations in the subcontinent brought about by several years of effort beginning with Inder K. Gujral's tenures as foreign minister and then prime minister and carried on by the Vajpayee and Manmohan Singh governments. The Nepalese polity was faced with a civil war with the Maoists and a strong democracy movement against the Nepalese king. In 2005 all the Nepalese parties chose to turn to India as an honest broker to help them work out an agreement charting a way forward and mainstreaming the Maoists. That was a far cry from the strained state of India-Nepal relations today.

This was also the period when India began to play a much more active role in Indian Ocean security. When the Indian Ocean tsunami struck in December 2004, the Indian Navy was among the first to respond in Indonesia, Sri Lanka, and elsewhere. With real capacity to help, India cooperated actively with the U.S., Japanese, and Australian navies in the Indian Ocean Tsunami Core Group. By May 2007 India was engaged in the first Quad Dialogue with these countries, all powers with an interest in keeping the Indian Ocean free, open, and secure. The 2007 Malabar exercises in the Indian Ocean involved over twenty-five naval vessels and 20,000 personnel from the navies of India, United States, Japan, Australia, and Singapore. India also began to institutionalize cooperation in maritime security with Sri Lanka and the Maldives, building up from maritime domain awareness to joint operations and cooperation. This cooperation has since grown to include Seychelles and Mauritius, the Bay of Bengal, and initiatives in the Indian Ocean region as a whole.

The amelioration of relations within the subcontinent and in the broader periphery during this period coincided with a resumption of growth in the subcontinent that made Bangladesh one of the fastest growing economies in the world along with India, pulling along the subcontinent's economies. The end of the civil wars in Nepal and Sri Lanka, and Myanmar's moves toward democracy and an accommodation with most of its ethnic insurgencies and groups, helped to improve the political climate in the subcontinent. It was thus a period of progress and hope in the subcontinent, as it was in many parts of the world.

~

India's periphery changed in another important respect during this period. The collapse of the Soviet Union and its shrinking into Russia had brought central Asia back into geopolitical play. India was unable to participate meaningfully— still physically cut off from central Asia by Pakistan and the aftermath of the de facto division of Jammu and Kashmir. China, on the other hand, was quick to seize the opportunity to "go west," as Jiang Zemin said, working the open spaces in the west to compensate for U.S. containment in the east, investing in Xinjiang and building links with the five new "stans" of the former Soviet Union—Tajikistan, Kyrgyzstan, Uzbekistan, Kazakhstan, and Turkmenistan. Given the close and continuing links between the "stans" and Russia, in the persons and ideology of their rulers and economically, China worked with Russia, set up the Shanghai Cooperation Organization, initially as a group to settle post-Soviet boundaries with China, and then build security, a priority of China's authoritarian leaders, and to boost economic links between the "stans" and China.

Russia-China relations strengthened steadily. Russia was more comfortable with a Chinese presence than with the United States or the West in the sensitive Russian "near abroad," where China shared Russia's interest in fighting terrorism, extremism, and Muslim fundamentalism. As U.S. and Western pressure mounted on Russia, promoting "color revolutions" and bringing NATO and the EU to Russia's doorstep, despite promises made to Gorbachev, Russia was steadily driven into a tighter Chinese embrace. The result was a consolidation of the Eurasian heartland under joint Russian and Chinese auspices in the decade since 2010. Today the United States and the West are absent in the continental heartland, apart from the stalemated war in Afghanistan from which the United States has pledged to withdraw. Though the Russia-China partnership may appear opportunistic and shaky, it is real and will remain so as long as the United States and the West follow shortsighted policies of opposing Russian interests in its periphery and denigrating its status as a world power.

~

The globalization years or the unipolar moment were marked by U.S. dominance of Asia's maritime periphery but not of the heartland. The political tone and course of global politics in the new century were set by the American reaction to the September 11, 2001, attacks on three targets in the United States by Al Qaeda mounted from that heartland. In response the United States chose to declare a global war on terror and turned to the military instrument to achieve its ends in Afghanistan and Iraq.

The Indian government under Vajpayee reacted immediately and positively to the 9/11 attack, making unconditional offers to the United States of logistical support, overflight clearance, and staging of combat assets including aircraft, quite apart from political expressions of solidarity and support.[14] There was hope in India that the United States would now better understand terrorism and Pakistan's role in furthering it. These hopes were only partially fulfilled in respect of Pakistan, but India-U.S. counterterrorism cooperation and intelligence sharing improved immeasurably after 9/11.

Addressing Congress on September 20, 2001, President Bush said: "Either you are with us or you are with the terrorists." This was a far cry from the cautious deterrence-based approach to action of the Cold War. It was a call to a universal mission with no limits in space or time. For a while it determined U.S. policies and alliances even though it had not been adopted as Western policy. Bush pushed for democracy in the Middle East, thus moving away from the realpolitik practiced by Kissinger and advocated by others at this time.[15] The neoconservative assumption was that changes in the values of a society as well as in its domestic politics would alter the country's international posture and actions. The claim was that democracies do not wage war on democracies. Thus, promoting democracy was seen as promoting stability and preventing wars.

The 9/11 attack made Samuel Huntington's analysis of the clash of civilizations appear prescient. It had been overshadowed by Clintonian liberalism and triumphant globalization when it first appeared in 1993. For many American neoconservatives Huntington seemed to have outlined the new ideological confrontation of the 2000s as well as the assertive U.S. policies required after

9/11. Huntington had also faced some justified pushback, which was forgotten as emotions ran high after the attack. Edward Said wrote an article called "The Clash of Ignorance," pointing out that Huntington was oversimplifying and treating Islam as monolithic.[16] Indeed, the scale of violence in Iraq after the U.S. invasion would demonstrate the depths of animosity within Islam—in every half-century of Islamic history, more Muslims have been killed by other Muslims than by non-Muslims.[17] Naturally, the clash of civilizations was also pushed vigorously by Osama bin Laden.

The September 11, 2001, attacks, or, to be precise, the U.S. reaction to them bought China and India a decade to build factories, economic alliances, and, in China's case, to stake out and enforce its claims in the South China Sea. China got a free pass to label Uighur separatists in Xinjiang as terrorists, and it tried, with less success, to also label Tibetan agitators for autonomy and freedom as terrorists. After 9/11 the United States chose to push for democracy in the Middle East rather than in China, both probably equally hopeless tasks. In effect, the war on terror masked the issue of China's rise for the United States but not for India. The United States neglected the Asia-Pacific balance as first Iraq and Afghanistan, and then Libya, Syria, and the Ukraine, preoccupied its attention. The Americans went into Iraq for poorly thought out reasons and came out with nothing good and are still engaged in the longest war in American history in Afghanistan. West Asia was reduced to a series of dysfunctional polities, civil wars, and terrorist threats. In the meantime, the Asia-Pacific, particularly India and China, concentrated on their economies.

The world economy, however, changed direction once again in 2008. The world economic crisis can be said to mark the end of not just the "globalization project," as originally conceived, but of the political order that went with it.

Excessive risk taking by American banks led to a crisis in U.S. subprime mortgages beginning in 2007, resulting in a global financial meltdown in 2008, and the worst global recession since the 1930s. On September 15, 2008, Lehman Brothers went bankrupt, prompting the largest-ever bailout of banks by the U.S. government. The follow-on effects of this banking crisis included a European debt crisis, a crisis in the eurozone, and a crash in commodity prices affecting the entire world. Pretty soon the world was in full-fledged economic crisis and deep recession. Raghuram Rajan had predicted the crisis in 2005 when chief economist at the International Monetary Fund, but there are still fundamental differences in the explanations economists offer for why the crisis occurred, ranging from a structural crisis of capitalism to regulatory laxness and cyclical factors.

Whatever the causes, the world reacted to the crisis with bank and other bailouts for stressed financial institutions, along with unprecedented pump priming and fiscal and monetary policies injecting liquidity into national economies. These, however, did not prevent a global recession in 2008–2012, with global trade and output shrinking, and debt and liquidity crises thereafter, and stagnation in industrialized economies other than the United States. The Bank for International Settlements and central banks adopted Basel-2 standards for capital and liquidity of banks internationally to prevent a recurrence of the subprime crisis and its knock-on financial effects, but many economists believe that the larger economic risks revealed by the crisis of 2007–2008 have yet to be addressed, and other steps put into place to prevent another such crisis have recently been dismantled.

The financial crisis of 2007–2008 was an important inflection point in world politics. It brought an end to what Cornell University economist Kirshner calls the "second U.S. postwar order," the period of American hegemony after the Cold War marked by domestic and international financial deregulation. Every financial, monetary, and economic regime rests on a particular political order. During the globalization decades it was the U.S.-run world political order that sustained the so-called liberal economic order where money and goods were free to roam the earth but not people and intellectual property. In its political effect the crisis accelerated two international political trends: the erosion of U.S. power and influence, and the increasing economic influence of other states, particularly China. It also brought in "a new heterogeneity of thinking" on how best to manage domestic and international economies.[18]

One political fallout of the crisis was the first leaders' summit in 2009 of the BRIC countries, namely Brazil, Russia, India, and China, followed by its formalization into an institution and the addition of South Africa in 2010. Conceived as a non-Western rather than an anti-Western grouping that had previously met desultorily at the official level, both India and China initially saw it as primarily an economic forum of emerging countries. As beneficiaries of the existing order, it was hardly likely that India and China would see the BRIC forum as an anti-Western grouping. For Russia first and later China, however, the forum was seen as politically useful as their relations with the West worsened. They attempted, over Indian and Brazilian objections, to introduce anti-Western and political elements into the BRIC forum. China invited South Africa to join in 2010, thus making it a four-continent grouping that has since gained a political profile and role in the much more fluid situation that exists since the 2008 crisis.

The 2008 shock hit both India and China significantly. Both had insulated their financial sectors and limited convertibility on the capital account. The direct financial impact on them was therefore not great. But the collapse of Western markets and demand wreaked havoc on their trade. China was particularly hard hit as it was more integrated into global supply chains. China's exports declined by one-third in a few months and the government estimated that 20 million workers lost their jobs.[19]

In their immediate response to the crisis China and India chose to match the United States by stimulating their economies with major injections of liquidity and thereby avoided a recession as technically defined. But this laid in store future trouble for themselves, creating real estate and stock market bubbles and nonperforming assets with their banks that still had to be fully deflated ten years on. Both countries were fortunate that commodity and oil prices that had boomed before 2008, crashed thereafter. For instance, the price of oil nearly tripled from $50 to $147 from early 2007 to 2008, before plunging as the financial crisis began to take hold in late 2008, as demand dropped and as fracking and other technologies greatly increased supply. For both China and India cheaper energy was a bonanza in a difficult economic situation.

In China, the 2008 crisis was seen as further proof of the dangers of completely unregulated finance and provoked what Kirshner calls "buyers' remorse" about a development model that left China with massive, historically unprecedented holdings of U.S. dollars binding it tightly to the American economy.[20] China, like other countries, has since moved to create financial space for itself, internationalizing the renminbi (RMB)—which has its own limitations—and creating its own financial institutions and arrangements, reducing somewhat its dependence on the dollar.

India and the subcontinent, to the extent that it was integrated to India, were not as greatly affected by the 2008 financial crisis as Europe and some others. India, like China, had never completely bought into the "globalization project," had kept some capital controls, and took quick action to stimulate demand in its own economy. The immediate economic impact of the crisis was averted. But the slowdown in the world economy and world trade meant that Indian exports had still to reach precrisis levels in 2018. Besides, India was certainly affected by the world and its geopolitics that emerged after the crisis.

The crisis moved both India and China to the lower growth trajectory that they exhibited until the pandemic and economic crash of 2020. Trend rates of growth for both economies came down. For India, this lower trajectory falsified earlier optimistic forecasts about eliminating the worst of mass poverty in two decades by 2025 and necessarily postponed the transformation of India. Much of the accelerated economic growth in India in the last thirty years has come from increased productivity and has therefore been jobless or relatively jobless growth. India has been relatively frugal in the use of capital and maintained high capital output ratios. (This is unlike China where most growth has come from very high levels of investment and the involvement of surplus labor and women in the formal economy rather than increases in productivity. Today, the marginal utility of capital is dropping rapidly in China.) In a young Indian society, which is adding about 11 million people to the labor force every year and where the overwhelming majority of the population is below the age of 25, jobless growth risks turning the demographic dividend that we were relying on for our future growth into a demographic disaster.

As Kirshner points out, the Bretton Woods system of 1948–1973 was a Keynesian influenced liberal order, encouraging an orientation toward an expanding international economy and seeking to "embed" market forces in the national management of economies. The "globalization project" of 1994–2007, on the other hand, was market fundamentalist, assuming that markets, even for financial assets, always knew best and that one economic model defined by markets fits all. Each of these orders naturally reflected the geopolitical ambitions and assessments of its creator, the United States, at that point of time. The Bretton Woods system sought to strengthen allies and the Cold War coalition against the Soviet Union. The globalization project sought to advance U.S. interests much more directly. The former collapsed when it had served its purpose and American allies like Germany and Japan had recovered, Cold War tensions had eased and were now managed differently under the Nixon administration—by a de facto U.S. strategic alliance with China, by detente with the Soviet Union, and by arms control agreements. When the Soviet Union collapsed and Japan stalled, and the U.S. economy underwent a resurgence in the late 1980s and early 1990s, talk in the 1970s and 1980s of a U.S. decline was replaced by that of U.S. dominance. Now U.S. power and ideology went hand in hand with the American globalization project. In the post–Cold War world of U.S. unipolarity, the promotion of globalization, financial and otherwise, was recognized as further enhancing the American geopolitical position.

Trouble with the globalization project was visible in the serial currency and financial crises in emerging economies like Mexico and Brazil in the 1990s, but the first systemic shock was the Asian financial crisis of 1997–1998. East and southeast Asia had always treated the market driven economic model with some skepticism. When southeast Asian and south Korean financial markets went into crisis in 1997, the United States and the IMF imposed deflationary policies on them as the price of support. By their reactions, and the fact that those who did not follow their prescriptions like Malaysia came out better, the IMF and the United States delegitimized the globalization project. It was also clear that economies that had maintained capital and currency controls like India and China were less affected by the crisis. Japan and most of Asia saw the cause of the crisis in the "inherent instability of liberalized capital markets," as Japan's "Mr. Yen," Vice Minister of Finance Eisuke Sakakibara, put it. Japan therefore proposed an Asian Monetary Fund in 1998 in the Miyazawa initiative, but it was quickly squashed by a U.S. exercise of power. It was clear that there were marked differences in approach and understanding between Asia and the United States.

The financial crisis of 2008 altered China's role in the Asian economy and the world. China kept growing as a result of the stimulus. All China's neighbors today see China as their market and source of capital and cheap goods, rather than as another emerging market or competitor, as they did before the crisis. In geopolitical terms, the removal of Saddam Hussein in 2003 reflected the height of America unbound, free, and capable of removing anyone anywhere even when much of the world disapproved. After the 2008 crisis, the Arab Spring and events in Libya, Syria, the South China Sea, and elsewhere showed the limits of American power in the new configuration. Geopolitically, the world after the financial crisis of 2007–2008 is one where the Asia-Pacific is both the political center of gravity and the main driver of the global economy.

The world today is therefore a very different world from that of the globalization decades. Equally, it is a product of those forces of globalization, and we are still in a globalized economy, and in the single geopolitical unit that it has made of our world. How the effects of globalization on India played out, and what globalization did to Asian geopolitics, is what we look at next.

PART II

The Present

9

What Globalization Did to Asia's Geopolitics

G lobalization transformed the world through the 1980s through the 2008
world economic crisis. In many ways, globalization was two-faced, giving
credence to both its fiercest critics and its most ardent advocates. The truth,
as always, was somewhere in between. In essence, the globalization decades
changed the global balance of power, increased instability, brought new authoritarians to power in several major countries, and enabled the spectacular rise of
China.

Much of the good that the latest round of globalization did in its heyday
was economic and was concentrated in a few emerging or, more precisely, reemerging economies.[1] China was the greatest beneficiary, followed by India.
China grew by over 9 percent for three decades, while India grew at over 6 percent for over thirty years. And they were not alone. Other Asian "tigers" and
"dragons" grew by tapping into global markets. Indonesia, Bangladesh, Africa,
Mexico, and many others grew too. Korea, Singapore, and Taiwan attained the
living standards of developed Western economies. While inequality between
and within societies increased, globalization improved human welfare on a scale
never seen before in history—a scale that seems unlikely to be matched in the
foreseeable future. The proportion of the world's population living in extreme
poverty halved between 1993 and 2015, from 35 percent to 11 percent, and bil-
lions have been pulled into the middle class.[2]

Objectively speaking, economic growth and progress in the 1990s and
2000s resulted in more people in the world living longer, healthier, more secure,
and more prosperous lives than ever before in history. Women are freer, and
class barriers and discrimination, though still horrendous, are less than before.
There has never been a better time to be young. Since the early 1990s global
child mortality has been cut in half, there have been massive reductions in cases

of tuberculosis, malaria, and HIV/AIDS, and polio incidence has decreased by 91 percent. More people are living healthy, productive lives than ever before.[3]

The paradox, of course, is that at the same time inequality has grown and has sharpened deprivation. Technology has brought awareness of higher standards of living elsewhere. Over 750 million people still live in extreme poverty, mostly in south Asia and Sub-Saharan Africa. The openness to foreign influences and ideas involved in global contact threatened long-standing cultural identities, even in societies that gained the most from globalization. More people feel anxious, more states feel insecure, and fewer people feel that their aspirations are being fulfilled than in previous generations. We live in an age of anxiety, in what Pankaj Mishra calls an age of anger.

Globalization has not been a purely economic phenomenon. Like all previous economic orders, the globalized world economy dominated by the United States was allied to an ideology and a political order. But it did have features different from earlier rounds of globalization. From the 1980s on, the world was increasingly interconnected by economics, technology, capital, trade and investment flows, and an increasingly dominant political liberalism. Unlike past waves of globalization, the primary agents of globalization were now not governments but private actors outside government such as transnational corporations and institutions. These included the five information technology majors—Microsoft, Apple, and so on—and private corporations such as ICANN, which assigns internet domain names. It is hard to assign a corporation a national identity: it can be incorporated, create its products, pay taxes, generate employment, and be owned in entirely different countries or a series of them. This was an age when technology brought other people's lives and ideas into our homes and palms. By doing this, information and communications technology fed both aspiration and resentment, driving demand and anger at the same time. Where that demand could be met in large part, and there was realistic hope of it continuing to be met, as in India and China, societies were stable and transformed. Where that demand could not be met and there was little hope for the future, as in western Asia, people turned to radical and extreme solutions; societies imploded, and overthrew strongmen and political parties that had been in power for decades, as in the Arab Spring of 2010–2011 and its chaotic aftermath.

∽

India, China, and Asia were fundamentally transformed by globalization. Manufacturing and trade moved from the advanced industrialized countries, and economic power went with it. In 1950 the G-7 share in world GDP (on a PPP basis) was 51 percent and emerging markets were 36 percent. By 2012 those proportions were reversed, and the center of gravity of the world economy continues to move east.[4] China began its rapid accumulation of hard power, rising to near superpower status. By 2018 China was the world's largest manufacturing and trading nation, the third largest military power on earth, and well on course to become the world's largest economy, overtaking the United States in total output but not in per capita income. India rose to become the fifth largest economy in the world. The world now faces the prospect that in a few decades two of the three largest economies will have poor populations, with unsatisfied aspirations, and revisionist politics to go with them. This is not a situation that the world is used to.

The world economic crisis of 2008 showed that no countries could be "decoupled" from the global economy—both a successful result and an undesirable consequence of the globalization decades. In the United States the Troubled Asset Relief Program (TARP) of 2008 with its US$787 billion stimulus included a "Buy American" clause, signaling that the pushback on an open global economy had begun. Both China and the United States began a process of onshoring production from global production chains that are so large a part of the globalized world economy. For economies like China and India, which were increasingly dependent on exports for their growth, the crisis meant a major adjustment toward reliance on domestic demand and consumption to drive their economies. China still is attempting that transition, but has only managed to implement a small portion of the market-oriented economic reforms that were approved at the third plenum of the 18th Central Committee in 2013. India turned to "Make in India" and domestic infrastructure development, on top of pump priming, and has been reviewing its experience of free trade agreements. In sum, the crisis put an end to the decades of evermore open and increasing trade and investment and to building out global supply and marketing and value-added chains that had been key to the globalization decades.

The crisis deflated Western liberal triumphalism. The recession and the fact that emerging economies like China and India were consistently outperforming the West led directly to the rise of protectionism in advanced countries. Their long stagnation and the radical politics that recession produced were part of a Western loss of faith in the post–World War II economic system, the so-called liberal order, that they had built and managed successfully for sixty years. For a few years after the crisis it appeared that the rest of the West would also be like Japan and enter extended stagflation and economic stasis. World economic growth has been patchy since the crisis and recovery unusually slow. Europe and the Middle East saw the largest declines in output during that recession, unlike China, the United States, and India where output kept growing. Latin America's output fell by about 8 percent. Ten years later, world trade was just about back to peak levels before the crisis.

Advanced economies led global economic growth prior to the financial crisis with "emerging" and "developing" economies lagging behind. The crisis overturned this relationship. The International Monetary Fund found that "advanced" economies accounted for only 31 percent of incremental global GDP, while emerging and developing economies accounted for 69 percent of incremental global GDP from 2007 to 2014.

~

The single greatest change that globalization brought to the world balance was, of course, the rise of China. The specific goals that Xi Jinping set for China within a month of coming to power in 2012 are the "Double Hundred": building a "moderately prosperous society," doubling per capita income to around US$10,000 between 2010 and 2021, the 100th anniversary of the founding of the CCP, and, making China a "modernized, fully developed, rich and powerful" nation by 2049, the centenary of the founding of the People's Republic of China. (In PPP terms China has already achieved the first goal, which required her economy to grow at 6.5 percent before 2021.) The achievement of these goals is described as the "China Dream," to enable the "Great Rejuvenation of China,"[5] which also translates as renaissance. In essence, the sentiment echoes the Trump administration's "Make America Great Again."

China steadily accumulated hard power and reached near global power status in significant metrics: In 2014 China achieved GDP parity with the United States in PPP terms and two-thirds U.S. GDP in standard exchange rate terms[6]; China is the world's top manufacturer by a considerable margin and has a decisive influence on most world commodity and manufactures markets; China has the second greatest military budget in the world and has modernized and streamlined its armed forces while equipping them with high technology; and China also has an apparently stable internal leadership. The nature of the regime and its survival as a one-party state have so far outlasted all prophets of doom. This is an impressive list of achievements in the forty years since China began the process of reform and opening up to the world. The sheer speed and scale of change and churn in China had significant consequences and side effects.

Externally, China has put the hard power accumulated in the last thirty years to several uses: to expand its security perimeter, consolidate the Eurasian landmass, transition to becoming a maritime power for the first time in its history, and to attempt some, still limited, order building in the global economy. China is remaking the PLA, following the model of the American armed forces, into an expeditionary force through extensive reform and modernization, giving the PLA a capability to project power well beyond territorial and coastal defense of the country's borders and periphery.

By expanding its security perimeter and militarizing the South China Sea, China has complicated the unrestricted freedom of maneuver that the United States has enjoyed in the western Pacific and seas near China since 1945. China has successfully changed the military balance in its immediate periphery in its favor. Its new strategy has been profitable, increasing its influence among southeast Asian countries and in its maritime periphery. It is difficult to see why it would change this approach unless its domestic condition changes drastically or if responses from its neighbors and the United States were to shift drastically from the last decade. China's neighbors are increasingly wary of being caught in a China-U.S. competition or to be seen opposing China. For several years the Association of Southeast Asian Nations (ASEAN) has not found an acceptable approach to controversies surrounding territories in the South China Sea, where several of its members regard various islands as their own. The United States has so far displayed no effective counter to China's militarization and enforcement of claims in the South China Sea and has avoided confrontation in these waters. In the East China Sea, however, the United States has steadfastly and publicly extended protection to the Senkaku islands citing the U.S.-Japan defense treaty, while privately counseling caution to Japan in its dispute with China.

The signature initiative that uses China's economic strengths while seeking to secure its geopolitical position in Asia is the Belt and Road Initiative (BRI). In essence, Xi's proactive policy in Asia offers a straightforward deal: China will deliver trade, investment, and economic benefits to partners that accommodate, or do not challenge, its core interests. China under Xi Jinping initially relied on economic diplomacy and coercion because it lacked political leverage. Hence the design and rollout of the BRI in 2013. But this is changing as China develops military and political leverage in its Asian periphery and shows an increasing willingness to be involved in the internal affairs and politics of its neighbors.

It is far too early to judge whether the BRI meets its stated economic and connectivity goals. These are long gestation projects. More interesting is the question of whether Beijing's infrastructure diplomacy is winning China friends across Asia. Here the record is mixed. While most countries, particularly their leaders, welcome the projects and financing, opinion is hardening against China across the continent, as China pursues her interests with increasing assertiveness in "wolf warrior" diplomacy, named after a series of popular action movies. In Pakistan, for instance, the initial announcement of the China-Pakistan Economic Corridor (CPEC) in April 2015 was greeted with considerable enthusiasm. But public support has weakened, particularly since May 2017 when Pakistan's *Dawn* newspaper published the CPEC master plan drawn up by China Development Bank, CPEC's main financier. The plan envisaged deep Chinese penetration of Pakistan's industry and society, leasing out thousands of acres of rural land to Chinese enterprises, and building a round-the-clock surveillance system in cities from Peshawar to Karachi. It would leave Pakistan both bankrupt and financially tethered to China. Almost 24 percent of Pakistan's external debt was already owed to China in 2018, and that proportion will go up rapidly with CPEC. It is uncertain, then, whether the BRI is China's new Great Leap Forward or the equivalent of a Marshall Plan.

As for order building in the global economy, China has leveraged its financial, manufacturing, and trading strengths once the 2008 crisis demonstrated the limits of U.S. economic power. The economic crash of 2020 with the COVID-19 pandemic, and China's relatively quick recovery, are accelerating China's economic order building, particularly in Asia. This had begun through the Asian Investment and Infrastructure Bank, the BRICS New Development Bank,[7] the BRI, Chinese investment and acquisitions abroad, and attempted internationalization of the Chinese currency, the renminbi. Also, the Trump administration's decision to exit the Trans-Pacific Partnership left the region open to the increasing influence of China. China has signaled an intention to join the Comprehensive and Progressive Agreement for Trans-Pacific Partnership (CPTPP) that Japan and other members of the TPP set up in 2018 without the United States. The new Regional Comprehensive Economic Partnership (RCEP) will now serve as an instrument to tighten Asia-Pacific economies' integration with China's and to build up global supply and manufacturing chains centered on China, though it is considerably less detailed and demanding than the CPTPP. The physical infrastructure for this China-centered economic order would be created by the BRI. When offers of cheap finance and infrastructure building are allied with a comprehensive security package—including "safe cities," cyber security, personal security for leaders, and total surveillance on the Chinese model—we are witnessing a new type of potential dominance, a "China model" that could be attractive to developing country leaders and aspiring autocrats around the world, but not necessarily to their citizens.

Today, China is central to the world economy. It manufactures one-fourth of global industrial production and is the largest consumer of several commodities and products. China consumes one-fourth of the world's energy, 59 percent of the world's cement, 50 percent of the copper and steel, 31 percent of the rice, and one-third of the semiconductors.[8] This creates a two-way dependence that drives China to try consolidating Eurasia while also attempting the transition to becoming a maritime power for the first time in its history so as to secure its sea-lanes and overseas interests. These new goals compete for resources and leadership attention with internal stresses in China's society and with traditional mindsets in China of a continental Asian power, and come up against the reality of China's still-limited ability to create outcomes in her periphery.

Taken together, Xi Jinping's policies represent a marked shift away from Deng's 1991 strategy expressed in the phrase "hide your capacities and bide your time"[9] to a much stronger push for China's interests and great-power status. Chinese officials have stopped describing China as a developing country, using instead "major power" or even "global power." Deng Xiaoping's accommodationist external political strategy left China free to concentrate on economic reform at home while slipstreaming the United States abroad. During his first term from 2012 to 2017 President Xi Jinping staked out independent positions on global issues while trying to work with the United States on climate change, the Korean nuclear issue, and other questions in a "new type of great-power relations," and simultaneously putting in place the pieces (such as bases in Djibouti, the Belt and Road Initiative, and so on) for a more independent Chinese policy. Since President Trump came to power in 2016, China has faced an unpredictable United States that behaves as a revisionist power in some respects and that explicitly identifies China as a rival. That has led to much sharper China-U.S. strategic contention and the beginnings of economic contestation. So far, the political contention is real only in the Asia-Pacific and is largely verbal outside the Asia-Pacific. Economic contention, however, recognizes no regional boundaries given China's global economic reach, which extends well beyond the range of its political and military influence.

In Asia, China's rise has both benefited and discomfited its neighbors and aroused growing U.S. concern. China has abandoned the military strategy of asymmetry that Mao and Deng followed. Instead, in response to the 1996 Taiwan Strait crisis and the display of U.S. capabilities in the Persian Gulf, China has pursued its own revolution in military affairs. The U.S. Quadrennial

Defense Review of 2006 described China as having "the greatest potential to compete militarily with the United States and field disruptive military technologies that could over time offset traditional U.S. military advantages." That potential has become a significant reality in that China now operates militarily at sea as well as on land in the Pacific and Indian oceans as well as in southeastern and central Asia. It has greatly raised the cost to any potential opponent of moves in its immediate periphery.

China is able to act assertively in the adjacent seas because it is now secure on land to a degree never seen before, a significant change from the 1960s and 1970s, or even in its long history. Globalization, with its emphasis on sea-lanes of communication, has necessitated Chinese power projection into the blue-water oceans around the country. Hence the Belt and Road Initiative. Hence also the Chinese sensitivity to potential threats to its permanent hold over Tibet and Xinjiang.

~

China's rise is only the most striking aspect of what globalization has done to the balance of power in Asia. This poses an issue. As a beneficiary of globalization, China is a status quo power in the world economy but is politically revisionist, wishing to change the political order in Asia to reflect its primacy. It seeks adjustments in its own favor in running the existing global economic order; it seeks a fundamental reordering of the political dispensation in Asia. Meanwhile, the world's greatest power, the United States, which has so far taken credit for the order, is now a revisionist power in economic terms, and President Trump was less committed to the political and military order that has given the United States global primacy without a peer competitor for so long. The question therefore is not whether the post–Cold War order will continue or be restored, but how it will change.

The 2008 crisis brought into question the political order that underpinned the last wave of globalization, namely, U.S. military and political dominance, because it marked a shift in the balance of power between and within states. Besides, globalization also led to the return of identity politics and rise of authoritarian leaders, shifts in the balance of power, and the reemergence of several significant global actors. Previous waves of globalization in history had always been accompanied by heightened diplomacy and conflict. Late-nineteenth-century globalization was an integral part of European imperialism at its most rapacious—of the Great Game between Russia and England, of the 1885

Congress of Berlin scramble for Africa, and the turn-of-the-century carving up of the Chinese melon, and led up to World War I.

The so-called liberal international order after World War II was always something of a myth, being neither liberal nor very orderly in practice. During the Cold War it was only orderly in that each superpower imposed order within its sphere of influence without interference by the other, as the Czechs and Hungarians discovered in 1956, and the British and French found when the United States disapproved of their Suez adventure. After 1989, with the collapse of the Soviet Union, the order was actually based on the overwhelming predominance of Western and American power. Both before and after 1989, if there were rules, they were for others. The superpowers did not consider themselves bound by them and practiced exceptionalism in every sphere from the UN Charter to nuclear nonproliferation to the law of the sea to their political and military interventions around the world. The more canny developing countries such as China and India chose to go along with the political manifestations of the "order" internationally after 1989, so long as it did not affect their ability to manage their own affairs, while using the opportunities opened up by the free flow of trade and capital after the fall of the Soviet Union. This is not to deny the undoubted utility of the panoply of institutions such as the UN's specialized agencies, the World Trade Organization, and others. But their ability to determine or change great-power behavior since the end of the Cold War has been limited and shrinking. Instead, great-power behavior can be explained equally well or better by balance of power considerations and calculations of self-interest rather than by international norms or institutions.

The defenders of liberal internationalism have offered a mythic rendition of America's ascent to global power, specifically what Andrew Bacevich termed the myth of the reluctant superpower.[10] The United States focused on globalization, and therefore the state became a protection system for an economic worldview that, in turn, helped fund the U.S. state. Even if one discounts the more extreme manifestations of liberal intellectual hubris—such as interpretations of the "end of history" and "clash of civilizations" unintended by their authors—the so-called Washington consensus and the dominant liberal political economy created inequality and discontents in both advanced and developing economies that fueled rage against the elites and expertise, leading ultimately to the loss of power of traditional establishments and a declining public confidence in global institutions. Politically, whether it was classical western liberal interventionism or its later forms of Western trans-governmentalism in the

1990s and thereafter—making sovereignty porous on the pretext of judicial or regulatory norms, a "right to protect," or "democratization"—the effect was the same: to provoke resistance and a loss of identity in several parts of the world. Across most of the world, identity and conflict in the 1990s were shaped and expressed in terms of aggressively ethnic politics that did not accord with Western or U.S. views of geopolitics. We are watching political pushback today from the Middle East to Russia to China and Africa and southern Asia, not to mention from the United States and Europe.

The other political consequence of globalization was growing inequality within and among societies at all levels of development. Alexis de Tocqueville's brilliant insight was that revolutions are produced by improved conditions and rising expectations, not by mass immiseration. This is exactly where globalization has left us—a time when everything is amazing and nobody is happy. The life of most people on earth is better than it ever has been in history, and yet the sense of uncertainty, dissatisfaction, and anger has never seemed higher.[11] By historical standards, the world today is much less inequitable, unfair, capriciously oppressive, murderous, and imperial than before. Paradoxically, deep racial, cultural, and ethnic panics are evident in all societies, including the most advanced. The tension and the dynamic continue between cosmopolitanism versus nostalgic reaction, between regimentation versus an open society. India's recent experience has shown that with economic growth and social change, states can be both more prosperous and plural and still be insufficiently equal and less tolerant.

~

In sum, globalization changed the balance of power in unforeseen and uneven ways. It made the world economy multipolar with the rise of China and other Asian economies, but left it unipolar militarily as the United States still outstrips every other power and possible combination of powers in military strength, technology, and the ability to project power on a global scale. Politically, the globalized world is confused. The will to power, strong in China and Russia, is not equally evident in the United States and other traditional great powers.

We are in a situation of multiple imbalances in the international system: between the global distribution of economic power as against that of military and political power; between regions like the Asia-Pacific dominated by the rise of China as against a global order that is still primarily Western; and, between the Western order's needs as against a United States unwilling to provide global public goods and leadership that had sustained that order. Not all these global imbalances can be laid at the door of globalization, but it certainly contributed to exacerbating them, just as it accentuated domestic inequalities in societies and economies around the world.

The beneficiaries of globalization included not just India and China but even the terrorist and radical groups that used the digital and physical connectivity of globalization to make the world less safe. The scholar Robert Kaplan describes this as the return of the Marco Polo world, unified by the Mongols, where tremendous profit went along with great danger and insecurity.[12] Those benefits were shared unequally between and within societies. And rising inequality meant that for a growing number of people the world was an unfair place, an awareness that was fed by the new social media, thus making the world less stable and secure than before.

In the five centuries since Vasco da Gama came to Kozhikode in 1498, the Western powers overthrew local orders in Asia and imposed their order on the world. The last in line was the United States, who, after defeating Germany and Japan in the Second World War, established primacy over both the Atlantic, where the center of gravity of world politics was located, and the Pacific. That era is now over.[13]

Globalization and the 2008 crisis that it produced and spread through the world left a politically fragmented world. The old Western order can no longer cope and no new order has emerged to replace it. There is no longer a central global balance, as the Soviet-U.S. balance was during the early Cold War, as the China-U.S. balance only operates in east and southeast Asia, not in west Asia or the subcontinent, and functions more as rivalry than as a stabilizer. Consequently, regional and subregional powers have come into their own, the United States and the West have ceased to be the sole deciding factors in global and regional disputes and struggles, and the international agenda has turned increasingly to a new security agenda, enabled and sometimes created by new technologies. This is a world of contradictions: where culture, from clothing to ideas, is global, provoking local assertions of identity and even the manufacture of a new chauvinist past; where a new global economy provides the means for local reassertions of chauvinism; and, where the objective fact of better lives does not seem to be reflected in politics.

And each of these destabilizing trends has been accelerated by the pandemic of 2020 and the resulting global economic crash. While it is difficult to foresee all of its consequences when we are still in the midst of the pandemic, the World Bank estimates that globally more than 100 million people will be pushed back into poverty and growth will only resume after a year or so.

~

Asia is the archetype of our paradoxical age, the best of times that are also the most uncertain times.[14] Nowhere have lives improved faster since World War II than in Asia. The same forces that created progress have also created inequalities, aspirations, and discontents. Having stoked fears of loss of identity and jobs in populations, globalization has created a world where Asia's leaders perceive increasing uncertainty about the future.[15]

Asia is once again central to the world's prosperity and security. Asia is the driver of the world economy. It is the cockpit of major power rivalry, where the foremost rising power, China, contends and cooperates with several rising neighbors and the world's single superpower, the United States. The world's geopolitical center of gravity has returned to Asia—a region of revisionist powers, none of whom was entirely satisfied or considers itself entirely bound by the geopolitical settlement imposed after the Cold War—not Russia, not China, not Iran, not, partly, India, and now, perhaps, not Japan. As a result, Asian politics have returned to national rivalries, territorial claims, naval buildups, and other historical patterns. Asia is witnessing a rapid and continuing shift in the balance of power. What the classical geopoliticians called the heartland or Eurasia is being consolidated under new auspices, the rimland has come into its own with the rise of China, India, and others, and the maritime space around Asia is increasingly contested. We are between orders, in transition, and this explains the pervasive sense of uncertainty in Asia today.

The shifting balance of power in Asia is now a truism and, like all truisms, expresses a truth. Power has shifted to Asia and within Asia. Economic power is more widely held than before globally and is relatively more concentrated in Asia. The preponderant change is the rise of China and India. What seems to have disoriented most people is the rapidity and scale of the shift. Within the Asia-Pacific itself, relative economic power has been concentrated in fewer hands, though there is no country that has not gained from globalization. By 2014 India and China together accounted for about half of Asia's total GDP.[16] In PPP GDP terms they are the world's largest and third-largest economies. Most of this, of course, is accounted for by China. How the location of economic activity has shifted is apparent in the fact that of the world's total nominal GDP of $74.1 trillion in 2016, Asia accounted for 33.84 percent, North America for 27.95 percent, and Europe for 21.37 percent.[17]

The consequence of shifting power has been the return of traditional power politics as Asian states, which for decades concentrated on their economies, now seek political weight and military protection commensurate to their economic success. Symptoms of this shift include the arms race in Asia and balancing and hedging behavior by all the states in the region. Internal balancing is evident in the military buildups and increasing security and intelligence capabilities. New military and maritime doctrines have been announced by several countries in recent years. While no one in Asia can prevail on or ignore China's power, there is no vacuum in Asia for China to fill, because India, Japan, South Korea, Vietnam, Indonesia, Iran, and others are powerful independent states. External balancing is evident in the increased frequency and scope of defense, intelligence, and security exchanges between Asian states, particularly India, Japan, Vietnam, Indonesia, Singapore, and Australia. China's rise has provoked natural strategic responses. China's attempt to assert its position in its near seas has provoked the return of Japanese nationalism and countervailing defense and security links between its neighbors, Japan, India, Vietnam, Indonesia, Singapore, and others. Disputes and flashpoints are alive again from Korea to the East China Sea, the South China Sea, and the India-China border. The navies of India, Japan, the United States, and Australia exercise together in the Indian Ocean and the seas near China.

Power political questions of territory and military power are back to dominate the international agenda. Earlier concerns surrounding world order and global governance of trade liberalization, nuclear nonproliferation, human rights, climate change, rule of law, and the like have taken a back seat. Asia and the Middle East have moved from win-win to zero-sum issues. Old-fashioned power plays are back. Consider the headlines in 2008–2019: South China Sea, North Korean nuclear weapons and missiles, Crimea and Ukraine, Syria and Yemen. This is a fundamental change and was described by Walter Russel Mead in 2014 as the revenge of the revisionist powers and the return of geopolitics.[18] We now deal again with boundaries, military bases and alliances, and spheres of influence.

Asia makes clear the breakdown of the Western-led international order's capacity to deliver security and prosperity to most of the world. Neither the traditional dominance of the United States' "hub-and-spokes" alliance system as a provider of security in eastern and southeastern Asia, nor a potential China-U.S. understanding or G-2, can settle or manage issues like the North Korea nuclear weapons program, the consequences of the return of geopolitics, the arms buildup, territorial and maritime disputes and flashpoints like the South China Sea, or the balancing behavior that we see in the Asia-Pacific. In western Asia, Syria, Iraq, Libya, and Yemen prove the same point. Equally in doubt is the post–Cold War order's ability to continue to provide global public goods such as freedom of navigation in the closed seas from the East China Sea to the Mediterranean, to secure cyber and outer space, or to prevent the fragmentation of the world economy. Nor is the multilateral system doing so. The present order is simply no longer seen as delivering security in Asia. States are therefore taking matters into their own hands, building up their own military strength, and finding new partners and allies.

The redistribution of power threatens the balance that has kept the peace in the Asia-Pacific since the Vietnam War. U.S. naval supremacy is now challenged by China; the continental balance is upset by Russian decline; Iran's rise threatens U.S. and Western allies' positions in west Asia; and Japan, India, Vietnam, and Indonesia are responding to contention in the maritime domain. The order that so benefited India can no longer be maintained by the United States alone. Since 2000 every U.S. election has been won by the candidate promising less rather than more American involvement abroad.

The last few years have shown that the order between the most powerful states in the world is no longer stable or agreed. The international community, if it exists at all, is anarchic. A breakdown in international order is signaled when the great powers start to disagree about the rules, as we see in the South China Sea. In the South China Sea, China is showing that she can break rules set by others, namely, the Law of the Sea, and that the United States and the international community choose to do little about it. The three pillars of the Westphalian order—states, sovereignty, and non-intervention—are all breaking down, and are under attack from both sides of the spectrum, by the Western proprietors and initiators of the order and by those who present themselves as its victims in west and east Asia. The purposive fictions that build community are no longer agreed, accepted, or acquiesced in. Fictions serve a purpose to make powers conform to rules of the road even when they do not fully share goals. It is not that revisionist powers are directly confronting or challenging the status quo. With the United States under Trump disengaging from the world, they hardly have to. Rising powers like China have successfully chipped away at norms and relationships that sustain the western order in Asia.

~

The rise of ultranationalism and new authoritarians in power and the return of power politics and security issues work against the economic integration that globalization had brought about, as well as against China's attempt to consolidate the Eurasian landmass through the Shanghai Cooperation Organization, its Belt and Road Initiative, and its links with Russia and Europe. In the emerging Asian order, Eurasia is being consolidated. For the first time a power other than the United States is attempting to dominate both the Eurasian heartland and the Asian rimlands, and the oceans from Africa to the American West Coast. We are witnessing the consolidation of the Eurasian landmass in various ways, through trade and investment, the building of physical infrastructure such as railways, roads, and pipelines, and the integration of central and western Asia into global production chains as producers of primary energy and raw materials and end consumers in their markets. In other words, globalization has promoted Asia's integration and consolidation into trade and other networks tied to great powers like China and Russia. China is now the largest trading partner of every one of its neighbors on land, except Afghanistan and Bhutan. China's emerging area of influence in Eurasia is growing not in a nineteenth-century imperialist manner but more subtly, as befits an economically globalized world. In geopolitical terms the heartland is being consolidated and secured by China with Russian assistance or acquiescence.

For most of its land periphery, unlike at sea, China is filling vacuums rather than ramming up against competing states, except for the Indian subcontinent and Korean peninsula. Such limitations as there are on China's continental strategy are primarily its neighbors' desire for independence and its own limited capability. In 2008, when the People's Liberation Army had to simultaneously deploy for the earthquake in Szechuan, insurgencies in Tibet and Xinjiang, and the Beijing Olympics, China found that it could move troops around the country rapidly but could not move the equipment and supplies those troops required. Such a limitation on power projection on land and sea has prompted China's recent acquisitions and fundamental PLA military reform since 2015. The Belt and Road Initiative increases modes of contact and communication in the large single area of Eurasia with new roads, railways, pipelines, and ports, in addition to overlapping missile ranges and ideologies. A changed geography is the result and that gives power politics more play.

For the first time in several centuries, China is secure enough on its inner Asian land frontiers to be free to turn to the maritime domain and attempt to become a maritime power. The maritime domain, however, is still overwhelmingly dominated by American sea power, and several other powers have significant and growing naval capabilities in their own near seas, such as Japan, India, and Vietnam. Unlike the continental domain, where territory can only belong to one country or another, security in the maritime domain is not a zero-sum calculus. Secure sea-lanes benefit all trading nations, and trade itself is positive-sum for all participants. Since World War II, the United States has provided the global public good of secure sea-lanes around the globe for its friends and neutrals. It is that U.S.-led security order that successive waves of Asian countries, including China, have used to benefit from export-led growth.

That China is no longer happy to rely on the United States for the security of the seas has been apparent for some time. In August 2018 China released the draft of the Code of Conduct for the South China Sea, for instance, which proposes that no companies from outside the region be involved in the economic exploitation of the South China Sea, that military exercises with third parties only be undertaken with the consent of the other parties, and that China enjoy "sovereign military immunity" for her own vessels. For China to attempt to be the sole arbiter in the seas near its borders, which are major carriers of international trade and energy flows, is to upset the present U.S.-based order and balance that has benefited most if not all the countries of Asia. For the present, the United States has no realistic economic, military, or political counter strategy in the South China Sea. China, on the other hand, is putting in place the military and political means to enforce its claims, building and militarizing islands, increasing its naval presence, and asserting its claims in every way possible short of war.

At the same time, with the Eurasian littoral crowded with warships, and Chinese, Japanese, Indonesian, and Indian maritime ambitions alongside the United States, China faces a much harder task in achieving primacy at sea than on land. It faces an organized string of U.S. allies in the first island chain running from Japan through the Ryukyus to Taiwan, the Philippines, and finally Australia. Both the South China Sea and the East China Sea are closed seas, and China's egress is limited and under hostile surveillance. China is not risk averse and its solution to this problem has been aggressive. Facing the grim seascape of a "Great Wall in reverse," as James Holmes calls it, China has sought to build anti-access and area denial capabilities in the near seas, raising the potential cost to others of naval interventions. In the Indian Ocean region it is building bases and ports with potential military uses should it succeed in changing the balance of maritime force in its favor. Its present concentration, though, is on the near seas where her land power extends, in the form of missiles, artillery and shore-based fighter aircraft. The intent is not to fight a naval war or to confront the United States under the present adverse balance of forces, but to dissuade and to affect the calculus and behavior of the United States and others in her near seas while building strength and changing the disposition of forces.

~

To my mind the key to Chinese political and military ambitions remains Taiwan. A 2009 Rand Corporation study had predicted that by 2020 the United States would not be able to defend Taiwan against a Chinese invasion. This is disputed by other analysts. Taiwan is doing to China what China is doing to the United States. Taiwan is hardening herself to raise the cost to China so as to dissuade an invasion. For China, the humiliation of the 1996 Taiwan Strait crisis, when it was forced by the presence of two U.S. aircraft carriers to back off from trying to influence the Taiwanese elections, was a spur to much of what we have seen China do around Taiwan in the South China and East China Seas, with a naval buildup and assertion of claims. Taiwan is critical to China breaking out of its containment by the first island chain and gaining free access to the Pacific and Indian Oceans. If China can consolidate Taiwan, its strategic position would improve dramatically. Unification with Taiwan remains a tempting way of securing a place in history for any Chinese leader. (Tibet, which may be the world's largest store of fresh water, is the other core interest for China. By 2030 China will be falling short of its water demand by 25 percent.) But in considering unification by force, the Chinese leadership must reckon not just with Taiwanese resistance and international opinion but also with the possible U.S. reaction. The United States has acknowledged since 1972 "the Chinese position that there is but one China and Taiwan is part of China."[19] The U.S. Taiwan Relations Act of 1979, spelling out the U.S. commitment to Taiwan, states that America would "consider any effort to determine the future of Taiwan by other than peaceful means of grave concern to the United States," stopping short of an explicit commitment to defend Taiwan but keeping the possibility open by maintaining ambiguity about what the United States might do. It also committed the United States to support Taiwan's self-defense and maintain capacity to come to Taiwan's aid. As one U.S. official said privately, Taiwan could not assume the United States would actually come to Taiwan's aid; the mainland could not assume it would not.

China's strategy with regard to asserting its power over Taiwan and the first island chain has its contradictions. If China were to deny others access to the seas near China, without the ability to protect the sea-lanes it relies on, China risks having its energy and other supply lines cut in the event of actual conflict with the United States or another serious naval power. In effect, this makes China's military threats less credible. But China is using multiple forms of national power—political, diplomatic, economic, commercial, demographic—alongside its military buildup to achieve its aims. Its maritime strategy is directed at separating American allies and other states on its periphery from the United States. China seeks to influence U.S. behavior, not to attack and defeat her today, given the military imbalance. The next stage is for China to achieve a true blue-water capability to defend its own sea-lanes of communication, first in the South China Sea and East China Sea and then in the Indian Ocean and western Pacific Ocean.

What is true of China and the United States is not true of China's maritime balance within Asia. For countries like India, Indonesia, Vietnam, and Japan, China's naval buildup has already changed the maritime balance irreversibly. In the last fifteen years China has built more naval vessels in numbers and tonnage than Japan, India, Korea, and Indonesia put together. China has cultivated navies throughout the Indian Ocean region, from Pakistan to Bangladesh to Thailand and elsewhere. Its first overseas military base in Djibouti is on the Indian Ocean. China is a presence in the northern Indian Ocean since its participation in anti-piracy operations off the Horn of Africa began in 2008, and it has regularly sent submarines into the Indian Ocean. Once again, the aim is not to start a conflict but to use a presence and threat of force to influence the calculus and behavior of other powers. The reaction has been along predictable lines. Japan shifted from "forward defense" since the early 1980s and 1990s to "active denial" in the face of China's military modernization. In 2010 Japan adopted a "dynamic defense concept."[20] India too has adapted its maritime doctrine and forces. But while China's defense budget has grown 665 percent from 1996 to 2017, adjusted for inflation, and now totals some $153 billion, Japan's has grown by 22 percent in this period to $47 billion, less than one-third of China's, and India's by much less.

~

The reordering of Asian geopolitics is also driven by the search for legitimacy and changing domestic compulsions of the leaders of the larger Asian states, and by the diminishing capacity of governments and leaders to deliver high economic growth, to manage new domains like cyberspace, or to control the political narrative. Since 2012, new authoritarian Asian leaders have claimed to be outsiders to the existing political establishment and tapped into popular fears and xenophobia. In effect they rely on nationalism, sometimes chauvinism, for their legitimacy. Max Weber defined legitimacy as coming from three sources: charisma, competence, and the Church or religion, which today means ideology. The new authoritarians rely on personal charisma for their legitimacy in politics. As a result, all these leaders also display an extreme sensitivity to criticism. None of them are institution builders since institutions would go against the personal nature of the power they exercise. Since 2008 we have seen variations on this theme in Japan, China, India, Turkey, Russia, and a host of other states.

In China, the 19th Party Congress in October 2017 dismantled several of the institutions and conventions that Deng Xiaoping had put in place after the Cultural Revolution and the fall of the Soviet Union to restrict the accumulation of personal power and prevent the emergence of another Mao Zedong or Gorbachev-type figure who might destroy the party and its rule. These included abolishing term and age limits and bypassing selection processes and internal balances within the party. In one basic respect Xi is true to Deng's legacy of tight control of politics and absolute control over the PLA. He has, however, yet to show Deng's talent or stomach for economic innovation and reform, which makes his political consolidation and centralization of power brittle. With China's external dependencies and internal tightness, external successes acquire greater significance internally, and the apparent price of failure is magnified.

India too is under a government whose overwhelming priority is domestic, whose ideological commitment is to remake the plural, liberal social contract and institutional basis on which India has so far been run, replacing the polyglot post-independence establishment with another drawn from a narrower social and religious class and geographical base. India, short of raw materials and linked to the world in many more ways than at the start of reform in 1991, has no option but to prioritize shaping the external environment, but must of necessity do so with other partners since it lacks the economic and hard power that China has accumulated in the recent past.

Both India and China now operate much more explicitly based on nationalism, and foreign policy is used for domestic political effect to a far greater extent than before. Because of the nature of the internal politics what we are witnessing is not the return of cold realpolitik based on calculations of national interest but the politics of emotion based on predilections and prejudice—not Bismarck but Kaiser Wilhelm II. The reliance on ultranationalist legitimacy by an increasing number of regimes has led to heated rhetoric and emotional outpourings, which find wide amplification in the social media. In other words, we are seeing the radicalization of internal politics across a unified world system and an increasing reliance on nationalism and chauvinism for legitimacy by governments. This has lessened the international system's ability to undertake the diplomacy necessary to avert crisis and conflict.

Developments in internal politics such as the rise of the new authoritarians or the shift to ultranationalism might not matter in a pure Westphalian world where internal politics is limited within and protected by the boundaries of sovereignty. But we are not in a purely Westphalian world. Globalization has ensured that our economic fates are interlinked, and information technology has obliterated social and national boundaries. Equally, and significantly for our politics and diplomacy, the rise of ultranationalism and the new authoritarians' reliance on it for legitimacy reduces the space for the give and take, compromise, and mutual understanding that are essential for diplomatic negotiations and peaceful coexistence. It is less likely today that we will arrive at peacefully negotiated solutions to international issues.

All in all, the current situation in Asia is fundamentally more complicated and therefore more unstable than at any time in the decades since World War II.

~

Why are we seeing a new resurgence of power politics in Asia? Economic globalization, abetted by technology, has converted the entire world into one closed system in geopolitical terms. Today, for the first time in history we can talk meaningfully of the global system. Barring catastrophe, it seems that economic globalization is here to stay. Technology has collapsed time and distance, in effect filling in the empty spaces on the world map, and creating a "crisis of room," in Paul Bracken's phrase, particularly in Asia.[21] Missile ranges overlap across the continents. For instance, ever since North Korea fired a missile across Japan into the Pacific Ocean in 1998, Japan is now part of the Asian military space, not an offshore outlier for Asia's geopolitics. Japan has no choice but to be involved in military and strategic developments on the continent, in China, Korea, Russia, and elsewhere. In other words, Eurasia has been reconfigured by technology and globalization's political effects into an organic whole. For example, China's assistance to North Korea's nuclear weapon program has found its way to Iran via Pakistan and to Syria, provoking reactions by Israel. What happens at one end of Asia affects the security calculus at the other end. If the United States reneges on its nuclear deal with Iran, that is one more reason why no effective understanding will be reached on dismantling North Korea's nuclear weapons program.

The growing appeal of nationalism and militarism is visible right across Eurasia, uniting the continent. The last two decades have seen the world's and history's greatest arms race ever in the Asia-Pacific—led by China's military modernization and with other countries not far behind. This is clearest in the pattern of naval buildups through the Asia-Pacific. Offensive weapons such as submarines and missiles, and power projection instruments like aircraft carriers, are now platforms of choice for China, Vietnam, India, Japan, and others. Armies are being rebuilt and repurposed from instruments of national consolidation to instruments of power projection and dominance. This is as true of the PLA as the Japanese Self-Defense Forces and should push India to catch up on long-neglected military reforms that are necessary. Weapons of mass destruction—nuclear and chemical, and ballistic missiles to deliver them—are present in an unbroken belt of countries from the Mediterranean to the Pacific, from Israel to North Korea.

Demography too has contributed to the creation of a closed global geopolitical system of which Asia is the most significant part. Today, for the first time in history, half the world's population lives in cities. By 2025 two-thirds of the world's population will be urban. (It was only 14 percent in 1900.) We have seen the rapid growth of megacities, with populations over 10 million. Of the over forty megacities in the world, only two are not in what used to be called the Third World. What this does to politics and military affairs is nothing short of revolutionary, for it makes crowd psychology the driving force of politics and enables the mass media, and now social media, to work on autonomous and alienated individuals outside their traditional social and familial structures. New ideologies, whether good or bad, can proliferate in this atmosphere. Urban crowds or mobs demand maximalist foreign policies, as we see in the viewership of the most rabid television stations in India, as, what Robert Kaplan calls "a resentful hot-blooded nationalism" spreads. And this reverberates across borders. In effect, the Asian rimland has been radicalized.

History tells us that crowded environments, such as what we see in Asia today with competing states adjoining each other, bred militarism and pragmatism, as happened after the thirteenth century in crowded continental Europe, which experienced five centuries of continuous warfare—the result of geography not character. Bound by a continent, Europeans then could not ground their foreign policy in a universal morality as the United States and Britain chose to believe and project about themselves in the twentieth century. In this respect Asia is more like early modern Europe than Britain or the United States, as it transitions from separate multiverses to a crowded environment as a result of globalization, technology, and the economic rise of its several nations.

~

Does this situation make conflict inevitable in Asia? Probably not, since nuclear deterrence should continue to keep the peace between the great powers, while other forms of conflict—civil wars, proxy wars—increase in number and lethality. Much will depend on the future course of U.S.-China relations. The Trump administration, with its transactional approach and effective disengagement from the world, witnessed in Asia by the U.S. withdrawal from the Trans-Pacific Partnership, and U.S. fatigue in maintaining the international order and providing global security and public goods, opened political space for other countries like China to pursue their own interests and goals in the international system. At the very least this led to a fragmentation of international politics, which is increasingly local and regional, and is no longer conducted within a broader international template such as the Cold War or the so-called rules-based liberal world order.

China has no intention of accepting a secondary role in global affairs, nor will it accept the current degree of American influence in Asia. "Ultimately, Asian affairs should be decided by Asians, and Asian security should be protected by Asian nations," said Xi Jinping in May 2014 at the Shanghai Conference on Interaction and Confidence-Building Measures in Asia. At the same time, his control over the PLA and ability to remake it into an expeditionary force, modeled on the U.S. armed forces while adjusting for China's particularities, has given Xi Jinping an instrument that was not available to his predecessors. The risk, of course, is that if you only have a hammer, every problem looks like a nail. We have seen this process at work in the United States for some time as its own foreign policy has become increasingly militarized. As American economic, and to some extent political, influence declined, the United States has come to rely increasingly on military options in Afghanistan, west Asia, and elsewhere with limited success. Under Xi, China has built up its internal security apparatus and armed forces, even as the civilian party and government have seen over 1 million cadres penalized in the anticorruption campaign. The PLA's role in policymaking has grown under Xi. Chinese policy already attempts seamlessness between politics, economics, diplomacy, and the threat or use of force. There is a real prospect of future Chinese policy exhibiting the same symptoms as the militarized foreign policy we have got used to from the United States.[22]

Despite the rhetoric about China as a strategic rival in the National Security Strategy of the Trump administration in 2018, an America First policy of isolation works for China. Trump's initial approaches to China were transactional, asking why he should respect the One-China policy if China did not give him what he wanted on trade, jobs, and manufacturing. He subsequently backed off on One-China and then showed considerable deference to Xi and China in the hope of Chinese cooperation on the North Korea nuclear issue. Since then, however, he has imposed tariffs on Chinese goods on grounds of national security and sought structural changes in China's industrial and technology policies, sparking fears of an economic competition that would affect the entire global economy. Vice President Mike Pence's October 2018 speech to the Hudson Institute clearly marked out China as a strategic competitor not just economically, politically, and militarily but also technologically. The evolution in the U.S. approach, and its concentration on the tactical and the transactional, made the Trump administration's China policy hard to predict. While the disruption opened opportunities for others, this approach may well be short-lived and not survive beyond the Trump administration. What is, however, clear is that China-U.S. relations have entered a new phase of higher levels of contention.

What we are witnessing is not a classical power transition from one superpower, the United States, to another, China. That may be how some see it in the United States, such as Graham Allison of Harvard.[23] But the United States remains dominant in military and also in technological power, and the two nations are codependent economically. Any economic downturn in one will affect the other. This was clear during the 2008 financial crisis when, according to the then U.S. Treasury secretary, Hank Paulson, Russia suggested to China after the collapse of Lehman Brothers that they work together against the U.S. dollar. Instead, China chose to work in daily coordination with the U.S. Treasury to prevent a run on the American dollar, in which most of China's external reserves are held.[24] Besides China is not the only power that is rising, and Asia is a crowded neighborhood, so a simple transition of power or hegemony, as occurred peacefully over time between Britain and the United States, is neither likely or possible.

The basic issue is what strategic adjustment is the United States willing to make to China's rise. This remains unclear. American policy since World War II has been to prevent the emergence of a peer competitor. It is hard to see how the United States can jettison this goal and now agree to change that for China. Besides, the present causes of friction are structural, and unless the United States shifts its goalposts, American demands would affect the nature of the Chinese economy and society. My sense is, therefore, that we are witnessing a longer-term paradigm shift in U.S.-China relations of which the "tariff war" is only one symptom. Elements of contention now predominate in the relationship. There will, of course, be deals and understandings, but they will not change the underlying dynamic. How will China react? The immediate economic impact on China of the Trump administration's measures was considerable, as was the shock of the unanticipated behavior of the United States. The short-term Chinese response was, therefore, muted, and the country will attempt to ride out the storm. For the long term China is likely to work to ensure that it can never be put in this position again, building capabilities and leverage wherever and however it must. While decoupling its economy from that of the United States is unlikely, building the ability to influence U.S. behavior and self-reliance in technology will be a large part of China's response.

A country's leaders often rely on what they perceive without necessarily having a complete picture or accurate information. Perceptions can be as important as reality. Now two competing narratives are making the rounds in Asia:

+ the inevitability of China's rise and a return to a historical norm of a predominant China in the Asia-Pacific replacing a declining United States, and

+ the dependance of Asia's future prosperity and stability on a continuation of the existing order.

If the South China Sea is a proxy for the larger strategic adjustment playing out between China and the United States across the region, China's intentions and U.S. responses are on display for the region and the world to draw their own conclusions. China argues that it is a geographical fact in Asia and the Asia-Pacific, while the U.S. presence is the result of a geopolitical calculation, making China a permanent feature and the United States a temporary one. The United States maintains that the region should rely on its auspices to prevent Chinese hegemony. Both narratives tell other countries to choose sides or risk being marginalized. But I believe this is a false choice. The U.S.-China competition actually gives those in the region room to maneuver. Each nation can balance, hedge, or even bandwagon, as needed, and also work with other rising and established powers in the region—most of whom reject assumptions of hierarchy, centrality, and superiority. In other words, each can pursue its interests independently. Most states in the region want the U.S. presence for security reasons but will not loosen their economic ties with China in return. Both China and the United States, therefore, bring different strengths and base their attractiveness on different criteria. Equally, in light of the attitude of the two recent U.S. administrations for a lighter footprint, regional powers will need to step up their contributions if maritime security and other issues in the contested global commons are not to result in interstate conflict.

~

Asia is a continent in transition. Not surprisingly, it can be difficult to describe the exact nature of this transitional period, including the different forces at work and the players and their roles.

New terminology has emerged such as *Indo-Pacific* to describe a part of the region and *Quad* for the United States, Japan, India, and Australia, a grouping revived in 2017 after initial meetings in 2007–2008. As a description of the security situation, however, the term Indo-Pacific is unsatisfactory. The western Pacific is a U.S. lake, the seas near China are enclosed waters that are contested, and the Indian Ocean is an open maritime space that no single power can dominate. The concept of an Indo-Pacific is dangerously out of touch with reality if it suggests that there is a one-size-fits-all security solution for these contiguous expanses of water. But the concept could be useful if we think of it differently.

Security is increasingly linked across a much broader region in Asia, and maritime security is certainly indivisible across the oceans girdling Asia. The idea of the Indo-Pacific would be useful as a means to signal consideration of new security issues, new cooperative solutions, and a broader open and inclusive security architecture in the maritime zone from east Africa to the western Pacific. A forum for such work already exists, thanks to ASEAN's forethought, in the East Asia Summit (EAS), a leaders' forum that needs to turn its attention to the security of this extended region.

Of the conceivable futures for Asia as a whole, both continental and maritime, several scholars have spoken of a reversion to historical norm, but they differ in how they see that norm. My sense is that before the arrival of Vasco da Gama in 1498, Asia consisted of coexisting multiverses—an east Asia centered on China, an Indian Ocean rim anchored by India, and a west Asian order held together by Iran and later Turkey. These multiverses traded with each other and exchanged people, ideas, religion, science, and technology but were politically distinct and did not affect each other's security calculus directly. Others see the historical norm differently. Robert Kaplan defines it as a globalized Marco Polo world,[25] and Robert Kagan as an anarchical jungle.[26] But the idea of a reversion to what there was in history ignores what empire and globalization have wrought and how this round of globalization differs both qualitatively and quantitatively from previous episodes in history. There is no going back and no good parallel in Asian history for today's situation.

At the systemic level, Asia faces at least three possible geopolitical futures:

- a regional order centered on one power, either the United States or China,

- an open, inclusive, multipolar concert of powers or a collective security architecture of some type, and

- a region of several powers of varying sizes and capabilities, each contending for primacy and influence to maximize its individual interests—a pattern familiar to nineteenth-century Europeans.

Consider first a China-centered order. Over the last few years China has been investing in order building in the global economy, leveraging its financial, manufacturing, and trading strengths to make strategic investments abroad, to internationalize its currency, to counter the Trans-Pacific Partnership in bilateral arrangements and the Regional Comprehensive Economic Partnership, to found the Asian Infrastructure Investment Bank and the BRICS New Development Bank, and, above all, to implement the Belt and Road Initiative. Since the 2008 financial crisis China has used every opportunity in its neighborhood to demonstrate the limits of American power and inability to moderate China's behavior toward its neighbors. Whether the Scarborough Shoal or Chinese naval and "fishing" boats in the East China Sea and the waters off South Korea, the message was clearly that the Philippines or Japan or South Korea should come to terms directly with China and could no longer rely on the United States for their security. It has replaced its conciliatory policy toward Taiwan with direct economic and military pressure on the Tsai Ing-wen government, even threatening an invasion if the U.S. Navy makes port calls at Kaohsiung, while following a soft policy toward Taiwanese business and society to induce a split and move away from growing support for Taiwan's independent identity on the island. China has also supported regimes in internal crisis to create dependencies and stakes for itself in the periphery. In several ASEAN countries, China has been successful in forcing a favorable recalibration of their relationship with China—countries like the Philippines, Malaysia, Thailand, and even Vietnam are showing more deference to China's sensitivities than they did a few years ago. Both processes, of order building and consolidating the periphery, have accelerated after the 19th Party Congress in October 2017. It is not inconceivable, given the exclusivity that China has sought in its draft of Code of Conduct for the South China Sea with ASEAN, that China will propose an east Asian or even an Asia-Pacific security or military arrangement against a threat from outside the region.

But does this mean that a China-centered order is inevitable? Certainly not. Chinese scholars today say that while China might overtake the United States economically, it is unlikely to do so militarily or politically. In trying to convert its accretion of influence into an order, China would face three issues: the desire of other countries in Asia to expand rather than contract their options, an order's need for legitimacy, and China's own domestic preoccupations and its likely trajectory. China does not enjoy the preponderance of power and the blank slate abroad that the United States did after World War II.

The second possibility of a multipolar order in Asia underpinned by collective security arrangements might appear to match the situation best, but is only slightly more likely than a China-centered order. Asia is crowded geopolitically with several rising and established powers, and an open multipolar architecture could theoretically accommodate rapid changes in the balance of power and several revisionist powers at the same time. Besides, while China is rising, the United States is not necessarily declining: it is the U.S. willingness to use American power that is in question. In practical terms a multipolar order in the Asia-Pacific would be best placed to address current issues: maritime security, cyber security, and military doctrines and postures. A multipolar approach could agree on confidence-building measures and crisis management, as well as cooperate in countering terrorism. It could be flexible and open to countries to participate in those steps that they find most useful and agree with. Its degree of formality could vary depending on the nature of the issue and the inclination of the powers. Working from the bottom up, it could build habits and institutions of cooperation in the region.

But it seems unlikely that any single power or combination of powers will construct a security order for all of Asia. West Asia's problems are different from those of the Asia-Pacific. Nor is it likely that the United States and China would cooperate in building such an order for subregions of Asia. Unlike west Asia, Asia-Pacific security is still primarily an issue between states, though terrorism spreading through the region is best dealt with by state structures with multilateral support. In west Asia a variety of means are required just to keep the peace. In the Asia-Pacific, China lacks the capacity and has not so far sought to build an order outside its immediate environs. The United States is largely absent, coming off a period of intense military and political engagement in west Asia that has eroded popular support at home for American order building abroad. It therefore seems more likely that we will see several single or regional power-centered or multipolar orders in subregions of Asia rather than one Asia as a whole. In western Asia a single power order could hypothetically be centered on the United States or on one or several of the regional powers: Iran, Egypt, or Turkey. In the Asia-Pacific the obvious candidates are the United States and China. An order centered on one power in either the Asia-Pacific or western Asia would be unstable, would not reflect the present or likely balance of power, and, history shows, has difficulties being rule-based or legitimate.

On the other hand, multiple orders in western Asia, the Indian Ocean, and the Asia-Pacific, differently designed to deal with the many issues facing each subregion, could be relatively stable. Asia's own past of coexisting multiverses and the history of the Concert of Europe suggest that. Multiple orders would reflect the economic multipolarity of Asia that has emerged in the last twenty years. They would be a natural evolution from the American-led order. In sum, they would reflect the existing balance of power in the subregions and their likely future evolution and are therefore more desirable.

All in all, it will not be easy to build multipolar, open, and inclusive security orders in Asia, given mutual suspicions and the ambitions of the great and rising powers, even though it is clearly in their best interest. It requires recognition by major powers that this is a desirable goal and that the attempt may have value in itself. The quest itself would be a significant confidence-building measure and would change the framing of several issues and hotspots from zero-sum to positive-sum. But that is a path less likely to be taken.

The third possibility seems to me the most likely, namely, that Asia becomes, willy nilly, like late nineteenth-century Europe, where several large countries of differing size and power contend to defend their interests and vie for influence and mastery. War was the result when a nineteenth-century European power sought a European order centered on itself, such as Napoleon's Continental System. Peace prevailed when Bismarck built a multipolar system of alliances or Metternich a Concert of Europe that united the major powers. Besides, Europe exported its rivalries, wars, and violence to Asia, Africa, and the colonies through the long nineteenth century, thus preserving peace at home but not abroad. Europe's peace was kept by eternal balancing between the powers, which broke down, despite globalization and interdependence, when the restraints and the requirements of balance were no longer understood or respected by leaders like Kaiser Wilhelm II. It is possibly the fate of the Asia-Pacific to see shifting balances and alliances of convenience, as already seems to be the case in west Asia, where debilitating conflict, both internal and external, has led to a relative decline in the region's global role and significance. But it is hard to argue that this is a desirable state to aim for, given the uncertainty and higher risk of conflict that comes with it.

In the Asia-Pacific we could be reverting to a pattern where politics and security are local, while economics, science and religion, culture, and ideology are global or regional. That would significantly alter the region's ability to deal with the issues of the day—an Asia-Pacific where the power balance continues to shift rapidly for decades to come and in which contention for mastery and advantage are chronic. Even so, I believe that there is still no very great risk of direct conflict between the major powers in Asia, despite their contention. But the fact is that the most powerful powers in the world, the United States and China, are contending for primacy, not to build a multipolar world or to bring order. And in that there is danger for us all.

No matter which of these futures comes to pass, today's situation—a crowded, changing, and unstructured balance of power in the Asia-Pacific—means that the region's goal cannot be strategic stability but managing change—putting in place the habits and institutions to ensure that shifts in the balance of power, which are inevitable and rapid, occur peacefully.[27] A more modest agenda that includes all significant players probably stands the best chance of enhancing security and averting conflict. The way to do so would be by building issue-based coalitions of the willing and interested, open to all states who wish to participate or contribute.

There is little comfort here for those who wish the world to return to the trajectory it was on before 2008. Nor is there much comfort for those who wish for a new Asian order with a clear hegemon and the certainties that come with that, whether they are partisans of China or the United States. I believe that neither China nor Asia is ready yet for a China-centered order. China may have the will and desire but lacks the objective power, and the United States seems incapable of exercising the will though it may have the power. Nor is a bipolar order the likely result in Asia. Instead, the facts of geography and history will probably result in separate arrangements and fragmented orders in the subregions of Asia: east Asia, southeast Asia, south Asia, the Persian Gulf, central Asia, the Levant, and west Asia. Each of these areas has local or regional powers to determine political and military outcomes, and we shall look at them next.

10

Viewing Asia from India

The views from India to the east and west differ markedly. To the east are the fastest growing economies in the world, rapidly industrializing and urbanizing, with strong state structures and hoary but modernizing societies. To the west are economies that rely on extracting natural resources, primarily oil, with fragile state systems under threat, fractured polities, and half-made societies, in author V. S. Naipaul's phrase. No west Asian economy figures in the top five Asian economies by GDP, in nominal or PPP terms. Looking east one sees a region with which India's ties have grown in the last thirty years since P. V. Narasimha Rao announced the "Look East" policy in April 1992. That endeavor has now morphed into "Act East." For three decades, India, Bangladesh, and other parts of the subcontinent have sought to emulate east Asia, while Pakistan and Afghanistan increasingly resemble west Asia.

~

In northeast Asia, the main driver of contemporary international relations and politics has been the rise of China, changing the balance in its own favor and provoking countervailing reactions. Japan and others have rearmed, the U.S.-Japan Security Treaty has been strengthened, and U.S. President Barack Obama made it clear that the U.S. security commitment covers the Senkaku or Diaoyu islands in the East China Sea that are disputed by China and in Japan's possession. The Trump administration had gone further to declare China a strategic rival and used technology and tariffs to push back against China's rise. While China has activated its disputes and claims in the East China and South China Seas and India-China border, and raised the costs of intervention for other powers, it has yet to achieve dominance.

The contention and disruption that the rise of China has caused has opened space for smaller, regional powers to explore new options. The United States and North Korea now deal with each other directly, as do North and South Korea, reducing China's position from being the world's exclusive interlocutor with North Korea to one of the important, but not the only, powers influencing North Korean behavior. There are limits to what China can achieve in its immediate periphery in northeast Asia where North Korea has land boundaries and direct land access to Russia and China and is hemmed in by the military presence in the area of some of the world's major military powers—Japan, the United States, Russia, and two formidable Koreas. This geography gives each of the powers balancing options and opportunities.

The train to peacefully denuclearize the Korean peninsula left the station some time ago, even though that is still the publicly stated goal of Chinese and U.S. policy. If North Korea's leadership learned anything from the example of Libya, Iraq, Ukraine, and Syria, it would be that giving up one's nuclear weapons leads to regime change or worse. And North Korea is not the only one to draw that conclusion. No military path to denuclearization of the Korean peninsula is possible without unacceptable damage to several states and peoples. And negotiations that threaten a regime's perception of its own survival are unlikely to succeed. The best way forward would be to construct a stable structure of deterrence in northeast Asia. This could be done in two ways. One is to accept the fact of North Korean nuclear weapons and externally deter their use. That is what U.S. extended deterrence could provide, except that people in South Korea and Japan must wonder whether the United States will risk San Francisco and New York, which North Korea can now hit with missiles, for Seoul and Tokyo. The other way would be to create local nuclear balance and deterrence on the Korean peninsula itself. The polls show that a large majority of the population in South Korea already believe that they should have nuclear weapons if North Korea does. That could make further proliferation in northeast Asia a matter of time. If South Korea nuclearizes, can Japan be far behind? A nuclearized peninsula could see nuclear deterrence limit the likelihood of full-scale conventional war in Korea. Rationally, armed conflict on the peninsula appears unlikely as it cannot create good outcomes for any side. Besides, armed conflict would damage Korea fundamentally, change the nature of security relationships in the region, have economic consequences for the rest of the world, and accelerate the arms race in northeast Asia.

In essence, China's rise has shaken loose the certainties of alliance politics in northeast Asia. South Korean policy in this century is a good example of how countries try to both accommodate and hedge against it, using the economic opportunity offered by China's manufacturing and market, while seeking to leverage China's influence to manage North Korean behavior. In neither attempt has South Korea been entirely successful, both because of the asymmetry between South Korean and Chinese economic power, and because of limits to China's political influence over North Korea. Another consequence of China's rising power in east Asia is Japan's evolution into what Ichiro Ozawa, the Japanese politician called the "shadow shogun" who split the long-ruling Liberal Democratic Party, would call a normal nation, shedding some of Japan's inhibitions about defending itself and playing a role in the region. Japan now works with multiple partners in security, defense, and intelligence matters, including India.

~

Bilahari Kausikan, one of the most astute observers of the region and a former Singapore diplomat, sums up the situation in southeast Asia by saying that "sovereignties are relatively new and other, still tender, historical enmities not yet forgotten, and the region lies at the intersection of major power interests."[1]

For southeast Asia the rise of China did not pose a problem so long as the tacit China-U.S. alliance meant that the two great powers operated in tandem, providing political cover for the Association of Southeast Asian Nations (ASEAN) on Kampuchea and other regional issues. This left ASEAN and others in the region free to concentrate on their economies, becoming part of global production chains. Today, however, the fraught relationship between China and the United States, plus a slow world economy and China's assertiveness, poses southeast Asian countries with two problems: choosing between China and the United States and risking irrelevance and lack of agency in determining the political and military future of their region. Their answer has been to balance, hedge, baulk, and collaborate with China and the United States, all at the same time, and to seek to strengthen regional security institutions, setting up the Asian Regional Forum and the ASEAN Defense Ministers' Meeting to which other states are invited. Still, the overall trend line over the last decade for most of southeast Asia shows ever stronger economic links with China leading to political accommodation of its influence. This is most evident in the South China Sea where several ASEAN countries have claims that contradict China's, with a solid legal basis that was reaffirmed by the Permanent Court of Arbitration on July 12, 2016. However, for several years ASEAN have been unable to find a common way to describe the issue in public statements, while China has proceeded to turn the area into a Chinese lake, building islands, militarizing the area, and steadily enforcing her writ.

The balance of power in southeast Asia is more in China's favor than in northeast Asia, where several of the world's major military powers are present in strength. For some ASEAN states like Laos and Myanmar, their land borders with China are porous and open to Chinese influence through migration, trade, or the use of insurgencies. China's levers of influence in southeast Asia are now manifold, and it can therefore push for exclusivity in its 2018 draft of the South China Sea Code of Conduct, agreed as the basis of negotiation with ASEAN, by asking that outside companies not be allowed to work in the area and that military exercises with outside powers only take place with consensus among local powers, thus giving China an effective veto. It is far from clear how this push by China will end, since the limits of Chinese power and of ASEAN forbearance are still not clear, but present trends work in China's favor.

The Chinese diaspora, numerically large and economically powerful, gives China a unique place in southeast Asia. During the 1980s and 1990s China moved to treating *Nanyang* Chinese as owing allegiance to their host countries and abandoned support for long-standing communist insurgencies. In Myanmar, China supported the Burmese Communist Party until 1989 when its war with the Myanmar Army ended. The Malayan Communist Party, sheltering in southern Thailand, surrendered the same year. Thailand was told by China that support for the Communist Party of Thailand would be withdrawn if Thailand turned a blind eye to China arming the Khmer Rouge in Cambodia. China's more recent interventions have been as intrusive though subtler than those in the 1950s, 1960s, and 1970s. In early 2015 war broke out on the Kokang border between the Myanmar National Democratic Alliance Army (MNDAA) and the Myanmar Army; more than 200 Myanmar officers and about 1,000 soldiers were killed. The MNDAA consists of about 5,000 fighters who are mostly ethnic Chinese, well-armed, trained, and funded on the Chinese side. Indian insurgent groups and leaders too, like Paresh Barooah of the United Liberation Front of Assam are also still hosted, armed, and funded by China through a web of private trading companies and underground intelligence contacts. Recently, small mercenary bands of Chinese People's Liberation Army veterans have begun offering their services around the world, operating much as Western mercenaries have for decades.

～

In central Asia, the coincidence of the end of the Cold War and globalization's high tide had profound, dangerous, and contradictory impacts. Central Asia is where Turkey and Iran, the most coherent states in west Asia after Israel, and

China and Russia, the neighboring great powers, abut each other. The Anatolian land bridge and the Iranian plateau have natural geographies that have played key roles throughout history. And the collapse of the Soviet Union and the new independence of the central Asian republics again provided Iran and Turkey, despite their internal problems, considerable opportunity to project military, political, and ideological power in this subregion.

There is a difference between Turkey and Iran: the former's imperial tradition (Seljuk and Ottoman) lies wholly within the Islamic age; the latter's imperial tradition predates Islam. The exception was the Safavid dynasty whose adoption of Shia Islam in the sixteenth century led to a war with the Sunni Ottoman empire that cut Iran off from Europe. Iran is traditionally as much a central Asian power as a west Asian one.

The Russian invasion of Georgia in 2008 changed central Asian geopolitics. At that point Armenia was allied with Russia and Georgia with the United States and Europe, as was energy rich Azerbaijan, whose oil and gas pipelines bypassed Russia running from Baku through Georgia and Turkey to the Mediterranean. The Muslim Azeris saw the Americans abandon Christian Georgia in 2008 in its hour of need and realized they could not rely on Washington in a crisis. The Azeri leadership as well as the leaders of Uzbekistan, Kazakhstan, and the other former Soviet republics were all alarmed by the Arab Spring and the Islamic uprisings that resulted. They were also worried by Russia's actions in Ukraine as well as by Russian-Turkish tensions and the fall in energy prices. With no friends in the world and an unreliable United States far away, they all turned to China, quietly removing pro-Russian elements from their bureaucracies and polity and delinking their economies from Russia. Russia is today pivotal only in Kazakhstan (where almost 50 percent of the population is ethnically Russian, and sizeable Kazakh and Uighur populations are alienated by China's repression in Xinjiang) and in Kyrgistan, but elsewhere in central Asia it shares influence with China. In 2013 China moved ahead of Russia in terms of regional trade, doing US$50 billion in trade with the five former Soviet republics, compared to Russia's US$30 billion. Chinese companies now own almost a quarter of Kazakh oil production and more than half of Turkmenistan's gas exports.

"Central Asia is unique in that it is the only place where all the great powers converge," a Chinese scholar notes.[2] The United States has a toe-hold in Afghanistan but otherwise plays little or no economic, political, or military role in central Asia. Historically the region included Xinjiang, Mongolia, and Afghanistan. What happens there is therefore a good measure of what happens to power relationships between the great land powers. Putin's Eurasianism and quasi-alliance with China has historical precedent in Russia's past, in the medieval tzars' alliance with the Mongols in the face of invasions by Swedes, Poles, and Teutonic knights. For Russia the rimland from the Baltic to the Black Sea basin is one integrated region; anarchy in west or central Asia is linked to what happens in eastern Europe and cannot be ignored. This is why Russia is in Syria, working with Iran to pacify the region and to keep a hostile West away from Russia's "near abroad."

For Robert Kaplan, "The Black Sea is no less a conflict system than the Caribbean was in the nineteenth century and the South China and East China Seas are today."[3] Russia's influence in the extended region, from the Baltic to Xinjiang and Afghanistan, today is restricted by China, not the United States. Having managed the Tibetan, Uighur, Mongol, and other peoples outside the arable Han heartland by subjugation, demographic pressure, and co-option, China now extends its influence beyond her late-eighteenth-century imperial boundaries in central Asia. China hopes to recruit Iran and others through the Belt and Road Initiative and Shanghai Cooperation Organization to stop radical Islamists, who have gained strength in west and central Asia by extending their reach into Xinjiang. Xinjiang and Tibet are part of an extended central Asian area where ethnic and cultural tensions are manifest and drive local developments and great power involvement in the region. All in all, China is consolidating the Eurasian landmass through a twenty-first-century combination of trade, finance, infrastructure, connectivity, and security webs and is increasingly the predominant continental power in inner Asia.

~

If central Asia is geographically open from east to west, the Indian subcontinent, with its 1.7 billion people, has a bounded geography only to the north, where the high Himalaya mark a clear geographic, cultural, and political boundary between what lies north and south of the mountains—a barrier or boundary that has lasted over history and is only now becoming porous as a result of modern technology. To the east, west, and south, whether through Afghanistan and Iran, or Myanmar, or the Indian Ocean, the subcontinent has been open to influence, immigration, and economic contact throughout its history.

The subcontinent has been most open to the world through the Indian Ocean. For the greater part of its history, the prosperity of the subcontinent has been as dependent, maybe more so, on its maritime dimensions as on the continental order. The Indian Ocean is not a closed ocean, not landlocked like the Mediterranean, the Aegean, the Black Sea, or the seas near China around which other civilizations grew. Thanks to predictable monsoons, the Indian Ocean did not have to wait for the age of steam to be united, unlike other oceans, and deep water sailing probably developed here first. The maritime domain by definition is a positive-sum one, and water transport has historically been easier and cheaper than that by land. For the greater part, therefore, southern Asia is maritime.

As a consequence of this geography, throughout history the subcontinent has been an autonomous strategic unit that was also part of a larger multiverse, connected but separate from the universes of the Levant and Persian Gulf, central Asia and Persia, the southeast Asian maritime kingdoms, and east Asia and China. And through history, the subcontinent was most prosperous and stable when its external connections to these regions flourished alongside its internal strength. This is very different from northeast Asia or northern Europe or north America, which were relatively isolated in history and unconnected to other regions for their security and prosperity for most of their past. One of the subcontinent's connections, that with central and western Asia, was broken at India's independence with the partition of India and creation of Pakistan, which having gained its independence from India, chose to define its identity in opposition to India from the beginning. This connected geography means that the security of the subcontinent is better thought of as a series of concentric but overlapping circles. What happens in southeast Asia or east Asia or west Asia directly affects the security of the subcontinent. And given the open geography of the Indian Ocean, what happens in southern Asia affects the rest of Asia as well.

The other geopolitical consequence of the open geography is linked fates and open societies within the subcontinent. Every southern Asian country has crossborder ethnicities and shares deep religious and strong linguistic, ethnic, and cultural affinities across its state boundaries. State boundaries are new and recently defined; the ethnicities, languages, religions, and cultures are ancient. There is a shared history of openness to each other within southern Asia that is stronger than in many other regions of the world. The region's affinities far outweigh its differences. Languages, foods, religions, and ethnicities cross all the state boundaries in southern Asia. Paradoxically, that affinity across formal state boundaries is one reason why nationalism is high, but nationhood is still a work in progress everywhere in southern Asia. Bhutan and the Maldives are exceptions in their relative homogeneity in ethnic, religious, and linguistic terms. India and Afghanistan are the other extreme, where every group is a minority in terms of either language, religion, region, or ethnicity. India, exceptionally, chose to base its nationalism not on a common religion, ethnicity, language, or enemy, but on an idea of India. Given the plural and diverse nature of its society, India chose after independence to be a democracy, where every social segment has a say. That idea of Indian nationhood is under political attack now, by an attempt to redefine it in nineteenth-century European terms using religion or "Hindutva," but it seems likely to endure as it objectively serves the interest of most of the population and is seen to do so by most Indians. The short geopolitical point is that the very high degree of cultural and other affinities across state boundaries in the old nations but new states of south Asia make for sensitive and touchy nationalist reactions and strong declaratory defenses of sovereignty by states.

In practice weak state structures mean porous borders, smuggling often exceeds formal trade, and large-scale migration for economic and other reasons is common throughout the subcontinent. There are an estimated 20 million Bangladeshi economic migrants in India according to conservative estimates, quite apart from refugee flows. The UN estimates a total of 5.29 million refugees in India of which about 3.1 million are from Bangladesh. These include over 100,000 Tibetans, 64,000 Sri Lankans, 36,500 Afghans and Myanmarese, and about 16,500 Rohingya. (The government of India has also used a figure of 40,000 Rohingya in India.)

India's geopolitical situation, though apparently similar to China's in some respects, is also fundamentally different. Like China, India is both a continental and maritime power. And India too faces a historically unprecedented geopolitical situation. Unlike China, however, it has always been an active maritime power. The peninsula has been the source of much of India's wealth, creativity, and power in history, and the keeper and disseminator of its cultural core. That the country emerged "sea-blind" from British rule, when British Indian governments in Calcutta and New Delhi obsessed about the Great Game and left maritime security to London and the Royal Navy, cannot change the facts of its geography and history or where its comparative advantages lie. The geopolitician would say that India's problem is that its present borders do not conform to the geographic borders of the subcontinent and that Pakistan, which is within the subcontinent, poses security challenges to India that rob India of vital political energy that it could otherwise harness in Eurasia.

Since India's independence in 1947, contemporary politics in the subcontinent have been broadly determined by two influences: the formation of independent nation-states in the region in the twenty-first century, and the disparity in power and the overwhelming weight of India in the area. Pakistan was a new state created in 1947; Bangladesh is an even newer one since 1971; Burma was separately administered from India only after 1936; Nepal and Bhutan were in ambiguous subordinate relationships with British India; and Ceylon was administered as a crown colony and has always had political arrangements separate from India unlike some other south Asian states. Given India's weight in the subregion, and the fact that every border is crossed by language, religion, ethnic groups, and myriad affinities, it was only natural that the consolidation of state structures on the basis of nationalism in these countries would take the form of identity politics that would be defined and measured against India and the Indian experience. This took two forms. On the one hand there were those who imitated the Indian freedom movement and the Indian experiment with democracy, a socialist pattern of development, and nonalignment. On the other, national politics in India's neighbors took the form of standing up to Indian influence or defining one's identity in opposition to India. Both phenomena varied in degree from country to country.

The process of nation building in the subcontinent has thus taken many forms. At one extreme is Pakistan, whose identity is propagated almost entirely in opposition to India and on the basis of religion. This has had several consequences: the outsize role of the army, the steady weakening of democratic political parties, civil society, and the left, and the increasingly radical role of religion in Pakistani politics. To justify Islamization policies, Zia-ul-Haq is said to have remarked that if a Turk was not a Muslim he was still a Turk, but if a Pakistani was not a Muslim he was an Indian. The result is an increasing role for religion and extremism and space for terrorist groups to masquerade as social organizations and political parties.

State consolidation and the formation of a national identity are still works in progress but have taken more benign forms in most other south Asian countries. Bangladesh's rich cultural heritage and Bengali identity and the strength of political parties with mass support have prevented Bangladeshi politics from going the Pakistan way. Sri Lanka and Nepal, despite long civil wars, have emerged more democratic than before and are now settling into more normal politics. Myanmar is attempting a difficult transition to democracy while protecting its unity from separatist demands of multiple ethnic insurgent groups. The Maldives is institutionalizing democracy and working out the role of religion in political life there. Bhutan, relatively homogenous ethnically, has made the smoothest transition to becoming a modern nation-state.

Their overwhelming domestic preoccupations mean that intra-south Asian cooperation among these countries has been limited. Despite affinities and porous borders, by formal indicators southern Asia is the least economically integrated region of the world. The World Bank says that intraregional trade in south Asia is less than 5 percent of its total trade, compared to 35 percent for east Asia and 60 percent for Europe. Intraregional investment is less than 1 percent. These formal figures may overstate the lack of economic integration. Informal trade could be more than three times formal flows, and the size of remittances suggests that migration and other transfers are large. But the lack of formal institutions means that the subcontinent has quite a way to go in integrating itself economically. The absence of local sources of investment and finance, especially since the 2008 crisis, make investment projects promised by China's Belt and Road Initiative alluring to all southern Asian countries except India. Clearly, if India wishes to take itself and the region to prosperity and minimize outside influences, it must first connect with and economically integrate with its neighborhood.

The first real attempts to institutionalize subregional cooperation beyond bilateral cooperation with India in a multilateral or subregional way began in the 1980s with the formation of the South Asian Association for Regional Cooperation (SAARC), which has underperformed since then. It has found it difficult to build beyond the significance of bilateral links with India for each of its members. SAARC has not produced a proportionate increase in intra-south Asian economic cooperation despite several efforts to reintegrate the subcontinent economically, such as through the South Asia Free Trade Agreement signed in 2004. Instead, India has taken unilateral and bilateral steps to open its markets to other south Asian countries, offering zero duty access to its neighbors under free trade agreements and special arrangements with Nepal, Bhutan, and Sri Lanka. Border markets have been opened with Bangladesh, some free movement by residents in a zone near the border takes place with Myanmar, and the common use of crossborder waterways has begun, as has the interconnection of electricity and other grids and the first steps to freer transport across borders.

~

The subcontinent's concentration on domestic politics also meant that its energy has largely been concentrated inward, rather than on broader Asian and global issues. During the Cold War, the superpowers' interest in south Asia was limited to its utility in their quarrels. The outside world was relatively uninterested in the subcontinent geopolitically, once India chose to be nonaligned and not participate in either Cold War bloc. Pakistan made itself useful to the United States as an ally against the Soviet Union, hosting U-2 reconnaissance flights and joining the Baghdad and Southeast Asia Treaty Organization (SEATO) pacts. Later Pakistan also made itself useful to China then having difficulties with India, signing a boundary agreement for portions of Kashmir's boundary with China in March 1963, just after the India-China war of 1962. South Asia also became momentarily significant to Nixon and Kissinger when the birth of Bangladesh threatened to complicate their plans for an opening to China.

During the Cold War, most southern Asian states were happy to opt out of the world's quarrels and alliances and to concentrate on their own development. Every southern Asian country was nonaligned in practice, except Pakistan. For a Pakistan with an identity deficit, joining a great power or an alliance and seeking outside support was, and remains, a way of seeking parity with a much larger India. This remains a Pakistani imperative despite fundamental changes in the international situation since the end of the Cold War. For the rest of southern Asia, however, changes in the international situation meant that the decades after 1990 have been the best in history for their economic development, for the growth of the middle class, and for their increasing integration into the world economy. Its open geography meant that southern Asia, and maritime southern Asia in particular—Bangladesh, coastal India, and Sri Lanka—did very well during the globalization decades. India is now the world's fifth largest economy in nominal GDP and third largest in PPP terms, and its society and economy have been changed fundamentally by reforms since 1991. In the two decades of open trade and investment that followed the end of the Cold War, the acceleration of growth has been broad-based among the south Asian economies. Bangladesh, Sri Lanka, Bhutan, and others have experienced unprecedented rates of growth.[4]

Globalization also changed the relative distribution of power among the subcontinent's countries. While India's preponderance remains or has grown, since 2006 Bangladesh has exceeded Pakistan's overall growth rate by 2.5 percent annually, its population growth at 1.1 percent per year is lower than Pakistan's 2.5 percent. With higher GDP growth and lower population increase, Bangladesh's per capita income is growing 3.3 percent faster than that of Pakistan. India's population has grown at 1.2 percent each year in the last decade. Roughly half of Indian's population in twenty-four states has achieved the so-called replacement fertility rate of 2.1 children per woman, at which rate population stabilizes. Bangladesh overtook Pakistan in terms of per capita GDP in 2020 and could soon overtake India. Driven by social change and improvements in the status of women, life expectancy in Bangladesh is seventy-two years compared to Pakistan's sixty-six years and India's sixty-eight years. Bangladesh has an inclusive economy (where only 10.4 percent of bank accounts are dormant, while 48 percent are in India), and its garment industry took advantage of a globalized world to build large garment firms and generate employment for women.[5]

What has also grown rapidly in the last decade is security cooperation between countries of the subcontinent (other than Pakistan), in the form of increased military diplomacy and training, some supply of defense equipment, and maritime cooperation between navies. Intelligence sharing and liaison have also improved considerably as part of a common effort against terrorism.

India's weight in the region because of its larger economy and population, and because most of its neighbors are only connected to each other through India, has several political consequences. For one thing, India's neighbors, save for China, seek to balance and hedge against the overwhelming Indian influence in their internal politics as much as in their dealings with the rest of the world. As India's power has increased, so has their need to balance this by building links with outside powers such as China and the United States.

India and China have had a complex pattern of cooperation, competition, coexistence, and contention in the subcontinent and the Indian Ocean region. India-China relations were easier in the 1990s and early 2000s, when the subcontinent was not a major arena for India-China competition. Now that the power dynamics have changed, both Delhi and Beijing seek to maximize their influence in the other countries of southern Asia and are increasingly rubbing up against each other. India's and China's extreme sensitivity about their territorial integrity and internal security makes contention in the periphery a visible source of friction in India-China relations and is reflected in India's relations with individual southern Asian neighbors. The first Modi government's closer alignment with the United States, its deference to China, and its assertive diplomacy in the subcontinent produced the very outcome that it sought to prevent: a much stronger Chinese presence in the subcontinent. The Modi government's susceptibility to U.S. pressure on Indian dealings with Iran and Russia and hedging by India's neighbors have further constrained India in its own periphery.

As China's power has grown, it has become an increasingly important trading and development partner to most south Asian countries. China's influence in the subcontinent is a relatively recent phenomenon, apart from the special and separate case of Pakistan, but is growing rapidly. China's investment in the subcontinent far exceeds India's with, approximately, more than US$2.3 billion each in Pakistan and Sri Lanka, US$2 billion each in Myanmar and Bangladesh, and US$3 billion in Nepal since January 2016, while India has invested less than a total of US$800 million in the same period. China's pledges under the Belt and Road Initiative are more than US$100 billion in investment and loans to south Asia: $62 billion to Pakistan, US$32 billion to Bangladesh, US$11 billion to Sri Lanka, and US$1.5 billion to the Maldives.[6] In trade, India is still the largest training partner for Sri Lanka, Nepal, and Bhutan, although the gap has been closing, and in the last decade India and China have switched places several times as Bangladesh's largest trading partner. The World Bank estimates that with the right steps, India's trade in goods with south Asia could amount to US$62 billion instead of the US$19 billion that it was in 2017. Remittances from India to south Asian countries amounted to over US$7.5 billion in 2014 (when remittances from China were US$700,000 in total). In the same year India received remittances worth US$9 billion from all of south Asia, while China received less than US$1billion mainly from Chinese workers. India clearly has much more to do economically in the subcontinent if it is to feel comfortable in its immediate periphery and to be an integral part of their economic future and prosperity.

Today, southern Asia and the Indian Ocean are a higher, but not the highest, priority for China in its contention with the United States, for its energy security, for its internal security concerns in Tibet and Xinjiang, and for its quest for primacy in Asia. China has shown a new willingness to be involved in the internal politics of Nepal, Sri Lanka, and the Maldives. Since China's and India's ascent has been combined with the simultaneous reemergence of powers like Korea, Indonesia, and others, and with Japan now behaving as a more normal power, politics around and within southern Asia has become more complex. Outside great power interest in southern Asia, limited in the 1980s to Afghanistan as an arena of U.S.-Soviet rivalry, has broadened to include the subcontinent's potential as a market, and as a source of military power, and now extends to an interest in its stability, but not necessarily to its rise to real power in the international system. When piracy became a problem off the Malacca straits in the late 1980s and early 1990s, local powers dealt with the problem, led by Singapore with India, Malaysia, and others. When piracy off the Horn of Africa became a problem in the mid-2000s, NATO, the European Union, the

United States, and regional and local powers such as India, China, and others all deployed their naval assets.

The limited interest of outside powers in the politics of south Asia changed with the end of the Cold War, with India and the subcontinent's improved economic performance, and with the rise of China. The global war on terror declared by the United States after the 9/11 attacks, and the resulting wars in Afghanistan and Iraq, made Pakistan necessary to American strategy. But China's rise and India's economic progress meant that the United States could no longer ignore India. Besides, India and Pakistan were declared nuclear powers after 1998. The U.S. answer was "de-hyphenization" of her relations with India and Pakistan. Through the late 1990s and early part of this century, under the Vajpayee and Manmohan Singh governments, India-U.S. relations were transformed, and for a while the United States took an interest in affairs of the subcontinent other than India-Pakistan relations. U.S. interest in other south Asian countries has declined with the end of the civil wars in Nepal and Sri Lanka and with President Donald Trump's domestic preoccupations, 2016–2020, with an "America First" policy and other distractions taking priority. Growing U.S. contention with China has, however, reversed this trend and made Bangladesh, Sri Lanka, and the Maldives more significant to the new U.S.–Indo-Pacific strategy, and Nepal because of its border with Tibet. Since 2018, the United States has begun discussions with these countries on greater maritime security assistance and increased economic commitments and undertaken a series of visits. India is now seen by the United States as a potential but so far unsatisfactory counterweight to China in the Quad group (composed of Australia, India, Japan, and the United States) and as a future Indo-Pacific partner. India is also a target of U.S. economic policy to open up her civilian and defense markets. Unlike the past, however, the United States has not sought to intervene on issues such as the fate of the Rohingya population that divide and consume south Asia. That could conceivably change with increasing U.S.-China contention or a change of administrations in Washington.

On the other hand, China has offered itself as an honest broker to Bangladesh and Myanmar on the Rohingya issue and is brokering the Myanmar government's negotiations with its ethnic minorities and insurgencies. There is now a much stronger political dimension to China's interest in the region. China is also much more active in shaping outcomes in Afghanistan, working with Pakistan, Russia, and Iran. China has worked hard to bring and keep the Nepalese communist parties together and in power, and has made its sympathies for some Sri Lankan politicians quite evident by funding and supporting them. Its influence in south Asia is rising and is unlikely to diminish in the near future. For most south Asian countries China offers a welcome alternative and balancer to excessive dependence on India, the eternal and looming presence in their lives. China also serves to make them attractive to the United States, the more occasional visitor.

In the larger Indian Ocean region, the balance and geography are different from the South China Sea and East China Sea. The Indian Ocean is not a closed sea. No power in history has controlled all ten of its choke points at the same time. China is today putting in place means for the future, building ports and bases at Djibouti, Gwadar or Jiwani, Hambantota, Khyaukpau, Malacca, the Maldives, and so on, preparing for a time when the balance can be worked in its favor. But here, given the distance from home, China is likely to first work with allies and partners, like the Pakistan Navy, while deploying psychological, political, economic, and other pressure to change the calculus of existing maritime powers in the Indian Ocean, namely, India, the United States, Singapore, Indonesia, Australia, and others.

The overall prospect is for the subcontinent to be increasingly connected to the outside world and influenced by outside powers. China's south Asian policy seems driven primarily by its security interests in the Indian Ocean and Tibet and by its political and strategic interest in its periphery and in keeping India preoccupied in the subcontinent. It is only recently that the subcontinent has become an object of China's economic interest. Increasing Chinese involvement is welcomed by most countries of the subregion, but not always by India. So far, the India-China fault line in the subcontinent has not achieved the salience or nature of the India-Pakistan one, which has prevented subcontinent-wide cooperation from gaining momentum. The subcontinent's Asian or global significance remains largely a function of India's role, one that would be strengthened if India worked with, rather than against, her neighbors.

∿

To India's west is a fragmented region where the politics of religion and identity are stronger than nationalism. West Asia is also an area of rapid change. Since the 1970s west Asia has transitioned from a rural society to one of megacities, and religious and rightist politics have trumped socialist and secular varieties in country after country, fueled by an influx of wealth from petroleum exports. There is a religious question at the heart of the politics of the region that other regions have either answered or finessed. That is whether religion takes precedence over reasons of state and, indeed, whether the state exists only to perform God's will, whatever that may be and by whomsoever defined. An Indian Muslim is an Indian first and Muslim in his or her personal practice not citizenship. No western Asian state can yet make a similar assertion or give a conclusive answer to this question.

The issue goes beyond the use of religion as a source of legitimization of leadership or state power to its role in determining issues in western Asia that are secular in much of the rest of the world. The twentieth century saw several different attempts in west Asia to answer this question, ranging from Ataturk's separation of Islam from the modern Turkish state (which lasted until a few years ago, longer than most other such west Asian experiments), to the 1979 Iranian revolution's creation of a theological republic based on *velayat-e-faqih* (or guardianship of Islamic jurists), to the Saudi example of rule after conquest through alliance by a ruling family with Wahhabi clerics, to multiple variants in between. None of these has served as a stable basis for political and economic progress. The one that came closest to finding a lasting answer has been the Iranian experiment, which, within a shifted frame, came about relatively peacefully,[7] and which, of all the political dispensations in western Asia, allows the greatest degree of freedom to women and the most popular say in the choice of leaders, not as a gift from the regime but because of Iranian history and cultural and political tradition. The fundamental challenge that the 1979 Iranian revolution posed to autocratic Arab regimes like Iraq and Saudi Arabia, which rule over large Shia populations, and to continued Western control of the sources of oil, has meant that Iran has been under military or other forms of pressure throughout its existence. It is hardly surprising if some Iranian leaders today are paranoid. Indeed, what I find surprising is the fact that there are still "reformists" among Iran's leaders with a considerable popular following who are willing to enter into agreements on their nuclear program with the West and who still look to the West rather than to Asia. To my mind that is proof of the fundamental pragmatism of Persian statecraft, a pragmatism honed by millennia of practice, not evident in the rest of the region.

Because the fundamental question of religion and politics is unresolved, states in western Asia are fragile, and often weaker than non-state actors, particularly those that claim religious legitimacy like the Islamic State or Caliphate and groups that combine religious authority with armed power like Al Qaeda. The overlay of ancient rivalries and the patchwork of minorities who straddle state frontiers have further weakened the authority of the state and added to the fractious nature of the region's politics. Take the Kurds, for instance, who straddle Iran, Turkey, and Iraq, or Shia populations under Sunni rule in Iraq, Bahrain, and eastern Saudi Arabia, or the absence of a clear majority in artificially created states like Lebanon. This phenomenon is what provides justification for the outsize political role of militaries in the state structures of western Asia, militaries that have often been the main instrument used by outside powers to manage and interfere in the politics of the region.

The history of outside interference in the region's politics has been prompted by its rich oil resources and its proximity to Europe, as the former center of gravity of world politics, and by great power rivalry ever since the Ottoman empire began showing signs of weakness. Fractured internal politics gave rise to proxies with whom outside powers could work, and this phenomenon became even more pronounced with the creation of Israel. State boundaries drawn by Western powers after World War I have remained the nominal boundaries because of the fragmented politics of the region. Baathists and Arab nationalists offered a secular alternative as political opponents, which the Wahhabis, Muslim Brotherhood, and other religious groups ignored or rejected. In practice, these Western drawn boundaries mean less and less, because they do not reflect the distribution of power, of political authority, of religion, of language or ethnicities, let alone an incipient sense of nationalism that has to compete with the other claims on identity.

The tradition of outside interference and the cocktail of fragilities that I have mentioned can together explain much of what we see in the region today: the attempted dismemberment of Syria; the dismantling of Libya; the consolidation of army rule in Egypt; the failed Turkish attempt to use the Muslim Brotherhood to extend its reach into the internal politics of the region; the rivalry between the larger regional successors to ancient empires, Turkey, Iran, and Egypt; and so on. With the elimination of Iraq from the regional geopolitical equation after the first Gulf War in 1990–1991, Iran's natural preeminence began to assert itself in the region and was furthered by the American invasion of Iraq in 2003 and the Arab Spring that began in 2010. By 2018, Iran had influence in a belt stretching across the region from Afghanistan to the Mediterranean and through the Persian Gulf, helped by the internal weakness of regimes that oppose it. Iran's opponents rely on terrorist and extremist groups to push back against growing Iranian influence in Syria, Iraq, Yemen and elsewhere, and on an alliance between Israel and the Sunni Arab monarchies, with U.S. backing. What is presented as a Shia-Sunni conflict is an attempt to prevent Iranian predominance from manifesting itself. There is now less Western interest in stability in west Asia, as oil and energy are available elsewhere. The

United States has become a significant exporter of oil and gas. Local forces in western Asia creating social fragmentation, state failure and religious extremism seem to be strengthening.

For India this situation in western Asia generates a series of concerns. India's security has always been intimately linked to what occurs in western Asia. Although the east is again more important to India's future prosperity than the west, India's prosperity, security, and defensive interests in western Asia remain. Over 7 million Indians live and work in the Persian Gulf and Saudi Arabia and remit money home, more than 63 percent of India's crude oil imports come from the region, and there remains the risk of radical or political Islam spreading to India from western Asia, which is already the major funder and inspiration for jihadi terrorist groups in India. This combination of interests makes Iran, Saudi Arabia, and the Gulf Cooperation Council Arab states around the Persian Gulf critical to India's security. India has no option but to be engaged with all the powers in western Asia and to work with all possible partners against radicalism and terrorism wherever possible. In that effort, Israel is an essential partner too, quite apart from the strong defense supply relationship that has made Israel one of India's major sources of defense equipment.

India had opposed the partition of Palestine in the UN in 1948, given its own unhappy experience with Partition, but recognized the state of Israel soon thereafter. A sizeable number of Indian Jews, many of whose ancestors came to India after the destruction of the First Temple, made *aliya* to the new state of Israel and relations between the two nations grew in agriculture, defense, and other functional areas in the 1950s and 1960s. Israel had stepped in with defense supplies during India's 1962, 1965, and 1971 wars with China and Pakistan. As a consequence, India faced an eight-day oil boycott by Saudi Arabia in 1974 because of dealings with Israel. By the mid-1970s, however, India was repositioning its relations with Israel. The PLO established an office in Delhi in 1975 after India recognized the PLO as the "sole legitimate representative of the Palestinian people." India, however, still sought to maintain balance in its relations with both Israel and the PLO, and if it recognized the Palestinian state in 1988, it also upgraded relations with Israel to ambassadorial level in 1992, with progress in the Middle East Peace Process.

India's economic interests demand that it work with all the powers in the region, Israel, Saudi Arabia, Egypt, Iran, and Turkey, as well as the Gulf Cooperation Council. Since 1947 India has been largely successful in that attempt by not choosing sides in their quarrels with one another, and by staying out of their internal politics (unlike Pakistan's army, which chose to provide internal security to regimes in Jordan, Saudi Arabia, and elsewhere). As the West's interest in and ability to provide order and security in west Asia diminishes, India will have to engage more. In today's situation, India should probably consider expanding its role as a provider of security, particularly maritime security around the Persian Gulf, where India's oil imports come from, as it did with its contribution since 2007 to the elimination of piracy off the Horn of Africa—as will China, for similar reasons, since this is an area where Indian and Chinese interests coincide.

In geopolitical terms, India's interests have often aligned with Egypt since the 1950s and with Iran since the 1980s. In the immediate neighborhood, in the fight against Al Qaeda and the Taliban in Afghanistan, and in the broader attempt to contain the more extreme sectarian Sunni groups and terrorists coming out of Pakistan with state support, India and Iran have worked together. Iran also offers India access to central Asia and Afghanistan that Pakistan has cut off. India's economic complementarity with Iran in the energy sector is growing. Of the regional powers in western Asia, Israel, Iran, and Egypt are those that have refrained from promoting sectarian extremism among India's minorities, and, since the early 1980s, from supporting Pakistan in it quarrels with India.

~

Can we today speak of Asia as one? From India it seems that apparent differences between the subregions of Asia mask a growing unity across the continent. Western Asia is indeed unstable. But the picture to India's east is not unmixed. The Asia-Pacific has seen the greatest and fastest improvement in human welfare. And yet, at the same time, as aspirations have grown, demands on leaders are higher than ever before, and governments are less confident of the future than before. Growth has slowed. Local power politics are back, after being subsumed into a bipolar framework by the superpowers in the Cold War and suppressed during the United States' unipolar moment. There is a mismatch between individual lives and the politics around them. Despite great economic progress, eastern Asian states are displaying many signs of insecurity in their behavior, or at least they perceive that they are less secure and face uncertainty that now imperils their future prosperity.

West and east Asia are increasingly linked, and these links are growing. One is the economic consolidation of infrastructure, connectivity, trade, and investment through central Asia that is being built through China's Belt and Road Initiative. How Russia and Iran react to China's consolidation of the Eurasian landmass will bear watching, for it is unlikely that they will be happy to see their immediate neighborhoods organized under other auspices, even if Western and American policy continue to drive them into China's embrace. West Asia's four largest customers for its oil and gas are in Asia: China, India, Japan, and South Korea. Other uniting bonds include the global supply chains that tie together the subregions of Asia, particularly in the northeastern and southeastern regions. Today's military technologies also make the continent as a whole one theater of operations, not just the maritime spaces or the Indo-Pacific around the Eurasian landmass. Ballistic missile ranges and satellite surveillance are not limited by conventional boundaries or geographical features like mountains, and new domains of contention like cyberspace and outer space also know no boundaries.

Asia is also increasingly united in another way: by the spread of radical Islamic ideology from western Asia to south and southeast Asia. Much of this had leapfrogged India, until the polarization of politics in India, Myanmar, Sri Lanka, Thailand, Kampuchea, and elsewhere through the radicalization of political Hinduism and Buddhism, and the attempt to make these religions more like those that arose in the Levant with a single credo, proselytization, conversion ceremonies, and rigid orthodoxies of dogma. The Rohingya pose this problem most directly to India. Arguing about which came first, radical Islam or radical Hinduism or radical Buddhism, only feeds the narrative of proponents of these political cults. Radical Islam is rising in southern Thailand and in Indonesia and has seen militant offshoots in the Philippines.

In any case, located as it is, India cannot segment its thinking or ignore either east or west Asia, both of which deeply, directly, and immediately affect its prosperity and security.

11

China Rising

India's interests, like Asia itself, are greatly affected by how a rising China chooses to behave.

As China turns to the sea, it is in a more comfortable geopolitical position than at any time since the high Qing conquest of the Dzungars in central Asia at the end of the eighteenth century. Through its long history, its preoccupation was to defend a geographically open inner Asian frontier against the nomads of the northern steppe belt that hatched several dynasties that ruled China—from the Tang to the Manchu or Qing. That is now changed. China's task of neutralizing and managing the Eurasian heartland has been considerably eased by the division of that steppe belt into smaller and weaker states, and by the retreat and diminution of Russia after the collapse of the Soviet Union. For the most part, Chinese power has been pushing at an open door on land, with the exception of south Asia, where India too is rising and expanding its interests, and in Korea, where partition of the peninsula and a U.S. military presence limit China's ability to shape outcomes.

China's turn to the sea is a consequence of the pattern of its recent development. Having relied on export-led growth to build its own manufacturing, China's future growth now requires continued access by sea to the world's energy, essential raw materials, food, markets, technology, and capital. Like India, external merchandise trade accounts for a little less than half of China's GDP. And to defend these interests China seeks to transition into a maritime power. But it faces more difficulty at sea than on land. What is new for China is that it now must think as a maritime power, something it has never done for any extended period of time, if at all.[1] Zheng He (1371–1433) is often cited as the exception for he voyaged in the Indian Ocean during the early Ming with a large "treasure fleet." But it could equally be argued from his conduct and the Chinese record itself that these voyages were a maritime variant of the overland expeditions to barbarian lands in central Asia that the Ming and other Chinese dynasties undertook to obtain control of trade routes, receive submissions and bring back treasure, and that they do not provide a guide to how China will act as a maritime power at this very different stage of its history.[2]

After 2008 China, apparently acting on the presumption that a West in decline would accommodate its drive for primacy in Asia, attempted a two-track strategy, neither track of which succeeded entirely. The first was to increase its commitment to its two de facto allies, Pakistan and North Korea, while bearing down in its immediate periphery on Japan, Vietnam, those aligned within the Association of Southeast Asian Nations, and others in the South China Sea and the East China Sea. The other was to offer a cooperative understanding based on parity to the United States in the guise of "a new type of major power relationship," which, in the Chinese understanding, would leave each to pursue its own "core" interests in its own spheres of interest.[3] Though initially tempted, the United States soon realized that accommodating China's definition of its own core interests in the South China Sea and elsewhere would circumscribe U.S. ability to operate throughout the Asia-Pacific, lose it allies, and offered little in return on core U.S. concerns. Besides, it went against the grain of U.S. grand strategy since World War II to prevent the emergence of a peer competitor in the international system. The balancing responses to these Chinese actions were a U.S. "pivot" to Asia and the formation of informal countervailing coalitions by powers in China's periphery: India, Japan, Vietnam, and others have increased their defense, security, and intelligence cooperation considerably.

China reacted to the initial pushback by readjusting its strategy in 2012 from a largely political and military strategy, focused on the South China and East China Seas, to a broader geo-economic strategy using its economic strengths, crystallized in Xi Jinping's One-Belt-One-Road proposal of 2013, subsequently renamed the Belt and Road Initiative (BRI).

A third policy option was logically available, though China has not yet tried it, which was to work with significant local powers in the region and its periphery—consulting with Japan, India, Indonesia, Vietnam, and South Korea, for instance—to evolve a new security order in the Asia-Pacific, based on mutual respect for core concerns and managing differences that exist. This would require an accommodation (and redefinition) of China's and others' core interests, but this may be politically difficult for leaderships in the present ultranationalist climate. While awaiting such a process of redefinition and agreement on core interests, confidence building measures, crisis management mechanisms, and communications arrangements between the powers would be required to restore a sense of security in the Asia-Pacific. It would be logical to start such a process with maritime security, where all the major Asian powers, including China and the United States, have a common interest as significant trading nations in maintaining security and freedom of navigation throughout the region. The more difficult issues that any collective security system would have to address would be the effects on the Asia-Pacific of terrorism and non-state actors, of new military doctrines and postures, of nuclear proliferation and deterrence, of cyber security, and of political and state fragility in west and southwest Asia, and its spread to southeast Asia, since states like Pakistan are themselves involved in abetting and creating some of these phenomena.

Instead, China has chosen to go its own way, relying on its own economic, political, and military power to secure its interests in Asia and to remake the Asian order.

For its neighbors, the most evident symbol of China's new power, and of its intention to project that power, is the People's Liberation Army (PLA). China's military is the transformed product of three decades of double-digit budgetary growth and the building of infrastructure to support it. The military reforms of the last few years have transformed the PLA from an instrument of national consolidation into an expeditionary force, an instrument of power projection with joint theater commands based on the U.S. model. For India one direct consequence is that mobilization times in Tibet have shrunk from two seasons to two weeks, as shown by PLA exercises in Tibet in the last decade practicing for contingencies on the border with India and within Tibet, and displaying China's rapid mobilization capabilities. China has also modernized its nuclear and missile forces into a more capable second-strike force and developed medium-range ballistic missile and cruise missile capabilities and systems that are altering the regional military balance, even with the United States. A repeat of the 1996 Taiwan Strait crisis is no longer possible. China's merchant marine fleet is built to PLA specifications. A large fleet of Coast Guard vessels and modern diesel submarines can project power and threaten surface vessels in the western Pacific, East China Sea, South China Sea, and, to a lesser extent, into the Indian Ocean. Its fighter aircraft inventory has grown to the point where China felt strong enough to declare an Air Defense Identification Zone in the East China Sea in November 2013, with hints of one to follow in the South China Sea. China has built up significant offensive capabilities in asymmetric warfare, in cyber war, in missile and strategic forces, and in power projection platforms such as submarines and aircraft carriers.

The ports and other infrastructure that it has built or is buying in the Indian Ocean littoral and the Mediterranean are now useful to the PLA Navy. China established its first PLA base at Djibouti, has access to Gwadar and Karachi, and is building or managing ports at Hambantota, Kyaukphyu, and other locations around the Indian Ocean and around the world. At the southern end of Laamu atoll in the Maldives, the island of Gaadhoo guards the one-and-a-half degree channel through which most Indian Ocean shipping passes. Gaadhoo was said to have been secretly promised to China by former Maldives president Abdullah Yameen and was cleared of its inhabitants during his presidency.

China's accumulation of the hardware of power is accompanied by a shift in China's declared willingness to project and use power, described in the May 2015 White Paper on Military Strategy.[4] The strategy gives military effect to Xi Jinping's shift away from Deng Xiaoping's twenty-four-character strategy of "hiding one's light and not taking a leadership role." PLA reforms since 2015, not just of the military commands and regions but in the role of the political commissars, and functional and other military changes, show a determination to change the PLA in fundamental ways into an instrument for power projection able to fight short, intense, high-technology wars in "informationalized" conditions outside China's own territory and immediate periphery. It has therefore further developed maritime and air capabilities. We have seen a regular presence of the PLA Navy in the Indian Ocean since 2008, including nuclear missile submarine patrols after 2014.

These steps provide the military underpinnings for the larger economic and political role that China seeks for itself in its periphery and the Asia-Pacific today and in the world tomorrow. Xi Jinping's signature connectivity and economic integration of the BRI, binding China and Eurasia overland to Europe and by a maritime route, will soon have Chinese military capacity to back and protect it. If the BRI fails, it will not be for lack of enforcement capability or top-level Chinese leadership commitment.

～

The slow global economy since 2008, further affected by the COVID-19 pandemic, makes China even more important to the world as one of the few sources of global growth. The International Monetary Fund estimates that China accounted for 25 percent of world GDP growth in 2017, and India for 15 percent. But its own economy has been slowing too, and could pose an internal challenge to the legitimacy of the Chinese regime. The legitimacy of single-party rule by the Chinese Communist Party (CCP) was originally based on socialism, nationalism, and communist ideology in the 1950s and 1960s. The Great Proletarian Cultural Revolution gave ideology a bad name, and was a form of political inoculation that gave mass politics a bad reputation in China. After Deng Xiaoping's reforms began in 1978, the Communist Party's claim to rule was based primarily on delivering rapid economic growth. This has now slowed to less than 6 percent according to the regime, or 2 to 4 percent, according to some foreign observers. The regime therefore increasingly relies for its legitimacy on nationalism, verging on ultra-nationalism or nativism, and on the leader's charisma and personality cult.

Internally, the CCP's ability to control a much more complex society and economy was under threat with the rise of a middle class and incomes outside the state sector. Technology, particularly information and communication technology, compounded this problem. China today spends more on internal security than on national or external defense. Ever since the 1989 Tiananmen Square killings, the Chinese state has explicitly prioritized "stability above all else."[5] Since 2012 under Xi Jinping, CCP command and control has been tightened with a drastic recentralization. Patronage networks and systemic corruption had weakened the party considerably. The anticorruption campaign has served as a political tool to eliminate rivals and build a Xi faction in the party. As the legitimacy of party rule weakens, Chinese leaders have also used external threats to justify domestic controls.[6]

We are now dealing not just with a changed China but with changed Chinese statecraft. A reconstructed history and the contemporary environment drive a more assertive Chinese external engagement and complex statecraft. China today fields less-sensitive diplomats, who seem not to count for much at home, and whose recent actions, called "wolf warrior diplomacy" after a popular series of action movies, are calculated more to show loyalty at home than for their effect abroad. As far as we can tell the PLA has considerably increased its role in policy formulation. The security hierarchies—PLA, state security, public security—and the central party departments have much greater policy weight in relation to the economic ones—the State Development Research Council and others—which were supreme in the 1990s and early 2000s under Deng Xiaoping, Jiang Zemin, and Zhu Rongji. And decisionmaking has been centralized to an unprecedented degree. Regime stability and the maintenance of one-party rule remain the highest priorities of the Chinese regime.

The second priority for China is continued economic growth. China is now more dependent on the outside world than at any point in its history, needing the world's raw materials, markets, technology, and exports to grow its economy and maintain internal social stability. There are few traditional models or historical precedents for this situation of a relatively strong China that is also dependent on the outside world.[7] While China has been dependent when weak, today's combination of power with dependency has not occurred before. There is thus an inbuilt tension between the demands of interdependence and the nationalist rhetoric that legitimizes Chinese Communist Party rule and leadership.

The Chinese leadership is convinced that China must shape its external environment if it is to prosper. And China's rise has given it the means or power to shape the environment immediately around it. The regime appears convinced that China faces multiple enemies abroad, some of whom, like the United States and the West, seek regime change in China, and others in the periphery who seek to encircle China and limit its natural predominance. The desire to shape the external environment takes two forms: China seeks control of its periphery; further afield it seeks a say.

In the last decade, Asia has become more Asian in its economic, trading, and financial arrangements and much more integrated with China. At the same time, China (and the United States) have tried to increase their share of manufacturing by on-shoring global production and value chains, a trend accelerated by the COVID-19 pandemic. In China's case this is not so much by moving manufacturing plants home as by China moving up the value chain and doing progressively more valuable work at home. China's exports have become more Chinese. Fifteen years ago only 55 percent of their value was added in China. Now it is 67 percent or so. East and southeast Asia are more intertwined than ever before. U.S. and western firms are now largely absent in central Asia and southern Asia, except India, and risk irrelevance in mainland southeast Asia, except in Vietnam and Singapore. The United States is therefore left largely as a security balancer in the Asia-Pacific. It is an open question how long the United States will continue to do so when its economic interests are so bound with those of China and are limited to the larger Asian economies—Japan, India, and South Korea. Besides, the United States is self-sufficient in energy, and isolationist sentiment in the country, represented by Trump, is ever stronger. It is unreasonable to expect a return to the liberal interventionist internationalism of the past four decades by the United States in Asia when its interests no longer seem to demand it and its internal politics do not support it.

∼

China's leaders identified the first two decades of this century as a period of strategic opportunity, during which regional conditions and the global balance of power enable China to best advance its interests.[8] At the 19th Party Congress in October 2017 President Xi Jinping noted, "Currently conditions, both domestic and abroad, are undergoing complicated changes. Our country is in an important period of strategic opportunity in its development. The outlook is extremely bright; the challenges are also extremely grim." He added that China has now "become a great power in the world" and has played "an important role in the history of mankind." The conclusion he drew was that "it is time for us to take center stage in the world and to make a greater contribution to humankind." These were strong statements of intent and confidence, addressed to audiences at home and abroad. Some have seen this as "defining a new world order and restoring to Chinese culture its former esteem."[9] I am less certain. I see President Xi's statement as a careful formulation recognizing that the American retreat has opened up an opportunity for China's continued economic success but, at the same time, acknowledging dangers and grim challenges ahead. These have only become more difficult in the years since 2017.

There is no question that the present situation presents China with an opportunity. It faces no existential threat, its nuclear deterrent has been effective, separatism in Tibet and Xinjiang is controlled and manageable, although with considerable effort, and the balance of power in its vicinity has not been so favorable to its for well over two centuries. What Marxists call the international correlation of forces works for China. Its agency and role in international society have grown considerably. The year 2017 was a moment of relative freedom and strength for China. There is a wave of popular support in China for assertive steps to enhance China's standing abroad.

Speaking at the 2017 meeting, President Xi also offered China as a model of development for the rest of the world to follow, an ideological challenge to the West that it had not posed since Mao's time. The world is now dealing with an outward-looking China, ready to project soft and hard power. The official Chinese media use many different terms in English for the same Chinese phrase, such as "Chinese method," "model," or "way." Perhaps China's successful spurt of modernization is indeed something to be emulated by others. It adapted the experience of Western capitalism applying "Chinese characteristics," staying pragmatic and "feeling the stones underfoot while crossing the river," adjusting as needed. If, however, a Chinese template is to be applied abroad, as was the Chinese-type Maoist permanent revolution that China exported in the 1960s, that would be another story and the world would react differently. China has never claimed to be a "city on the hill," an American mythology, but has always been acutely aware of its uniqueness and superiority. Xi's statements, therefore, represent a return to a Maoist past with considerable implications for how China will deal with other countries.

How this will play out is uncertain. Some Chinese scholars such as Yan Xuetong speak of reshaping the international configuration to one of China-U.S. bipolarity, but that assumes a degree of pragmatism and acceptance by the Americans of China's preferred role.[10] That China is now speaking of its model for export suggests a shift away from the constant experimentation of the Deng Xiaoping era.

~

Kevin Rudd, the former Australian prime minister who has known Xi Jinping for some time, describes Xi as "a man in a hurry."[11] That hurry is expressed clearly in the "Double Hundred" goals for China established by Xi Jinping in 2012 and in China's more assertive behavior with its neighbors and internationally. The conventional explanation for this Chinese assertiveness is that the 2008 financial crisis in the West led China to believe the time had come to firmly work toward the country's key interests, especially to restore a greatness the nation had enjoyed generations earlier. This sentiment was fed especially by the slogan "never forget national humiliation," which has nurtured a Chinese nationalism based on victimhood that seeks payback. To this push factor could be added these pull factors: that the United States has steadily vacated space in Asia since 2000 and is no longer interested in maintaining the balance of power or international order and that Europe's economic troubles and Putin's difficulties in Ukraine and near abroad have opened up space for China. While Russia accommodates China in Central Asia and allies with it globally against the U.S.-led order, Europe welcomes a greater Chinese economic and political role, seeing economic benefits in doing so.

The United States' diminishing interest in maintaining order and balance in the Asia-Pacific, beginning with the Obama administration and accelerating under President Trump, created a vacuum that left China with significant advantages in east and southeast Asia. This eased the way for China's transition to a strategy of "striving for achievements." So far as we can tell, this approach appeared a success to most Chinese until recently. There could also be a deeper explanation for China's hurry, however. Is it possible that China sees its relative power as being at its height now and as possibly declining in the future? Is the moment of strategic opportunity that China's leaders speak of limited? Is it actually a closing window of opportunity that China faces?[12]

By this logic, China knows that the future will not be a straight-line extrapolation from the present. Its economy is slowing and reverting to mean; its society is aging rapidly—by 2040 China's demographic profile will be like Japan's today—and the international balance could shift again and is likely to be more crowded with several powers rising in its vicinity. It also now faces pushback from the United States for the first time. It would be logical for China to feel that it must put in place and consolidate changes in the internal, regional, and global order now, so that Trump and his successors cannot remove or roll them back. China's relatively rapid recovery from the COVID-19 pandemic gives her an opportunity to pursue her goals now.

Beyond the narrative of national humiliation propagandized by the CCP and through Chinese textbooks since the early 1990s, from China's point of view, several elements remain unsatisfactory: unification with Taiwan is unfinished; China faces the world's greatest armada, the U.S. Navy, twelve nautical miles off its coast; its relations with its larger neighbors have deteriorated in the last decade; economic integration with its periphery could be improved; and the Western liberal alternative still exerts domestic political, social, and economic pressure. China is a revisionist power, seeking to change and adapt the present U.S.-led order in its own favor, preferably peacefully and without endangering its economic stakes in the present structure of the world economy.

If one were to characterize China today, it is a global power in economic terms, it is a regional power in military terms, a dominant power but not a hegemon in the Asia-Pacific, and it betrays an obsessive defensive worry about the effect of others' soft power on its polity and society that suggests a real internal sensitivity and weakness. This is an unusual and unique combination of attributes for a great power and leads to exceptional behavior by China.

~

Another significant driver of future Chinese behavior will be the course of China-U.S. relations. Pessimists in the Chinese leadership who had argued that the international balance might shift adversely can point to the turn that U.S.-China relations took under President Trump.

It is perhaps ironic that China's rise to global power was facilitated by the United States, by the policies that Henry Kissinger and Richard Nixon put in place. But this was a period of China's opening when it lacked the attributes and wherewithal of a great power. And it has seemed that U.S.-China policy has been almost on autopilot since then, until recently. Today, China has accumulated sufficient hard power to challenge America in northeast and southeast Asia. Contrast the situation in and around the Taiwan Strait during the 1996 crisis with that in 2018. South Korea has put off further deployment of THAAD radars in deference to China's sensitivities, while recent South Korean presidents have found China essential for their diplomacy related to their overwhelming preoccupation, North Korea. China has changed the balance and militarized its near seas, the South China Sea and the East China Sea. On the broader stage China respects its inferiority to the United States in practice, but never acknowledges it. Since 2008 China has used issues like the South China Sea to effectively weaken U.S. credibility in the region. ASEAN countries, once U.S. allies, then reluctant to choose between the two, are now unable to agree on a common public position even on their own issues with China such as the South China Sea, let alone stand with the United States against China.

China-U.S. relations were until recently the primary dynamic in the Asia-Pacific. For the present they are characterized by strategic contention with deep economic interdependence. Do not underestimate China-U.S. codependence. The balance between contention and dependence is what has shifted recently. Under President Trump the Obama combination of a pivot to Asia with broader engagement with China had ended, but it is far from clear what will replace it. Trump, with his isolationist tendencies and his desire to make deals, made U.S.-China accommodation possible but unlikely. He first announced a major unthinking concession to China in the form of his decision not to pursue the Trans-Pacific Partnership (TPP) agreement, thus shifting the balance of economic power in Asia further toward China and leaving the Regional Comprehensive Partnership (RCEP) as the only game in town for a while, until the other TPP members revived it without the United States. Trump simultaneously indicated a willingness in his early statements to do a deal with China and made Taiwan a bargaining chip in his pursuit of Chinese help to boost U.S. jobs and manufacturing.

As I write, the United States has, for the first time since 1971, attempted to use its economic and technological leverage with China to change China's behavior. It imposed tariffs on some Chinese goods and raised demands for fundamental structural changes in Chinese industrial and technology policies and in the running of its economy. The "asks" made by the United States were impossible for China to accept in totality. They would have meant changing the way China grows and acts, whether in the "Make in China 2025" program, in market access, in its IPR practices and forced technology transfers and so on. In addition, the United States has tightened technology transfers to China, limited Chinese investment for national security reasons, and sought changes in China's technology acquisition and development strategies. These are reminiscent of U.S. demands on Japan in the 1970s and 1980s, but as the Chinese have reminded the United States, China is not Japan, an ally dependent on America for its security, and is not willing to sign the equivalent of the Plaza Accords as Japan did. Implementing the U.S. demands would mean changing China's manufacturing economy, slowing its technological progress, and, ultimately, curtailing the CCP's capacity to control the economy and could cost it its rule. These fundamental demands would make it difficult for China to emerge as a true peer competitor to the United States in sensitive and critical areas. It is therefore hard to see how the Chinese leadership could acquiesce in them.

It is also not clear whether and how long the United States can sustain such a tactic, given the relatively high level of codependency between the Chinese and U.S. economy. For several large U.S. corporations and for Wall Street, China is the most important external factor in their bottom-line profit and their manufacturing base. A quick look at the profits of major U.S. corporations in 2017 is enlightening. For technology companies the dependence on China is high, as you would expect—over 24 percent of profits for Apple, for instance. Even for more traditional companies, like DuPont, it is as high as 9 percent. The proportions are particularly high for aerospace and soya bean and grain producers. But the shift in bipartisan U.S. sentiment in Congress and among U.S. corporations, its strategic justification, and U.S. statements of policy suggest that what we are witnessing is more than just an effective negotiating tactic to reduce the U.S. trade deficit with China. On October 4, 2018, Mike Pence, Trump's vice president, delivered a blistering attack on the Chinese government that might one day be compared to Churchill's 1946 Iron Curtain speech at Fulton, Missouri, which launched the U.S.-Soviet Cold War. Labeling Beijing authoritarian, Orwellian, and expansionist, Pence accused it of "employing a whole-of-government approach, using political, economic, and military tools, as well as propaganda, to advance its influence." He said that the Trump administration would no longer attempt to cajole and persuade China to play by the rules; instead, it would emphasize "strong and swift action" to penalize Beijing for any perceived infractions.

The U.S. attempt to change China's behavior cannot be described as a success, for China has responded with a much more assertive diplomatic pushback

and a turn inward economically. U.S. actions only confirm Chinese paranoia
that the West and United States are bent on regime change in China and on
preventing its rise, containing it within the first island chain, and embroiling
it in its periphery. The impact of U.S. tariffs and the prospect of the United
States confronting China have complicated China's calculus. In the long run,
China will work to ensure that it cannot be placed in this position in the future,
not only by some decoupling from the United States but by building its own
leverage and capabilities, by creating countervailing opportunities for itself in
the world, and by building parallel orders as it has done with the internet. The
best analogy may be the Chinese reaction to the 1996 Taiwan Strait crisis when
it was humiliated in its own backyard. Since then it has militarized the seas
around Taiwan (the South China and East China Seas), built up its naval forces,
tightened Taiwan policy, and raised the costs of intervening in the enclosed seas
near China. With the United States, China will seek dominance in strategic
sectors, and we can expect an accelerated Chinese military buildup, concentration on artificial intelligence, cyber and "assassin's mace" technologies, and a
rapid buildup of its political, military, and economic strengths.

The root problem in U.S.-China relations today is that neither country
can be seen to give way on the issues that matter: technology, sovereignty, and
regime survival. China cannot afford to accept American terms that would
effectively prevent China's continued rise. China itself has little choice but to
continue on the path it has chosen. And the United States cannot abandon
its policy of preventing the emergence of a peer competitor on the world stage.
This is not to say no deals and understandings will emerge between the two
countries. There will be. But the deals, like President Trump's June 2018 understanding with Kim Jong Un in Singapore, will not change the fundamental
dynamic on issues that matter.

In the short term, heightened China-U.S. contention should have made
China tactically more accommodating in Asia. While it works toward dominance in the longer term, it should try for an amelioration of relations with
Japan, India, and other neighbors it has alienated since 2008 so as to be free
to manage the United States. But that is not what occurred in 2019 and 2020.

In south Asia, I see two direct effects. First, in the binary geopolitical competition between China and the United States, the subcontinent will not be
marginal, unlike the Cold War. The United States will work with India on
maritime issues, having conceded the continental order to China already. China
will work to maximize its influence in south Asia and the Indian Ocean rim,

to keep the United States out or minimize U.S. influence, as it is attempting in Nepal, Sri Lanka, and Bangladesh. The more contentious China-U.S. relations become, the harder it is for Pakistan to be a strategic ally of both. Instead, it will rely more on China, the ally it considers reliable, unlike the United States, which "abandoned" it in 1965, 1971, and 1989, according to the Pakistani narrative. Once the United States withdraws from Afghanistan, Pakistan's tactical utility to the Americans will also diminish. U.S. actions so far also would have convinced China of the longer-term utility of making an alliance of what is now a short-term arrangement of convenience with Russia. As Western pressure on Russia and China has mounted, it has cemented their common interest in working in concert in Asia, magnified their resentment at the present international order, and increased the likelihood of their creating institutional and structural alternatives. In other words, from an Indian point of view, heightened U.S.-China contention would complicate India-China relations, make India potentially significant to U.S. Asian strategy, and have negative second order effects on India's relations with Russia, Iran, Pakistan, and others, such as Japan.

During the Trump administration, uncertainty about American behavior in the region made the U.S.-China dynamic, while still the most important relationship in the Asia-Pacific, no longer the determinant of developments here. Most regional powers are hedging and balancing against both China and the United States, although none will admit it. The major security issues facing the Asia-Pacific today—disputes in the South China and East China Seas, maritime security, North Korea's nuclear weapons program, or cyber security, for instance—will not be settled by either U.S.-China cooperation or by their contention. Regional issues will depend to a considerable extent on the decisions of local or regional actors. President Trump had been less than consistent on U.S. security commitments to allies South Korea and Japan, indicating during the 2016 campaign that he would ask them to fend for themselves and even go nuclear. But once elected, he affirmed that he is with them to the end in meetings and conversations. American tariffs aimed at China have also hit U.S. allies in the European Union, as well as South Korea and India.

The Trump administration also affected the credibility of U.S. extended deterrence for South Korea and Japan. Japan and South Korea would consider acquiring their own nuclear weapons, if failed attempts to negotiate with North Korea leave them at a disadvantage with no reliable deterrence against Chinese and North Korean nuclear weapons. A nuclearized northeast Asia is now a real prospect. And this is of real concern to China, as is the steady modernization of U.S. capabilities. In 2006 Keir Lieber and Daryl Press predicted that "growing U.S. capabilities will pressure Russia and China to reduce the peace-time vulnerability of their forces" through "logical" precautionary steps, including larger nuclear forces coupled with more offensive postures.[13] Taylor Fravel and Fiona Cunningham, after considering the evidence and Chinese reactions to improved U.S. counterforce capabilities, came to the conclusion that ambiguity in posture is likely to be the best Chinese response rather than a shift to first-use or other changes in Chinese doctrine.[14] Recent American political unpredictability probably reinforces the probability of China's shift from no-first-use to counterforce in response to the precision and sensing accuracy of American conventional weapons.

Much, of course, depends on the United States' own trajectory. If the past is a guide, the United States will right itself, though the rest of us may pay a price. It has reinvented itself at least four times in my lifetime—building the Great Society under President Lyndon Johnson, after the Vietnam War, expanding the technology revolution in the 1990s, and again after 2008—and is capable of doing so again. Its internal growth and development have leveraged serial crises and constant social renewal and immigration to propel the country forward and accumulate power. The American problem now, however, is to get used to dealing with a peer competitor in China. After thirty years without a competitor in sight, it now faces a world in which power is being diffused as a result of changes in technology and the globalized drivers of the economy.

There is one respect in which the United States and China have grown more similar in the last two decades. That is the steady militarization or securitization of foreign policy, the increasing role of the military in policy formulation at the expense of traditional civilian hierarchies, and the growing tendency to see issues in zero-sum terms. This congruence is not one that bodes well for their relationship or the region.

∿

Historians seek to understand China's future behavior and how a rising China will use its growing power by looking to its past. Traditional Chinese thought, whether of Confucians' stressing "humane authority" or Legalists' stressing hegemony, maintained that the establishment of a hierarchical system based on a leading state's superior strength is the sole method of preserving interstate order.[15] While humane authority tends to the use of carrots, hegemonists emphasize the stick. In history, there has never been a *Pax Sinica* or, for that matter, a *Pax Indica* in Asia or the Asia-Pacific. Nor has India or China traditionally sought to impose one for any length of time. Such hubris was the exception. The brief exceptions were Han emperor Wudi (reigned from 141–187 BCE) in Central Asia, who relied on alliances more than the projection of force and direct administration, and Ming emperor Yongle (reigned from 1402–1424 CE), who sent out the "Treasure Fleet" under Zheng He between 1405 and 1421 to achieve recognition of Ming preeminence among the polities of the known maritime world.[16] Both these attempts were soon aborted, with Zheng's voyages stopped by Yongle's successor on the very day he ascended the throne for reasons of internal Chinese politics. The century or so when Britain imposed a *Pax Brittanica*, and when the United States established what we might consider a *Pax Americana* after World War II, was a brief historical aberration in Chinese eyes.

Today, some see the Asia-Pacific reverting to its historical norm. That norm is differently defined by various historians. In the official Chinese telling it is one of natural Chinese preeminence, exercised benignly, and deferred to naturally by others. For me, that norm was an Asia, before the coming of the West, of multiple power centers, trading circles, and interconnected universes—a plural multiverse. Historians disagree on China's role in east Asia in history.[17] Where they do agree is the hierarchical view of the universe that China operated under, a "Sino-centric hierarchical order" seeking respect and obedience.[18] They also mostly agree that relative power concerns were at the heart of Chinese strategic choice. Imperial China acted opportunistically and coercively in east Asia.[19] As Yuan-Kang Wang says, "China tended to adopt an offensive grand strategy when its power was relatively strong and a defensive one when its power was relatively weak. In addition, Chinese leaders have not restricted their war aims to deterrence and border protection but at times adopted expansive goals such as acquisition of territory, destruction of enemy power, and total military victory. . . . In short, anarchy trumps culture."[20]

If any of these versions of history is any guide, China is unlikely to be a net provider of security in Asia as the United States has been, or to set norms, or to open its own markets and society to the outside world. Instead, it will seek to build a China-centered hierarchical order modeled on itself, as far as possible and as far as its power will reach. This is not incompatible with China becoming a net provider of knowledge to the world as it and previous hegemons were and sooner than the world expects. And, as liberalism declines, it will be tempted to offer alternate ideological justifications for the order it prefers, derived from its traditional thinking.

Unlike China, traditional Indian thought was used to a pluriverse or multiverse. China had limited historical experience of living in a world of equals and no traditional theory of a multiverse. Compare Chanakya and Han Feizu, who probably lived within a century of one another. Han Feizu envisages a universe or "all under heaven" that is homogenous not plural, in China's own image, hierarchical, obedient, unipolar not multipolar. Han Feizu seeks primacy, status, deference, and recognition of that primacy. This is very different from a Kautilyan universe of several kingdoms, city states, confederations, and republics of differing power but equal legitimacy contending among themselves, rather like the world we see today. Both these conceptions were in turn very different from modern Western ideas of international order, based as they are on the Westphalian state and concepts of sovereignty and legitimacy.

The question today is to what extent China's strategic thinking and culture has been Westernized. If it draws on the Western tradition of exclusive nationalism, of sovereignties struggling for mastery, of closed regionalism and mercantilism that led through four centuries of European war to two world wars and ultimately devastated European power, China will presumably behave as badly, probably with the same disastrous results. If, instead, the change and adaptation of China's thinking fits circumstances in the region and the world, there is hope. The debate is still on in China, within and outside government.[21] The jury is still out as countries like China and India struggle to come to intellectual grips with their present situation and to develop a vocabulary and theory of international relations that matches the particularity of their cases. But well before that theory or understanding emerges, we can expect China to be in the front rank of powers as the world's largest economy and the dominant military power in the Asia-Pacific.

To my mind China's ancient past can only be an imperfect guide to its future behavior. The situation that China is in today is unprecedented, making the past largely irrelevant, except for the history that Chinese choose to tell themselves. History tells us that China has consistently adjusted its behavior to the balance of power between itself and other powers. As Zheng He memorialized the new Ming emperor in the fifteenth century:

The strength of our dynasty has surpassed all previous [dynasties]. It controls the northern and western barbarians, but has not had to marry princesses to foreigners as the Han did, has not had to make allies [with equal powers] like the Tang, has not had to pay annual tributes like the Song, and has not had to engage in an etiquette of treating enemy states as brothers. They all come to pay tribute and are received with courtesy. . . . How grand this is!

Ever since Chengzu [Yongle] pacified all under heaven [tian xia] with
military power, [he] wanted to control the world [wanfang] with force,
[so] he sent envoys to all directions to solicit [them]. Thus all the large
and small countries in the Western region [xiyu] came to kowtow and
submit and compete in presenting tribute. [The Ming envoys] reached
all the places that could be reached by water and land, as far north as the
remotest desert, as far south as the farthermost sea, as far east and west
as the sun-rising and sun-setting places.[22]

Today, China feels stronger than it has for several centuries, the world
around it has changed, and it sees a window of strategic opportunity. It should
not surprise us today when China chooses to behave as Ming Yongle did, rather
than as the Han, Tang, or Song did from positions of relative equality or inferiority with their neighbors.

~

Apart from the relative balance of power, one gets a sense of what to expect of
China from the long-term drivers of Chinese foreign and security policies and
its geopolitical situation, which were major determinants of China's behavior
in the past.

While China is willing and able to partly fill the economic vacuum that it
sees in Asia and globally, its political and military situation is more complex.
China has certainly increased its military power and effectiveness, increased
spending on the PLA since the Tiananmen killings in 1989, and restructured
its armed forces into instruments of power projection. However, other powers
too have risen in this period. The Asia-Pacific has seen the world's and history's
greatest arms race over two decades, most of it in offensive weapons.[23] The military balance in the Asia-Pacific does not reflect the economic preponderance
that China now enjoys.

From China's point of view, while the relative power calculus in its immediate periphery has improved considerably, China is still not militarily predominant. Take two examples: Taiwan and the South China Sea. China is not in a
position to impose a Monroe Doctrine of its own even in the closed geography
of the South China Sea. It lacks the kind of military dominance—70–80 percent of all naval assets and control of most of the coastline—that the United
States and, briefly, Japan enjoyed when they were able to impose one. Nor is
the military balance such that it can be sure of taking Taiwan relatively pain-
lessly, unless there is internal chaos in Taiwan and it is virtually without a

government.[24] That may explain why the present Chinese approach is of unrelenting pressure on the Tsai Ing-wen government while going soft on Taiwanese business and society, as against the earlier policy of co-opting Taiwan economically and through kinship when Ma Ying-jeou and the Kuomintang were in power. The negative consequences of a forcible takeover of Taiwan for China are considerable, including the resulting shifts in Japan's security policy and reactions among other countries in the region. With shrinking popular support on Taiwan for reunification, resistance and killings in Taiwan would affect the legitimacy of the People's Republic of China (PRC) leadership. China has therefore consistently stayed its hand. In the meantime, China builds up the PLA's capability to invade the island, which enables coercion and intimidation. China has built up its anti-access/area denial capabilities in the near seas, which give it the ability to embarrass the U.S. Navy in the seas near China and to prevent a recurrence of the 1996 Taiwan Strait crisis. But there remain practical limits to Chinese military assertiveness. In the South China Sea it does everything possible to incrementally change facts on the ground and at sea in its own favor, while being careful to stay below the threshold of provoking an outright military response or conflict. Today, freedom of navigation, fishing, and other activities by other countries continue in the South China Sea, and other claimants have not surrendered their claims. For the present the Chinese goal seems to be to create the impression that these activities occur because China allows them. That goal is not yet achieved or entirely in sight.

We have seen a similar phenomenon of China attempting to change the situation on the ground by military means while staying below the threshold of outright conventional conflict on the India-China border in Ladakh in spring 2020. How that will end, and the nature and success of India's pushback to restore the situation to what it was previously, still hangs in the balance as of this writing.

In the short run, military power is the cutting edge of change, and the military balance is a measure of immediate opportunity. But long-term outcomes and the ability to sustain them depend more on underlying factors: demography, the economy, technology, geography, internal politics, and diplomacy, namely, on the popular and dictionary definition of geopolitics. The efficacy of external policies also depends on political structures that convert capability and intent into outcomes. In China's case, that "power train" or transmission is untested militarily since the unsuccessful 1979 war against Vietnam and has been changed and reformed continually since.[25] Its political "power train" has produced mixed political outcomes for China in the last few decades. Economically it has proved most productive and efficient. Besides, the success or effectiveness of the apparatus of China's foreign and security policies is secondary to the directions in which the drivers, the real strategic underpinnings of China's external policies, take China.

Regime stability remains the abiding concern in China because its internal structure is still unsettled, undergoing constant change, and because the process of reform and opening up has complicated the task of governing China. In the last few years, China has consistently spent more on internal security than on national defense. Chinese official statistics show 8,700 "mass incidents" in 1993, 32,000 in 1999, 58,000 in 2003, and 180,000 in 2010. (A mass incident is defined as a demonstration involving over 100 people.) When the number of incidents reached about 200,000 in 2012, the government stopped publishing these statistics and began speaking of 80,000 to 100,000 such incidents each year. The last few years have seen demonstrations by large numbers of PLA veterans as well. At the same time non-coercive means of control available to China's government have declined as a result of reform. The central government delegates most social functions such as health and education to the provinces, which disburse over 70 percent of total government spending, with 55 percent spent below the provincial level. Between 1978 and 2011 the share of industrial output produced by state firms fell from about three-quarters to one-quarter, retreating in all product lines. By 2019 this had risen under Xi Jinping to over 36 percent. Only 13 percent of urban employees work for state-owned enterprises now.[26]

The Communist Party leadership has responded by tightening state control of society and individuals. It uses digital technology to mine big data, has developed facial recognition, and has improved surveillance to the point where China is able to introduce a "social credit system" where each individual gains or loses credits depending on his or her behavior, down to littering on the street. This requires comprehensive and consistent tracking and monitoring of every individual's behavior, a capability that no state has had in history. The likely effects on individuals, society, and governance boggle the mind and are probably best understood in dystopian Chinese science fiction, which has seen a great efflorescence recently.

In the longer run the core political issue is not state-owned enterprise reform or anticorruption but whether a sense of opportunity and fairness will sustain the legitimacy of the CCP. That requires fundamental economic and political reform, for which there is little appetite in the Chinese leadership after 2008, with opposition from power holders in the system. The deep reforms planned and announced at the third plenum of the 18th Central Committee in 2013 are conspicuous by their lack of implementation. The risk to China is that it becomes like Japan, stagnant economically, but at a lower level of prosperity, and therefore less socially stable and likely to behave erratically abroad.

The rise of China's middle class, a product of globalization, has made China harder to govern. The new middle class makes a different set of demands of its government, and votes with its feet or its money when dissatisfied, as we saw when US$1 trillion left China in 2016. Social change is evident in the return of popular religion and superstition in China, as well as the rise of proselytizing faiths like Christianity. These seem to reflect a sense of spiritual emptiness and a revulsion among the middle class against the lack of morality and the get-rich-quick mentality spawned in globalizing China. The CCP has attempted to co-opt Buddhism, which is seen as indigenous and less threatening in not having an external focus of loyalty like Islam or Christianity.[27] China has, in effect, told the Dalai Lama by law that he will reincarnate with the approval of the Chinese Communist Party—a peculiar demand from a party of professed atheists. All priests in China are civil servants appointed and paid by the state. The rise of large, powerful business interests, some of whom the regime is now acting against, adds to social complexity. Chinese society has thus grown considerably more complex and less malleable than before.

Long-term demography suggests that these social trends will continue. China's ratio of working people to total population peaked in 2010–2011 and began to decline as the burden of elderly pensioners rose. From 2010 to 2018, China's population grew at 0.5 percent a year. India's population grew at double that rate, at 1.2 percent a year, marginally higher than the global average of 1.1 percent. By 2020 China was already deep into the problems of a graying society like Japan, South Korea, and Italy, and by 2040 its population will have the age structure of Japan, the most aged of all advanced societies.[28] On present trends, China will be old before it gets rich.

According to the UN, India will overtake China as the most populous country in the world around 2024, with a significantly younger population. India's working-age population will continue to grow till 2050, while Japan, China, and western Europe age. By then, Japan's median age is expected to stand at fifty-three years, China's at nearly fifty, and west Europe's at forty-seven years. The median age in India will be just thirty-seven years.[29]

This will have more than domestic economic consequences, such as the need to set up a welfare system and concentrate on health and pensions from now on. It also affects military preparedness for the world's largest army and its capacity to recruit, which might explain the PLA's stress on artificial intelligence and autonomous weapons systems. If history is a guide, older societies do not display the same intent and willingness to project power, to take risks, or to pay the price for primacy that younger ones do. We will have to see how this works in China's case. Besides, aging societies see a slowdown in innovation and economic growth. China's demographics therefore suggest that China may be working within a relatively short window of relative opportunity and advantage. Hence the haste with which it pursues the Belt and Road Initiative and others.

The second long-term driver of China's external policies is its economy. The relative strength and security of its economic power are today the main underpinning of China's policies in its periphery and further afield. But the conditions that created China's economic miracle have already changed and are unlikely to return. The high tide of globalization, of which China and India were among the greatest beneficiaries, has passed. The effects of the 2008 crisis linger in a low-growth global economy, exacerbated by the pandemic economic crash of 2020, and countries are displaying increasing protectionism or mercantilism. The globalized economy is fragmenting into regional trading blocs, and protectionist sentiment is on the rise in the United States and Europe. The 2018 imposition of tariffs on Chinese goods by President Trump on national security grounds and China's retaliation marked increasing pushback by advanced economies to China's economic success. China's own economic slowdown and reduced Chinese and foreign demand, from aging demographics and declining productivity growth, make it hard to identify future sources of global growth. A fundamental restructuring of the world economy is underway, with changes in the energy economy, digital manufacturing and artificial intelligence, genetic engineering and biotechnology, to name just some prominent changes. What William Overholt calls China's crisis of success has created inequality, corruption, and pollution and a dependence on the outside world, none of which seems amenable to command economy solutions from China's recent past.[30]

For three decades export-created surpluses made possible China's investment-fed miracle growth spurt of about 10 percent GDP growth. As China's economy reverts to mean, global trade has shrunk. China's share of global exports has been dropping (to 13.5 percent in 2016 from 13.9 percent in 2015) and was less than 13 percent in 2017 (first eleven months). Exports made either a negative or a neutral contribution to China's GDP growth in those three years. In a post-pandemic world, China faces the double task of restructuring its own economy to rely more on domestic demand and consumption and of restructuring its economic engagement with the world. And unlike Deng in 1978, Xi is not writing on a blank slate.

The shift to domestic consumption as the main source of economic growth will not prevent China from remaining the world's greatest trading nation. It still needs to deal with the excess capacity created in the past and to ensure that jobs are preserved to avoid social unrest. What will change is the increasing degree to which China seeks to manage and shape the external environment. China's leadership has a strategy for successful economic transition, but struggles with the politics of implementing that strategy. It is trying to implement an economic reform that will damage the interests of every powerful group in China—state-owned enterprises, party cadres, local government, private entrepreneurs—while simultaneously alienating the foreign business community and challenging China's maritime neighbors and the U.S. Navy. Actual implementation of the set of economic reforms announced at the third plenum of the 18th Party Congress in 2013 has been minimal, despite the bold reforms it presaged and the association of President Xi's prestige with the package. The problem is not just state capacity in economic management, which is constrained, but also the intervention of events such as the Shanghai stock market crash of 2015 and capital flight in 2015–2016, which led to reactive and traditional economic policy responses. If China fails to reform, there is a real risk of its falling into stagnation with high inequality. Economic failure of that magnitude would almost certainly force changes in the political structure.[31]

The pattern of its economic success, China's resource endowment, and its need to import energy mean that isolation is not an option for China. It will have to actively pursue resources, markets, technology, and access across the world. China's sensitivity to outsiders controlling any of its lifelines will only grow, the greater its stake and the more it has to lose. But while foreign trade and investment will be a necessity for China, we are likely to see its reaction to protectionism abroad and the end of the high tide of globalization manifested in increasingly mercantilist behavior, which it now has the power to indulge in. This explains the more ambitious RCEP that China sought after the United States left the TPP, both as an instrument to further bind the region to itself and as a means of raising the bar for reluctant partners like India. And China has also expressed a willingness to join the new TPP, or CPTPP.

Its economic condition also makes it unlikely that China will provide the global economic public goods that the United States used to provide for the financial and trading system. So far China has sought to use the U.S.-run system while adding parallel institutions where it feels the need. The test is whether China will set up rival institutions and make the investment in them necessary for their success as alternatives, and whether it will have a set of rules and norms of its own to propose. Present signs are mixed. The implementation of the Belt and Road Initiative so far would suggest that China seeks to manage Belt and Road Initiative projects centrally through separate bilateral relationships, funded by Chinese banks and implemented by Chinese companies, and building them to standards unique to China. It also seeks to settle all Belt and Road-related disputes through arbitration in China. At the same time, it lacks an overall framework or set of norms that applies across BRI. The Asian Infrastructure and Investment Bank (AIIB) is outdoing the World Bank in its conditionalities and the rigor of its processes before lending to Asian countries, applying standards and norms developed by the Bretton Woods institutions in its work. Incidentally, over a quarter of all AIIB lending commitments so far are to India.

A similar logic applies to China's need for foreign technology and products, not just to meet China's present demand but to avoid being relegated again by revolutions in energy, digital manufacturing, biotechnology, artificial intelligence and information and communication technology, and transportation that are still primarily Western intellectual property, even if Chinese and Indians in Western firms and universities play a major role in their creation in the West. The OECD estimates that over 76 percent of R&D by the top 2,500 firms of the world is in the West. Today, even the iconic symbols of China's success such as the skyscrapers of the Pudong skyline have Western or Japanese elevators, electronics, cooling and heating systems, and so on. In 2017 China imported US$260 billion worth of semiconductors and related products, more than it spent on the import of crude oil. This is a dependency on the advanced economies for critical high-technology products created by globalization that is unlikely to be slaked soon. We have seen the effort that China has put into renewable energy, given its own shortage of oil, and its ambitious goals in artificial intelligence. A similar effort in water, in which much cutting-edge work being done on the U.S. West Coast by Chinese-origin scientists, should also be of great interest to India. Energy and water are already significant drivers of China's foreign and security policies and will become even more important in years to come.

For the Chinese leadership, technology represents its hope of breaking through the constraints on continuing China's growth and development. China is making a major effort in artificial intelligence, bioengineering, and genetics.

It has aggressively pursued intellectual property rights by means ranging from R&D to acquisitions to cyber espionage. The ultimate success of China's efforts to absorb high technology, now that other countries are more sensitive to the protection of their intellectual property rights, remains to be seen. But if history is any guide, China could well be successful in building an innovation economy under a tightly controlled political order.[32]

China's role in global technology chains is changing fast. Restrictions on technology transfers to China imposed by the Trump administration forced China to develop internal capacity more rapidly. China's own history of great innovation during politically troubled times, as under the Song Dynasty or under autocratic regimes such as the Sui and Ming, shows that neither the nature nor structure of its politics has prevented China from leading global innovation in history. Those who argue that only an open, democratic China will be able to innovate are wrong and ignore the tremendous effort that China is putting into cutting-edge technologies that it believes will determine its future. China is betting on a model of innovation that is different from that which has succeeded so spectacularly in the West, relying not so much on rule of law as on very high incentives and rewards for successful innovation, whether in private or state entities.

These fundamental drivers, demography, the economy, and technology push China into being more involved in the world, unlike its historical self-image of a China sufficient unto itself, dealing with the world on its own terms when it chooses to. But the strongest driver for China not behaving in the international system as previous Western hegemons, Britain and the United States, have done, even if the balance of power makes that tempting, is geography.

Unlike the United States, China is in a crowded and confined neighborhood, with thirteen neighbors on land, many of whom it has difficulty with, and its near seas are enclosed by island chains outside its control. China's power differential with its larger neighbors has varied over time, but it has never had the luxury of hegemonic power in its own continent that the United States has enjoyed for over a century, or of being separated from the rest of the world by two of the world's greatest oceans. That is why China has historically been an inward-looking power, preoccupied with internal order, regarding the outside world as a threat rather than an opportunity for most of its history. Its geography also means that preoccupations in its immediate neighborhood have consumed much of China's energy, and that pacifying the periphery, or barbarian-handling, remains a primary preoccupation. Its geography makes economics and technology all the more important to China to overcome the limitations that geography places on its reach. We see this in its attempt to consolidate the Eurasian landmass through the Belt and Road Initiative, leapfrogging over or reaching through its neighbors to markets, raw materials, and global partners in Europe, Africa and elsewhere. The Belt and Road Initiative can be seen as a logical response to its geographical containment by the first island chain and the U.S. alliance system, and to its need for the world, using its undoubted economic strengths to break out and tie its periphery and regions further afield to itself.

$\sim$

The overriding goal of the present regime in China remains survival, and international primacy is now seen by the Chinese leadership as necessary for its goal of securing China's rise or, to use its words, China's rejuvenation. Internal politics in China too will ensure that China will not behave like the United States. The 19th Party Congress in October 2017 marked the overturning of several institutions and conventions that Deng Xiaoping had put in place after the Cultural Revolution and the fall of the Soviet Union to restrict the accumulation of personal power, thus preventing the emergence of a disruptor like Mao Zedong or a dismantler like Gorbachev. How long the attempt to change Deng's arrangements will last is an open question. As performance legitimacy becomes harder to claim, there is an even greater centralization of power, a personality cult, and a new authoritarian leader whose legitimacy is increasingly based on nationalism. The centralization of power brings with it a concentration of responsibility, so that should things go wrong, as they certainly will sometimes, blame will fall on the leader.

The internal dynamic affects China's foreign policy in three ways, none of them unique to China. First, the capacity to negotiate, compromise, give and take, and bargain that diplomacy requires is constrained by the ultranationalist legitimacy such leaders assume.[33] Second, foreign policy is used for domestic political purposes to a much greater extent, with foreign policy considerations playing second fiddle to how actions will play to a domestic audience. Third, the more the internal pressure, the harder the external line, and the greater the Chinese leadership's propensity to take risks. That dynamic reinforces the more assertive Chinese policy that we have seen in recent years.

$\sim$

If China succeeds in the China Dream, in making China great again, do not expect China to behave as Western powers have in the past. It will not necessarily be another United States setting international rules, norms, and institutions and providing security and public goods for an order that it manages. The idea that China will do so by proposing an alternative order is today's equivalent of the Western wish-myth of the 1990s that China's market-based economic development would bring about a Western-style democracy and a pro-Western regime.[34]

Will China replace the United States as a net provider of security, as an expeditionary power projecting power across the globe? I think not. It cannot and will not be able to for some time. Will China seek to determine the nature of regimes and successfully implement regime change in other countries across the world? The United States has apparently done so seventy-two times since 1950. China today has the necessary combination of soft and hard power only in its immediate periphery, where it now shows clear preferences between local leaders and supports them financially and otherwise in moments of transition. The 2018 Malaysian elections and Nepal and Sri Lanka's internal transitions saw this phenomenon. Will China open its markets to the rest of the world to promote globalization to the extent that the United States does? This is most unlikely as it will affect China's internal economic structure based on state-owned enterprises and state-run finances on which the power of the CCP is built. The desire for regime stability will prevent this.[35] Will China design, invest in, and run the global financial and trading institutions that undergird the global economy as the United States did? Not if its domestic needs for constant infusions of capital and technology remain as they are, if it can get what it wants from present institutions, and if the sources of its growth continue to shrink. Will China exert the kind of cultural influence and be a net provider of knowledge to the world that every previous hegemon has been? This could actually come about first but is still a few years away.

None of this precludes China's developing a capacity to project power globally in permissive environments, while concentrating on building up sustained operational capabilities in its periphery—east and southeast Asia, central Asia, south Asia, and subsequently the Indian Ocean rim. By using humanitarian and disaster relief, nonmilitary evacuations, and peacekeeping, China presented its military modernization as nonthreatening with a softer image. Weaknesses in airlift, sealift, and logistics have been addressed in the last decade, thus enabling more effective military expeditionary purposes. Today, China is adding the space-based ocean and land surveillance systems, large transport aircraft and tankers, ports, bases, amphibious combat ships, special forces, and other requirements to project force beyond its periphery, a capacity that so far only the United States has. Organizational reform of the PLA since 2015 and changes in training also point in the same direction. Under Xi Jinping, the ideological and doctrinal barriers too have been loosened for the PLA to intervene and be more assertive, particularly in what it regards as its "own" region.

This new assertiveness's popularity in China is evident in the record box office receipts of films like *Wolf Warrior-2* about the PLA using force abroad to save Chinese citizens. As China's investment abroad grows, as more Chinese travel, and as China increasingly provides security services to local governments in Africa and Asia, the PLA's motivation to intervene militarily abroad will only grow. More than half of Chinese investment abroad is in energy assets and another large proportion is in real estate. In 2013 China owned more than US$3 trillion abroad. Most of this investment is either from the state or by state-owned companies, thus increasing the motivation for the government to intervene abroad. Over 20,000 Chinese companies operate in over 180 countries. And over 130 million Chinese traveled abroad last year spending about $115 billion. There have been attacks on Chinese workers and citizens around the world and the number of incidents is increasing. In 2014 the Chinese Foreign Office said that it handled 100 incidents of Chinese nationals in danger every day.

Besides, China has begun to provide security services, both as part of securing its Belt and Road Initiative projects, as in Pakistan, or as an investment in the local government, as in Zimbabwe. The security tools and practices that China has developed since Tiananmen to manage internal security and maintain stability are now being exported to eager authoritarians in Asia and Africa. China naturally sees advantage in improving its image abroad as a great power committed to peace, while creating the means to deter, compel, and punish those who might be tempted to oppose it. In the near future, China will have a limited global expeditionary capability to project power and will be able to militarily dominate parts of its own periphery. This could lead to a militarization of China's foreign policy, as has occurred in the United States. Certainly, the temptation for China to use force will increase.

The fundamental drivers of its policy will lead China to a unique pattern of behavior in the near future. Its economics, technology, and internal politics require a China much more actively engaged in shaping the world than it has ever been before, in ways that will be different from previous powers like the United States or Britain. At the same time its internal stresses, geography, and demography suggest that the scope for China's activism or interventionism will be limited in both space and time. Neither space nor time are necessarily in China's favor. It will remake them while it can, in what Xi has called "strategic opportunity." Like good gamblers, they will make the most of the moment, while the cards run their way. The question, however, is whether China knows when to leave the table and cash in its chips, or whether there will be a precipitate withdrawal. The danger is that the dichotomy between its needs and what is practical could result in a frustrated but powerful China. The Chinese are realists; they expect others to respect their power, as they respected U.S. dominance for over three decades. But realists are often disappointed, which is why so many of them become pessimists.

~

We have argued that a rising China is and will be more assertive due to the internal push to tighten control and the external pull of opportunity. The world now depends on China for global economic growth and Asia-Pacific stability. Of course, that dependence is mutual. If China is a global economic player, it also needs the world for its own continued growth and stability. It needs markets, raw materials, commodities, energy, and technology from the world if it is to continue to grow and maintain domestic tranquility. The issue is no longer one of accommodating China in a U.S.-led international order, as some U.S. administrations did in the past. The twin questions are whether China will ride roughshod over others in the Asia-Pacific, as it can, and whether the United States will share global leadership with China, as it must to avoid conflict. Recent history offers no cases of peaceful retrenchment by a hegemon, except Britain after World War II. What, however, makes China-U.S. conflict unlikely is the fact that unlike the U.S.-Soviet Cold War, China and the United States are economically joined at the hip, operate under nuclear deterrence, and are part of a single global system.

The Belt and Road Initiative, "string of pearls" port building and acquisition, and other Chinese actions abroad have led many in Asia to ask whether a China-centered Asia is now an inevitability. It should be clear from what I have said that I do not think so. Instead, several futures and at least three scenarios can be envisaged for Asia. China's behavior and choices may well be the single largest determinant of which scenario comes true, but they are not the only ones. There is no dearth of predictions. We could be returning to Marco Polo's world as Robert Kaplan believes, or China could rule the world as Martin Jacques is convinced, or China could finally fulfill the ever-postponed predictions of its collapse and fall by Gordon Chang and others, or we could face some combination of all these predictions.[36] Take your pick depending on your predilections.

Objectively, China is a hemmed-in power in a crowded neighborhood with limits to its power. It has overwhelming domestic preoccupations and regime survival issues. Has it overreached, made its move too soon like Wilhelmine Germany? That question cannot be answered conclusively yet. But what we can say is that the constraints on China today are primarily internal and physical, and it is hard to see how it will overcome them. Therefore, there are good reasons to test the hypothesis that China has actually overreached and made its move for primacy too soon. If, on the other hand, China succeeds in making China great again, it will still behave differently from Western hegemons or powers in the past. Either way, China will be in the front rank of powers, the world's largest economy, with the willingness to exercise preponderant military power in the Asia-Pacific. China will naturally play a larger role in international society as it continues to develop.

The key for India's "China problem" is that China's periphery is also India's. It is here that China seeks primacy and projects power. This same periphery is critical to India's security and, potentially, to our prosperity. China could behave either like the benign hegemon that it says it was in history, or as a frustrated and disappointed power, externalizing its internal shortcomings, displaying a touchy and hypersensitive nationalism. The power that it has accumulated will compound the effects of such a Chinese trajectory on its neighbors and the rest of Asia. India, with its own set of interests, capabilities, traditions, and strategic culture, will be among those most directly affected. As Deng Xiaoping famously told Rajiv Gandhi in December 1988, the twenty-first century would not be the Asian century if India and China did not both develop together.[37]

12

India and China

Two narratives prevail in the telling of India and China in history, neither of which is objective or a credit to the historian's craft.[1] One, popularized by the national movement in India and by some pre-communist intellectuals in China, tells of a continuous series of positive, peaceful, and friendly exchanges between two nations through centuries. The other, mainly by Western and postmodern historians, describes two inward-looking civilizations that had nothing to do with each other. Both are incomplete renditions of a common past.

There is a long history of positive India-China interaction in history from antiquity onward. It is an inspiring story of contact through traders, pilgrims, and monks, of two open societies exchanging learning and ideas, overcoming the perils of travel by land and sea that took years. The life stories of Kuma-rajiva, Bodidharma, Xuan Zang, Fa Xian, and others are known, recognized, and admired to this day in both countries. China's first contact with India, and its admiration of this equivalent civilization from Han to Tang times, despite considerable internal opposition, is in vivid contrast to the nineteenth-century "opening" of China by the West. And in India, the number of words in Sanskrit and Prakrit with the prefix *cina*—meaning China—is proof of the two-way nature of these exchanges. This is the stuff that makes history attractive to subsequent generations and to national movements.

Until the twentieth century, however, China was peripheral to or absent from the security and political calculus of Indian polities, as was India to the Chinese, because of the absence of a common border until 1950. Before the late-nineteenth-century wave of globalization, Asia consisted of separate, multiple universes, or three multiverses—one in east Asia centered on China, another in the Indian Ocean region linked to India, and a third tied to Persia, Mesopotamia, and Egypt in western Asia. These multiverses were in economic, cultural, and technological contact with each other, exchanging goods, traders, pilgrims, ideas, ideology, and religion. But they were not part of each other's political or security calculus. Before the nineteenth century, China's greatest external security challenges were its inner Asian frontiers beyond the Great Wall where a series of dynasties tried to manage the "barbarians" and work with a string of vassal states.

A possible exception to the absence of political or security connections between India and China in antiquity was the series of Ming naval expeditions led by Zheng He. On balance, the voyages appear to have been imperial, colonial projections of power, and attempts to impose trading monopolies in important commodities like pepper and porcelain. For instance, Zheng He used the rivalry between Cochin and Kozhikode (or Calicut) in Malabar to try to set up an alternate pepper trading node under Chinese control in Cochin. The attempt failed within a few years. Today, the official Chinese projection of Zheng He's voyages is an idealized picture of a peaceful trading and civilizing mission, a precursor of the Belt and Road Initiative, as it were.

Zheng He's voyages are fascinating precisely because they resonate with today's Chinese statecraft. In the fifteenth and sixteenth centuries, Ming China and Portugal did not seek to occupy territory (that came later), but to control sea-lanes, ports, and nodes through which trade flowed in the Indian Ocean region—a "Go" strategy rather than one of chess or Monopoly. Zheng set the pattern that the Portuguese and others followed and used in the next century. But one should not overestimate Zheng's impact or underestimate how ephemeral his interventions in local politics were: Cochin reverted to Calicut's control as soon as Zheng left, while Majapahit, the kingdom in Java, soon controlled Malacca again, and the wrong king was in power in Sri Lanka within a few years of the voyages. The king whom Zheng He installed in Sri Lanka was rapidly overthrown in a coup, but since the usurper used the same name as the overthrown one, the Chinese kept dealing with and supporting him under the impression that he was still their man. When the truth was discovered, the voyages had been stopped by the Chinese emperor and there was little to be done.

Even in the early nineteenth century, when the British were in India, the Manchu court did not connect the British traders and gunships pushing to open trade and selling opium to the Chinese empire to the British presence in India. When Nepalese rulers sought Chinese intervention in their quarrels with the British in India in the nineteenth century, repeated Imperial edicts reiterated that the Qing empire would not intervene or expend treasure and soldiers on this frontier. It was only much later that Chinese frontier policy, which treated Tibet as personally linked to the Manchu emperor, evolved by the end of the nineteenth century into a foreign policy that saw the threat from the British in the opium wars on China's coast as linked to the Tibetan frontier and the British presence in India.[2]

As for Tibet itself, which was India's neighbor until 1950, it basically ran its own affairs. Chinese general Zhao Erhfang's 1908–1910 occupation of Lhasa was the first time a Chinese army did so against Tibetan wishes. When Zhao's Chinese soldiers were repatriated to China in 1912 after the Xinhai revolution in China, most of them went home through India. Thereafter, Tibet reverted to its de facto independence.

In other words, between the spread of Buddhism in the first millennium and the middle of the nineteenth century, communication and exchanges between India and China were conducted largely via intermediaries and were overwhelmingly mercantile. With no political, military, and security contact, the postcolonial states that emerged, the Republic of India and the People's Republic of China, had little experience of dealing with each other.

This is not to deny that each, independently, played a significant role in the world system until the late eighteenth century. Until 1800 India and China dominated the Asian economy and were the motors of the world economy. Angus Maddison's estimates suggest that India and China together accounted for two-thirds of world manufacturing in 1750. Peninsular India under the Cholas was the essential link between China's markets and the other subsystems of what Janet Abu-Lughod has described as the "thirteenth-century world system."[3] This role persisted for well over six centuries after 1000 C.E. Until the end of the eighteenth century, there was little to distinguish the economies of Europe, China, India, and Japan; they were surprisingly similar.[4] This was not reflected in a political or imperial relationship between India and China. Nor did it result in the India-China relationship finding a place in the popular imagination of either country in the twentieth century. It is possible that the political economy of India and China diverged during Mughal and Ming times, before the rise of capitalism in the West created the great divergence between the West on the one hand and China and India on the other. There is work to be done by historians on the parallel and then divergent economic paths and roles in the world economy of India and China before the nineteenth century.[5]

~

In effect, little in their pre-colonial history, separate or together, prepared India and China to cope with the international situation and with each other when they emerged as modern nation-states in the second half of the twentieth century. History provided little experience and no parallels to guide postcolonial statecraft in India and China. Instead, in their initial interactions in the early and mid-1950s, both India and China fell back on what they had learned under the impact of Western imperialism. It was the Western impact on their thinking rather than any common history that guided their behavior as nation-states with each other and in their dealings with the rest of Asia.

Both India and China took the form of the nation-state from their encounter with Western imperialism. Britain's imperial occupation of India brought the instruments, ideas, practices, and accoutrements of a modern Western state to India. In China, the Western powers chose to keep a weakening Manchu Qing dynasty in place (but not in power) to prevent any one of the Western powers from dominating this huge market and originally rich economy. Large sections of Chinese sovereignty, like the imperial customs, and areas, called the treaty ports, were taken over and directly administered by the imperial powers. It was therefore only natural that in both India and China the national goal became, in one form or the other, how to build strong, prosperous, modern states.

Today, both India and China share the humiliation of colonial occupation, of once being among the richest and most advanced societies in the world in 1750, to becoming among the poorest, weakest, and least industrialized countries in two centuries. This history has been a powerful spur for their development into modern states. It has also had a powerful corollary in their determination to achieve power and agency in the international order to make renewed subjugation or humiliation impossible in future. That same drive for agency and power and control of their own fates brings contention into the relationship between the modern states of India and China. Today, India and China have embraced modernity, characterized politically by the nation-state, economically by industrialization, and ideologically by an emphasis on progress and liberation. Profoundly different from each other, their development after the eighteenth century was historically contingent on differing experiences of decline and imperialism. As a result, India and China are today huge societies with deeply rooted cultures and new nationalisms following different pathways.

History also left India and China with very different perspectives on the India-China border—and Tibet is at its center—which created the largest boundary dispute in the world, involving over 138,000 square kilometers of territory.

~

Despite romantic ideas of the other propagated as part of the process of nationalist awakening in both countries in the first half of the twentieth century, the fact that the Republic of India and the People's Republic of China brought little historical baggage to their relationship in 1950 was both an opportunity and a risk. It meant that the two states could write on a tabula rasa to build a relationship as they wished. But it also meant that they had little real understanding of each other and were prone to make mistakes in building that relationship. And that is exactly what happened in the 1950s and early 1960s.

The Asia in which India and China emerged as free nation-states in the post–World War II world was also new: a bipolar Cold War world, with much of Asia still fighting for freedom in Indonesia, Malaya, and Indochina, where the ideological lines between communism and patriotism were visible to the great powers but were not always so evident to Asians. In their initial approach to a southeast Asia still under colonial control, India sought to export freedom and decolonization, while China exported revolution and communism.

Given their weak economies and the need to build their fragile new polities, it was natural that both India and China sought to harden their own sovereignties and to promote Asian solidarity as a hedge against outside powers. Nehru was first off the mark, organizing the Asian Relations Conference in Delhi in March–April 1947. Nehru saw a new era and hoped for a resurgent Asia, with newly independent countries coming into their own. China wanted a more structured and formal arrangement to organize the Afro-Asian countries. When Indonesia organized the Bandung Conference (Asian-African Conference) in April 1955, Zhou Enlai proposed that there be a permanent Afro-Asian Secretariat and revived the idea in the early 1960s. Most others, including Nehru, opposed this idea, seeing it as creating yet another bloc rather than addressing the issues facing newly independent nations. Both India and China found the idea of Asian solidarity useful to their pursuit of independent space in the international system. But their goals diverged. For China, Asian solidarity was a useful defense against the West; for India, it was meant to promote its engagement with both East and West and to strengthen its hand in dealing with both.

Internally, the Chinese state under the communists launched a much more radical and successful attack on agrarian hierarchical society, including its religious aspects, than anything the Indian state was able or willing to do, paying a much higher cost in human lives, stability, and freedom than India. The effects were clear from the resulting literacy rates, relative income levels, land cultivation rights, and gender relations in rural India and China. To some extent this explains the differing effects on the Indian and Chinese economies and societies of the liberalization and opening up that both countries introduced during the 1980s and pushed into high gear in 1991 and 1992. The social effects of economic growth in China have been radical, with implications for one-party rule and state control that are far from fully understood. India, on the other hand, enjoyed over 6 percent growth for over thirty years with relative social and political stability, and the disruptive effects on social order are only now becoming evident. In India these policies have been implemented in a vibrant civil society and open public sphere, unlike China. The result is an issue of legitimacy in China for the one-party system since the Cultural Revolution, which India has avoided. But the price of maintaining the old social order in India has been considerably less flexibility in the choice of policies going forward, a slower pace of economic reform and social change, and less change in traditional ways of thinking.

When it came to their foreign and security policies, again each followed a different path. While India chose nonalignment, China chose alignment. Nehru struck out on his own, outlining a policy independent of the Soviet and Western blocs, even before India was politically free, and to create an "area of peace" or geopolitical space for India. China, in a pattern that it was to repeat in the future, chose to align with one superpower, the Soviet Union, signing a defense alliance. China used that alliance for its own development and to manage its periphery in Korea and Indochina. China's decision to enter the Korean War against the United States was both a defense of its new communist regime and an attempt to polarize the situation to catalyze Soviet support.

On the other hand, India's relations with both superpowers and their allies remained relatively fluid and open until alliance structures like the Central Treaty Organization (CENTO) and Southeast Asia Treaty Organization (SEATO) came to Asia in the mid-1950s. Many Indians saw these alliances as a mortal blow to Asian unity and resurgence, an imperial divide-and-rule effort again. Time was to prove them right about the politics but wrong on the economics. Even thereafter, Nehru tried to maintain balance in India's relations with the two superpowers. China, on the other hand, saw Asian diplomacy and solidarity as offering it a way of increasing its options, locked as it was into the Soviet bloc, a position that it found increasingly constricting and unsatisfactory. China especially became concerned after Khrushchev's 20th Party Congress de-Stalinization speech in 1956, and its implicit attack on Mao's status and policies, and when expected Soviet support for China's policies on Taiwan, Indochina, and India was not automatic or complete.

The different policies and paths that the Indian and Chinese states chose in the mid-twentieth century greatly influenced China's place in postwar global governance structures. If China retained a seat on the UN Security Council through the Cold War, whether occupied by the Republic of China or the People's Republic of China, it was because it was allied to one or other superpower. India was not. There have been persistent reports of China's seat having been offered to India in the 1950s, but this was unlikely to ever be a real prospect in a bipolar world where China was allied to one superpower.

Both new states, the Republic of India and the People's Republic of China, tried in the 1950s to build a positive relationship. They each had major tasks of internal consolidation and development to undertake and did not see advantage in indulging in a confrontation. That initial attempt to build constructive relations did not succeed. For all their similar experience of imperialism, difficult as it was, and their professed commitment to Asian solidarity, they still had to reconcile their interests and deal with external power balances. The Chinese People's Liberation Army's entry into Tibet in 1950–1951, whose "return" to the motherland China undertook while postponing similar actions for Taiwan, Hong Kong, and other claims, brought Indian and Chinese troops face to face across a border for the first time in history. Dealing with this fact and reconciling their interests and positions on the boundary and in Tibet were among the first issues the new states had to address. This they failed to do. The consequences of that failure were the border conflict of 1962 and the long freeze in India-China relations that followed. Their inability to reconcile their interests or to overcome Chinese suspicions of Indian objectives in Tibet led directly to the Chinese decision to initiate the 1962 conflict. After the 1962 war, India and China followed active adversarial policies against each other until the first moves to normalize relations in the mid-1970s. That antagonism also spurred India's nuclear weapon program, making it a cross-party national effort within India. India became the strategic glue in China's ever closer ties to Pakistan, stretching to the internationally unparalleled Chinese supply of nuclear weapons and missile technology to Pakistan.

China's tacit alliance with the United States after 1971 against the Soviet Union saw its first application in their combined opposition to India and the birth of Bangladesh. Through the 1970s and 1980s, China's tacit alliance with the United States included working to exclude India from southeast Asia, an approach that continued for China but not the United States through the 1990s, even when the original justification and logic of the Cold War no longer applied. India had chosen then not to be part of Asian economic integration or of political integration efforts like the Association of Southeast Asian Nations (ASEAN) but reversed course after 1991. In the 2000s, worried about China's rise, the United States began seeing merit in India's naval and diplomatic presence in southeast Asia, though this has not yet extended to Indian membership in the Asia-Pacific Economic Cooperation (APEC) and economic integration with the region is no longer as influenced by the United States.

~

For three decades, from the late 1970s on, beginning with then foreign minister A. B. Vajpayee's February 1979 visit to China, India-China relations progressed steadily if slowly, incrementally improving, building a functioning bilateral relationship, managing differences, keeping the disputed border peaceful, and working together, where possible, on the international stage. China ceased overt support to insurgents in India's northeast, as Deng promised Foreign Minister Vajpayee in 1979, and by the mid-1970s armed Tibetan resistance to Chinese rule had ended. Irritants and contention remained, particularly in the periphery that India and China share, and the boundary dispute remained unsolved. However, both sides kept the border peaceful and built up a structure of confidence-building measures under the Border Peace and Tranquility Agreement of 1993. Bilateral trade grew from less than $2 billion in 2000 to over $93 billion in 2018, and China became India's largest trading partner in goods, with India becoming China's sixth largest export market. More than 23,000 Indian students now study in China. Since 2014 China has invested over US$26 billion in India, mainly in the IT, financial payments, and smartphone sectors. India and China worked together in international negotiations on climate change, the World Trade Organization's Doha Round, and in the BRICS organization (composed of Brazil, Russia, India, China, and South Africa). India-China interdependence has grown rather than diminished. Increased trade relations have resulted in predatory pricing and bidding for power and telecom projects by China, and the effect of cheap Chinese imports on small-scale industry in India have become bigger concerns. When the trade deficit ballooned, it accounted for over half of India's overall trade deficit. The two governments were careful in what they said that might affect the relationship.

The mutually agreed strategic framework, or modus vivendi, for the relationship that was evolved through the 1980s was formalized during Prime Minister Rajiv Gandhi's 1988 visit to China. In essence the framework established

+ negotiations on a boundary settlement while preserving the status quo on the border;

+ agreement that bilateral differences such as a boundary should not prevent bilateral functional cooperation; and

+ cooperation where possible in the international arena.

In practice each stayed out of the other's way internationally while concentrating on internal development and growth.

The steady course of relations from the 1980s through the 2000s continued despite geopolitical headwinds. While they resumed meaningful bilateral communication, and some level of coordinated action internationally, India and China were on opposite sides of major Asian issues, such as Afghanistan and Cambodia through the 1980s.

For a while after the Tiananmen killings, it remained important for China to keep India on its side when communist regimes were falling elsewhere and China feared becoming the target of regime change efforts by the United States. The 1980s proved a seminal period for the upgrading of the bilateral relationship, including public recognition by Deng Xiaoping of India's role in Asia alongside China. Through the 1980s, Indian and Chinese troops came into increasingly frequent contact along the border and tensions grew, eventually leading in 1986 to a prolonged face-off at Sumdorongchu. This was the spur for both sides to negotiate the 1993 Border Peace and Tranquility Agreement. The 1993 agreement committed both governments to respect the status quo on the border pending a negotiated settlement of the boundary and put in place the first in a series of confidence building agreements and understandings to reduce the risk of conflict. As a result, the India-China border was generally peaceful and stable until 2014 despite lack of clarity even on where the line of actual control lies in some sectors.

In effect, the collapse of the Soviet Union and the end of the Cold War shook India and China into a form of cautious engagement. Their reaction to the end of the bipolar world order was similar—to strengthen ties with the new hegemon, the United States, to begin a 360-degree foreign policy of multiple engagements with major powers, while attempting to pacify their own peripheries. Each of these policies had some success in itself. Their overall effect on China and India's economic transformation was phenomenal. The two decades between 1989 and 2008 saw the most successful economic development and growth of both countries in history.

But while India may have benefited from the globalization decades, it is the growing gap between India and China that now worries policy elites in India. In 1979 China was economically and technologically on par with India. Forty years later, it is a global economic power with a GDP four times India's, second only to the United States.[6]

India and China drew different conclusions from the 2008 crisis. Both saw an increased global role for themselves in a revived G-20 and elsewhere, though actual change in international governance has been slower and less evident than either hoped for. Some in China's leadership saw opportunity in what they considered the terminal decline of the West after 2008, and acted assertively as though China's moment had come. India, on the other hand, reacted defensively to what it saw as the end of the supportive external environment that it would have preferred to continue for many more years of internal transformation. The new government in India after 2014 chose to double down on its relationship with the United States, strengthening strategic partnership and declaring a joint vision for the Asia-Pacific with the United States, and adjusting energy policy and climate change positions to ease the relationship with the United States, reviving the Quad group (Australia, India, Japan, and the United States), and adopting the U.S. concept of an "Indo-Pacific," but simultaneously raising tariffs since 2017 and opting out of the Regional Comprehensive Economic Partnership (RCEP).

Despite differences in political and economic systems and between their societies, both China and India turned to strong, authoritarian, and conservative leaders in their last leadership transitions (as did Japan). In all three countries the new leaders used the opportunity created by the post-2008 crisis to centralize power in their own hands and to increase the stridency of their appeals to nationalism as a source of political legitimacy. Populist ultranationalism is flourishing in Asia, on the internet, and otherwise, even though governments remain careful in what they say on the record about each other.

~

From 2012 onward, India-China relations, which have always had elements of both cooperation and competition, began showing multiple signs of stress. Today, the modus vivendi of 1988 is no longer sufficient to manage the relationship and prevent conflict. Face-offs and intrusions along the border, which were handled quietly and managed smoothly before 2012 are now more frequent, publicized by both sides, and led in 2020 to the first death of troops since 1975 in clashes on the border.

When Xi visited India in September 2014, China tested the new Modi government's reactions in two ways. Over 1,000 Chinese troops entered Chumar, a disputed area in the middle sector of the border, on the day that Xi landed in India and stayed there during the visit before withdrawing and restoring the status quo. In the same month, a Chinese diesel submarine paid a first-ever port call to Colombo port, and the Chinese Foreign Office also confirmed that a Type-093 Shang-class Chinese nuclear attack submarine had been deployed in the Indian Ocean.

The face-off in Doklam in the summer of 2017, which took seventy-two days to resolve, saw both sides choosing a negotiated face-saving solution, but it was different from previous incidents in two respects: voluble and threatening commentary in the Chinese media and official statements and the incident occurring on territory disputed by China with a third country, Bhutan. Ultimately, the issue was resolved as in previous cases since 1986 by the restoration of the status quo through quiet diplomacy and ambiguity so as not to affect either side's substantive position on the boundary question. But unlike the past, while Chinese troops vacated the face-off spot, they soon established a permanent year-round presence on the plateau itself, where previously they had only patrolled occasionally. The solution thus left several loose ends to be sorted out, including a changed ground situation and the effect on Bhutanese opinion.

Other frictions also grew. Since 2015 China has made known publicly its opposition to India's membership in the Nuclear Supplier Group. This was in contrast to China in 2008 going along with the consensus in the NSG to make an exception permitting cooperation with India. India has criticized China's Belt and Road Initiative (BRI) and was one of the few countries not to attend the Belt and Road Forums in Beijing in 2017 and 2019 even though invited to do so—despite India's interest in Asian connectivity and its founder membership of the Asia Infrastructure Investment Bank (AIIB) started by China. Negative narratives in India are also fed by a perception of a new burst of Chinese activism in the Indian subcontinent, particularly the commitment to the China-Pakistan Economic Corridor, involving a Chinese presence on sensitive Indian territory abutting Afghanistan under Pakistani occupation, at Indian Ocean ports like Hambantota and Gwadar, and in the internal politics of Nepal, Sri Lanka, and other neighbors. Media and public narratives on the relationship in both countries have become much more negative and strident. Events that in the past saw muted Chinese reactions, such as the Dalai Lama's visits to Arunachal Pradesh, now elicit strong and vituperative commentary in the official Chinese media. Negative accounts in the public domain today feed a narrative of rivalry and possible conflict between India and China. The old modus vivendi is broken as both countries expand their definition of their interests with rapid development and growing capabilities. Both now see the world as critical to their domestic development, and China tries to actively shape its periphery shared with India and the world economy that is critical to India's future.

In India the narrative feeds on concern that India is falling behind China. It is little consolation that China is the only major power that India has fallen behind in the last three decades. As one of the fastest growing economies over an extended period, India increased its economic and political weight in the world in the years unto 2012. Besides, the objective reality of the India-China relationship is far more complex than simple binary narratives suggest. The 1:4 economic disparity, China's growing military strength, and its economic and political weight in the world do affect Indians directly. But, in terms of usable power, such as power disposable on the border, India may not be as badly off as the aggregates suggest; the global political balance was, until recently, also a factor in its favor. There was an effective or working balance on the border—no death occurred on the India-China border between October 1975 at Tulungla and June 2020 in the Galwan Valley, when Indian and Chinese soldiers died in clashes. Chinese actions in the spring of 2020 to move troops forward in several areas and to prevent Indian troops from patrolling in areas they have controlled for years have fundamentally changed the situation and suggest that deterrence has broken down on the border, and the series of confidence building agreements since 1993 are in question. India-China relations are in crisis in 2020.

Both India and China have developed and changed since the strategic framework was put in place in the 1980s. New issues such as maritime security and cyber security have come to the forefront. As a result of development, their interests have grown and expanded, and they now rub up against one another in the periphery they share, extending to the South China Sea. About 38 percent of Indian trades transits the South China Sea, making freedom of navigation there vital. As a consequence, India's stakes in the peace and stability of the area have grown, and India works with partners in the region such as Singapore, Japan, and Vietnam in new ways extending to defense and security issues.

Certainly, China's military modernization arouses legitimate concerns in India. The People's Liberation Army (PLA) is now the transformed product of two decades of double-digit budgetary growth, the building of hard infrastructure to support the military, and military reform under Xi Jinping to convert it into an expeditionary force. China has modernized its nuclear and intercontinental ballistic missile forces into a more capable second-strike force and developed medium range ballistic missile and cruise missile capabilities and systems that are altering the regional military balance. The PLA is now an in-strument for power projection, tasked to fight short, intense, high-technology wars in "informationized" conditions, outside China's own territory, dominat-ing its periphery.

And China has chosen not to do things to ease the relationship with India. For instance, the Indian trade deficit with China has steadily grown over sev-eral years to the point where it was US$52 billion in 2017, amounting to 45 percent of India's total trade deficit with the world. China could have addressed this. China has a 16 percent overall share in Indian imports, and much higher shares in certain sectors: 57 percent in electronics, 35 percent in machinery, 36 percent in organic chemicals, 60 percent in furniture and lighting, 36 percent in steel products, and over 80 percent in toys. India is dependent on China in the areas of electronics, bulk drugs for medicines, power generation equip-ment, and digital payment services. Over $26 billion of Chinese investment has come into India in the last six years—mostly through Singapore, Malaysia, and other countries. (The official figures only show $1.8 billion of Chinese invest-ment into India.) Chinese venture capital funders such as Alibaba have invested in Ola, Pay™, Snapdeal, bigbasket, Oyo, and Zomato.[7] India is also one of the major destinations for Chinese project exports. One-quarter of AIIB financing is presently committed to India, the most to any single country. This interest will grow as China-U.S. relations get more difficult.

Besides, the international context in which the relationship developed has also changed. Before the 2008 crisis, the main economic issues on the mul-tilateral negotiating agenda were north-south issues in the Doha Round, and international trade and investment flows were supportive of India and China's development. It was relatively easy and natural for India and China to work together on those north-south issues, to work up a common front. The same was true of climate change negotiations where India and China earlier worked with the BASIC group to preserve the advances of the 1992 UN Framework Convention on Climate Change.[8] More recently, however, as the world economy fragmented, each major economy attempted to preserve its own growth and prevent contagion, and China's industrialization accelerated. As the run-up to the 2015 Paris climate conference showed, China's interests in climate change negotiations could now be reconciled with those of the United States. It was the China-U.S. joint announcement and statement that largely produced the Paris outcomes. With the post-2008 rise of protectionism, and with China's rise to become a great manufacturing and trading power in the world, the issues on the international economic agenda are now of opening up domestic markets to each other in negotiations like RCEP, or trade facilitation, and are no longer developmental in nature. Energy security issues have come to the fore in the climate change negotiations with far less flexibility displayed by the industrialized countries, and a middle-income and highly industrialized China finds its interests are now more aligned with those of the United States and Europe.

To these changes that require a recalibration of India-China relations should be added the trajectory of domestic politics in both countries. Populist, authoritarian, and nativist leaders in most major powers are more mercantilist than their predecessors. We live in an age of ultranationalism where politics precludes many sensible economic choices. The emergence of leaders who rely on a heightened sense of nationalism for their legitimacy, who present themselves as strong leaders, represents both an opportunity and a danger. As strong and decisive leaders they could take the decisions required to deal with difficult issues in the relationship. At the same time a reliance on nationalism limits their ability to compromise and be flexible, or to counter the negative narrative that is emerging in both countries on the relationship. Public opinion in either country is unlikely to take kindly to any one-sided attempt to redraw the relationship in favor of one side or the other. Both governments had so far escaped this trap and been careful in their rhetoric about the other. However, the India-China crisis of 2020 has made this unlikely to continue.

On the Chinese side, the role of the PLA in decisionmaking on India-China relations has increased steadily over the last thirty years and seems to have accelerated under Xi Jinping. This may partly explain the increasing frequency with which China asserts its military presence in disputed border areas. The face-off in Depsang in 2013, when PLA pitched tents in an area that has always been patrolled by India but that lacked a permanent presence from either side, was finally defused after two weeks of diplomacy by restoring the status quo and the PLA withdrawing. In the next border commanders meeting, the PLA told the Indian Army that the issue would have been resolved much earlier if we had just spoken to them rather than to the officials in Beijing. Face-offs and intrusions are now much more frequent, and patrolling patterns are evolving with better access and technologies available to both sides. At a time of high nationalism, these incidents acquire a political and psychological salience in the relationship far beyond their immediate military implications.

∼

One factor above others that brought renewed stress into the Indian view of China is China's much stronger strategic commitment to Pakistan since President Xi Jinping's 2015 visit to Pakistan which announced the US$62 billion China-Pakistan Economic Corridor (CPEC). With China's broader activism, Pakistan has gained in importance for China. India was and remains the strategic glue to Pakistan-China relations since at least the late 1950s and definitely since 1962. This is certainly true for Pakistan, perhaps less so for China. The March 1963 China-Pakistan Boundary Agreement was a public manifestation as it sought to dispose of Indian territory under Pakistani occupation in Kashmir.

Less often noticed in India are the limits to China's commitment to Pakistan, not always to Pakistan's liking, and how they have changed over time. China has been ready since the 1960s to build Pakistan's military, nuclear, and other capabilities as a check and hedge against India, tying India down in the subcontinent. The first known case of a nuclear weapon state sharing nuclear weapon and missile technology and materials with a non-weapon state is between China and Pakistan. With each Indian advance in missile technology, China ensured that Pakistan stayed a close step behind. China has been less willing, however, to actually expend its own blood or treasure in defense of Pakistan. In none of Pakistan's wars with India did China intervene militarily, not even in 1971, when Pakistan was breaking up and Kissinger tried his best to get China to act against India, guaranteeing that the United States would neutralize any possible Soviet response against China. Sensibly, China was ready to fight to the last Pakistani, but preferred that not a single Chinese be involved. It remains to be seen whether this is still so with China's new and extensive stakes in Pakistan, including the military base in Gwadar/Jiwani, and after the remaking of the PLA into an expeditionary force.

In December 1996 President Jiang Zemin told the Pakistan National Assembly that Pakistan should do with India what China was doing, discussing bilateral disputes without allowing them to prevent the development of normal relations, and cooperating where they could. This echoed Indian advice to Pakistan and is something Pakistan has never been ready to do. That period of public Chinese neutrality between India and Pakistan was made possible by the end of the Afghan War, China's need for internal consolidation after Tiananmen, and Deng's accommodationist external policy toward the United States, all of which reduced Pakistan's immediate utility to China. China's signing of the Border Peace and Tranquility Agreement with India in 1993 also made overt hostility unnecessary, even though China's covert support to Pakistan's nuclear weapon program and army continued. For India, China's stance created space that Prime Ministers P. V. Narasimha Rao, A. B. Vajpayee, and Manmohan Singh utilized in their dealings with the world and Pakistan—a space that is no longer available to the present Indian government.

Today's situation is clearly very different from that period between 1988 and 2008, even if one discounts Pakistani claims in 2017 that China is now ready to sign a defense treaty committing for the first time to Pakistan's protection. After the India-U.S. nuclear deal, and more so after China adopted a more assertive policy after the 2008 world economic crisis, Pakistan is a significant part of the strain in India-China relations.

China's commitment to Pakistan is today broader and deeper than it has ever been. For China strong reasons for an increased commitment include a restive Xinjiang, balancing India, access through Gwadar to the Indian Ocean sea-lanes carrying her energy imports, a base for the PLA Navy at the mouth of the Persian Gulf, and Pakistan's role in the Belt and Road Initiative and in Afghanistan. For India, this enhanced Chinese commitment to an inveterately hostile neighbor is in itself a game-changer. China's long-term presence in POK as part of the CPEC is a Chinese bet on Pakistan's continued hold on Indian territory, and has deepened the Chinese interest in the longevity of a Pakistan dominated by its army. As a consequence, Pakistan has less incentive to be responsive to Indian overtures. Besides, the implications of a Chinese military presence in Gwadar, Djibouti, and other ports around the Indian Ocean coincide with a shift in declared Chinese strategy toward power projection and an accretion of Chinese capabilities that changes India's security calculus.

Since 1990 Pakistan's agency within the international system has declined, India's has grown, and China's has risen phenomenally. Along with this decline, Pakistan has seen poor economic prospects along with an increasing reliance on terrorism and religion as instruments of state policy. While Pakistan uses terrorism as a weapon against India and Afghanistan, it manages intelligence and terrorist groups for the various interests of the United States, China, and Russia. Meanwhile, there is an increasing intertwining of terrorist and extreme religious groups within Pakistan's own establishment and political parties. China's dependence on the Pakistani Army has also increased to fight Uighur groups and to protect assets in Pakistan and Afghanistan.

As Pakistan has declined economically, China has had to do more to support this client. Before Xi Jinping's China-Pakistan Economic Corridor (CPEC) commitment in April 2015, which has since risen in some accounts to US$72 billion, China's economic assistance to Pakistan was negligible and limited to strategic projects like the Karakoram highway and Gwadar port and to strengthening security ties. A RAND study puts total financial assistance pledged by China to Pakistan between 2001 and 2011 at $66 billion but finds that only 6 percent of it ever came through.[9] China has never kept Pakistan from having to go to the International Monetary Fund, not even when explicitly asked to by Pakistan in 2008. Pakistani officials put total Chinese investment in Pakistan before CPEC at $25 billion, but official Chinese figures speak of pre-2010 direct investment of $1.83 billion.

China's interest in Pakistan is still primarily strategic rather than economic. Within the CPEC, Gwadar port was developed first to enable China to secure its oil and gas supplies from the Persian Gulf and to project power into the Indian Ocean. The Chinese media itself has downplayed the commercial significance of an oil pipeline from Gwadar to Xinjiang saying that oil using this route would prove 16.6 times more costly than alternative sea routes through Shanghai. It is clearly not the economics of road or rail or pipeline connectivity that is driving the CPEC through some of the earth's most hostile terrain, highest mountains, and least secure places. It is strategy. As India develops, the incentives increase for China to buttress Pakistan for balance of power reasons.

∽

India's biggest strategic challenge today is managing its relationship with China and dealing with the consequences of China's rise. The former has to be done with China; the latter must include other powers that share India's interests.

Heightened China-U.S. contention should have led both China and the United States to ameliorate points of friction in their other relationships such as that with India, not picking new fights and postponing old ones to concentrate on their primary preoccupation, each other. There were some signs of this in China's behavior toward India and Japan in the Wuhan summit and the Abe visit in 2018, but China's behavior on the border in 2020 has changed that fundamentally. India's goal in the India-U.S.-China triangle should be to be closer to both China and the United States than they are to each other. The question is whether China's accommodation of some Indian concerns could amount to anything more than a tactical response to an immediate situation. To the extent that medium- to long-term factors drive India-China relations, it is in the interest of both sides to explore and create conditions for a new strategic framework for the relationship, to manage and solve core issues such as the boundary, and to monitor behavior in our common periphery. Both countries use outside balancers in their relationship with each other.

It is in the periphery that India and China most rub up against one another. China's emerging area of influence in Eurasia is growing not in a nineteenth-century imperialist manner but more subtly. In geopolitical terms the heartland is being consolidated and secured by China with Russian assistance or acquiescence. China's neighbors wish to have other hedging options to keep China honest, and they have turned to Russia, the United States, and regional powers like Iran and Turkey. There is an opportunity here for India, for instance, to build its own connectivity to central Asia, such as Chabahar port in Iran and the North-South Corridor with Iran and Russia. There is also an opportunity to offer the central Asian oil and gas producers, Turkmenistan and Kazakhstan, an alternative market, swapping on the international market if India cannot organize transport.

There are possible uses for India of Chinese-built connectivity so long as it is open, available, and economically viable. Consider the contrast between the Colombo and Hambantota ports in Sri Lanka, both expanded by China. Most of what goes through Colombo port, which is thriving, is to or from India. Thus, India enjoys the use of infrastructure built by Chinese money and effort in Colombo, and the Sri Lankans are able to pay back the cost of Colombo port expansion. Hambantota, on the other hand, has been unable to pay back the Chinese loans because very few ships berth there. So the Sri Lankan government had no option but to convert the debt into a lease to China, turning the port over to China for ninety-nine years. But frankly, that only converts a Sri Lankan dud into a Chinese one, and I do not see how that improves the situation from Sri Lanka or China's point of view. Given issues of viability and sustainability for several Belt and Road projects, it seems likely that those with internal rates of return that justify the investment and some of the strategically significant ones like Gwadar with basing for the PLA Navy will be implemented. The rest will labor against their own contradictions. Either way, these projects will fundamentally change the environment in which India operates. The threat of the military use of Hambantota will have to be part of the Indian calculus and provided for, even if that does not come about. The commercial uses of these ports would present India with opportunities for transshipment and competition that should make ports in south India more efficient.

In the broader maritime domain, India's interest for the present is not in attempting to exclude maritime powers from the Indian Ocean, which is impossible today, but to ensure the safety and security of the sea-lanes that carry its energy and trade, not just in the Indian Ocean but in the seas near China and to its west. To do so India must work with all the maritime powers. To the extent that the larger ones like China, the United States, and Japan share the Indian interest in freedom of navigation in the high seas, it should be possible for India to take the lead in working out a regime, formal or informal, that ensures this in the areas of its primary interest.

It also is in India's interest to work for an open, inclusive, and plural security order in the Asia-Pacific to replace the one that is no longer working. It would seem logical that as China seeks to play a greater role in the region and the world, it should work with other powers who share a desire to improve the world order and to concentrate on general economic betterment at home. This would require not just the fact of bilateral economic cooperation but addressing the sources of insecurity in the Asia-Pacific. This could be accomplished by integrating China into the political and military order of the region in a cooperative manner, just as China integrated itself into global and regional value and manufacturing chains in the last thirty years. If China chooses to work for an open, inclusive, multipolar concert or architecture in Asia, it would need to work with partners. So far this has not been China's choice. Given its history, experience, and recent behavior, it also seems unlikely.

Judging by China's actions in its periphery and with India in 2020, China has instead chosen to build a China-centric hierarchic order in the Asia-Pacific. Clearly, this diminishes India-China convergence on regional and global issues, particularly if China tries to change the global economic and political agenda to suit its particular interests. It is unlikely that globalization with Chinese characteristics will suit India. More abiding shared interests may lie in counterterrorism, maritime security, and other security issues rather than the economic issues that they worked on together in the past. To the extent that a Chinese attempt to build a China-centric order would be opposed by the United States, India would be asked by both sides to choose one side or the other, and each would seek to use India in its own negotiation with the other. Such a Chinese attempt would certainly provoke reactions from other regional powers like Japan, Vietnam, and Indonesia, though each would, like India, seek to work with China while minimizing the damage to its own interests—cooperating and competing at the same time.

If China sees the window of opportunity for its rise to primacy as limited, and if it is also convinced that the world is essential to its future growth and prosperity, we can expect a continuation or even a doubling down on China's assertive policies. In the short to medium term of five years or so, we will see a China in a hurry, changing facts on the ground in its favor and seeking friendly or pliable regimes in its periphery. It will set up alternative international institutions as its own instruments rather than wait for reform of existing multilateral institutions to be accommodated. PLA deployments and resorts to the threat and use of force abroad will become more frequent. Loyalty tests and demands for public recognition of its status will increase. And China will be demanding of other rising powers, seeing them as obstructions. All in all, China will seek to shape its external environment in more active ways. This would certainly mean that India-China relations are in for a period of turbulence and uncertainty.

The very reasons for China's haste would mean that such a policy could not be sustained for more than a decade or so. Whether this will indeed happen as described here depends on many imponderables, most significantly the Chinese Communist Party's primary interest in staying in power, China's domestic imperatives, and the extent to which Sino-U.S. contention forces a scaling back of Chinese pressure on its neighbors. If at any stage this activist policy is seen as hurting Communist Party rule, it will be abandoned forthwith. However, from what little we know of opinion in China, this activist stance is popular. It has helped the CCP to deal with discontent and to offset its declining legitimacy.

~

What does the present state of the India-China relationship suggest for India-China relations going forward, when older understandings no longer work, as Doklam has shown, and are inadequate to deal with issues that development and a new situation have thrown up? At the end of 2020, India-China relations are in crisis because of Chinese actions on the border, despite eighteen meetings between Prime Minister Modi and President Xi Jinping as well as the care that the Modi government displayed after 2017 regarding China's sensitivities about Tibet, the BRI, and the Indo-Pacific.

The present prospect is for tenser and more adversarial India-China relations. One consequence of more difficult relations between India and China is the increasing attempt by smaller neighbors to play the two off against each other, getting from each what they can. To several Indians this seems like containment or encirclement of India by China, as they watch a communist coalition supported by China in power in Nepal, as the Maldives entered surreptitiously into a free trade agreement with China and possible basing arrangements for the PLA Navy at Gadu island next to Gan, and as Sri Lanka handed over Hambantota port to China for ninety-nine years. The absence of a commercial or economic rationale for much of what China does in southern Asia fires Indian suspicions that these projects are strategically motivated. Whatever the intent, they are certainly creating infrastructure that could be available to the Chinese military. To that extent, China's activism in southern Asia will make India's relations with its smaller neighbors more fraught and contribute to the worsening of India-China relations.

In my opinion, the regional and global situation suggests that the next few years may be more difficult than the last three decades for India-China relations. The more India rises, the more we must expect the balance to shift from cooperation to competition with China. India will have to work with other powers and in the subcontinent to ensure that its interests are protected. The most important thing, for me, is the need for India to rapidly accumulate usable and effective power, even while the macro balance takes time to right itself. Even so, my personal sense is that the bilateral relationship could be managed by the two countries, despite the complications created by an evolving international context and China's drive for primacy in Asia. But this requires more than a reactive strategy or even just preventive engagement with China. It is hard to think of possible gains from conflict for either side that are not outweighed by large costs. The very uncertainty of the geopolitical situation around them, at a time when they each must undertake major domestic adjustments in their economies and societies, impels them to find a way to manage the relationship in the new situation. The causes that led them to first work out a modus vivendi in the 1980s and to successfully implement it thereafter remain valid, namely, their domestic preoccupations and concerns about their relations with the rest of the world and the sole superpower, the United States.

But the balance of power with India has shifted in China's favor since the 1980s. The economic complementarity that underlay the political understanding between them has increasingly turned to Indian dependence on China—for power generation and telecom equipment, and for the vast infrastructure needs of the Indian economy. India is the biggest beneficiary of the Chinese-led Asian Infrastructure Investment Bank in its first two years, taking a quarter of its investment commitments. In its first two years the AIIB approved US$4.3 billion of funding more than US$1 billion of which is to go to schemes in India.[10] China is a potential investor and builder of the infrastructure that India needs. And the trade imbalance itself makes clear the demand for Chinese goods in India.

~

Could India and China evolve a new framework for their relations? Theoretically it would include respect for each other's core interests; new areas of cooperation like counterterrorism and maritime security and crisis management; a clearer understanding of each other's sensitivities; settling or at least managing differences; and, a strategic dialogue about actions on the international stage. New security issues, like maritime security which is increasingly important to both India and China, can be positive sum issues, if not looked at territorially. Both have an interest in keeping the sea-lanes open and secure for their trade and energy flows and should be discussing them and cooperating. The hardest part will be coming to a common understanding of each other's core interests, which, for India would include its security in the subcontinent and the Indian Ocean.

India too will need to adjust to new economic realities. For example, the rise of China and its economic strength make the extent of India's engagement in RCEP a matter of debate in India, at a time when trade in goods accounts for almost half of India's GDP. Equally, India now has an interest in freedom of navigation in the South China Sea, since US$66 billion worth of its exports and about 33 percent of its trade passes through that waterway; the nature and manner of safeguarding that interest are still an issue in India. If India stays away from the RCEP, it is much less likely to achieve its own economic goals.

Today, China-U.S. contention—which I think is structural and therefore likely to continue for some time—opens up opportunities and space for other powers. Initially, both China and the United States looked to put other conflicts and tensions on the back burner while they deal with their primary concern, each other. We saw this effect in the April 2018 Wuhan informal meeting between President Xi and Prime Minister Modi and the apparent truce and dialing back of rhetoric by both India and China, even though this did not extend to a new strategic framework or understanding or to a settlement of outstanding issues. Their second informal summit in December 2019 at Mahabalipuram suggested that the truce would continue. These hopes have been belied in 2020.

Therefore, the Chinese attempts in spring 2020 to change the situation on the border by occupying areas on the Indian side of the Line of Actual Control and prevent Indian troops from patrolling where they had before marked a significant change in China's behavior. It came when India and the world were preoccupied by the COVID-19 pandemic and the economic crash it produced. India's reaction has naturally been to resist the changes and to increase the deployment of forces on the border. Today, both sides are in a tense military standoff involving several divisions. While both sides seek disengagement, several rounds of talks have so far not resulted in any relaxation. The India-China border is alive again, after many years. Risks are heightened by the fact that both sides are claiming victory in the military confrontation.

More significantly, the political relationship, after several years of sliding toward increasing confrontation, is being reset in a more adversarial frame. Public opinion in India is overwhelmingly critical of China. Though calls to boycott Chinese goods in India have so far not led to economic decoupling, the Indian government has announced a turn to self-reliance, is working to lessen dependencies on China, and is building more secure and resilient supply chains along with Japan and Australia. India is now far more willing to be seen working closely with the United States in the region. The shift from pure balancing between China and the United States to a more aligned posture will not, according to the external affairs minister, extend to an alliance. Neither the United States nor India wishes to enter into the mutual defense commitments that are at the heart of an alliance. Short of an alliance, a further strengthening of India-U.S. defense, security, and intelligence links is now a certainty, thanks to recent Chinese actions.

The international situation and correlation of forces also give India a chance to strengthen its own capacity, to build coalitions of the willing to shape China's behavior, and to work with other Asians to achieve desired outcomes in India's issues. These become even more important as a new modus vivendi with China will be even harder to achieve if the power gap between India and China continues to grow.

Will reason prevail in India-China relations and can the two countries manage their bilateral relations successfully after the crisis of 2020? In the midst of the crisis it is hard to see India and China finding a way forward that is better than their recent past. That requires a degree of pragmatism and a strategy of simultaneously balancing and actively engaging with China that enables India to get on with what is really important, creating outcomes that transform India and improve the well-being of its people. It was done once before between 1986 and 1988. But then there was a balance of economic, political, and military power between India and China. That is no longer true. Whether or not India and China are successful will affect not just India's future prospects, but also the course of Asian geopolitics in years to come.

13

India's Tasks

Independent India's foreign policy has managed three geopolitical phases and their transitions: from 1947 to the 1960s, a bipolar, nuclearized, Cold War world to which India responded with nonalignment and advocacy of decolonization, disarmament, and multilateralism; from the early 1960s to the mid-1980s, drastic shifts in Asia with the Sino-Soviet split in the early 1960s and a Sino-U.S. alliance from 1971, to which India responded by consolidating its immediate periphery and tightening links with the Soviet Union; and after 1989, the unipolar globalization decades when India reformed itself, integrated its economy with the world, and transformed its relations with the United States.

We are now in the midst of yet another transition. It is time that we thought afresh about the practice of Indian foreign policy and its theoretical underpinnings. We face three critical challenges: the intellectual one of understanding the present-day world and developing a concept of India's place in it; the practical one of devising policies that enable India's continued transformation; and the broader challenge of devising a workable grand strategy for India.

~

The intellectual challenge is to develop concepts of India's place in the world and of the order we should seek. Free India has a geopolitical dilemma all its own. Independence in 1947 meant a fundamental change in India's geopolitical circumstances. India is not the geopolitical heir to the Raj, neither is its situation like that of any other country. India cannot, should not, and will not behave like others. Take China, for instance. India's geopolitical situation is similar to China's only in the broadest sense of a rimland power to Eurasia, but it is the product of a fundamentally different geography and history. While India has an open maritime geography, China does not. The Indian Ocean balance and geography are very different from those of the South China Sea and East

340

China Sea. The Indian Ocean is not a closed sea. China is trying to put in place the means for future predominance in this open oceanic space, building ports and bases at Djibouti, Gwadar-Jiwani, Hambantota, Kyaukphyu, Malacca, the Maldives and elsewhere, preparing for a time when the balance can be worked in its favor. But here, given the distance from home, the United States and China are each likely to work with allies and partners, like the Pakistan Navy, while deploying psychological, political, economic, and other pressure to change the behavior of existing maritime powers in the Indian Ocean, namely, India, Singapore, Indonesia, Australia, Japan, and France.

India also carries a unique strategic mindset and inheritance. Indian thought has been comfortable with multistate systems, with a pluriverse or multiverses. The Kautilyan universe was rather like what we see in the world today, multiple political units each differing in its power, internal arrangements, and potential. Kautilya's was a conception very different from modern Western ideas of international order, based as they are on the Westphalian state and ideas of sovereignty and legitimacy. The present Indian establishment is not educated for imperium or to rule, as were Curzon and his ilk, and is still undergoing rapid social churn.

Halford Mackinder and Alfred Mahan's best disciples are today to be found in Asia and not the Europe and America for which they wrote. In classical geopolitical literature, India was the ultimate pivot state. This may have been true when the subcontinent functioned as a single geopolitical unit. Today, India's borders do not conform to the geographic borders of the subcontinent. That is the heart of India's continental dilemma. Pakistan, for instance, poses a security challenge to India within the subcontinent, robbing India of political energy that it would otherwise harness for Eurasia and the Indian Ocean.

India must deal with a world and an Asia in which its major geopolitical challenge is the rise of China and the reactions and effects of that displacement on the balance of power in the region and in the immediate neighborhood. The global economic slowdown, technological change, the return of power politics, and the effects of globalization have made more complex and difficult the international context for the realization of India's transformation. Since Indian independence, the primary function of Indian policy has been the great national task of transforming India into a prosperous, strong, and modern country. The task of the foreign and security policy apparatus is to identify, deter, and defeat threats to national security that could prevent that transformation and to create an enabling environment for India's transformation. This will remain the nation's purpose for a long time to come, so long as India has poor, illiterate people who live insecure lives threatened by disease and who cannot fulfill their potential. Why should many Indians live in what Juvenal called "a state of ambitious poverty," which affects all Indians in so many ways?

Some in India think that the transformation of India is too defensive a goal, that we should make it clear that we wish to be a great power or a superpower. Frankly, being a great power will follow, not precede, success in building a strong, prosperous, and modern India. Our purpose is the outcome in India, not some notional status or recognition by others. We should never confuse our national interest in creating outcomes at home with international prestige. We have a long way to go, despite all that we have achieved since independence. All rising powers in history have chosen to keep their heads down while building their own strength, rather than inviting resistance to their rise to great power status by proclaiming their power and its uses. Those that followed the path of flaunting their ambition and their growing power too early, such as Wilhelmine Germany and Japan in the 1930s, were frustrated in their rise and paid a heavy price. Whether China has made the same mistake recently remains to be seen.

With thirty years of over 6 percent growth and the accretion of hard power, India has improved its relative position vis à vis all powers except China. India now has some economic influence, and the local political and military balance is not as unfavorable as it was for most periods after independence. There are no existential threats to India from abroad. If there are threats to India's existence, they are primarily internal. The magnitude of the remaining task of transforming India means that the primary focus must still be creating an enabling external environment for the transformation of a resource-poor but people-rich India. It is likely to remain so for quite some time to come.

Until recently India had a vision of both its place in the world and of the order it preferred. That was of an order that was rule-based, democratic, and plural, that would assist in the transformation of India. To this end, India saw itself as a responsible stakeholder in the international system, was a willing contributor to international peacekeeping and to solidarity among developing countries, and was an active participant in the multilateral order. India was one of the greatest beneficiaries of globalization decades. Now, the Narendra Modi government desires to be seen as new and to overthrow what it sees as the Nehruvian legacy, but it has not described an alternative in practice or theory. The Nehruvian legacy in foreign policy was of expanding what Nehru called "the area of peace." This involved working within the existing order to create an enabling environment for India's development and to encourage an open, plural, and democratic international order, while improving the order, and India's say in it, where possible. That policy, adjusted to circumstance by Nehru's successors, worked. It delivered sufficient security for India to grow faster than it had ever done in history, to take more people out of poverty than any other country except China, and to have a realistic shot at ending India's underdevelopment.

For the last few years, however, India seems adrift in terms of a vision of India's role and place in the world.[1] There has been an obsession with India as "a leading power" and its standing in the international order. Spokespersons for the Modi government have spoken of statecraft as a "battle of civilizations, battle of cultures, basically the battle of minds."[2] They have also concentrated on India's civilizational glory and spoken of regaining it. Prime Minister Modi has spoken since 2015 of India as a *vishwaguru*, or world teacher. This is a noble soft-power goal but ignores the fact that soft power is useless without the sinews of hard power to back it up, and that whatever India may have been in the past, it is far from being a provider of knowledge to today's world. The idea of a *vishwaguru* probably plays well with Modi's core Hindu constituency at home but is hardly a realistic goal when contemporary India is a net importer of knowledge, is not known for its innovation, and must still do a great deal to spread primary education to its people and raise educational standards to acceptable levels in its institutions of learning. Nor is it clear how *vishwaguru* status would address the immediate problems of livelihood and security that the Indian people and nation face. Becoming a *vishwaguru* is hardly the answer to India's security, economy, and development needs and what they require from the international system. In any case, the first Modi government saw precious little done to move India toward this nebulous goal, which may be just as well.

In the last decade a domestic narrative has taken hold across the Indian political spectrum that India must be a superpower or a great power. But very little is said of the purposes of that accumulation of power and of the uses it should be put to. Nor is it clear how it will enable India's transformation into anything but a nineteenth-century European power. It is worth wondering what the quest for great-power status will do to the polity and society within India, not all of which is likely to be for the better. Implicit in terms like "rising India" or "India the great power" are ideas of hierarchy and perception, both of which are hardly defined or measurable by agreed metrics or standards. Such terms reduce international relations in the popular mind to some kind of macho contest between states of who can throw a shot or missile furthest or can do the most damage to our planet and people. India is and has been an important player on the world stage with its own interests and will continue to be so. And yet, the purpose of our participation in the international community is not to see how many people we can outdo or push down. It is to uplift our own people and to improve their condition from the abject state that we were left in after two centuries of colonialism. That is not achieved at someone else's expense. Instead, it requires us to work with others in international society to achieve an enabling environment for India's transformation.

The narrative about India as a great power seems driven more by a desire for status and recognition than by the outcomes the quest for great-power status is likely to produce for the Indian people, society, state, the subcontinent, and the world. What is missing is a vision of India's place in the international system and its goals, as Nehru was able to articulate in his time, even though he was not always entirely in touch with the realities of power and therefore saw some of his policies fail.

One reason for that absence may be that India is still in the process of developing a vocabulary and theory of international relations that suits the particularity of the Indian case. This is not a uniquely Indian problem. China, Japan, Russia, and others face the same issue of devising the scholarship and concepts necessary for an understanding of their countries' places in the world. For some years before and after independence, a body of Indian scholars contributed to global international relations scholarship. From the mid-1970s onward, however, standards of international relations scholarship in India declined, although several Indian academics made reputations abroad. Today, again, young scholars are doing outstanding work on India's relations with the United States, with the rest of the subcontinent, about the Nehru years, and on the drivers of Indian foreign policy. Most are products of today's globalized world, many have brought their scholarship home, and they represent the beginning of a new wave of India studies.

We tend to forget that international relations theory, like much theory in the liberal arts, is the product of a very specific time and place, and the intellectual expression of a certain economic and political dominance, in this case of a limited slice of European and north American experience and history. If international relations scholarship is to be relevant to India, it will need to adapt and change too. It would need to draw on India's own traditions, for one, and must look at other traditions, in east Asia for instance. Today, the world that created international relations theory as we know it is rapidly fading. The center of gravity of the world economy and politics is returning to Asia. And it is time for those of us in India to think afresh and for ourselves again about India and its place in the world.

As described earlier, India is fortunate in having a tradition of strategic thought that, unlike China's, prepares it for the polycentric or multipolar world of contention among today's powers of differing capabilities. A scholarship tradition and framework allows India to reconceive its place in the world. The role India seeks should not be of a "great power" or "middle power," or a transactional and instrumental "swing state" or a "balancer" in a hierarchically ordered world. It must be one derived from the kind of India that is the common goal. If it is a plural, democratic, secular country for all Indians that is to be built, can India accept anything less as its goal in the world? For the present, while capacity is limited and resources finite, India's domestic transformation will override any attempt to remake international society. But this will not always be so as India's power and agency in international society increases.

~

The practical challenge for India is to pursue a foreign policy that will continue to transform the country in an uncertain world. India has learned from failures in the early years, as well as its increasing success from the 1990s on. Now it must recalibrate some of its major relationships yet again. The world is now multipolar economically, but India's region is being pulled in two directions by the United States and China.

At a time of rapid change, it would be foolish to think that what has worked before will work now. That would be a variant of Einstein's definition of insanity: doing the same thing over again expecting a different result. And yet, that has been India's recent course. In essence, in its early years the Modi government followed the foreign policy practices of past governments, renaming and repackaging them, with three significant deviations: moving India's foreign trade and economic policies toward a more closed and protectionist stance, opting out of the Regional Comprehensive Economic Partnership; weakening relations with neighbors in the subcontinent; and stepping up strategic commitments to the United States and to U.S. allies in west Asia. Yet, if this was seen as a tilt by India it was corrected in the last two years of the first Modi government. Prime Minister Modi's speech on the Indo-Pacific at the Shangrila Dialogue in Singapore in 2018 could have been delivered by any Indian prime minister of the last thirty years. However, as circumstances have changed, the results have not matched those achieved by previous governments. India's relationships in the subcontinent are more fragile and challenged than they were five years ago; relations with our largest neighbor, China, are fraught; and India risks missing the economic development bus in the harsher economic climate today. In 2020, the crisis on the border provoked by China's move to occupy territory previously under Indian control has led to a renewed emphasis on ties with the United States and partners on China's periphery, such as Japan, Australia, Vietnam, Indonesia, and Singapore.

Some of the effects of hypernationalism and domestic politics in India and in its neighbors on relations between competitive powers are visible in India-Pakistan relations and in India-China relations. Neither relationship is as predictable as it was a few years ago. These complicate southern Asian politics and India's relations with its other neighbors, giving each of them more balancing and hedging options to get their way with India and to compensate for the disparity in power. India therefore has to be much more skillful in managing relationships in the subcontinent and resist a recent temptation to use these relationships for image building or political advantage at home. Most successful Indian diplomacy in the subcontinent in the past has been silent, not broadcast in public or tweeted, and has publicly respected the sensitivities of smaller neighbors. This seems no longer to be the case.

How should India conduct itself in a subcontinent where economies are not integrated, where nationalisms are defined against and by India, and where existing institutions of cooperation are not viable? The answers are several: by making economic integration an overriding goal of policy, by building connectivity and by being willing to pay a price for it; by being a contributor to the security of its neighbors; and by ensuring through its actions that India is seen as an agent of positive change; and by tempering its proconsular instincts. Unfortunately, the last few years have seen Indian inaction or actions that run counter to previous Indian practice and policy in Nepal, the Maldives, and elsewhere in the subcontinent. The result is a marked deterioration in India's influence and the increasing role of powers such as China and the United States and of west Asian states in India's periphery.

An obsession with Pakistan and boycotting the South Asian Association for Regional Cooperation (SAARC), when China is an active presence in south Asia, have led neighbors with whom India has close affinities to hedge their bets. Nepal is the most obvious example, but this is also true of the Maldives and Sri Lanka. In Nepal, the quest to restore a "Hindu rashtra" and monarchy in Nepal by some Indian political parties and organizations has confused Indian policy and further alienated Nepalese ruling parties and the Kathmandu elite, while facilitating the marginalization of Madhesi parties in the *Terai*, the belt of lowland that constitutes the India-Nepal borderlands, where India's traditional links and friendships have been particularly close. For India to be seen in 2015 publicly pressing for changes in a Nepalese constitution already adopted by the country's own assembly, then to be seen to fail, and then to impose a blockade, was the epitome of ugly and ineffective Indian neighborhood diplomacy. Domestic politics and communal polarization in India, with threats by ruling party president Amit Shah to expel Bangladeshi immigrants whom he described as "termites," the National Register of Citizens in Assam, and India's ham-handed response to the Rohingya crisis have affected ties with Bangladesh, diminished India's credibility, and lowered its ability to integrate the subcontinent. And this at a time when Bangladesh has been most cooperative with India on security and economic and political issues since 2008. Despite talk of "neighborhood first," the actual delivery of Indian development cooperation has diminished recently. South Asia has seldom seemed so disunited or less integrated. This is a pity when the economic performance of south Asia, particularly of Bangladesh and of Sri Lanka after its civil war, is the basis to build a much more prosperous and integrated region. The more the overall uncertainty in the global system, the higher the priority that India should accord to stabilizing and managing its immediate periphery, particularly the subcontinent.

India's presence and influence in the Indian Ocean, the Maldives, and Sri Lanka have now to compete with many more powers, and its strategic space is shrinking. India is treating important relationships in the neighborhood, which are significant in themselves for India, as subsets of other issues such as those surrounding China and Pakistan, thus affecting relations with Nepal, Bangladesh, Myanmar, and possibly even Bhutan. These are examples of the kind of diplomacy that India cannot afford when external circumstances have sufficiently complicated the neighborhood environment. India cannot today restore the subcontinent's ability to act as a single geopolitical unit in the world, but it can aim for a peaceful periphery, keeping relations on an even keel with its neighbors, integrating economies, and working for the subcontinent to act together on the many international development and political issues that unite us.

For most Indians the fly in the subcontinental ointment is Pakistan. The 2003 ceasefire along the Line of Control between India and Pakistan has broken down, and political communication between the two states is minimal today. We are a long way from the promise of the 2004–2007 period, when India and Pakistan appeared close to addressing the issues between them, when terrorism declined, and it seemed possible that the two countries would find a way to live together in peace, no matter how fragile. As a consequence of India-Pakistan differences, the SAARC Summit, which was to be held in Pakistan in 2017, has been postponed. Cooperation in SAARC has been driven down to subregional levels that exclude Pakistan. Polarized local politics in both countries will probably ensure that this chill continues for some time, despite a shared fondness for theatrical gestures of reconciliation.

The Modi government's declared "muscular" policy and reliance on the public use of force have re-created opportunity for Pakistan in Jammu and Kashmir (J&K). According to those who track the data, the number of terrorist incidents in J&K climbed from 208 in 2015 to 342 in 2017; terrorist killings doubled and, according to the state government, so did the number of Kashmiri deaths, which rose from 66 in 2015 to 126 in 2017. Clearly "surgical strikes," retaliation, and tough policing in J&K had the opposite effect of the peace that was promised.

Since then, after winning a second mandate in the May 2019 general elections, the Modi government reduced the level of provincial autonomy in J&K and reorganized the state into two union territories, administered from the center in August 2019. This necessitated a considerable tightening of security, the arrest of prominent politicians, and a prolonged lockdown, as well as provoked local resistance. The second Modi government's Pakistan policy and actions within J&K have effectively internationalized the Kashmir question again, handed Pakistan and China a lever to raise the matter in the UN Security Council after more than forty years, and occasioned negative reactions across the Muslim world.

From an Indian point of view, a peaceful periphery requires managing Pakistan or neutralizing its hostility. In the best scenario, Pakistan's utility to other powers seeking to check or limit India's rise would be limited, and India's fear of a two-front war against Pakistan and China would be neutralized. In pursuit of that goal, most Indian governments have chosen a two-track policy—to keep Pakistan engaged, while actively countering Pakistani hostility and terrorist and other violence against India. This has the advantage of recognizing that Pakistan, the Pakistan Army, and its Inter-Services Intelligence organization have a vested interest in a managed level of tension with India, but that India has no quarrel with the Pakistani people. It has also limited outside interference in India-Pakistan issues, which for the most part India has handled bilaterally since the 1971 war.

The card that Pakistan uses to make itself useful to great power patrons, such as Afghanistan, will no longer work once the United States withdraws its troops from there. But, as China's concerns in Xinjiang grow, and Russia's fears of a destabilized central Asian "near abroad" increase, Pakistan is turning to them. The United States is willing to bring the Taliban to power in Afghanistan in order to avoid the humiliation of admitting military defeat, leaving the Afghan government and other stakeholders to their own devices. It is hard to predict, as of this writing, how this will turn out. Afghanistan, its society, and its neighbors are not what they were when the Taliban were helped to power in 1996 by international neglect and the Pakistan Army. The Taliban itself is changed, factionalized, and outflanked by the more extreme Islamic State, or Da'esh. While these developments will change the dynamic in Afghanistan, India's security and crossborder terrorism problems have always been a Pakistan problem rather than an Afghan problem. Whether today's Pakistan, much more fragile and politically extremist than it was in 1996, will be able to limit and deal with the consequences of a stronger Taliban in Afghanistan is moot.

In a strategic sense, Pakistan is a distraction, dangerous primarily because of the uses that other powers put Pakistan to. India has better and more important things to do than engage in pointless conflict with Pakistan. For most of its life, Pakistan's own survival has been a question. By dealing with every leader of every military coup in Pakistan, India has strengthened and lent legitimacy to them, and they then consolidate their hold on power after Indian recognition. And as long as the Pakistan Army dominates governance and the construct of Pakistani nationalism is what it is, there will always be new issues, as Pakistani general and former President Pervez Musharraf used to say. The underlying causes of tension—crossborder terrorism from Pakistan and Pakistan's quest for "strategic parity" with India and strategic depth in Afghanistan—are rooted in Pakistan's internal condition. Therefore, they are likely to repeatedly assert themselves, and any warming is likely to be limited and temporary until the nature of Pakistan's politics changes fundamentally.

If there is one thing that the past should have taught India, it is that Pakistan is its problem to solve and that it is one that other powers find convenient to use. No other power is willing to do the heavy lifting on Pakistan for India. For more than seventy years the United States and Pakistan have aligned their security interests sporadically and partially, finding some tactical congruence during the Cold War 1950s, in the war against the Soviets in Afghanistan, and after the 9/11 attacks. Meanwhile, Pakistan has found increasing commonality with China on security interests vis à vis India and others since the late 1950s, culminating in the transfer of nuclear weapon drawings, technology, and materials from China to Pakistan since 1975. Today, Pakistan uses its nuclear weapons, and the fear of their falling into the wrong hands, to ensure U.S. and international interest in supporting the Pakistan Army and state.

India's primary strategic focus must be Asia. Here, China is a fact of Indian life. As China transitions to greater political and military power, and an increasing presence in the neighborhood, India meets China in every sphere of activity. The China-U.S. relationship is playing itself out around India. China is not something that can simply be opposed. Nor is it something that can be ignored or lived with passively. India must actively deal with and try and shape its relationships with China and the United States to moderate their behavior in India's interests. Ideally, this requires India actively engaging with both China and the United States, not choosing sides, and having better relations with each than they have with each other. This was the policy that India followed from the 1980s onward. It meant more than just maintaining India's freedom to judge and react to events on the basis of its interests and not their preferences, the classic definition of nonalignment. It also meant actively working with others and shaping the environment.

That attempt has clearly been overtaken by China's actions to militarily change the status quo on the border in the spring of 2020. Instead of active engagement or the evolution of a new strategic framework for India's relations with China, we are faced with the prospect of a much more adversarial India-China relationship.

On the other hand, India-U.S. relations have gone from strength to strength in the last decade. Although the United States may have been preoccupied internally and limited its external engagements, India doubled down on the relationship. The Modi government has chosen to depend strategically on the United States to a far greater extent than any previous Indian government. For instance, it has signed four foundational defense agreements for interoperable military communications and bases, resisted by earlier governments.

The U.S. response to China's rise is today described as an Indo-Pacific strategy. The Quadrilateral Security Dialogue of four regional democracies—Australia, India, Japan, and the United States—was revived in 2017 to act as a counterpoint to a more aggressive China. However, this is only a partial answer to India's challenges. For one, the so-called Indo-Pacific strategy is a purely maritime strategy that implicitly concedes the continental order to powers other than the United States, namely, China and Russia. India is both a continental and maritime power with significant security interests on the Asian landmass. The only American presence in continental Asia is its unsustainable embroilment in Afghanistan, which will end as soon as it can find a way of withdrawing without the stigma of defeat. India's major points of contact with China are on land and include the world's largest boundary dispute. Any Indian strategy for continental Asia must therefore work with Asian powers, Russia, Iran, China, and others. More important, the geography and security issues of the Indian Ocean, the seas near China, and the western Pacific are different from one another. They require different solutions and approaches. To be effective the Quad must involve countries in the region, ASEAN, particularly Singapore and Indonesia, in its work. As the Quad begins to explore a set of practical steps, its agenda for the future will keep evolving. India's future security has to be based on much more than such a weak and indeterminate reed.

None of this is to question the strategic underpinnings of the India-U.S. relationship. Both sides had their reasons to be skeptical of each other during the Cold War. Since then, however, there has been a growing congruence between Indian and American interests for more than two decades, which has produced a remarkable transformation in the relationship. The Modi government has taken the defense and security relationship to new levels. As in any relationship of unequals—and the disparity in power and capacity between India and the United States is indeed great—the stronger power is often frustrated by the weaker's ability still to follow its own, different interests. But the basic economic complementarity and congruence in wanting a predictable rule-based security order in the Asia-Pacific, and their shared disquiet about the effects of the rise of China, have enabled India and the United States to manage differences and build positive cooperation in Asia, particularly in the maritime domain.

The United States remains critical to the transformation of India, its effort to manage and shape the external environment, its internal and external balancing in response to the rise of China, and to the shape of the evolving international order. Given the differences in geography, development levels, and interests, the United States might not provide all the answers to India's strategic needs, but it is the one power that affects all of India's critical interests. The relationship will need to be carefully nurtured by India, quite apart from how Asia and American strategy and views evolve. India and the United States are therefore moving toward a partnership that increasingly has some of the characteristics of an alliance, but without the commitment to mutual defense that is the heart of any alliance.

Tighter India-U.S. relations seem likely even though questions remain regarding how and to what extent the United States will remain engaged in Asia. The steps that the Trump administration took signaling a U.S. unwillingness to maintain the so-called liberal world order were loud and clear. The United

States has withdrawn from the Trans-Pacific Partnership, has refused to implement its treaty commitment under the nuclear agreement with Iran and imposed sanctions, has begun an economic and tariff offensive against China and others, has barely resourced the military and economic wings of its Indo-Pacific strategy, has announced troop withdrawals from Afghanistan, Syria, and elsewhere, has increased reliance on local proxies like Saudi Arabia to deal with Iran in Yemen and the Gulf, has withdrawn from the Paris climate accord, and has crippled the WTO dispute settlement process, just to name a few of the Trump administration's actions. The United States is no longer the engaged partner of the past. This shift is not necessarily just the result of President Trump's personality, but to the extent that it reflects structural changes in U.S. internal politics it seems likely to last, at least in terms of the unwillingness to engage militarily abroad, a reliance on allies and partners, and the reluctance to provide global public goods. Other policies of the present American administration, such as its stance on climate change and free trade, which in time will begin to affect U.S. interests adversely, will presumably not be as long-lasting or extreme.

The United States has been written off before and has shown a capacity to repeatedly adapt and shift shape, remaking its external and internal policies. The United States was the only Western economy to successfully mitigate the consequences of the 2008 world economic crisis. The same can happen if America uses information technology, artificial intelligence revolutions and digital manufacturing, and its technological and energy resource dominance to again change the rules of the game to its advantage.

What is in doubt today is U.S. political commitment and understanding of the post–Cold War order that it built and ran. The United States seems to be deglobalizing, on-shoring production where possible. Given how the Trump administration treated loyal allies like Canada and the European Union, Germany and others have come to the conclusion that they must now go their own way and build their own capabilities. The Trump administration seemed to wish only to deal with allies who follow and clients who obey. For it to learn how to work with partners, which was what India seeks, was to expect a great deal. This was a transactional America under Trump, looking for immediate gain and victories, most of them tactical. India's rise is not seen as a strategic interest. None of this means that India-U.S. relations will not grow. Indeed, the congruence in interests means that they will. But they will not follow the trajectory of the past, and the role of governments and leaders is not going to be as decisive as before as the relationship acquires depth.

It is for India to independently use the disruption that the new U.S. approach to global politics creates to further its own interests and influence. There is opportunity here for India to work with a broad set of partners, augmenting its influence and building coalitions of the like-minded. This is true of new security agenda issues such as space security, maritime security, cyber security, and counterterrorism, and in terms of balancing behavior, strengthening bilateral defense, and other ties. In other words, there is opportunity for India.

The idea of working with those who share India's interests on particular issues and circumstances is particularly relevant in west Asia. Traditionally India has managed to work simultaneously with several regional powers even when they were at loggerheads with each other—such as Iran and Saudi Arabia today, and Egypt and Israel in the 1960s and 1970s. The politics of west Asia are now so fragmented that the regional powers are involved in direct and proxy wars against each other in Yemen, Syria, Libya, Iraq, and parts of the Sahel and central Africa. With a diaspora of some 7 million citizens and given Indian interests in the steady flow of energy, counterterrorism, and access to central Asia and Afghanistan, as well as warding off possible blowback against India's minority population if they get involved in west Asia's complex internal quarrels, it would be prudent for India to continue its cooperative approach with its west Asian neighbors and stay out of their internal politics and regional quarrels. But worsening relations among the regional powers, and the fatigue and disinterest of the United States and West in promoting stability in west Asia, means that India must also now seek ways to directly bolster security itself, as, say, in securing energy imports at sea and possibly working with the other major importers, Japan, China, and South Korea. This situation also requires India to work more closely with regional powers such as Iran, Israel, Egypt, Saudi Arabia and Turkey, and with outside influencers like Russia. Iran is a crucial partner for the Indian interests mentioned here. Iran's natural geopolitical weight in the region, enhanced by the weakness of the other regimes and diminishing Western interest and capacity in west Asia, and its geographical position, make Iran critical to the attainment of Indian objectives. It has previously shown a willingness to work with and accommodate India, whether in the matter of oil imports, on Chabahar port, in Afghanistan, or elsewhere. While that may not suit the Americans, that is no reason not to pursue Indian interests. Indeed, a strong relationship with Iran could also incentivize the United States to accommodate those interests.

For a credible neighborhood policy, India must also develop a workable approach to Asian economic integration, particularly to the Regional

Comprehensive Economic Partnership (RCEP), led by China. The India-ASEAN Free Trade Agreement in goods, in effect since 2010, has set a goal of US$200 billion in trade by 2022, which will not be met. While India-ASEAN trade grew twenty-five times in twenty-five years, it still only amounted to $70 billion in 2016–2017. ASEAN is India's fourth largest trading partner, while India is ASEAN's seventh. For three years running, the government of India has raised customs duties, and protectionist sentiment in India is on the rise. India's existing free trade agreements are being reviewed by government and attacked by members of the ruling party. This inward turn to protectionism has been strengthened by the COVID-19 pandemic and the economic crash of 2020, even though it flies in the face of India's experience of benefiting from globalization and of having tried autarchic alternatives without success. In the meantime, China has begun canvassing ASEAN for an alternative free trade area in Asia composed of ASEAN, China, Japan, and Korea. India has chosen to leave the RCEP negotiations in their final stages. India's choice of how to deal with the most dynamic economies in the world in the geopolitical center of gravity of the international system is a strategic choice that will have great and long-term consequences.

~

Critical to India's future is also the Indian Ocean. Today, many countries have vested interests there, because it accounts for transport of 70 percent of oil, 50 percent of container traffic, and 35 percent of bulk cargo of the world. How to build capacity and create international will to keep the Indian Ocean region open and free and secure must be one of India's foremost tasks going forward. The maritime domain around India is still overwhelmingly dominated by American sea power. Apart from China, several other Asian powers have significant and growing naval capabilities, such as Indonesia, Singapore, Japan, India, and Vietnam in their own near seas.

India's interest is not in attempting to exclude maritime powers from the Indian Ocean, which is impossible, but to ensure the safety and security of the sea-lanes to the east and west that carry Indian energy and trade, not just in the Indian Ocean but in the seas near China and further. To do so India must work with all the maritime powers. Unlike the continental domain, where territory can only belong to one country or another, the maritime domain is not subject to a zero-sum security calculus. Secure sea-lanes benefit all trading nations, and trade itself is positive-sum for all participants. The larger ones like China and Japan share the Indian interest in freedom of navigation in the high seas, and it should be possible for India to work with them to develop a regime, formal or informal, that ensures India's primary interests. It would be logical for India to engage with all the major maritime powers in these seas—who are not the same in the Indian Ocean, the western Pacific, and the seas near China—to work out rules and arrangements that would enhance security and ensure freedom of navigation. This would include working with the United States, Japan and China, and with ASEAN partners like Singapore and Indonesia, and with Australia. In the Bay of Bengal, the Arabian sea, the South China Sea and elsewhere, India could build on existing associations and working relationships with local partners.

Other domains like cyberspace, by their very nature, are more complicated. Codes of conduct and intergovernmental agreements have only limited utility in regulating individual, corporate, and state behavior in cyberspace, where attribution is difficult, and the speed of attack overwhelms deterrence and escalation control. New ways of thinking about contention in the virtual domain are required. Prudence demands that India build its own capabilities and defenses, which in cyberspace are indistinguishable from offensive capabilities, staying abreast with technology and its uses.

India is not alone in its approach to these commons—whether maritime, outer space, or cyberspace—of keeping them free of any single power's dominance and in trying to keep them open and secure. Japan, ASEAN, Australia, and others share India's interests in the global commons, despite U.S.-China contention there, and in countering attempts by some to treat these commons in cyberspace as subject to sovereign jurisdiction and to territorialize the high seas. It should therefore be possible to work with other powers to further our common interests.

~

India built up nuclear deterrence faster than any other nuclear weapon state did. India's nuclear capabilities helped to keep the peace since 1971, and drove its adversaries to use asymmetric and nonconventional means against it. Since India became an overt nuclear weapon state in 1998, there has been no credible threat of using nuclear weapons against India nor attempt to use nuclear blackmail to change its behavior. To that extent, India's nuclear weapons have served their declared purpose.

There are, however, those who believe that India should change its no-first-use policy and begin to think of nuclear weapons as war-fighting weapons to compensate for India's conventional military inferiority against China. The present government came to power suggesting that it might do so. Three reviews by previous governments of the no-first-use doctrine have so far only led to the doctrine being reiterated and reconfirmed. But that does not mean that the doctrine should not be regularly reviewed and postures adjusted.

Potential adversaries in the region are steadily developing and improving their nuclear arsenals. In addition, advances in remote-sensing technologies and in the precision of conventional weapons are rapidly changing deterrence calculations. If an adversary can locate all of your nuclear weapons and has the ability to hit them with precisely targeted conventional weapons, as present trends in technology could make possible, deterrence breaks down and the line between nuclear and conventional war is erased. Any such adversary would be tempted to take out your weapons with a preemptive first strike. Attempts to preclude this possibility, by developing newer, more effective, and better hidden nuclear weapons, while defensive in your mind, will not appear so to the adversary and will set off a nuclear arms race.

India has so far avoided such scenarios, but is faced with the only nuclear weapon program in the world that is under military control in Pakistan. It is also the one most likely to fall into terrorist hands. Chinese reactions to U.S. technological developments, improving their nuclear weapons and changing their possible uses, also affect India's strategic nuclear calculus. Regular review of India's nuclear doctrine and postures is therefore essential.

$\sim$

India faces no existential threat from abroad any more. The real future threats to India's stability and progress are from within. The consequences of rapid urbanization and globalization have changed global and Indian politics: 70 percent of humanity lives within 200 miles of the coast, and of the forty-three megacities (over 10 million population) only three are outside the Third World. By 2025, 75 percent of the world's population will live in cities. In India by then more than half of its population will live in cities. This has huge social, political, and security consequences. Socially we will be dealing with an aspirational and young population, cut off from traditional family and social structures, alienated and alone, open to new ideologies, good or bad. The marked political effects of rapid urbanization are already evident in India. Politics becomes an exercise in mob psychology and mobilization, abetted by the mass media and social media. This is an environment where social violence, polarization, and the militarization of policing are likely, and where traditional policing is ineffective. Today, we see social violence on the rise across the globe, enabled by the new technologies and easy availability of traditional weapons. Of the 560,000 violent deaths around the world in 2016, 68 percent were murders, while wars caused just 18 percent.[3]

Equally worrying is the fact that the nature of violence in our society seems to have changed, with increasing crimes against the person, against women, accompanying social and political polarization and violence between communities. The Ministry of Home Affairs and South Asia Terrorism Portal websites show that the number of deaths among civilians and security forces from jihadi terrorism, or in the North-East and Jammu and Kashmir, or from left wing extremism declined steadily in the decade and a half before 2014. However, communal violence and crimes against the person have been growing since 2012. We are becoming an increasingly lawless society. My worry is that we do not have the right tools to deal with the phenomenon of social violence, which is much more than a law and order problem. It cannot be dealt with by traditional policing in a society that is now very different from the agrarian settled one our policing institutions were designed for.

These internal security issues matter to India's dealings with Asia in two ways. For one, the nature of violence and its social roots are shared with India's neighbors. In addition, they detract from India's ability to conduct coherent foreign and security policies and reduce domestic support for external engagement, which, as we have seen, is essential for India's future. They diminish the effective power and energy that India can bring to bear on issues abroad.

~

Twenty years ago, in 1998 India was the first parliamentary system in the world to experiment with a National Security Council (NSC) and a national security adviser (NSA) to the prime minister.[4] Since then several other parliamentary democracies such as the United Kingdom (2010), Japan (2014), and Spain have also appointed such advisers and established these councils. The Indian model emerged at a time when the nature of threats and security issues managed by states had long outgrown the silos of individual ministerial responsibility in the parliamentary or cabinet system of government. The NSC's primary function is to identify cross-cutting and strategic national security issues and suggest holistic policy responses. In doing so it is assisted by a National Security Advisory Board (NSAB) composed of outside experts and professionals. The implementation of responses and policies approved by the NSC is entrusted to a Strategic Policy Group originally led by a cabinet secretary, and now by the NSA under this government, which has given the security adviser an increasingly operational rather than advisory role. Over time the NSC has become more involved in daily or routine matters rather than long-term assessment and thinking. The NSAB exists in a new, smaller version.

The immediate spurs that led to the creation of the NSC were crossborder terrorism that peaked in J&K in the 1990s, the lessons of the Kargil conflict of 1999, and India's overt nuclear weapon–state status after 1998, all of which required holistic and coordinated national direction and management. India had also begun to face new security issues such as cyber threats, which were both everyone's business and no one's. Kargil had shown that while raw intelligence was available, it was not shared, understood, analyzed, or acted on in time. Besides, the nature of war in South Asia had changed, with Pakistan trying for the first time to use its nuclear weapons to cover its traditional mixture of conventional and jihadi force. The intensity and nature of crossborder terrorism from Pakistan in the 1990s in J&K and the rest of India had shown that India's response could not be left to old-fashioned policing and politics. Instead, it required the coordinated application of force across the spectrum, including the army, the armed police, and the state police. It required new structures and formations like the Rashtriya Rifles and multilevel coordinated responses—intelligence, political, and social—if India was to prevail.

Besides, India's nuclear weapons and the development of the doctrines, structures, and practices for their use and management were neither a purely political nor a military or a scientific problem. Here India was in uncharted territory, and the NSAB did remarkable work in creating India's nuclear doctrine. No nation shares its real experience or knowledge of nuclear weapons programs. India has done in a little over a decade what the United States took forty years to do, and China thirty, namely, building up the Nuclear Command Authority, standing up the Strategic Forces Command (India's only truly joint command), and creating the staff, production, and scientific and military structures required to manage and build a credible deterrent based on a triad of sea, land, and air vectors. This has been a remarkable unsung achievement by scientists, the armed forces, and civilians working together, outside the glare of publicity.

The NSC has done good work, particularly in areas like cyber security. It is the only regular high-level policy forum where India's highest political leadership sits together with the three service chiefs and other top national security professionals and discusses national security issues in detail. In the years that I was directly associated with the NSC, it met regularly, never for less than two hours at each sitting, and discussed complex and major issues such as left-wing extremism, China policy, Afghanistan after 2014, the Indian Ocean region, cyber security, and the Naresh Chandra Committee report in great detail, considering options and actions.

None of these tasks was the work of one day or of one order or decision. The series of rolling reforms of the national security system begun by NDA-I and carried on by UPA governments that the NSCS midwifed included: the setting up of the National Technical Research Organization to deal with technical intelligence, critical cyber infrastructure and cyber intelligence; a national policy framework for cyber security in May 2013 that has led to the creation of a National Cyber Security Coordination Center in the NSC secretariat, the laying down of guidelines and rules and the strengthening of capacity; reforms in intelligence tasking, analysis, and monitoring under the Joint Intelligence Committee of the NSC secretariat; the creation and strengthening of covert and other capabilities to deal with crossborder terrorism and the support that it gets in our own society; and coordinated policies toward Afghanistan, Bangladesh, Nepal, Myanmar, Sri Lanka, and the Indian Ocean region.

~

Now in a region increasingly feeling the Chinese presence, what overall or grand strategy should India adopt, and with which tools? India has no choice but to engage with the world. Whether it is called preventive engagement, or strategic outreach or any other catchphrase, India must engage. The question is the manner of that engagement.

Today sees a much more uncertain world. Fear of the scale of change and uncertainty, and domestic-party political compulsions, leads some Indians to advocate shifts away from strategic autonomy to a much greater reliance on outside powers for security. Some recent actions by the government, adopting phraseology like the "Indo-Pacific," also give credence to this view. The faint of heart in India, fearful and mesmerized by China's rise, put their faith in various forms of alignment with the United States or in arrangements such as the Quad, without showing how India's issues are solved through these arrangements with powers that have bigger stakes in their bilateral relationships with China than in the Quad.[5]

Another response is to deny change and to retreat into domestic preoccupations, as appears to have happened to India's foreign trade and economic policies in the last few years, when faced with RCEP negotiations and demands to open the Indian economy from partners not just in the industrialized European Union and United States but in our immediate neighborhood such as ASEAN and the subcontinent. It is hard to see how India can hope to have a meaningful

"Act East" policy in politics and security if it lacks an economic and trade heart to keep it alive. Insularity cannot be the answer to a more complex and difficult geopolitical environment for an India whose economic prospects depend on its links with the world. After all, India is resource, capital, and technology poor, all of which are needed from the world if India is to be transformed. According to the International Monetary Fund, India provided 15 percent of world economic growth in 2017, giving the world a stake in India's growth. This is an opportunity for India and should give government confidence for greater rather than less economic engagement with the world.

Both of these approaches risk India losing the sense of its own unique destiny that guided India for seventy years. For me, the answer to India's present dilemmas would seem to be both more engagement and more strategic autonomy, no contradiction in terms. Strategic autonomy actively practiced simply means that on the larger issues that matter to India—national security, world trade, climate change, and so on—India will work with and engage with all those that it can work with, rather than taking sides between powers in disputes based on a prior alliance or alignment that constrains India's pursuit of its own interests. So long as the decision to work together as partners is India's, even in ways that allies do, strategic autonomy is maintained.

It is sometimes argued that India's interest lies in avoiding a situation where any one power dominates either the region or the globe, or that India should aim to be a swing or balancing state. I find this a distraction as a goal, an attitude left over from Cold War bipolarity, and hard to justify. Terms such as swing state or balancer from Western academic thought arise from a very different situation from what we face today. In a multipolar global economy and amidst political confusion, who is India supposed to balance or swing between? India's best years of growth, of agency in the international system, and of improving relationships with the United States and other countries were when the international system was unipolar. They were not easy years but, handled skillfully, opened opportunity for India.

What India needs, more than the tactical play that the anarchical absence of a hegemon or multiple-power centers offer, or the momentary glory or ego satisfaction that might be possible in the midst of flux, is strategic, namely, peace and a supportive external environment for India's transformation. India is therefore not a disruptive revisionist power, except where it is ready to reorder the international system in its own favor in specific areas. Even here it seeks not disruption for its own sake or to overthrow the existing order but to improve it, creating positive outcomes within a predictable and peaceful international order. That should be the goal of India's strategic autonomy.

The common thread running through the foreign and security policies of successive governments of India until the Modi government, irrespective of their various political persuasions and compositions and the predilections of different leaders, has been the pursuit of strategic autonomy for India. It has been called by different names: Jawaharlal Nehru's coinage of nonalignment for the most part, "genuine nonalignment" by the Janata government, and more recently strategic autonomy. In practice it has meant keeping decisionmaking power within India, avoiding alliances, and building internal capabilities while working with others when it was in India's interest to do so. Even in moments of dire peril, as in the immediate aftermath of the Chinese attack in 1962, when Nehru felt compelled to seek military assistance from the United States, he simultaneously attempted to maintain his freedom of maneuver by also turning to the Soviet Union for support and supplies.

Why has this pursuit been so constant since India's independence in 1947, despite changes in the international situation and in India's own condition and capabilities? Why has independent India never chosen to bandwagon or ally with a superpower or another great power? Clearly, India did not fight for independence in order to willingly hand over its decisionmaking, recovered at such great effort, to another power. That was a particularly strong motivation in the decades soon after independence when India's weakness and four wars led some at both political extremes like the Swatantra and Communist parties to urge alliance with one or the other superpower. But those voices were few and far from the mainstream. The pursuit of strategic autonomy also meets the fundamental needs of maintaining India's sovereignty and improving the lot of its people. Up to now, India's is the only nationalism and identity not based on religion, language, ethnicity, or ideology. Nor has India hitherto relied on bowdlerized or self-serving versions of its own history to build its nationalism, although I am not sure how long this will remain true. It is the awareness by Indians of their common destiny, and of all belonging to India, irrespective of language, religion, caste, or regional differences, that is the basis of Indian nationalism. This makes India unique. It also imposes a unique set of responsibilities and demands to maintain the democratic balances, pluralism, and diversity that are the necessary bases of its internal and external policies.

No other country shares India's precise set of interests for the simple reason that no other country shares its history, geography, size, culture, and identity, and our domestic condition, all of which determine what we seek from the international system. What we have sought is an external environment that supports the transformation of India, that enables us to build a modern, prosperous, and secure country, eliminating poverty, illiteracy, disease, and other curses of underdevelopment. That is the core interest. Strategic autonomy has served that core interest best despite changes in the international situation. During the Cold War, when the world was divided into two hostile camps, it obviously served India's interest not to be dragged into external entanglements. When the bipolar world ended with the collapse of the Soviet Union, India entered two decades of globalization, of an open international trading and investment climate. Once again India's interest was served best through the pursuit of a multidirectional foreign policy to help the country transform.

The results of India's approach are clear: Over thirty years of 6 percent GDP growth and a much more secure and capable India, which has pulled more of its citizenry out of poverty and grown faster than it ever did in history in terms of improving the quality of life of its people. As a result of that period of accelerated growth and change, India is today much more integrated into the world than when it began reform in 1991. India has a growing interest in the world and in creating, to the extent that it can, an enabling external environment for transformation. To my mind, strategic autonomy is the only way forward if the goal is for India to succeed in transforming.

We live in a time of rebalancing among all the powers and India's friends are reevaluating and readjusting their policies to new realities. For larger powers, like India, who want a greater say and an improved international order, disruption may open up possibilities. Smaller Asian states that see their space shrinking rebalance toward China, as Malaysia, the Philippines, and Thailand seem to be doing. Indeed, they hedge, balance, and bandwagon simultaneously. China itself uses the opportunity opened by uncertainty and U.S. disengagement to attempt to organize and consolidate the Eurasian landmass through the Belt and Road Initiative and other geopolitical means. This is a topsy-turvy world where, as China is rediscovering, Deng's advice of biding one's time and hiding one's light remains good counsel.

This is hardly the time for India to abandon strategic autonomy. The higher the uncertainty in the international system, the more important it is that India develop its own capability and be able to independently decide and respond to events and situations, and to work with those partners who share its interests. The purpose of policy is to increase India's power and hence its options, not to limit them.

Strategic autonomy is not autarchy. India has no choice but to engage both to its east and west. With internal reform in 1991, India chose to follow the eastern Asian pattern by concentrating on economic development while putting political and security disputes on hold as it built up strength and accumulated power. That policy has succeeded in making India one of the world's fastest-growing economies and has contributed significantly to the well-being of the Indian people. However, the time has probably come when that policy alone will no longer suffice, when India's engagement in western and eastern Asia needs to expand and be more active, both economically and in political-military aspects of security. But domestic politics in India and the new international environment make India's path forward problematic.

Despite its complexities, the present situation does have possibilities. This is a time to consolidate at home, while entering the spaces that are opening up in west Asia, Africa, and eastern Europe. India must step up its game in southern Asia, which affects security directly. I have already said how I think that relations with China can be managed. At the same time, heightened Sino-U.S. contention inclines the United States to work more closely with India bolstering its defense and other capacities. And an assertive China leads several partners in Asia, such as Japan, Vietnam, and others to work much more closely with India politically, in defense, security, and intelligence. To my mind the key, both with major powers and in subregions seeking India's greater involvement, is India's willingness to strike out on its own independent path and to have a clear agenda. India has leverage in the international system as the distribution of power flattens. At the same time, economic multipolarity means that the lure of India's large market in hard times will induce harsher pressure from the economic powers and neighbors to open that market, and India must adjust its way of doing business. I remain optimistic that India can think this through and find a way to use the political and economic spaces that are opening up.

India is not a status quo power but is invested enough in the system to want to see peaceful rather than revolutionary change in the order so that it has a say in its design and running that reflects its growing interests and capabilities. This will never be easy or fruitful if the approach is to prioritize institutional change such as a UN Security Council permanent seat. It is easier to bring about a change in others' behavior in specific sectors where India's independent capability and power have grown, as was apparent in the civil nuclear initiative with the United States in 2005–2008. There are international markets and areas like oil and gas, renewable energy, rare earths, ICT, international law, and cyber security where India has an objective opportunity to not only influence global trends but also to help to set the rules or norms.

Avoiding war and attaining one's goals is the highest form of strategy by any tradition or book—whether espoused by Kautilya, Sun Tzu, or Machiavelli. And if you look at India's record over sixty-eight years of independence, India has not done badly in moving toward its main goal of transforming India. India has weathered several storms over its history, and it is certain that it faces now will not be more of the same. This brings me to the last and most important improvement that I think India needs to do: introduce flexibility into its thinking and institutions. Change is the only certainty in life.

~

Is a stable Asian order emerging, different from the old?

For me, stability is not a realistic goal in an area where the balance of power is shifting almost by the day in a crowded geopolitical space that includes the rise of China and India and other powers like Indonesia, Vietnam, and South Korea, and where established powers like Japan and Australia are reevaluating their options and their defense postures and strategies. The U.S. administration seems unhappy with the present order and seeks to renegotiate its terms. If the greatest status quo power, the United States, is dissatisfied with the present order, is it realistic or reasonable to aim for strategic stability in Asia? Nor is stability a desirable goal for this part of the world. The blind quest for stability to perpetuate an unequal status quo—as represented by the Treaty of Versailles in 1919 Europe—flew in the face of fundamental changes in military technology and ignored several revisionist powers, thus contributing significantly to the explosion that was World War II. We must not make the same mistake. The Asia-Pacific is home to several rising, reemerging, and revisionist powers. While they may pay lip service to strategic stability, their actions belie their words. None of them is satisfied with the status quo. To try to bind them to stability sounds to them as though they are being told to know their place in the world and accept what they are actually trying to change.

In fact, stability as a goal prevents and distracts us from far more useful and practical steps that we can take to manage crises and improve security in the larger region. To be effective in both the Asia-Pacific and western Asia, any security order or measures should manage change rather than try to prevent it, providing for the shifting balance of power and the rise of powers like Iran and China. And there is indeed much that could be done to improve security from the bottom up in the Asia-Pacific. The India-China example of the last thirty years is a good one, of two wary neighbors using confidence-building measures and practical steps to keep the peace despite the world's greatest boundary dispute. The practical way forward in the Asia-Pacific would seem to be issue-based coalitions of the willing to deal with the multiple security issues facing the region.

This approach would mean that we in Asia build issue-based coalitions of the willing to strengthen regional habits of cooperation on specific issues and seek to manage change rather than try to freeze the present or force the future into preconceived notions. This would include forums for dialogue between regional powers to discuss the real security issues: military doctrines and deployments; cyber security; and security of the commons, particularly maritime security. It requires managing change rather than chasing the chimera of strategic stability. Institutions, such as the East Asia Summit and ASEAN, are available to coordinate any of these activities. We should set up crisis management mechanisms before crisis is upon us so that we have put in place and rehearsed channels of communications and responses to foreseeable situations. Out of these could evolve rough and ready, and practical, rules of the road, like the U.S.-China agreement on cyber-crime, which is far from comprehensive or watertight but is a working beginning.

Starting small seems sensible when no one has yet put forward a concept or idea that could serve the interests of all the regional and extra-regional stakeholders in Asian security. China, India, and other powers have so far sought adjustments and improvements in the present order, not its abolition or overthrow. This may be changing as China's power grows and as it attempts to create a China-centric order, starting in its immediate vicinity. Today, the vacuum or the absence of order and institutions is being filled through natural evolution from the bottom up, differently in different subregions. The Eurasian landmass is being consolidated and connected. A continental order is forming in Eurasia, and it is centered on China. The maritime order is contested and harder to envisage, despite its positive-sum nature and the common interest in freedom of navigation and security of sea-lanes, especially of trading nations, the largest of which are in the Asia-Pacific. And in western Asia it is hard to speak of any order at all.

Neither has the United States put forward a concept that takes into account the rise of India, China, and others in the region, other than an ill-defined and poorly resourced "Free and Open Indo-Pacific" strategy.

The only lasting way forward is to integrate the new powers into an international order that takes into account their essential interests, whether it is China or Iran or India or Indonesia or Brazil. The conventional, "liberal" wisdom is that this is less likely now after the Trump administration in the United States. My own feeling is that the disruption that the Trump administration caused could actually bring forward the adjustment.

We tend to argue by analogy. The two "great teachers" of Western thinking on international relations and politics have been World War I and the Great Depression. Today, we are told that the situation is like that before that first world war and that our globalized world risks stumbling into global conflagration.[7] But from an Indian point of view, we are watching relative U.S. disinterest, the dismantling of an idealized and imagined order that never truly was either liberal or rule-based when it mattered to India. Today's globalized world is different from that before World War I and has several powers rising like India and China. It was the declining powers, Austria-Hungary and Russia, that led the march into the conflagration of 1914. This suggests a different outcome in today's Asia from the half-century of destructive war and civil strife that destroyed Europe's centrality in the world.

Multipolarity is good. Asian history before European hegemony, and in Europe when the Concert of Europe delivered a long nineteenth century of peace, suggests that multipolar systems are actually more stable than systems dominated by one or two hegemons or superpowers. The traditional Chinese tributary system worked because it was not a system but a fiction convenient to participants. On the other hand, Napoleon's Continental System lasted less than a decade, and Cold War bipolarity four. Multipolarity is the goal that we should be aiming for if we seek to minimize uncertainty in today's world. Yet, the very factors that make multipolarity a desirable goal also make it difficult to achieve. It is hard to see authoritarian centralizers who depend on a heightened appeal to nationalism for their legitimacy making the sort of compromises and adjustments that building a new multilateral international order would require.

We live in a time when all the great-power relationships that we were accustomed to since the end of the Cold War are undergoing a reset—U.S.-China, U.S.-Russia, India-China, India-U.S., and so on. For me the risk is not so much from the likelihood of conflict arising from one of the issues. It is that as issues worsen, we are piling up kindling for a conflagration precisely when the broader political and international context has reduced the international system's ability to deal with issues and crises that inevitably arise.

We lack an agreed basis for such an order across Asia or even the Asia-Pacific, such as respecting the status quo (India-China, 1993) or respecting existing boundaries (Helsinki). I doubt that a single regional order can be constructed in the midst of such rapid change, when so many powers in the region want to change the status quo and believe that their position will improve in the future. China seeks primacy or at least parity with the United States; Japan to become a "normal" power; India to achieve the international status its domestic transformation requires; and so on. With so many revisionist powers making different demands of the order, the result could well be a lowest common denominator order, long on good sentiment and short of capacity to provide security. However, I do believe that the search for the order is worth undertaking in itself, to find solutions to the Asia-Pacific's security issues. Since these are unique in themselves, the solutions will also have to be singular and unique.

The changed security situation is manageable, if we show good sense, managing change and accommodate rising powers rather than trying to impose strategic stability. If not, the resulting insecurity is the enemy of solutions to the problems that previous economic success has thrown up for rapidly growing and changing societies and economies like India's. Indeed, the economic challenges should not be underestimated and may actually be harder to solve than the security challenges. I am not pessimistic; our geopolitical challenges are manageable if we show some good sense and stop making our so-called and newly discovered core interests non-negotiable. I believe that the international system can shift to accommodate new powers—this will take an effort but must be done. As someone said of old age, I prefer it to the alternative.

India's interests and condition dictate that it remain domestically focused for a long time to come, using foreign and security policy for domestic transformation, avoiding external entanglements when possible, and working with its neighbors, as it has with the United States, Russia, China, Japan, and others in the past. As noted, India needs the world for domestic purposes to encourage its continued economic transformation. Therefore, expect more interventions, expeditionary and activist external politics, playing to the nationalist gallery at home, and attempts to shape the environment, working with friends and coalitions.

All in all, we are in a different world, where the vocabulary and rules of wartime pervade ordinary life in the name of the "war against terror" or other such causes. History should have prepared India for this. The British enterprise in India, whether called the East India Company or Government of India, was, for most of its life profit seeking and making, part company, part government, part army, and it was not unique in history. In history the lines between all three categories, whether government, business, or the army, have been murky, as have the lines between private and public good. Today, again, these lines are confused in China, the United States, and other powers, making them less principled, less predictable, and less secure.

The same factors that ensured the "long peace" of the Cold War—namely, nuclear deterrence and the balance of power—will likely continue to prevent a global conflagration in the new situation.[8] The danger of annihilation remains should nuclear weapons be used in conflict, as does the rough balance of power where it matters between the United States and the West, on the one hand, and China and Russia, on the other. But just as the Cold War's "peace" was far from peaceful or orderly below the stratosphere of superpower relations, it is unlikely that the peace will be stable or certain at regional or subregional levels in the years to come.

As I've written, I hope that Asia is heading for multipolarity. This could take two forms. One is a reversion to the historical norm, a set of multiverses within which northeastern Asia, the Indian Ocean region, southeast Asia, America, and Europe live separate political and regional security lives, while interacting intensely with each other economically, technologically, and in culture and innovation. This may sound paradoxical but is possible and has indeed been a familiar pattern through much of recorded Asian history. Politics and security are local, while economics, science, religion, culture, and ideology are global. More likely in our globalized world knitted by technology and economics is a situation not unlike nineteenth-century Europe of several powers of differing size and power contending among themselves in shifting coalitions and alliances, and of multiple orders in different domains in a world that is as much geopolitically globalized as it is economically. What India should be aiming for is a world order "safe for diversity," as John F. Kennedy phrased it, that accommodates liberal and illiberal alike, so that India and others can focus on the home front.

I do not think that conflict between the great powers is inevitable, even though some see the situation purely as a transition of power from an existing hegemon, the United States, to a rising challenger, China, and speak of a Thucydides trap. Graham Allison argues that of the twenty cases of power transition in the last 500 years, only four were peaceful. But he also says that while conflict is likely, it is not inevitable.[9] There are several factors at play here, not all of which were true of previous power transitions. Taken together, these factors make it hard to escape the conclusion that uncertain politics and security dilemmas now endanger the prosperity that the old order created in the Asia-Pacific, but will not necessarily lead to great power conflict. This does not exclude conflict between larger powers and smaller ones, or between local powers, and civil wars in states.

The immediate dangers come from the inability to manage local conflicts and to navigate cross-sectoral issues related to the world economy, the environment and climate change, and energy, and to adjust to the pace of technological and economic change. But the fact is that the two chief powers in the world, the United States and China, are contending for primacy, not to build a multipolar world. And in that there is danger for us all.

But how serious is the risk? My overall sense is that the risk of great-power involvement in conflicts with lesser powers or in regional flashpoints in the Asia-Pacific is rising. (In Europe and western Asia, Russian and U.S. armed forces are already fighting in local conflicts.) In other words, the Asia-Pacific is unstable but not critical. We have too much to lose if we get our security wrong. Western Asia less so. I am relatively optimistic about the Asia-Pacific muddling through this period of uncertainty, just as it did in the face of economic crises in the past, finding practical solutions and ways forward. One can be much more optimistic about the Asia-Pacific than when looking west to western Asia or Europe.

The determinant of India's grand strategy should be what kind of India we want to build. Is it to be modern, prosperous, and secure, as we have long discussed and broadly agreed in our domestic politics? But social churn is manifesting itself in unpredictable ways within India, of polarized and communal politics, increasing religiosity and leadership cults, and an increased faith in authority.[10] This cannot but also affect Indian foreign policy. In its second term the Modi government has alienated elements in the neighborhood that see a future in working with India, liberal Western opinion, and certain influential Muslim states. Steps to reorganize Jammu and Kashmir, what the UN High Commissioner for Human Rights called "fundamentally discriminatory" steps, and changes in the citizenship law enacted for domestic reasons have had effects on India's dealings with the world. The government's domestic agenda has re-hyphenated India with Pakistan, and Kashmir has been discussed in the UN Security Council after forty years, an internationalization that Pakistan could not achieve until the Indian government's actions gifted this to them. This has happened when the world matters more to India than ever before. Yet India seems to be turning its back on the world, abandoning the RCEP negotiations, and disengaging. Going it alone in pursuit of a national goal, as happened in 1971, is one thing. But to do so in pursuit of sectarian, divisive, and party-political goals is another.

To take the longer view, since the beginning of the twentieth century Asia as a whole manifested three main responses to Western power. The reactionaries were convinced that if Asians were truly faithful to their religious traditions, which are presumed to be superior to others', they would be strong again. Moderates had the notion that only a few Western techniques were required for Asians, whose traditions and cultures already provided a sound basis for culture and society, to progress. And radical secularists and revolutionaries like Mao and Ataturk were determined that the entire old way of life had to be revolutionized in order to compete in the jungle-like conditions of the modern world.[11]

From independence until the 1970s, India sought radical change at home and abroad. In the 1980s, governments shifted to the more moderate goal of modernizing without remaking society or the world. Today, under the Modi government, Indian foreign and domestic policy is in the reactive or reactionary position of stressing tradition and a mythical past and chasing prestige, not outcomes, when the world is becoming more jungle-like and is changing faster than ever before. Quite apart from what it says about Indian polity, society, and economy, this evolution makes it less likely that India will be a great power, will modernize, or will accumulate sufficient power to conquer poverty and play the role abroad that its own development needs. In the short term, China's bid for primacy and the U.S. trajectory and choices in responding to the loss of hegemony and dominance in some spheres, as well as revolutions in technology, will be crucial. It is essential that India understands and uses these processes as they play out.

~

If history teaches us anything it is that nothing is permanent, that change is a constant. Just as globalization created the forces that now oppose it, today's policies will create their own counter. Change is inevitable but not necessarily always for the better, and the process may be neither pleasant nor gentle.[12] "Presentism" is the disease of pundits—the assumption that what is happening now is going to keep on happening without something to stop it. This ignores the first lesson of history. Good outcomes are possible too. History often surprises us, and realism can generate not only pessimism but also hope.

Finally, it would be clear from this account that any prognosis based on the present geopolitics of Asia can only be tentative. That is because, as I have said, we are between eras, when the old order no longer works and does not reflect the balance of power, but the new one is not yet fully formed. We live in a paradoxical world. There is little comfort here for those who wish the world to return to the trajectory it was on before. There is no going back, and the future is uncertain. That does not mean that the future is without hope. We live in a time of challenge and contradiction, one that is also an amazing era. Geopolitical problems are man-made and should not be beyond human ingenuity to solve. The same technologies whose effects challenge us provide the means to deal with those challenges. Mankind has always met previous challenges.

Nor is there much comfort for those who wish for a clear unipolar Asian order, one with a clear hegemon and the certainties that come with that, whether they are partisans of China or the United States. I believe that neither China nor Asia is ready yet for a China-centered order. China may have the will and desire but lacks the objective power, and the United States seems incapable of exercising the will though it may have the power. Nor is a bipolar order the likely result in Asia. Instead, the facts of geography and history—the basis of geopolitics—will probably result in separate arrangements and fragmented orders in the subregions of Asia, in east Asia, southeast Asia, south Asia, the Persian Gulf, central Asia, the Levant, and west Asia. Each of these areas has local or regional powers that will determine political and military outcomes, rather than relying on great-power rivalry and cooperation.

For India, if there ever was a time for strategic autonomy, for building up national strength and hard power, and keeping a cool head, this is it. In confused times like this it is essential to keep one's enemies close and friends closer— keep the periphery pacified, stay out of blocs, and work with coalitions of powers wherever India's interests coincide. This is not a time for drama, showy events, and the pursuit of status. India's power and capabilities have yet to peak, and no other power shares its interests. Influence, like power, is a means to an end. For the conceivable future the purpose of India's external policies is to assist its transformation, creating an enabling environment for that task. That requires doing what successful powers did at similar stages of development—China in the 1980s and 1990s, the United States from 1880 until the end of World War II, Tudor and Stuart England—namely, not to overextend ourselves abroad and to build ourselves at home. India faces no existential external threat today. If there is a threat, it is internal. Letting others carry a costly or heavy burden is also a strategy. Rather than seeking a grand and outsize role abroad—something that Germany and Japan tried and failed to do in the last century without the necessary power and geopolitical conditions—India should do what is most important, that is, to make it possible for every Indian to live a safe, prosperous, and dignified life with the opportunity to realize his or her potential. That is the only goal worthy of a great country such as India.

Afterword

India's Destiny

I ndia's future resides in the hands and heads of all of its citizens.[1] How we as
citizens perceive our situation and choose to build our narrative deeply affect
our future.

Free India inherited national confidence from the freedom movement, untouched by false pride, hubris, or ego. We sought no apology or reparations
from Great Britain for what that empire had done to us. Instead, we set out to
build our own future in our own way. When Jawaharlal Nehru chose nonalignment, it was with confidence that India was entering a new era and would grow
into a modern, secular, prosperous, and safe country for all Indians. That confidence was bound in a national narrative that accepted history for what it was,
without ridiculous claims, manufactured enemies, or exaggerated boasts. We
need some of that confidence and objectivity now, combined with logic, reason,
and clarity, if we are to deal successfully with the world as it is, building a better
India that is true to itself and its people.[2]

Today, more than ever we need to strengthen our autonomy while working with all the major powers and cooperating harmoniously with our neighbors. Instead, some Indians are so worried by the uncertain world that they
suggest India go cap in hand seeking security in alliance with others, chasing
status, glory, and approbation instead of the welfare and security of the people.[3]
As a result, relations with our neighbors have seldom been as difficult as they
are now. China and Pakistan have no compunction in acting together against
Indian interests and sovereignty, and India is being reduced to a bit player on
the international stage. We have lost five years. Our national confidence has
been replaced by bravado and extravagant statements.

We need to get back to our roots, to the clear well springs of our will and our
confidence. India is the country of Kautilya, Chandragupta Maurya, Charvaka,

Kalidasa, Panini, Ashoka, Kanishka, Harsha, Akbar, Gandhi, and Nehru. All of them threw open the windows of our home to the world. We should accept no less, no simulacrum of leadership, no prejudices masquerading as ideas. Some of us have lost the ambition to think big of ourselves, of India's role in the world. Dread and hate replace reasoned thought, leading to destructive social conflict in and around India. We are offered two pictures of our national destiny. One vision is born of fear and polarization and the other of national self-confidence and ambition. The former excludes many Indians and is based on a narrow, intolerant, and false sense of nationalism. The latter is a proudly patriotic, tolerant, modern, progressive, and secular vision of a confident nation that respects all its citizens. The former is inward looking and diminishes India in the world. The latter is a confident India that stands for something with universal appeal. It is time we rejected the former and rededicated ourselves unambiguously to making the latter real.

Notes

Introduction

1. *Cassell's English Dictionary* (Cassel and Co., 1962), p. 485.

2. Sir Halford Mackinder, 1861–1947, was an English geographer and director of the London School of Economics, who submitted "The Geographical Pivot of History" in 1904 to the Royal Geographical Society. Later, in 1919, Mackinder summarized his theory this way: "Who rules East Europe commands the Heartland; who rules the Heartland commands the World-Island; who rules the World-Island commands the world," in Mackinder, *Democratic Ideals and Reality* (Holt, 1919), p. 150. A man of his time with its prejudices, Mackinder expressed disdain for non-Europeans and believed in the civilizing mission of empire. Alfred Thayer Mahan, 1840–1914, U.S. naval officer and historian, who wrote *The Influence of Sea Power upon History 1660–1783*, (Little Brown & Company, 1890), stressed the importance of command of the sea and of a powerful navy. His policies were adopted by most major European powers and led to the naval arms race before World War I.

3. Klaus Dodds, *Geopolitics, A Very Short Introduction* (Oxford University Press, 2014), pp. 18–20.

4. Karl Haushofer was a professor at Munich University after retiring as a major general from the German Army in 1919. He committed suicide in 1946 after he learned that his son, Albrecht, had been executed in April 1945 for his part in the July 1944 plot to kill Hitler. Other controversial personalities have been associated with geopolitics more recently. Augusto Pinochet, the Chilean dictator, was a professor of geopolitics and wrote a book, *Geopolitica*, in 1968.

5. *Merriam-Webster* definition, www.merriam-webster.com/dictionary/geopolitics.

6. I have tried in this book to use the name of a country most prevalent at that time, such as the USSR (Union of Soviet Socialist Republics) or Soviet Union before its dissolution in 1991 and Russia thereafter, or Ceylon before it became Sri Lanka in 1972. As for personal names, I have used the form most familiar to readers in English-language texts today.

Chapter One

1. Contrast this with China's contained geography and relative isolation. China's natural routes to the outside world were much more limited, and really only two: the Gansu corridor (between the Qilian Mountains and the Gobi Desert) through Yumenguan; and, the narrow band of steppe running north from the Yellow River, around the Gobi Desert to the Mongolian steppe and ultimately to the Altai Mountains and the Kazakh steppe beyond. Being contained, China displayed tremendous continuity and conservatism through successive dynasties and centuries.

2. Chapter 1 of the *Cambridge History of India, Ancient India*, Vol. 1 (Cambridge University Press, 1922).

3. Graham P. Chapman, *The Geopolitics of South Asia; From Early Empires to the Nuclear* Age (Routledge, 2009), pp. 89–90.

4. Prime Minister Jawaharlal Nehru to Parliament on December 12, 1957, initiating the debate on the international situation. See, for instance, "Shashi Goel: Indian Foreign Policy; Nehru and Non-Alignment" at www.researchgate.net/publication/323167067_Indian_Foreign_Policy_Nehru_and_Non_Alignment.

5. Jawaharlal Nehru speech to Asian Relations Conference, March 1947, in Ramachandra Guha, ed., *Makers of Modern India* (Penguin India, 2012), pp. 340–47.

6. Under Akbar (1542–1605), the Mughal empire's urban population was 17 million people in 1600, larger than the urban population in Europe. By 1700 Mughal India had an urban population of 23 million people, larger than British India's urban population of 22.3 million in 1871. Nizamuddin Ahmed (1551–1621) reported that under Akbar, Mughal India had 120 large cities and 3,200 townships. Several cities in India had a population between a 250,000 and 500,000 people, with larger cities including Agra having up to 800,000 people and Dhaka over 1 million. Mughal India also had 455,698 villages by the time of Aurangzeb (1658–1707).

7. See, for instance, Richard H. Davis, *South Asia in Early World History: Global India circa 100 CE* (Association for Asian Studies, Ann Arbor, Mich., 2009), pp. 1–3.

8. Speech to Indian School of International Studies, February 13, 1961, in *International Studies* 22, no. 2 (1985), excerpted in *Pragati*, 34 (January 2010).

9. Kenneth Pomeranz, *The Great Divergence; China, Europe, and the Making of the Modern World Economy* (Princeton University Press, 2000). Pomeranz shows several surprising similarities in agricultural, commercial, and proto-industrial . . . development among various parts of Eurasia as late as 1750—between various core regions scattered around the Old World: the Yangtze delta, the Kanto plain, Gujarat, Britain and the Netherlands. For some historians, Europe could have been China, if it were not for the resources it plundered from the New World.

10. For the complete statistical series, Maddison Online Database, www.ggdc.net .MADDISON/oriindex.htm.

11. Sanjeev Sanyal, *The Ocean of Churn: How the Indian Ocean Shaped Human History* (Penguin Viking, 2016).

12. Immanuel Wallerstein, *World Systems Analysis: An Introduction* (Duke University Press, 2004). Also, Christopher Chase-Dunn and E. N. Anderson, eds., *The Historical Evolution of World Systems* (Palgrave MacMillan, 2005).

13. Halford Mackinder, *The Geographical Pivot of History* (1904).

14. Robert Kaplan, *The Return of Marco Polo's World; War, Strategy, and American Interests in the Twenty-First Century* (Penguin Random House, 2018).

15. S. B. Cohen, *Geography and Politics in a Divided World* (Methuen, 1963).

16. Thomas R. Metcalf, *Imperial Connections: India in the Indian Ocean Arena, 1860–1920* (Permanent Black, 2007), p. 210.

17. Ibid., p. 13.

18. Ibid., pp. 208–14.

19. Peter John Brobst, *The Future of the Great Game: Sir Olaf Caroe, India's Independence, and the Defence of Asia* (University of Akron Press, 2005)

20. Aparna Pande, *From Chanakya to Modi; The Evolution of India's Foreign Policy* (HarperCollins, 2017).

21. Jawaharlal Nehru, *The Discovery of India* (Penguin Random House India, 2004; first published, 1946), pp. 597–600.

22. Ibid., pp. 600–03.

23. Rajmohan Gandhi, *Rajaji, A Life* (Penguin Books India, 1997), p. 203.

24. "The Hindu," September 18, 1939, quoted in Rajmohan Gandhi, *Rajaji; A Life* (Penguin Random House India, 1997), p. 203.

25. Pankaj Mishra, *From the Ruins of Empire; The Revolt against the West and the Remaking of Asia* (Penguin Books, 2013), p. 3.

26. Jawaharlal Nehru, *An Autobiography* (1936; republished Penguin India, 1989), p. 488.

27. Pankaj Mishra, *From the Ruins of Empire: The Revolt Against the West and the Remaking of Asia* (Penguin Books, 2013), p. 247.

28. Christopher Bayly and Tim Harper, *Forgotten Armies: Britain's Asian Empire and the War with Japan* (Penguin Books, 2005), p. 40.

29. Jawaharlal Nehru, *The Discovery of India* (Penguin Random House India, 2004), p. 586.

Chapter Two

1. With India's independence on August 15, 1947, British India was partitioned into two states, India and Pakistan, by an Act of the British Parliament. States under Indian rulers, or the princely states, which had been under British "paramountcy" (with defense, foreign relations, and other crucial functions controlled by the British), were left free to join either India or Pakistan, or, theoretically, to branch off on their own when paramountcy lapsed with independence. See Ramachandra Guha, *India After Gandhi: The History of the World's Largest Democracy* (Picador India, 2008), pp. 36–58.

2. B. R. Ambedkar, final speech to the Constituent Assembly.

3. Sir Cyril Radcliffe, an English judge with no previous experience or knowledge of the subcontinent, headed the boundary commission that was given three weeks to draw the international boundary between India and Pakistan. Its results were published after independence on August 16, 1947, to condemnation in both countries. Radcliffe destroyed his papers before leaving India. As a result, the reasons for his choices remain a mystery.

4. Gyanesh Kudasiya, *A Republic in the Making: India in the 1950s* (Oxford University Press, 2017), ch. 2, pp. 31–72.

5. By 1939 the ICS had 759 Europeans and 640 Indians. When Nehru took over the Department of External Affairs in 1946, only 17 Indians were among the 124 officers of the Indian Political Service. See Dr. Sneh Mahajan, *Foreign Policy of Colonial India, 1900–1947* (Routledge, 2018), pp. 13–14.

6. Butler was a member of the Indian Civil Service, governor of the United Provinces of Agra and Oudh, governor of Burma, and first president of the Delhi Gymkhana Club.

7. David Gilmour, *The Ruling Caste: Imperial Lives in the Victorian Raj* (Pimlico, 2007) p. 159.

8. See, for instance, Thomas R. Metcalf, *Imperial Connections: India in the Indian Ocean Area, 1860–1920* (Permanent Black, 2007), for a description of the "empire of the Raj" and India's subimperial role.

9. Y. D. Gundevia, *Outside the Archives* (Sangam Books, 1984), pp. 18–19.

10. K. M. Panikkar, *Indian Nationalism: Its Origins, History and Ideals* (republished Ingrams Short Books, 2008, originally published in 1923).

11. K. M. Panikkar, *The Future of India and South East Asia* (republished by Life, 2019, originally published in 1943).

12. K. M. Panikkar, "The Defence of India and Indo-British Obligations," *International Affairs* 22, no. 1 (January 1946), pp. 85–90.

13. See Rahul Sagar, "Jiski Lathi Uski Bhains," in Kanti Bajpai, Samira Basit, and V. Krishnappa (eds.) *India's Grand Strategy: History, Theory, Cases* (Routledge, 2014), pp. 234–36, p. 242, pp. 244–45. And Golwalkar, *Bunch of Thoughts* (Sahitya Sindhu Prakashan, 2017), p. 260 and p. 270. On p. 277 Golwalkar says: "It is not the gun but the heart behind it that fights . . ."

14. Christopher Bayly and Tim Harper, *Forgotten Wars: The End of Britain's Asian Empire* (Penguin Allen Lane, 2007), p. 137.

15. Ramachandra Guha, ed., *Makers of Modern India* (Penguin India, 2010), pp. 343–45.

16. Andrew Philips and J. C. Sharman, *International Order in Diversity; War, Trade and Rule in the Indian Ocean* (Cambridge University Press, 2015), pp. 202–03.

17. SEATO or the South East Asia Treaty Organization, was formed September 8, 1954, and was formally the South East Asia Collective Defence Treaty or Manilla Pact. Its eight members were mostly from outside the region: Australia, France, New Zealand, Pakistan, the Philippines, Thailand, the United Kingdom, and the United States. It was headquartered in Bangkok and dissolved on June 30, 1977. CENTO or the Central Treaty Organization, formally the Middle East Treaty Organization, was formed on February 24, 1955, by Iran, Iraq, Pakistan, Turkey, and the United Kingdom. It was headquartered in Baghdad (1955–1958) and then Ankara (1958–1979) and dissolved in

1979. Dulles said that the United States could not participate because of the "pro-Israel lobby" and difficulty in obtaining congressional approval.

18. J. Nehru, *India's Foreign Policy: Selected Speeches* (New Delhi: Government of India, 1961).

19. Peter John Brobst, *The Future of the Great Game: Sir Olaf Caroe, India's Independence, and the Defense of Asia* (University of Akron Press, 2005), pp. 145–46.

20. See Chandrashekhar Dasgupta, *War and Diplomacy in Kashmir, 1947–1948* (Sage Publications, 2002), for an account of early Western diplomacy on Kashmir. See also Paul M. McGarr, *The Cold War in South Asia: Britain, the US and the Indian Subcontinent, 1945–1965* (Cambridge University Press, 2013), for a description of differences within the West on Kashmir and Pakistan.

21. Srinath Raghavan, *War and Peace in Modern India; A Strategic History of the Nehru Years* (Permanent Black, 2010), pp. 315–16.

22. With some exceptions. Maulana Maudoodi, of the Jamaat-i-Islami, decried what was happening in Kashmir as not a *jihad*. He said that instead of martyrdom, those killed there would "die a dog's death."

23. Caroe had been foreign secretary of British India, governor of the North-West Frontier province, and wrote, *The Wells of Power: The Oilfields of South Western Asia; A Regional and Global Study* (Da Capo Press, 1976), p. 64, p. 50.

24. See Pyarelal, *Mahatma Gandhi; The Last Phase* (Ahmedabad, 1968, Vol. II) p. 524, p. 476, p. 502. See also J. Nehru, *Speeches, 1946–1949*, vol. 1 (Publications Division, New Delhi, 1949), p. 184.

25. Mao chose to postpone taking Taiwan on Stalin's advice, and after the PLA was defeated trying to take Jinmen island in an amphibious operation. Instead, Mao chose to take Tibet and to get involved in the Korean War, effectively postponing the unification of Taiwan. Asia and international relations might have been very different if he had indeed moved against Taiwan in early 1950 once President Truman's secretary of state, Dean Acheson, indicated that it was outside the U.S. defense perimeter in Asia. If Mao had done so, China would have broken out of the first island chain containment and probably had an easier relationship with the United States much earlier.

26. Ranjit Singh Kalha, *India-China Boundary Issues: Quest for Settlement* (Indian Council for World Affairs and Pentagon Press, 2014).

27. See Kenneth Conboy and James Morrison, *The CIA's Secret War in Tibet* (University Press of Kansas, 2002); and Gyalo Thondup, *The Noodle Maker of Kalimpong; The Untold Story of My Struggle for Tibet* (New York: Public Affairs, 2015).

28. Zorawar Daulet Singh, *Power and Diplomacy; India's Foreign Policies during the Cold War* (Oxford University Press, 2019), p. 310.

29. A nuanced and rigorous examination of India's neighborhood policy is in "Inaction to Intervention: India's Strategic Culture of Regional Involvement," by Constantino H. Xavier, unpublished PhD thesis at Johns Hopkins University, Washington D.C., July 2016, which is forthcoming as a book.

30. S. D. Muni and Rahul Mishra, *India's Eastward Engagement from Antiquity to Act East Policy* (Sage, 2019), pp. 96–97.

31. Zorawar Daulet Singh, *Power and Diplomacy: India's Foreign Policies during the Cold War* (Oxford University Press, 2018).

Chapter Three

1. Odd Arne Westad, *The Cold War: A World History* (Allen Lane, 2017), p. 1. This chapter draws extensively on his insights.

2. George Frost Kennan (1904–2005), U.S. diplomat, scholar, and realist; best known for suggesting the U.S. policy of containment of the Soviet Union while posted in the United States embassy in Moscow in a "Long Telegram" in 1946 and in a subsequent article in *Foreign Affairs* on "The Sources of Soviet Conduct" in 1947. *Foreign Affairs*, 25 (4): 566–82.

3. Graham Allison, "The Myth of the Liberal World Order," *Foreign Affairs* (July–August 2018).

4. Joseph Nye, "Will the Liberal Order Survive?" *Foreign Affairs* (January–February 2018).

5. John Lewis Gaddis, *The Cold War* (Allen Lane, 2005), p. 40.

6. Paul Thomas Chamberlin, *The Cold War's Killing Fields: Rethinking the Long Peace* (HarperCollins, 2018), p. 1.

7. Ibid., pp. 1–3.

8. Quoted in Allison, "The Myth of the Liberal World Order."

9. K. P. S. Menon, *Many Worlds: An Autobiography* (Oxford University Press, 1965), pp. 250, 257, explain the reasons behind the change in India's attitude.

10. Zorawar Daulet Singh, *Power and Diplomacy: India's Foreign Policies during the Cold War* (Oxford University Press, 2019), p. 21.

11. India signed a separate peace treaty with Japan because it regarded the San Francisco treaty, signed while Japan was still occupied by U.S. forces, as victor's justice. India also waived war reparations from Japan.

12. Christopher Goscha, *The Penguin History of Modern Vietnam* (Allen Lane, 2016), p. 216. The British general involved was Gracie of the Indian Army who was Pakistan's chief of army staff during the 1947–1948 war with India.

13. Zorawar Daulet Singh, *Power and Diplomacy* (Oxford University Press, 2019) pp. 124–28.

14. Ibid., p. 144.

15. Matthew W. Mosca, *From Frontier Policy to Foreign Policy: The Question of India and the Transformation of Geopolitics in Qing China* (Stanford University Press, 2013).

16. Nehru's statement during the debate in Parliament on November 25, 1961, in *Prime Minister on Sino-Indian Relations, Vol. 1, In Parliament* (Government of India, Ministry of External Affairs, External Publicity Division, 1961).

17. This was in reply to Nehru's writing to him about the boundary for the first time on December 14, 1958. For full texts of letters exchanged between prime minister Nehru and premier Zhou Enlai, see *"Notes, Memoranda, and Letters Exchanged and Agreements signed between the Governments of India and China,"* White Papers, vols. I to VIII (Government of India, Ministry of External Affairs, 1959 onward).

18. Unlike India, Pakistan voted against seating China in the UN and voted for the UN to consider condemning the crackdown in Tibet in 1959. Ayub Khan had offered India a joint defense agreement, which was rejected by Nehru in the Rajya Sabha on May 4, 1959. The door had been opened for Zhou to begin working on Pakistan and its fear of India.

19. Longju was an odd case, possibly a local overreaction or mistake, as Zhou ordered

an immediate internal investigation in the PLA, the commanders were changed, and China did not ratchet up the verbal abuse as in other premeditated cases.

20. The full title of the White Papers, thirteen volumes of which were ultimately published, was "Notes, Memoranda and Letters Exchanged between the Governments of India and China," issued by the Ministry of External Affairs, Government of India.

21. Ambassador Liu Xiao's memoir, *Chu shi sulian ba nian* [Eight Years as Ambassador to the Soviet Union], reviewed by John Garver, "New Light on Sino-Soviet Relations: The Memoir of China's Ambassador to Moscow 1955–62," *The China Quarterly*, no. 122 (June 1990), pp. 303–07.

22. Paul M. McGarr, *The Cold War in South Asia: Britain, the United States and the Indian Subcontinent, 1945–1965* (Cambridge University Press, 2013), p. 75.

23. There is a fascinating account of the talks in Foreign Secretary Gundevia's memoir, *Outside the Archives* (Sangam Books, 1984), pp. 249–310, for those who are interested.

24. Paul M. McGarr, *The Cold War in South Asia* (Cambridge University Press, 2013), pp. 280–84.

Chapter Four

1. J. N. Dixit, *Across Borders: Fifty Years of Indian Foreign Policy* (Picus Books, 1998).

2. Duane R. Claridge, *A Spy for All Seasons: My Life in the CIA* (Scribner, 1977).

3. Paul M. McGarr, *The Cold War in South Asia: Britain, the United States and the Indian Subcontinent, 1945–1965* (Cambridge University Press, 2013).

4. Arjun Subramaniam, *India's Wars: A Military History, 1947–1971* (HarperCollins India, 2016), p. 276.

5. The Nathula (September 11–14, 1967) and Chola (October 1, 1967) clashes saw Chinese troops open fire on Indian soldiers laying barbed wire to mark the boundary at Nathula pass after the Chinese had crossed into Sikkim from August 13, 1967, and begun digging trenches. They had stopped and filled in one trench and withdrawn after adding loudspeakers, when Indian troops protested. The Chinese opened fire in Nathula on September 11 and Indian troops gave as good as they got. Dead soldiers were exchanged on September 15–16. On October 1 Chinese troops attacked an Indian post at Chola but were rebuffed. In both places Indian forces achieved "decisive tactical advantage," defeated Chinese forces, destroyed PLA fortifications, and drove back forces. China said that 32 Chinese and 65 Indians were killed at Nathula and 36 at Chola. The Indian Ministry of Defense said that 88 Indians were killed and 163 wounded, while 340 Chinese were killed and 450 wounded in both incidents. This was the most unstable period of the Cultural Revolution in China, and Fravel says that the "declining claim strength" of the Chinese may have been a factor. For me, it is striking that India was willing to fight conventionally despite the nuclear asymmetry. See Taylor Fravel, *Strong Borders, Secure Nation; Cooperation and Conflict in China's Territorial Disputes* (Princeton University Press, 2008), pp. 197–99.

6. Indira Gandhi to Kosygin, July 20, 1968, Haksar papers, Nehru Memorial Museum and Library, Delhi.

7. Zorawar Daulet Singh, *Power and Diplomacy: India's Foreign Policies During the Cold War* (Oxford University Press, 2019), pp. 21–22.

8. Michael Vatikiotis, *Blood and Silk: Power and Conflict in Modern South East Asia* (Weidenfeld and Nicolson, 2017).

9. Dixit, *Across Borders*, p. 93.

10. Chandrashekhar Dasgupta, private communication.

11. David Brewster, "The Expansion of India's Security Sphere" in Sumit Ganguly, Nicolas Blarel, and Manjeet S. Pardesi, eds., *The Oxford Handbook of India's National Security* (Oxford University Press, 2018), p. 498.

12. S. D. Muni and Rahul Mishra, *India's Eastward Engagement from Antiquity to Act East Policy* (Sage, 2019), p. 126.

13. McGarr, *The Cold War in South Asia*, p. 287.

14. A detailed description of the main issues in the negotiation of the NPT is in Bertrand Goldschmidt, *Le Complexe Atomique* (Editions Fayard, Paris, 1980). The relevant chapter was extracted in the IAEA Bulletin 22, no. 3/4 at https://www.iaea .org/sites/default/files/publications/magazines/bulletin/bull22-3/223_403587380.pdf.

15. According to Dixit in *Across Borders*, Foreign Secretary Rajeshwar Dayal and Joint Secretary Rikhi Jaipal were for signing, while Director S. K. Singh and the representative to the negotiations, V. K. Trivedi, were against.

16. To Morarji's credit, while he had originally supported the NPT in principle, when he became prime minister in 1977 and the discriminatory nature of the treaty was explained to him, he gave President Carter an earful when he broached the subject during his 1978 visit.

17. Dixit, *Across Borders*, p. 95.

18. Bertrand Goldschmidt, *Le Complexe Atomique* (Editions Fayard, Paris, 1980).

Chapter Five

1. Srinath Raghavan, *1971: A Global History of the Creation of Bangladesh* (Harvard University Press, 2013), p. 8.

2. Salman Rushdie, *Shame* (Jonathan Cape, 1983) p. 178.

3. Nixon saw Indians as "a slippery treacherous people," "devious," and "ruthlessly self-interested," and called Indira Gandhi a "bitch" and "witch" in White House transcripts. General Yahya Khan, president of Pakistan, he saw as "honorable." See ibid., p. 82.

4. For Gandhi's strategy during the Bangladesh crisis, see Chandrashekhar Dasgupta, "The Decision to Intervene: First Steps in India's Grand Strategy in the 1971 War," *Strategic Analysis*, 40, no. 4 (2016), pp. 321–33. See also Raghavan, *1971: A Global History of the Creation of Bangladesh*, pp. 67–70.

5. A U.S. National Security Council study in mid-February 1971 examined options if the independence movement gained momentum. See ibid., p. 88. On the cables, see Gary J. Bass, *The Blood Telegram; Nixon, Kissinger and a Forgotten Genocide* (Alfred A Knopf, 2013).

6. Foreign Secretary T. N. Kaul's note to Prime Minister Indira Gandhi and External Affairs Minister Swaran Singh, August 3, 1971 in the Nehru papers. Nehru Memorial Museum and Library, New Delhi.

7. William Burr, ed., *The Kissinger Transcripts: The Top Secret Talks with Beijing and*

Moscow (New Press, 1998), pp. 48–57. See especially "Memcon of Kissinger and Huang, 10 December 1971, CIA 'Safehouse' Manhattan."

8. There is a remarkable exchange between Nixon and Kissinger during the war that suggests a willingness to contemplate using nuclear weapons. When Kissinger argued, if the "Soviets move against them and we do nothing, we'll be finished." Nixon asked, "So what do we do if the Soviets move against them? Start lobbing nuclear weapons?" Kissinger did not reply. See Francis J. Gavin, *Nuclear Statecraft: History & Strategy in America's Atomic Age* (Cornell University Press, 2012), p. 116.

9. Hindu female deities, one representing power and might and the other the goddess of war.

10. For one of the Indian participants, P. N. Dhar, the Line of Control was an ethnic and linguistic frontier, leaving Kashmiris as an ethnic community undivided on the Indian side. *Times of India*, April 4, 1995, has Dhar recollecting Simla.

11. For a detailed account based on archival material and meticulous research, see A. S. Bhasin, *India and Pakistan: Neighbours at Odds* (Bloomsbury, 2018), chs. 20 and 21, on the Simla Agreement, pp. 231–45, and pp. 250–54, describe their unwritten understanding on Kashmir.

12. John Pomfret, *The Beautiful Country and the Middle Kingdom: America and China, 1776 to the Present* (Henry Holt, 2016), p. 432.

13. See, for instance the records of Kissinger's July 1971 conversations with Premier Zhou Enlai, available at https://proquest.libguides.com/dnsa/kissinger2; https://digitalarchive.wilsoncenter.org/search-results/3/%7B%22contributor%22%3A%221067%22%7D/date_desc?recordType=Record; https://china.usc.edu/getting-beijing-henry-kissingers-secret-1971-trip; and https://www.nytimes.com/2002/03/03/weekinreview/word-for-word-kissinger-in-china-beijing-1971-oh-to-be-a-fly-on-the-great-wall.html. For a flavor of the conversations, see also William Burr, ed., *The Kissinger Transcripts: The Top Secret Talks with Beijing and Moscow* (New Press, 1998).

14. Burr, *The Kissinger Transcripts*, p. 86.

15. Harsh V. Pant and Yogesh Joshi, *Indian Nuclear Policy* (Oxford University Press, 2018), p. 71.

16. G. B. S. Sidhu, *Sikkim: Dawn of Democracy; The Truth Behind the Merger with India* (Penguin Viking, 2018), is a detailed account by the R&AW's man on the spot during this crucial period. Pp. 16–21 describe the initial decisions.

17. Jairam Ramesh, *Intertwined Lives: P. N. Haksar and Indira Gandhi* (Simon and Schuster India, 2018), p. 222.

18. Zorawar Daulet Singh, *Power and Diplomacy: India's Foreign Policies During the Cold War* (Oxford University Press, 2019), pp. 21, 198, and 209.

Chapter Six

1. Narges Bejoghli, "The Hidden Sources of Iranian Strength," *Foreign Policy*, May 15, 2019 at https://foreignpolicy.com/2019/05/15/the-hidden-sources-of-iranian-strength.

2. M. H. Ansari, chapter on "Afghanistan" in *External Affairs: Cross-Border Relations*, edited by J. N. Dixit (Roli Books, 2003), p. 159.

3. The best account of this covert war is Steve Coll's *Ghost Wars: The Secret History*

of the CIA, Afghanistan and Bin Laden, from the Soviet Invasion to September 10, 2001 (Penguin Press, 2004).

4. For an account of the ISI's thinking and war-waging in this period, see Mohammad Yousaf and Mark Adkin, *The Bear Trap; Afghanistan's Untold Story* (Lahore: Jang Publishers, 1992). Akhtar Abdul Rehman Khan and Zia both perished together in a plane crash in 1988.

5. Ahmed Rashid, *Taliban: Islam, Oil, and the New Great Game in Central Asia* (I. B. Taurus, 2000) p. 186.

6. Avinash Paliwal, *My Enemy's Enemy: India in Afghanistan from the Soviet Invasion to the U.S. Withdrawal* (Hurst and Co., 2017), pp. 74–76. The book is a thorough recounting of the facts but is less reliable in its analysis of the motivations and assessments of the actors, particularly in India.

7. Rashid, *Taliban*, p. 195.

8. Barnett R. Rubin, *The Fragmentation of Afghanistan* (Yale University Press, 1995).

9. Milton Osborne, *Southeast Asia; An Introductory History* (Allen and Unwin, 2016, orig. 1979), p. 263.

10. Christopher Goscha, *The Penguin History of Modern* Vietnam (Allen Lane, 2016), p. 434.

11. Amitav Acharya, *East of India, South of China: Sino-Indian Encounters in SE Asia* (Oxford University Press, India, 2017), p. 49.

12. J. N. Dixit, *Across Borders: Fifty Years of India's Foreign Policy* (Picus Books, 1998), pp. 156–57.

13. Japan's share of the U.S. market was automobiles 21 percent; motorcycles 65 percent; radios 46 percent; cameras 29 percent; video recorders 100 percent; watches 14 percent; and machine tools 11 percent.

14. Richard McGregor, *Asia's Reckoning; China, Japan and the Fate of U.S. Power in Asia* (Viking, 2017) p. 100.

15. There is a chapter on the agreement in S. Menon, *Choices: Inside the Making of Indian Foreign Policy* (Brookings Institution Press, 2016).

16. For a readable account of the military aspects of Operation Pawan in Sri Lanka and Operation Cactus in the Maldives, see Sushant Singh, *Mission Overseas: Daring Operations by the Indian Military* (Juggernaut Books, 2017).

17. Ronen Sen, Foreword to *The Great Game in Afghanistan: Rajiv Gandhi, General Zia and the Unending War* by Kallol Bhattacharjee (Harper Collins, India, 2017).

Chapter Seven

1. Gurcharan Das, *India Unbound: From Independence to the Global Information Age* (Penguin Books, 2000), pp. 214–18.

2. In Mearsheimer's definition, a hegemon is the only power in the system that no other state can militarily act on.

3. Vinay Sitapathi, *Half Lion: How PV Narasimha Rao Transformed India* (Penguin, 2016), p. 257.

4. On December 6, 1992, the opposition BJP and its supporters destroyed a 400-year-old mosque that had been built on the site of a temple at a spot that some Hindus consider

the birthplace of the god Ram. The resulting riots and communal tensions in India were exploited and fanned by Pakistan.

5. Francis Fukuyama, "The End of History," *The National Interest* (Spring 1989), pp. 2–18; S. P. Huntington, "The Clash of Civilizations?" *Foreign Affairs* 72 (1993), pp. 21–49.

6. Richard McGregor, *Asia's Reckoning: China, Japan and the Fate of U.S. Power in the Pacific Century* (Viking, 2017).

7. Henry M. Paulson Jr., *Dealing with China: An Insider Unmasks the New Economic Superpower* (Hachette, 2015), p. 240.

8. Henry M. Paulson Jr., *Dealing with China: An Insider Unmasks the New Economic Superpower* (Hatchette, 2015).

9. Michael S. Chase and others, *China's Incomplete Military Transformation: Assessing the Weaknesses of the People's Liberation Army (PLA)* (Santa Monica, RAND, 2015).

10. J. N. Dixit, *Across Borders: Fifty Years of Indian Foreign Policy* (Picus Books, 1998), p. 213.

Chapter Eight

1. World Bank open data, "Historical GDP by Country, Statistics from the World Bank, 1960–2018," https://knoema.com/mhrzolg/historical-gdp-by-country-statistics-from-the-world-bank-1960-2018.

2. Montek Singh Ahluwalia, *Backstage: The Story Behind India's High Growth Years* (Rupa, 2020), p. ix.

3. Angus Maddison, *Contours of the World Economy, 1–2030 AD* (Oxford University Press, 2007), p. 379, table A4.

4. James Crabtree, *The Billionaire Raj: A Journey through India's New Gilded Age* (Tim Duggan Books, 2018).

5. Ahluwalia, *Backstage*.

6. Crabtree, *The Billionaire Raj*, p. 12.

7. I have written extensively on the civil nuclear initiative in *Choices: Inside the Making of Indian Foreign Policy* (Brookings Institution Press, 2016) and will not repeat that here.

8. For an examination of mixed U.S. motives in dealing with possible nuclear proliferation in allies like Pakistan, see Francis J. Gavin, *Nuclear Statecraft: History and Strategy in America's Atomic Age* (Cornell University Press, 2012), p. 138. See also Hassan Abbas, *Pakistan's Nuclear Bomb: A Story of Defiance, Deterrence and Deviance* (Penguin Random House India, 2018), pp. 71–74, 178–79, and 202–03.

9. Harsh V. Pant and Yogesh Joshi, *Oxford Short Introduction to Indian Nuclear Policy* (Oxford University Press, 2018).

10. The specific sanctions included termination of U.S. development assistance; termination of U.S. government sales of defense articles and services; termination of foreign military financing; denial of credit, credit guarantees, or other financial assistance by the U.S. government; opposition to loans or assistance by international financial institutions; prohibition on U.S. bank loans or credit to India and Pakistan; and prohibition on exports of "specific goods and technology." See the CRS report on sanctions at www.everycrsreport.com/reports/98-570.html.

11. Strobe Talbott, *Engaging India: Diplomacy, Democracy, and the Bomb* (Penguin Viking, 2004).

12. Ibid.

13. Steve Coll, "The Back Channel: India and Pakistan's Secret Kashmir Talks," *The New Yorker*, February 2009.

14. U.S. State Department cable, *http://www.esd.whs.mil/Portals/54/Documents/FOID/Reading%20Room/International_Security_Affairs/08-F-0039_SecDef_Phonecall_to_Indian_MOD_Jaswant_Sing_Sep-20-2001.pdf.*

15. See, for instance, John Mearsheimer, *The Tragedy of Great Power Politics* (W.W. Norton, 2001).

16. Edward Said, "The Clash of Ignorance," *The Nation*, October 22, 2001.

17. Jeremy Black, *Geopolitics and the Quest for Dominance* (Knowledge World Publishers, 2017), p. 219.

18. Jonathan Kirshner, *American Power after the Financial Crisis* (Cornell University Press, 2014), p. 2.

19. David Dollar, "The US-China Trade War has its Seeds in the Financial Crisis," *Order from Chaos* (blog), Brookings Institution, September 14, 2018, www.brookings.edu/blog/order-from-chaos/2018/09/14/u-s-china-trade-war-has-its-seeds-in-the-financial-crisis.

20. Kirshner, *American Power*, p. 13.

Chapter Nine

1. The World Bank says that from 1960 to 2012, 101 countries graduated from developing economic status to middle-income status, that is, US$9,000 per capita income each year; 89 have not graduated; and 12 became developed, with per capita incomes over US$18,000 per year.

2. Gideon Rachman, *Financial Times*, October 30, 2018; *Australian Financial Review*, October 31, 2018.

3. Bill Gates, "Gene Editing for Good: How CRISPR Could Transform Global Development," *Foreign Affairs* (May/June 2018).

4. Calculating the center of gravity of the world economy is simply finding the average location of economic activity measured on a globe across different geographies. For three decades after 1945 it was located somewhere in the mid-Atlantic. Now it has moved east, between Europe and Asia, and in 2050 will likely be between India and China. See Bruno Maçães, *The Dawn of Eurasia: On the Trail of the New World Order* (Allen & Lane, 2018), p. 7. See also "The World's Shifting Centre of Gravity," *The Economist*, June 28, 2018, www.economist.com/graphic-detail/2012/06/28/the-worlds-shifting-centre-of-gravity.

5. Zhonghua minzu weida fuxing is the transliteration of the Chinese term for "the Great Rejuvenation of China." By using "minzu," meaning race/people/nationality, the phrase implies that this is the duty of all Chinese or Han around the world, whether they are citizens of the People's Republic of China or not. It excludes non-Hans like Indians in Hong Kong and expects compliance from "Chinese" societies such as Singapore.

6. Edie Purdie, "Tracking GDP in PPP Terms Shows Rapid Rise of China and India," World Bank Blogs, October 16, 2019, https://blogs.worldbank.org/opendata/tracking-gdp-ppp-terms-shows-rapid-rise-china-and-india.

7. BRICS is the group composed of the five major emerging economies: Brazil, Russia, India, China, and South Africa.

8. See Ambassador Charles Freeman's speech to the St. Petersburg Conference on World Affairs, February 12, 2019, at https://chasfreeman.net/after-the-trade-war -a-real-war-with-china/.

9. The full Chinese slogan is to "observe calmly; secure our position; cope with affairs calmly; hide our capacities and bide our time; be good at maintaining a low profile; and never claim leadership."

10. Andrew Bacevich, *American Empire: The Realities and Consequences of U.S. Diplomacy* (Harvard University Press, 2004). This is a myth that all hegemons propagate. The British claimed to have acquired an empire in a fit of absent mindedness. The Chinese empire was presented as an inevitable consequence of nature, through the working of the mysterious Mandate of Heaven.

11. Pankaj Mishra, *Age of Anger: A History of the Present* (Farrar, Strauss and Giroux, 2017).

12. Robert D. Kaplan, *The Return of Marco Polo's World: War, Strategy, and American Interests in the Twenty-First Century* (Random House, 2018).

13. Coral Bell, "The End of the Vasco da Gama Era," Lowy Institute paper, November 15, 2007, at www.lowyinstitute.org/publications/end-vasco-da-gama-era.

14. Kishore Mahbubani and Larry Summers made the case for global optimism in *Foreign Affairs* (Spring 2016) at www.foreignaffairs.com/articles/2016-04-18/fusion -civilizations. See also Steven Pinker, *The Better Angels of Our Nature: Why Violence Has Declined* (Penguin Books, 2011).

15. See Pankaj Mishra, *The Age of Anger: A History of the Present* (Giroux, Farrar and Strauss, 2017).

16. *IMF World Economic Outlook* (April 2015) describes India and China as accounting for 52.77 percent in PPP terms and 48.99 percent in nominal terms of Asia's total GDP, https://www.imf.org/en/Publications/SPROLLs/world-economic-outlook -databases#sort=%40imfdate%20descending.

17. "Comparing China and India by Economy," *Statistics Times*, August 28, 2019, based on International Monetary Fund and World Bank datasets, http://statisticstimes .com/economy/china-vs-india-gdp.php.

18. Walter Russel Mead, "The Return of Geopolitics and the Revenge of the Revisionist Powers," *Foreign Affairs* (May/June 2014).

19. "Joint Statement Following Discussions with the Leaders of the People's Republic of China, Shanghai," February 27, 1972, https://history.state.gov/historicaldocuments /frus1969-76v17/d203.

20. Richard Samuels and Eric Heginbotham, "A New Military Strategy for Japan," *Foreign Affairs* (July 16, 2018), www.foreignaffairs.com/articles/asia/2018-07-16/new -military-strategy-japan?cid=nlc-fa_fatoday-20181012.

21. Paul Bracken, *Fire in the East: The Rise of Asian Military Power and the Second Nuclear Age* (Harper Collins, 1999).

22. See Rosa Brooks, *How Everything Became War and the Military Became Everything* (Simon and Schuster, 2016).

23. Graham Allison, *Destined for War: Can America and China Escape Thucydides' Trap?* (Houghton, Mifflin, Harcourt, 2017).

24. Henry M. Paulson Jr., *Dealing with China: An Insider Unmasks the New Economic Superpower* (Hatchette, 2015).

25. Robert D. Kaplan, *The Return of Marco Polo's World: War, Strategy, and American Interests in the Twenty-First Century* (Random House, 2018).

26. Robert Kagan, *The Jungle Grows Back: America and Our Imperiled World* (Knopf, September 2018).

27. See John Mearsheimer, "Why China's Rise Will Not Be Peaceful," in *The National Interest*, October 25, 2014, for a contradictory view arguing that conflict between a rising China and the United States is inevitable at https://nationalinterest.org/commentary /can-china-rise-peacefully-10204. His earlier prediction to the same effect is in *The Tragedy of Great Power Politics* (W.W. Norton, 2001), pp. 396–402.

Chapter Ten

1. Michael Vatikiotis, *Blood and Silk: Power and Conflict in Modern Southeast Asia* (Weidenfield and Nicolson, 2017), p. 264.

2. Zhao Huasheng, "Central Asia in Chinese Strategic Thinking," in *The New Great Game: China and South and Central Asia in the Era of Reform*, Thomas Fingar, ed. (Stanford University Press, 2016), p. 182.

3. Robert D. Kaplan, *The Return of Marco Polo's World: War, Strategy, and American Interests in the Twenty-First Century* (Random House, 2018), p. 23.

4. "The overall growth of GDP per capita of South Asia was 1.9 percent annually during the 1960s and declined to 0.6 percent in the 1970s (coinciding with the first oil shock); then it accelerated to 3.3 percent in the 1980s and 3.4 percent during 1990–2003. These accelerated growth rates of the later periods still lagged far behind those of East Asia, but represented a superior growth performance compared with other developing regions. The contrast is most striking with sub-Saharan Africa, which experienced decline or stagnation in per capita GNP during the 1980s and 1990s.

"India has led South Asia's growth acceleration since the beginning of the 1980s, not only because of its size (80 percent of the region's GDP and of the total population) but also because of its superior growth performance. Its GDP growth in the three years unto fiscal year 2005/6 averaged about 8 percent annually, and even conservative analysts put the country's current 'trend' annual GDP growth to be at least 6 percent—the rate it has achieved since 1991. The growth acceleration in India had started even earlier, with the growth rate of GDP averaging 5.5 percent per year in the 1980s, compared with the infamous 'Hindu rate of growth' of about 3.5 percent per year during the three previous decades.

In spite of India's leading role, economic growth has been broadly based among the South Asian economies. In terms of long-term growth, Sri Lanka has performed best, and Nepal worst, but even Nepal's per capita GDP growth at an average of 1.8 percent per annum over the decades of the 1970s, 1980s, and 1990s represents significant progress. In recent years the growth performance of the economies has withstood many adverse factors—natural disasters, internal conflict and external economic shocks—and this speaks to the resilience and robustness of the growth that has been taking place." See *Handbook on the South Asian Economies*, Anis Chowdhury and Wahiduddin Mahmud, eds. (Edward Elgar Publishing, 2008).

5. Kaushik Basu, "Why Is Bangladesh Booming?" Brookings, May 1, 2018,

https://www.brookings.edu/opinions/why-is-bangladesh-booming/amp/?__twitter _impression=true.

6. Tuneer Mukherjee and Premesha Saha, "India's Shrinking Influence in Littoral South Asia," Observer Research Foundation, April 30, 2018, www.orfonline.org /research/indias-shrinking-influence-in-littoral-south-asia/.

7. To those who would dispute this, I would only point out that the blood shed by the American, French, Russian, and Chinese revolutions proportionately far exceeded that shed by the Iranian revolution.

Chapter Eleven

1. Ong Kee Beng, *The Eurasian Core and Its Edges: Dialogues with Wang Gangwu on the History of the World*, Institute of Southeast Asian Studies (ISEAS), Singapore, 2015.

2. See Tansen Sen, *India, China and the World: A Connected History* (Rowman and Littlefield, 2017), pp. 200–216. The official PRC narrative of Zheng He's voyages as peaceful and harmonious trading voyages is belied by the official Ming record of violent and hegemonic projection of power and use of force to collect tribute, create alternate nodes on the Cochin coast and at Malacca and Malindi in east Africa, and the attempt to fix prices on precious commodities like pepper and porcelain across the Indian Ocean region and trading networks.

3. Interestingly, the Chinese choose to define unrealized ambitions, such as reunification with Taiwan and claiming the South China Sea as China's "territorial waters," as their core interests, thus making their ambitions non-negotiable.

4. Ministry of National Defense, People's Republic of China, "White Paper on National Military Strategy," May 27, 2015, http://english.www.gov.cn/archive/white _paper/2015/05/27/content_281475115610833.htm.

5. The Chinese characters for this expression can be transliterated as *wending yadao yiqie.*

6. See Jessica Chen Weiss, *Powerful Patriots* (Oxford University Press, 2014), for a nuanced analysis of how and when the Chinese regime permits, prevents, and uses nationalist protests domestically and externally. See also CCP Document 9 of 2013 at www.chinafile.com/document-9-chinafile-translation.

7. Except, perhaps, the Mongol or Yuan dynasty in the thirteenth and fourteenth centuries whose military, bureaucratic, and intellectual power were generated outside China.

8. See, for instance, *Global Times* of June 7, 2017, at www.globaltimes.cn/content /1050519.shtml?utm_content=bufferc912f&utm_medium=social&utm_source =twitter.com&utm_campaign=buffer.

9. Jia Yangfan, "At the Communist Party Congress Xi Jinping Plays the Emperor," *The New Yorker*, October 18, 2017.

10. Yan Xuetong, "Chinese Values vs. Liberalism: What Ideology Will Shape the International Normative Order?" *Chinese Journal of International Politics*, February 8, 2018, pp. 1–22.

11. Kevin Rudd, "How to Break the 'Mutually Assured Misperception' between the US and China," *Huffington Post*, April 20, 2015, www.huffingtonpost.com/kevin-rudd /us-china-relations-kevin-rudd-report_b_7096784.html.

12. Some see it the other way around. For Karnad, the time China takes to establish its *tianxia* concept of a harmonious world that it dominates is the time available to India and others to organize the resistance and thwart China's plans. See Bharat Karnad, *Staggering Forward: Narendra Modi and India's Global Ambition* (Penguin India, 2018), p. 3.

13. Keir A. Lieber and Daryl G. Press, "The End of MAD? The Nuclear Dimension of U.S. Primacy," *International Security* 30, no. 4 (Spring 2006), pp. 7–34, at p. 10.

14. Fiona Cunningham and Taylor Fravel, "Assuring Assured Retaliation, China's Nuclear Posture and US-China Strategic Stability," *International Security* 40, no. 2 (Fall 2015), pp. 7–50.

15. Yan Xuetong, *Ancient Chinese Thought, Modern Chinese Power* (Princeton University Press, 2011), pp. 43, 47–51, 86–88.

16. Howard W. French, *Everything under the Heavens: How China's Past Helps Shape China's Push for Global Power* (Alfred A. Knopf, 2017), p. 104 ff. "The Ming were busily constituting a sphere of influence based on the preponderance of force. It was not like the Portuguese and other empires that would follow in the sense that it does not seem to have regarded commerce for the pure sake of mercantile wealth as its central or primary objective. Nor were the Chinese preoccupied with using naval power to seize control of faraway lands for their own direct administration. . . . The missions of Zheng, though, constituted a clear type of imperial behaviour that placed politics at the centre, following the familiar principle that the strength of an emperor or dynasty in China was measured in good part according to the degree to which it could obtain the deference and submission of nearby peoples."

17. For a good summary of present scholarship and an original contribution to understanding the Tributary System, see Ji-Young Lee, *China's Hegemony: Four Hundred Years of East Asian Domination* (Columbia University Press, 2017).

18. The Chinese would describe the domain as "all under heaven." See also John King Fairbank, ed., *The Chinese World Order* (Harvard University Press, 1968); Mark Mancall, *China at the Crossroads: 300 Years of Foreign Policy* (Free Press, 1984); David Kang, *East Asia before the West: Five Centuries of Trade and Tribute* (Columbia University Press, 2010); Feng Zhang, *Chinese Hegemony: Grand Strategy and International Institutions in East Asian History* (Stanford University Press, 2015).

19. Alastair Iain Johnston, *Cultural Realism: Strategic Culture and Grand Strategy in Chinese History* (Princeton University Press, 1995).

20. Yuan-Kang Wang, *Harmony and War: Confucian Culture and Chinese Power Politics* (Columbia University Press, 2011), p. xiii.

21. See, for instance, Yan Xuetong, *Leadership and the Rise of Great Powers* (Princeton University Press, 2019), which develops a Chinese theory drawing on traditional Chinese and Western realist thinking on international relations.

22. Sun Laichen and Geoff Wade, eds., *Southeast Asia in the Fifteenth Century: The China Factor* (University of Chicago Press, 2010), p. 61.

23. David C. Kang disputes this in *American Grand Strategy and East Asian Security in the 21st Century* (Cambridge University Press, 2017). He argues that military spending in East Asia has gone down since the early 1990s as a percentage of GDP. He says that "defence spending of the eleven main East Asian states declined from an average of 3.35 percent of GDP in 1990 to an average of 1.84 percent in 2015." But this is just when their economies grew fastest. In absolute terms, what we are seeing is an arms race without parallel in scale, volume, and offensive capability and it is led by China. No military planner

can afford to base his calculations on the adversary's expenditure as a proportion of GDP. He responds and plans on the basis of the enemy's capabilities and intent.

24. See Michael Beckley, "The Emerging Military Balance in East Asia," in *International Security* 42 (Fall 2017), pp. 78–119, for a detailed analysis.

25. All PLA Group Army commanders and political commissars have been reassigned as of November 2017 after the PLA reduced the number of group armies from eighteen to thirteen in April. Over 90 percent of military officers from the original group armies and 40 percent from the combat brigades have been transferred to improve command and training.

26. Nicholas Lardy, *Markets over Mao* (Peterson Institute for International Economics, 2014).

27. Ian Johnson, *The Souls of China: The Return of Religion after Mao* (Allen Lane, 2017).

28. The 2017 "Blue Book" of the Chinese Academy of Social Sciences (December 22, 2017) says that China must fully relax birth controls, but even then China could struggle to meet President Xi's goals of a modern society by 2035 and a powerful modern nation by 2050.

29. McKinsey (2007) estimates the Indian middle class at nearly 600 million people by 2025—defining middle class as those with disposable household income of US$4,000–22,000. Already India builds only slightly fewer automobiles than South Korea and more than Mexico in 2016.

30. William H. Overholt, *China's Crisis of Success* (Cambridge University Press, 2018).

31. Ibid., pp. xxiv and 256.

32. Mark Elvin, *The Pattern of the Chinese Past* (Stanford University Press, 1973). In hindsight, the last paragraphs of the book are prophetic.

33. See Jessica Chen Weiss, *Powerful Patriots* (Oxford University Press, 2014), for an analysis of how and when the Chinese regime permits, prevents, and uses nationalist protests domestically and externally.

34. This seems to be a case of the wish fathering the myth. It is hard to find cases where postcolonial states have transitioned through market-based development to Western-style democracy and a pro-Western regime without Western military occupation and extensive social engineering.

35. It has been estimated that raising its trade surplus by 1 percent of GDP keeps China's government from having to take on between 10–15 percent of GDP more in loans. The offsetting surplus income counts for a great deal with high debt, and China therefore needs to maintain its trade surplus. See Gwynn Guilford, *China's Plans to Lead the Global Economy Are Being Foiled . . . by China*, in *Quartz*, December 31, 2016.

36. Robert D. Kaplan, *The Return of Marco Polo's World: War, Strategy, and American Interests in the Twenty-First Century* (Penguin Random House, 2018). Martin Jacques, *When China Rules the World; The Rise of the Middle Kingdom and the End of the Western World* (Allen Lane, 2009). Gordon Chang, *The Coming Collapse of China* (Random House, 2001).

37. Deng had actually expressed some skepticism about the "Asian century." What he said was: "In recent years people have been saying that the next century will be the century of Asia and the Pacific, as if that was sure to be the case. I disagree with this view. If we exclude the United States, the only countries in the Asia-Pacific region that

are relatively developed are Japan, the 'four little dragons,' Australia and New Zealand, with a total population of at most 200 million. . . . But the population of China and India adds up to 1.8 billion. Unless those two countries are developed, there will be no Asian century." Remarks from December 21, 1988, in Deng Xiaoping, *Selected Works of Deng Xiaoping*, vol III, pp. 182–83.

Chapter Twelve

1. When I use the terms *India* or *China* before the twentieth century, it is to refer to the polities, societies, and economies in the geographical area occupied by the modern states and not to refer to them as nations or states in those times, even though some scholars, such as Nicholas Tackett, *The Origins of the Chinese Nation* (Cambridge University Press, 2017), now trace the Chinese sense of nationhood and a nation-state for Han Chinese to Song China.

2. Matthew W. Mosca, *From Frontier Policy to Foreign Policy: The Question of India and the Transformation of Geopolitics in Qing China* (Stanford University Press, 2013).

3. Janet Abu-Lughod, *Before European Hegemony: The World System AD 1250–1550* (Oxford University Press, 1989).

4. Kenneth Pomeranz, *The Great Divergence; China, Europe and the Making of the Modern World Economy* (Princeton University Press, 2000).

5. Prasannan Parthasarathi, *Why Europe Grew Rich and Asia Did Not: Global Economic Divergence, 1600–1850* (Cambridge University Press, 2011).

6. Bharat Karnad, *Staggering Forward: Narendra Modi and India's Global Ambition* (Penguin Random House India, 2018), p. 272.

7. See *New Indian Express*, October 14, 2019, for details.

8. The BASIC group, consisting of Brazil, South Africa, India, and China, was formed by agreement on November 28, 2009, and coordinated the approach of these newly industrialized countries in international climate change negotiations at the Copenhagen summit and thereafter. It also brokered the final Copenhagen accord with the United States in December 2009.

9. Andrew Small, *The China-Pakistan Axis: Asia's New Geopolitics* (London: Hurst and Company, 2015), p. 97. In comparison, the United States delivered $17.12 billion in military ($11.74 billion) and economic ($6.08 billion) assistance to Pakistan between 2002 and 2011 in constant 2016 dollars, according to U.S. government figures.

10. *Financial Times*, March 20, 2018, p. 4.

Chapter Thirteen

1. There are some, like Ian Hall in *Modi and the Reinvention of Indian Foreign Policy* (Bristol University Press, 2019), who believe that Modi is a self-consciously transformational leader with a clearly ideological agenda that has structured priorities. Hall, however, concedes that Modi was not successful in reinventing India's foreign policy to his "Hindu nationalist" construct in his first term.

2. Ajit Doval, national security advisor to Prime Minister Modi, in the Lalit Doshi Memorial Lecture on "State Security, Statecraft, and Conflict of Values," August 2015.

3. *The Economist*, April 7, 2018, p. 9.

4. The NSC was created on April 16, 1999, on the basis of the Pant Task Force report. Subsequently some changes were made in the organization and the role of the NSA was enhanced after the Kargil Review Committee and the Group of Ministers recommendations. The National Security Advisory Board was created earlier in November 1998 while the other structures of the NSC including its secretariat (originally a renaming of the Joint Intelligence Committee that had existed in various forms since 1948), were set up the next year. A previous attempt to set up an NSC and appoint an NSA in 1990 by the V. P. Singh government had soon foundered.

5. See, for instance, Rajesh Rajagopalan, "India's Strategic Choices: China and the Balance of Power in Asia," Carnegie India paper, October 7, 2017, http://carnegieindia.org/2017/09/14/india-s-strategic-choices-china-and-balance-of-power-in-asia-pub-73108.

6. Martin Wolf, *Financial Times*, February 13, 2018.

7. Margaret MacMillan, "The Rhyme of History: Lessons of the Great War," *The Brookings Essays*, (Brookings Institution, 2014), pp. 109–33.

8. John Lewis Gaddis, *The Long Peace: Inquiries into the History of the Cold War* (Oxford University Press, 1987).

9. Graham Allison, *Destined for War: Can America and China Escape Thucydides's Trap?* (Houghton Mifflin Harcourt, 2017).

10. According to the Pew Organization's polls, among all the democracies, India has the highest proportion of people who support a strong leader untrammeled by a constitution or checks and balances, and that proportion is rising.

11. Pankaj Mishra, *From the Ruins of Empire: The Revolt against the West and the Remaking of Asia* (Penguin, 2013), p. 10.

12. Rosa Brooks, *How Everything Became War and the Military Became Everything: Tales from the Pentagon* (Simon & Schuster, 2016).

Afterword

1. Amos Tversky and Daniel Kahneman, "Judgement under Uncertainty: Heuristics and Biases," *Science* (New Series) 185, no. 4157 (September 27, 1974), pp. 1124–31.

2. A March 2018 Pew survey showed that only 2 percent of Indians are politically unaffiliated. Only 8 percent of Indians hold negative views of democracy. Indians and Israelis are among the least skeptical about democracy worldwide. We are not cynics and I hope we never will be.

3. As then U.S. general Ulysses Grant said of Abraham Lincoln's secretary of war, Edward Stanton, in a comment on the American Civil War, "He could see our weakness, but he could not see that the enemy was in danger."

Index

globalization and rise of, 214–17, 241–46, 278, 307; goals of, 242, 243, 245, 294–95, 312–13; Great Proletarian Cultural Revolution, 100, 292; history as predictor of future behavior, 301–04; India-China War, 97–98, 323; Indian independence and, 51–52; Indian Ocean, influence in, 282, 291, 341; India-Pakistan conflict and, 134; internal security and, 260, 292, 306–07; isolation of, 99–100, 140; Japanese economic growth and, 172–73; Korean War and, 56, 69–70; maritime power of, 20, 243, 253–56, 288–90, 305; middle class in, 307; military power of, 242–43, 245–46, 260–61, 290–91, 304–06, 313–14, 328–29; nuclear weapons of, 116–18, 137, 145, 218, 220; Panchsheel Agreement (1954), 76; security commitments of, 289–90, 314, 322, 335; Sikkim, accession to India, 147; south Asia, influence in, 279–82; Taiwan Strait crisis and, 201–03, 255, 299; Tiananmen Square protests, 175, 197–98; U.S. retreat from Asia and, 293–94; Vietnam-Cambodia conflict and, 164–67; Vietnam War and, 74, 114, 137. *See also* South China Sea; *specific countries for relations with*

China-India relations, 317–39; challenges for, 336–37; Cold War and, 88–92, 96; colonial legacy and, 319–20; future of, 335–39; future tasks for India and, 350–51; Indira Gandhi and, 147–49; Rajiv Gandhi and, 184; global financial crisis and, 326; history of, 317–19; internal and external policies, compared, 321–22; to manage stability, 364–65; media on, 327–28; Nehru and, 84–92, 321; Pakistan and, 331–33; pan-Asianism and, 320–21; recent stressors on, 326–30; superpower relations and, 322–24; Tibet and, 323; trade and, 177, 221, 324–25, 329–30, 334–35; United States and, 333–34. *See also* Border issues with China

China-Pakistan Economic Corridor (CPEC), 244, 327, 331–33

Churchill, Winston, 35, 43

"The Clash of Civilizations" (Huntington), 194

"The Clash of Ignorance" (Said), 231

Climate and geography of India, 11–14, 21

Climate change and environmentalism, 113, 170, 195, 329–30

Clinton, Bill, 201–02, 209, 220

Cohen, S. B., 21

Cold War, 65–102; deaths in Asia resulting from, 68–69; end of, 168, 186–89; Formosa (Offshore) Islands and, 77–78; India-China boundary and, 84–99; India-China War and, 97–100; Indian foreign policy on China

during, 88–92; Indian independence and, 43–45, 50–52; international ideologies during, 65–66; Korean War and, 69–72; nonalignment of Asian countries during, 78–79, 84, 278; nuclear deterrence and, 82–83; resolution of border with Pakistan, 101–02; Suez crisis and, 79–80; U.S.-China relations and, 137–43; U.S. strategy during, 66–67, 80–82; Vietnam War and, 72–77

Colonialism: Indian independence and, 33–35; institutionalized violence and racism, 26; legacy of, 33–35, 275, 319–20; Nehru and, 48

Communism: capitalism vs., 43–48; India and, 99; India-U.S. relations and, 50; post-war appeal of, 67, 113; southeast Asia and, 113; Soviet collapse and, 167. *See also* Cold War; *specific countries*

Comprehensive and Progressive Agreement for Trans-Pacific Partnership (CPTPP), 244, 309

Comprehensive Test Ban Treaty (CTBT), 190, 218

Connolly, Arthur, 21

Counterterrorism. *See* Terrorism and counterterrorism

COVID-19 pandemic: China and, 296; economic growth and, 233–34, 291; manufacturing on-shoring and, 293; poverty and, 249; protectionism and, 354

CPEC (China-Pakistan Economic Corridor), 244, 327, 331–33

CTBT (Comprehensive Test Ban Treaty), 190, 218

Cuban Missile Crisis, 96, 98

Cunningham, Fiona, 301

Curzon (Lord), 22–24, 27, 34, 41

Cyber security, 355, 358–59

Dalai Lama, 56–60, 89, 173–74, 307

Dasgupta, Chandrashekhar, 54, 115–16, 186, 190

Decolonization, 32–33, 47, 49–50, 73, 78–79, 83

Demography: of China, 307–08; globalization and, 278–79; of India, 14–15, 80, 259, 307; of Japan, 307

Deng Xiaoping: economic policies of, 197, 292; Indian relations and, 169; Japanese economic growth and, 172–73; nuclear weapons and, 145; political strategies of, 245; Russian relations and, 167; Tiananmen Square protests and, 174–76, 197–98; Tibet relations and, 174; U.S. relations and, 141–42

Desai, Morarji, 120